KLOOK

THE STORY OF KENNY CLARKE

KLOOK
THE STORY OF KENNY CLARKE

MIKE HENNESSEY

QUARTET BOOKS
LONDON NEW YORK

First published by Quartet Books Limited 1990
A member of the Namara Group
27/29 Goodge Street, London W1P 1FD

British Library Cataloguing in Publication Data
Hennessey, Mike
Klook : the story of Kenny Clarke.
1. Jazz-biographies
I. Title
785.42'092'4

ISBN 0–7043–2529–2

Typeset by MC Typeset Ltd, Gillingham, Kent
Printed and bound in Great Britain by
BPCC Hazell Books, Aylesbury, Bucks.

Contents

For Daisy and Laurent

Acknowledgements

My grateful thanks to all the musicians who contributed to this book: Benny Bailey, Charles Bellonzi, Lou Bennett, Walter Bishop Jr, Francy Boland, Ray Brown, Kenny Burrell, Donald Byrd, Mike Carr, Nathan Davis, Alan Dawson, Kenny Drew, Curtis Fuller, Slim Gaillard, Dizzy Gillespie, Benny Golson, Jimmy Gourley, Dusko Goykovic, Johnny Griffin, Roger Guérin, Joe Harris, John Hawkins, Marc Hemmeler, Billy Higgins, Nancy Holloway, Noah Howard, Milt Jackson, Philly Joe Jones, Quincy Jones, Al Levitt, John Lewis, Herbie Mann, Shelly Manne, Jackie McLean, Carmen McRae, Pierre Michelot, Red Mitchell, James Moody, Big Nick Nicholas, Henri Renaud, Max Roach, Red Rodney, Annie Ross, Ronnie Scott, Horace Silver, Hal Singer, Grady Tate, Clark Terry, Michel de Villers, Joe Wilder, Jimmy Woode and Phil Woods; and to my fellow writers and jazz enthusiasts, including those who responded to the letter I sent to various jazz magazines seeking material on Kenny Clarke: Pascal Anquetil, Jeff Atterton, George Avakian, Joachim Berendt, Pawel Brodowski, Tony Caldicott, Gigi Campi, Maurice Cullaz, Charles Delaunay, Gudrun Endress, Michel Faligand, Bill Fogerty, Michael Frohne, Yves Gagnon, Simone Ginibre, Jim Godbolt, Randi Hultin, Paul Keutgens, Louis Victor Mialy, Jim Motavalli, Francis Paudras, François Postif, Jenny Sheard, John Surber, Frank Ténot, Steve Voce, Valerie Wilmer, Mike Yates and Mike Zwerin.

Special thanks to Lisa Boulton for helping with translation; to Arthur Taylor for permitting me to reproduce material from *Notes and Tones*; to the Rutgers Institute of Jazz Studies, New Jersey, for access to the 1977 Helen Oakley Dance interview with Kenny Clarke; to Michael Haggerty for his enormous help with the discography and for allowing me to quote extensively from his 1982 interview, *A Flower for Kenny*; to Ursula Davis for permission to use passages from *Paris without Regret*; to Kenny Clarke Jr (Toby) and Samuel 'Speedy' Spearman for their invaluable assistance; to Chris Parker for his endless patience; to Dorothy Hennessey for helping transcribe some of the interview tapes; and to Olympia Werke AG, Wilhelmshaven, whose 1956 vintage portable typewriter stood up magnificently to my sustained assault.

I must acknowledge a huge debt of gratitude to Gisela Albers for undertaking the transcribing of a vast number of taped interviews and for doing it so speedily, so accurately, so graciously.

My grateful thanks to Daisy Clarke and Laurent for their co-operation, their kindness and their friendship, and for waiting so patiently for this book to be completed.

And finally I want to pay a special tribute to Jean Elliott, for her love and inspiration then, and to Gaby Kleinschmidt for her love and inspiration now.

Mike Hennessey
Durchhausen
German Federal Republic
December 1989

Foreword

I'm happy to have the opportunity to provide the introduction to this book because Kenny Clarke was a master drummer and a number-one human being. If anybody in jazz deserves to have his life story recorded for posterity, it's Kenny Clarke.

Kenny was a perfect example of mastering the old and combining it with the new. He was equally at home in a big band, small group or just a duo. He was right at the top of his craft and he made a huge contribution to the music. He knew what to do with the bass drum better than anybody. Everything he did was in the right place – and you don't find too many players you can say that about.

Klook had a perfect nature and all the guys looked up to him. We had lots of conversations about drums. I would show him some things and he would always listen. Anything I suggested he would try. He knew the secret of drums and he was always helpful to other musicians.

Kenny was a real professional, always on time and always immaculate on stage, appearance-wise and musically. And he had the gift of a great sense of humour. They only made one Kenny Clarke and I consider myself very fortunate to have been his musical associate and friend for fifty years.

Dizzy Gillespie

Preface

Kenny Clarke was one of the most honourable, admirable and supremely likeable persons I ever knew. I was privileged to be his friend from the time I met him in August 1960 up to his death in January 1985.

This long-overdue book – which I had promised Kenny I would write back in 1976 – has, quite genuinely, been a labour of love, if a slightly intimidating one. To do full justice to the career and character of this remarkable man represents a daunting challenge which I have done my best to meet. Happily, in any case, Klook's incomparable contribution to jazz over a career which spanned five and a half decades is abundantly documented on a vast array of recordings.

The most telling testimony to the great human qualities that Kenny Clarke possessed is the fact that, of the scores of people I interviewed in the course of gathering material for this biography, there was not a single individual – not one – who had an unkind word to say about him. Kenny was respected and revered by all who knew him – and, of course, by tens of thousands who knew him only through his music.

'Music' is a perfectly apposite word to describe what was produced when Kenny Clarke sat behind a drumkit – the one instrument created specifically for jazz. Nobody in the history of jazz did more to convert the drums into a musical instrument. I don't think it is too fanciful to say that Kenny Clarke's achievement in revolutionizing the rhythmic foundation of jazz is on a par, in its own way, with that of Frank Whittle's invention of the jet engine. Certainly, in my view, Kenny

Clarke's contribution to music was equal in its enduring significance to that of Louis Armstrong.

Though Kenny was always ready to give generous credit to Sid Catlett, Chick Webb, Cozy Cole, Jo Jones, Ray McKinley, Dave Tough and Max Roach for the parts they played in emancipating the drums, the new ideas that he brought to jazz drumming were predominantly his own, worked out over a long period that began ten years before he got to Minton's. He once said that he had changed his way of playing drums at least ten times in his career.

Kenny Clarke was a man of dignity and he was proud of his race and of its having made the gift of jazz to the world. He was also a man of charm and humility, possessed of a generous spirit and a great fund of compassion. He had an irresistibly infectious grin and a most affecting laugh which was a compound of a chuckle and a giggle – and although, throughout his life, he had to contend with more than a fair share of adversity, he was always ready to laugh. He was an inspiration to hundreds of his peers, not only as a master musician but also as a human being with considerable moral authority, a keen social awareness and a deep-rooted sense of justice.

For all the investment he made in life and music, Kenny Clarke has not, I think, been accorded his rightful position in jazz history. Perhaps the fact that he spent more of his professional life in France than in the United States has been a key contributory factor in the serious under-assessment of his contribution to jazz. I hope this book will go some way towards redressing the balance.

Mike Hennessey
August 1989

1
The Supreme Accompanist

The modest little two-storey terrace house at 142 bis, rue de Rosny in the suburb of Montreuil-sous-Bois to the east of Paris stands as a somewhat improbable and unprepossessing monument to one of the most gifted, influential and respected jazz musicians of all time. For almost twenty-three years, this was the home of Liaquat Ali Salaam, born Kenneth Clarke Spearman but universally known as Kenny Clarke. The house, with its small, trim back garden, pocket-handkerchief lawn and rose bushes, was the ultimate sanctuary of a man whose whole life was a search for peace, freedom and spiritual fulfilment.

'To discover Kenny Clarke,' wrote *Jazz Hot*'s François Postif in 1965, 'you have to go as far as Montreuil. And there, ensconced in the comfort of his suburban *pavillon*, with garden, Kenny lives a simple and tranquil life. The legend on the door reads, "Liaquat Ali Salaam", and, underneath, "*dit* Kenny Clarke".'

In the wood-panelled living room, an imitation Paris street sign on the wall, presented to Kenny by his son Laurent, bears the legend 'Place Kenny Clarke'. To the left are record shelves, packed with albums, and, above them, a shelf lined with books. They include *Webster's Seventh New Collegiate Dictionary; La Petite Larousse; Just Above My Head* by James Baldwin; *Le Défi Democratique* by French Communist leader Georges Marchais; *Bird Lives!* by Ross Russell; Dizzy Gillespie's autobiography, *To be or not to Bop* and *Il n'y a pas de Drogué Heureux* by Dr Claude Olivenstein.

This was the home of a man whose mission in life was not

only to liberate the function of the drummer in the music he loved so much, but also to liberate himself from alienation, exploitation, discrimination and conflict. The different phases of his life can be seen as a series of escapes as he searched for the path that would lead him to contentment. He escaped as a teenager from his native Pittsburgh because his early life there had been a painful, bruising ordeal of deprivation and rejection. He escaped, temporarily, from the regimentation and restrictions of the US Army when he went AWOL some months after being drafted. He 'escaped' from the Modern Jazz Quartet when he felt his creative freedom being threatened by the rigid dictates of commercialism. He very much resented John Lewis's having sole control of the music the Quartet played.

Finally, he made his escape from the United States and with application, perseverance and patience, and no little financial hardship, eventually found a way of life that put him at peace with himself and helped to heal most of the wounds he had suffered along the way.

Kenny Clarke's career as a professional drummer spanned fifty-five years; about thirty-one of those years were spent in France. It is largely because of his decision to exile himself to Paris permanently in 1956 that the full recognition of his stature as a major jazz innovator and influence eluded him.

Klook's contribution to the evolution of jazz was not only a matter of technical innovation; what made Kenny Clarke so special was his *attitude*, his conception of the role of the drummer in jazz. Kenny detested bombast in life and in music, and he always insisted that it was the drummer's function to *accompany*, to back soloists, to spur them on – and to get the band to swing. In short, in the eloquent phraseology of his good friend Nathan Davis, 'to kick ass'.

Kenny Clarke was a drummer for all seasons. He played everything from military music to *musette*, from dixieland to avant-garde jazz, passing through gospel, blues, swing, mainstream, pre-bop, bebop and cool. He could make any size of unit swing – from duos to big bands – and he would play for dancers, acrobats and singers with equal integrity and commitment. He was not only a peerless drummer and a tremendous source of stimulation for his fellow musicians, he was also a significant musical innovator. He didn't just *happen* to be the drummer with Teddy Hill, at Minton's, with the legendary Dizzy Gillespie Big Band, with the pacemaking Tadd Dameron Orchestra, with the MJQ, on those classic 1954 Miles Davis Prestige sides, at the Blue Note in Paris, and with the superb Clarke–Boland Big Band. He played a pivotal, formative role in all these phases of his career and his creative intelligence and imagination left jazz infinitely richer.

At Minton's it was Kenny who was the prime mover, the co-ordinator, the musical director. He provided the essential foundation on which the new music was built. And that foundation, that exhilarating new musical vocabulary, became universally assimilated into the jazz language.

Frank Ténot, chairman of the French radio station, Europe No. 1, a long-time jazz enthusiast and a friend of Kenny Clarke, says, 'Kenny has influenced all percussionists. Outside a few dixieland groups, no one after 1945 played the drums without drawing on Kenny's inventions.'

That is an enormous achievement, equalled by no other musician except Louis Armstrong. Kenny's role in emancipating the drums has been compared to that of Jimmy Blanton's with the bass and Charlie Christian's with the guitar. But Blanton and Christian were principal pioneers of a general movement. Klook initiated a movement all on his own.

In the book *Jazz Masters of the Forties,* Ira Gitler also points out that Kenny Clarke's 'experimentations began much earlier than most jazz fans realize' and he adds: ' . . . by the time all the tributaries of modern jazz were ready to join forces, he was there to contribute the very important stream of his drumming'.

Kenny had an amazingly prolific career. He probably played with more jazz giants than any other musician in history. Louis Armstrong, Duke Ellington, Sidney Bechet, Dizzy Gillespie, Charlie Parker, Thelonious Monk, Billie Holiday, Clifford Brown, Lester Young, Bud Powell, Charles Mingus, Stan Getz, J.J. Johnson, Miles Davis, Dexter Gordon, Cannonball Adderley, Ella Fitzgerald, Benny Carter, Count Basie, Sonny Rollins, Coleman Hawkins, Ben Webster, Tadd Dameron, Oscar

Peterson, Benny Goodman, Chu Berry, Stéphane Grappelli, Art Tatum – he played with them all. And they all loved to work with Klook because he didn't play over them, he didn't simply play *with* them, but he played *for* them.

The late Ralph Gleason once wrote: 'I have a suspicion that Kenny Clarke, placed in the rhythm section of almost any group, is the equal of half a dozen poll-winners, several thousand volts and the pocket history of jazz.'

Klook was a superlative catalyst and he was passionately dedicated to his craft. He was a most creative drummer, enriching every band he played with. When he worked in the Lonnie Simmons band in New York's Black Cat club, he drove a rhythm section that was the blueprint for the classic, interior-sprung rhythm machine of the Count Basie band; the constant flow of his inspiration at Minton's encouraged jazz musicians to scale new heights, explore new possibilities; his work with the explosively innovative Dizzy Gillespie Big Band was stunning and, in contrast, his drumming with the Modern Jazz Quartet was perfectly poised and restrained, totally in keeping with the group's musical orientation.

As house drummer and A & R consultant for the Savoy label, Klook helped a succession of fine jazz musicians to play at the top of their form; as he did when he was resident at the Paris Blue Note for nearly eight years. And for more than a decade he was the mainspring of the spectacular, multi-national big band which he co-led with Belgian pianist/composer/arranger Francy Boland.

Yet for all his outstanding musical achievements, Kenny Clarke was a man of genuine modesty and humility. It was not the kind of specious modesty that waves aside accolades in the hope of earning a further medal for being diffident. He was well aware of his capabilities, but he never went in search of approbation. He sought respect, fair treatment and a reward for his endeavours that was commensurate with his skill and experience. He was really not concerned to be famous, and neither did he have the remotest inclination to show off when he played. He told Helen Oakley Dance in a 1977 interview: 'I was never a soloist. I always thought drum solos were very stupid. I always concentrated on accompaniment. I thought that was the important thing. That was my basic function as a drummer: to accompany. And I think that's why a lot of musicians liked me so much.'

2
Little Haiti

Pittsburgh, Pennsylvania at the turn of the century was a thriving, industrial town – the main steel-production centre of the United States – which had enjoyed two decades of continuous growth and prosperity. Its population included large contingents of Poles and Italians, a substantial Jewish community and many black people who had come from the South to seek employment. Pittsburgh made railway lines, rolling stock and locomotives. It also made excellent musicians. Pittsburgh did not nurture a jazz movement or style, like New Orleans, Chicago, Kansas City and New York. But it was a rich source of jazz musicians and was to provide the world with some eminent individualists – pianists Earl Hines, Erroll Garner, Mary Lou Williams and Ahmad Jamal; trumpet players Roy Eldridge and Tommy Turrentine; saxophonists Stanley Turrentine and Nathan Davis; drummers Art Blakey, Joe Harris and J.C. Moses; guitarist George Benson; bassists Ray Brown and Eddie Safranski, and singers Billy Eckstine, Dakota Staton and Eddie Jefferson.

But by far the most important of Pittsburgh's jazz sons was Kenneth Clarke Spearman, known as Kenny Clarke, later as Liaquat Ali Salaam and, affectionately, as Klook. Kenny was born, according to most reference books, on 9 January 1914. It seems that Kenny's birth was never officially registered, although some accounts say that he was born in Pittsburgh's Mercy Hall Hospital, and certainly this is recorded on his birth certificate. Ursula Broschke Davis in her book *Paris without Regret*, which deals with the French sojourns of four self-exiled black Americans – Kenny Clarke, James Baldwin, Chester Himes and Donald Byrd – says that Kenny was actually born on 2 January 1914.

Kenny's father, Charles Spearman, came from Waycross in Georgia, where he was born in 1886. He was a trombone player of indeterminate skill but a ladies' man of some distinction. His father had played bass drum in a masonic band. Kenny's mother, Martha Grace Scott, was born in Pittsburgh in 1889 and, according to Kenny, was an accomplished pianist. Kenny had a brother, Charles – known as Chuck – who was two years his senior.

The family home was in Wylie Avenue, in the integrated, bourgeois neighbourhood of Lower Hill – known locally as Little Haiti. It boasted not only a piano but also an organ, according to written reminiscences which Kenny left behind: 'We weren't rich, but we managed OK. Our home was blessed with a good upright model piano and a fairly good, grand model organ.'

One of Kenny's earliest memories was of being put on his mother's knee while she played the piano and taught him simple tunes. 'This developed in me a great love of the instrument,' Kenny told Helen Oakley Dance in a 1977 interview initiated by the Rutgers State University Institute of Jazz Studies. He had a natural ear and apparently showed great aptitude for the piano – but was even more fascinated by the organ. 'The sound possibilities of it attracted me even more than the piano, and before long I was composing simple pieces and playing hymns. The family and neighbours were all very proud and impressed when I had a chance to perform my pieces in the parish church.' Kenny was an altar boy at the church along with another youngster destined to make his mark in jazz – Billy Eckstine.

Kenny would play 'Nearer My God to Thee' and 'Just a Closer Walk with Thee' on the church pump organ, and it is very probable that, had he continued to have lessons from his mother, he would have become a professional pianist. But his mother died suddenly in her late twenties and Kenny's world was shattered. It is not clear from Kenny's various recollections just how old he was at the time. In some accounts he has said he was four, in others five, and in yet others six and a half. What is certain is that he was emotionally scarred by the event, particularly since his father had already abandoned the family and moved to Yakima in Washington State to stay, according to Kenny, 'with a great-aunt who raised apples'. Whether or not this 'great-aunt' was a euphemism for his father's new woman friend is not clear, but certainly Charles Spearman began another family, fathering at least seven more sons and daughters, including Frank, later to become a bass player and work with Kenny.

After Charles Spearman left the family home in Pittsburgh, Kenny's mother began a relationship with another man, a Baptist preacher called George whose surname is not to be found in any of the archive material that I have examined. George eventually moved into the house and, when Martha died, found himself with two young sons on his hands. He found a home for them in what Kenny had described in one account as 'a boarding school'. In fact, it was a home for abandoned or delinquent black children.

In her perceptive and sensitive account of Kenny Clarke's home background in *Paris without Regret* Ursula Broschke Davis makes the point that, in recalling his childhood days, Kenny tended to soften the harsher realities of his early years.

> Even in the last interview with me before his death, Clarke did not reveal the hurt from his childhood. Instead, he insisted that everyone had treated him 'very, very good' after his mother's death. The questions remain: why did he totally reject his home town and his childhood memories? Why was it so painful for him to return to those childhood memories? He had blocked most of them from his mind and did not want to discuss them. In almost every interview he told a different story. Each time he spoke of those early years, he related a different sequence of events, variable and contradictory anecdotes. He seemed to go out of his way to paint a rosy picture of his childhood without acknowledging the burdens of being an orphan.

My researches also support the view that there were some aspects of his childhood that Kenny preferred to forget or to present in a less painful form, and this resulted in some conflicting recollections. For example, in one account of his father's departure from the Pittsburgh home, Kenny says that he took his brother, Chuck, with him. But in the Rutgers interview, he says that Chuck was with him in the boys' home. And this was surely the case.

Founded in 1907, the Coleman Industrial Home for Negro Boys was located in Pittsburgh's Hill District. It was an old, dilapidated house with two large bedrooms, accommodating thirty-three boys aged from six to fourteen. Fortunately for Kenny, the teacher at the home, a Mr Moore, was an accomplished musician, 'capable of playing all the instruments' and he was quick to spot Kenny's aptitude and affinity for music.

'They had all kinds of instruments there,' Kenny told Ursula Davis. 'They had all brass instruments . . . I played the trumpet there. I played baritone horn and the peck horn.' He also had a spell playing trombone. But the brass instruments didn't really appeal to Kenny, so Mr Moore suggested that he try playing the snare drum. It was probably at around the age of eight or nine that Kenny Clarke picked up drumsticks for the first time. If Mr Moore did nothing else in his life, he at least qualifies for a place in history as the man who first put Kenny Clarke within striking distance of a drum.

'I really wanted to play the piano,' Kenny told Helen Oakley Dance, 'but lessons were so expensive and we didn't have much money – so I knew my stepfather would never consent to giving me piano lessons.'

Kenny stayed at the Coleman Industrial Home until he was eleven or twelve, playing the snare drum in the home's marching band for parades on Independence Day, Thanksgiving Day, Memorial Day and other local events. And each summer, the local masonic lodge, the Syria Mosque, would have a cookout for the boys. Kenny recalled to Ursula Davis:

> We would just walk around and eat ice cream all day long. Ice cream and hot dogs. I used to love the Syria Mosque day. I would always ask, 'When is Syria Mosque day, man?' They would say, 'Be cool.' Waiting on that, that was beautiful.
>
> When my grandfather died – I guess I was about ten – he dressed all up in his masonic marching suit with his hat and all this stuff, you know. . . . I said, 'Pap, are you going to a lodge meeting?' He said, 'No, son. I am just going to lay here.' I said, 'What are you dressing up for, Pap?' He said, 'That's all right, boy. Get out of here.' So I went downstairs. He laid up on his bed and died. He wanted to die with his uniform on! So that stuck with me. Anybody that dedicated! . . . So one day, I decided, I want to be a Mason.

And he duly became one.

Throughout his five or six years in the home, Kenny spent many hours in the house of his Aunt Julia and his Uncle Wash (Washington Childs) who was a carpenter. They were apparently his only accessible relatives. He described his Aunt Julia as 'a hip eighty-nine-year-old – and beautiful'. Ursula Davis suggests that though Kenny spoke of his aunt with warmth and admiration, 'it is possible that in his attempt to suppress the bad memories of being abandoned in a children's home, he exaggerated the amount of time he spent with her'.

After leaving the home, Kenny and Chuck stayed with their preacher stepfather in an apartment in the Baptist church and attended the Washington School together. The school had a large number of Jewish pupils and it was here that Kenny first met a young French boy called Bernard Hilda, later to become a bandleader and impresario in Paris and a long-term friend. It was also at this time that Kenny, who had no great reason to feel attached to the environment of his boyhood, began to dream about fresh fields and pastures new.

Ursula Davis writes,

> Kenny's childhood experiences give the first clues as to why he ultimately left the United States. He spent his childhood in Pittsburgh, but he disliked the ambience of the steelmill town. He did not fit in; he felt uncomfortable in his environment and could not communicate with people around him. Alienated and isolated, he had dreams of being somewhere else . . . He could sense that there was something more beyond the boundaries of his community, and he reached out to this new and unknown world.

He told Ursula: 'I wanted to go to France. I had read about it. I kept thinking about it: France, Paris, must be nice. I was twelve.'

Whether this young mind was quite so closely focused on Paris as his ultimate destination is open to considerable doubt; more likely it was a case of retrospective rationalization. But unquestionably, Kenny was anxious to distance himself from the Hill District where he had suffered so much anguish and insecurity and where he had no settled home. Records show that between 1922, when he was eight years old, and 1929, Kenny had at least five different addresses, two on Webster

Avenue, two on Bedford Avenue and one on Francis Street.

The records also show that after attending the A. Leo Weil and Letsche Elementary School from February 1922 until February 1925, he was registered at McKelvy Elementary School from February 1925 to the summer of 1926. And between 1926 and 1927 he was transferred to Watts Elementary, to Madison Elementary and then back to Watts. Nowhere is there a reference to the Washington School that Kenny mentions, though there are some gaps in the records. What is certain is that the last year or so of his formal education was spent at Herron Hill Junior High School. Unlike brother Chuck, who went to Schenley High School and graduated, Kenny dropped out at fifteen and set his sights on becoming a professional musician.

It was at this point in his life that an unhappy domestic incident resulted in him and his brother leaving his stepfather's home. The preacher caught Kenny one day going through the drawers of his desk. Kenny has said that he was looking for a photograph of his mother, something by which to remember her. But his stepfather did not believe him. He started to hit Kenny, and when Chuck intervened in his brother's defence, both boys were ordered out of the house. Looking back on the incident, Kenny was not bitter about his stepfather. He said, 'He was a nice guy. He did the best he could.'

Chuck went to stay with the family physician, Dr John Buchanan Buse, and Kenny was placed in a foster home with a family called Dunmore, where he remained until he was sixteen. Dr Buse sent Chuck to West Virginia State University on a scholarship to study medicine but fate decreed that he was not to become a medical practitioner. After a couple of years of study, Chuck was obliged to drop out from the university, having made his girlfriend pregnant and been persuaded by her father, and a loaded shotgun, to marry her. 'But,' Kenny said later, 'Evelyn was such a beautiful person and so intelligent. I told Chuck that he couldn't have found a better partner – she was well worth sacrificing a medical career for!'

For a while Chuck took a job in the post office and then he

and Evelyn moved back to Pittsburgh. Chuck became a foreman for the Pittsburgh Housing Authority and later worked for the Pennsylvania Railroad. He also became a union official, a role in which he demonstrated the same compassion and concern to help his fellow men that was very much in evidence in his brother's character. Chuck became a pillar of Pittsburgh society, a community leader. 'He could,' said Kenny, 'have been a professional drummer. In fact he started to play drums at about the same time I did and I always thought he was much better than me.'

Chuck remained in Pittsburgh until his death in 1977.

In January 1930, Kenny Clarke had to leave the Dunmores because the Pittsburgh authorities would not pay for him to live in a foster home after he'd reached the age of sixteen. He now had to support himself as best he could – so he went in search of a job. His first employment was in a soda fountain run by a man called Cohen Sali on the corner of Center Avenue and Patrick. He allowed Kenny to live on the premises, in a room above the shop. But Kenny did not intend to spend too much time dispensing ice cream sodas. He had his heart quite irrevocably set on a career in music. During his time at the Herron Hill school, Kenny had played drums in the band and had been allowed to take a snare drum home to practise. But he was playing military-style drums and needed to learn how to adapt in order to play dance and swing music.

He had developed a friendship with a dancer in a downtown Pittsburgh club called Johnny Porcher, with whose family he sometimes stayed, and Johnny invited him to the club from time to time so that he could get familiar with the different dance rhythms. At the club Kenny met and mixed with dancers, singers and musicians, enthusiastically soaking up the show-business atmosphere. 'I saw all these wonderful people singing and dancing and playing,' he said, 'and I said to myself, "Oh, God, this is where I want to be."'

Kenny also frequented a cabaret where the resident drummer, Biddy Johnson, would let him sit in. As Kenny recalled to Ursula Davis, 'Biddy would say, "Hey, Kenny, I have this little girl I want to talk to – play a few numbers for me."' At this point Kenny had absolutely no experience in playing dance music, nor did he know how to hold the sticks. But Gene Jenkins, the understanding bandleader, helped and encouraged him, and Kenny's natural ability did the rest. Eventually Kenny took over from Johnson.

It was at about this time, when he was seventeen, that Kenny heard his first real jazz record.

> It was the Fletcher Henderson Orchestra playing either 'Black Bottom' or 'Mahogany Hall Stomp'. I couldn't keep still! And from that point on I started listening to all the records I could get my hands on: Duke Ellington, Louis Armstrong, Cab Calloway, Bessie Smith . . .
>
> I began going to local dances every chance I had, and since I rarely had enough money to pay the admission, I used to sneak in through the side window or the back door. To be able to shake hands with the musicians and to get advice from them more than compensated for the humiliation I suffered from time to time in the form of a boot in the pants from the dancehall owner.

It took Kenny some time to learn how to play a proper roll on the snare drum, but he got some expert tuition from two Irishmen, Hammond and Gurlock, who ran a big music store on Penn Avenue. And he also drew inspiration from the drummers he heard around Pittsburgh. 'I thought they were the best drummers in the world, although their names are little known: James "Honeyboy" Minor, Manzie Johnson, "Hot Sticks" Hackett and Joe Watts.'

It was through Joe Watts that Kenny got his first professional job as a drummer. Watts was working with Leroy Bradley, whose band operated on the nightclub circuit accompanying the floorshows and playing dance music in between. Joe was in the Pittsburgh Fire Department and he invited Kenny to sub for him when his duties as a fireman had to prevail over his band work. Kenny got to play with the Bradley band three or four times a month.*

Klook's first regular engagement was with a trio led by Gene Jenkins which was resident at a cabaret called Derby Dan's. Jenkins was a fine alto saxophone player and the pianist was Earl Brown. Kenny joined them in 1931 at the age of seventeen,

* This is the consensus version of Kenny's professional début. However, another scenario has it that Joe Watts was actually the drummer in the Jack Spruce band at the Loendi Club on Fullerton Street and that Kenny took his place in *this* band.

and even at this early stage, he was thinking about the need for a new approach to drumming, a concern that was intensified some years later when Kenny's bass-playing brother, Frank, played him a Duke Ellington record featuring a Jimmy Blanton bass solo.

Kenny felt, from the time he started playing and listening to other drummers, that the drums were always too loud: 'Drummers used to play like they were deaf.' He thought that this heavy-handedness had developed as a result of the use of the tuba in the early jazz bands.

> At this time, to keep tempo, it was necessary to choose a very loud instrument like drums to mark the beat without dominating the rest of the orchestra – but with the tuba it was difficult to play soft and staccato at the same time – to be heard, the tuba player had to play long notes; and this made the drummer change his style. But when Duke Ellington introduced the bass fiddle into his band, it became the instrument of tempo, and this induced the drummer to play more lightly. Or, at any rate, it should have done.

Kenny's recognition of this change marked the beginning of the revolution that was to transform jazz drumming so dramatically and comprehensively.

Although he worked mostly as a drummer at this period, Kenny was still torn between drums and his first love, piano, an instrument he played well enough to be able to take piano gigs with some of the smaller local bands. 'But,' he said, 'my drumlike punctuations at the keyboard often proved disconcerting for the other musicians. It was also confusing for the drummers, who were playing a steady four beats to the bar; any strong, out-of-the-ordinary punctuation would throw them.' And he told François Postif that it was partly because he got so frustrated trying to play piano with unsympathetic drummers that he decided to concentrate on drums.

In the same year during which he took over the Joe Watts drum chair, Kenny also played in the band of George Hornsby, a very fine pianist from Pittsburgh's North Side. 'He came in the club one night,' Kenny said, 'and asked me if I could read. I told him I could make out, so he said, "Well, let's hear something fast." So Gene Jenkins, who always took care of me, played something up-tempo. Afterwards Hornsby said,

"That's pretty good. Here's my address and here's where we rehearse."'

Kenny gigged around with Hornsby for quite a spell, until the bandleader got religion, left the band and thereafter played only in churches. Kenny, whose interest in the church had been strictly limited to the music played there, was dismayed. 'George was a wonderful pianist and he had a good band – about fourteen pieces. He wrote many of the songs in the Fletcher Henderson library,' he said later.

According to Kenny in the Rutgers interview, when Hornsby left, the band was taken over by Roy Eldridge, who at that time was playing and singing like Louis Armstrong. The band, which included Roy's brother Joe on violin and alto saxophone and a tenor saxophonist, Henry Gerald, who was later to work with Kenny in the Teddy Hill band, toured around Pennsylvania, West Virginia and Ohio. Then Kenny left to return full-time to the Leroy Bradley band, an ensemble with three saxes, four brass and three rhythm, in which he remained until 1935. This band was one of the first to be heard over the air via KDK, Pittsburgh's first radio station, both in the station's studio and in a live broadcast from the Club Mirador in Homestead, Pennsylvania. The broadcasts were heard across a wide area of the United States.

While on a weekend engagement in Cincinnati, Kenny bumped into Mary Lou Williams and drummer Ben Thigpen, stranded in the town after the Andy Kirk Orchestra had broken up because of lack of work. Mary Lou told Kenny that the highly regarded orchestra run by Jimmy Jeter and Hayes Pilars was looking for a new drummer because Walter Kirk was leaving to head for New York. The Jeter–Pilars band was resident at the Plantation Club in St Louis and, since Mary Lou and Thigpen were heading for Kansas City, they agreed to give Kenny a lift.

'We all packed into Ben Thigpen's Model A Ford and took off for St Louis,' Kenny recalled later. 'Mary Lou put in a good word for me and I got the job the night we arrived.'

But Kenny was a little disappointed that the band, though a good, professional outfit, played mostly show music and radio broadcasts. He had expected that with such musicians as

Walter Page, Harry Edison and George Hudson in the line-up there would be more opportunity to pay some real jazz. He remained with the band for only two months, then left with Harry Edison to stay in Harry's home in Columbus, Ohio for a couple of weeks. Kenny's place in the Jeter–Pilars band was taken by Sid Catlett.

When Kenny returned to Pittsburgh he was able to rejoin the Leroy Bradley orchestra, which had now secured a residency at the Cotton Club in Cincinnati. This engagement lasted for about three years, and the band accompanied such visiting stars as the Berry Brothers and Ethel Waters. Every week there would be a guest orchestra: Earl Hines, Duke Ellington, Don Redman, Fletcher Henderson, Jimmie Lunceford and others. It was invaluable experience for the teenage Kenny Clarke. He learned to read music well and to play all kinds of styles; he also had exposure to some of the greatest bands of the period. 'It gave us a chance to sit right under the "heavy guns" of the day, hoping that something would rub off,' he said later.

'Playing for those shows was really a test for a drummer. I had to take care of all the accents – and I knew how to do that. It might have had something to do with the bombs I dropped later on! Because when I started playing jazz, those accents stayed with me. I was cooking way back then when I was about nineteen.'

In the space of little more than two years Kenny had developed at remarkable speed into a superb all-round drummer. It says much for his dedication and commitment that he achieved this with hardly any formal instruction, just by picking up tips and ideas from watching and listening to other musicians.

When the Cab Calloway band came to the Cotton Club, Ben Webster was highly impressed with Kenny's playing and tried to persuade him to make the almost mandatory pilgrimage to New York, which was rapidly becoming the jazz capital of the United States. Ben told Kenny: 'Look, you're a bitch. Why don't you come to New York, man? We need drummers like you.'

It didn't take Kenny too long to accept the advice.

3
That Basie Beat

At this point in their careers both Kenny and his brother Frank had dropped the family name Spearman for professional purposes, deciding that Clarke was a more suitable name under which to work. And for their very first gig in New York the Clarke brothers were to have the pleasure of working together.

Kenny left Leroy Bradley a very much more accomplished and confident drummer than he had been when he first joined the band and, for a while, he freelanced around the Cincinnati area with a local pianist named Call Cobbs. They both worked for some time with a band that was a sort of black equivalent to Guy Lombardo. But the music was not too exhilarating and Kenny began to think more and more about trying his luck in New York. He'd had a good chance to assess drumming at the top level with all the great bands of the day making appearances at the Cotton Club and he was confident that he could handle the competition. By now he had acquired a vibraphone and was developing an impressive facility on this instrument. Cobbs was also anxious to see what New York had to offer – so, one day towards the end of 1935, they took the bus to the Big Apple, Kenny's drums and vibraphone stacked in the rear, wrapped in blankets.

'We came through the Holland Tunnel,' Kenny said later, 'and Call said, "Well, Kenny, here we are in New York." And I said, "My God!" – and started shaking. I was suddenly so afraid that I didn't know what to do.'

And, in fact, for the first few months in New York, Kenny and Cobbs didn't do very much at all. Kenny said he was lucky

> because I had an aunt who lived on Lenox Avenue and I was able to stay with her, so I only had to pay a minimal amount of those heavy New York dues. Happily, I knew many of the musicians in the city from having met them on the road or when they passed through Pittsburgh. But I was new and the youngest drummer in town, so I didn't get into anything of consequence until early in 1936. Then my brother Frank came up to New York from Kansas City and we formed a trio with Call. We gigged around New York and the group soon began to attract quite a lot of attention. I was doubling drums and vibes and the vibraphone proved to be a big drawing card at the time – in fact, when we got bookings the clubowners would always say, 'Make sure Kenny has his vibes with him.'

At this stage Lionel Hampton, primary advocate of the vibraphone in jazz, was still on the West Coast and had yet to be heard in New York, so the instrument had a great deal of curiosity value.

The group played for a period in a Harlem club on Seventh Avenue, between 122nd and 123rd Streets, but broke up after a few months when Cobbs left to work with Art Tatum. He was hired to read the music of the tunes that Art liked and to play behind Tatum, who was virtually sightless. Cobbs was acting as Tatum's eyes. However, Frank soon found alternative work with a band led by tenor saxophonist Lonnie Simmons from Charleston, South Carolina, and he persuaded Simmons to hire Kenny. In the band were guitarist Freddie Green – another native of Charleston who had come to New York with Simmons – trumpeter Bobby Moore, who at that time was one of the most gifted players in New York, and a remarkable pianist from Philadelphia called 'Fats' Atkins.

Kenny Clarke said later,

> What a band that was! We worked at the Black Cat in the Village and we always drew good crowds. The word got around and we used to have a lot of top musicians come in to hear us – Benny Goodman, Gene Krupa, Teddy Wilson, Vido Musso and Harry James, who was twenty at the time and had just joined Goodman. After we finished at four in the morning, the cats would get up on the stand and jam with us sometimes until 10 a.m. Harry James would sit right beneath my sock cymbal. It was something new at the time and I'm pretty sure the idea came from Pittsburgh originally because all the drummers around home used to make their own sock cymbals with a spring-loaded strap attached to the left foot and the end of the spring screwed into the cymbals. It was called a sock cymbal because it came up to the level of a pair of long socks – just below the knee. When the drum companies started manufacturing sock cymbals, they called them hi-hats and made them much higher.

Using his sock cymbal to good purpose, Kenny Clarke really galvanized that rhythm section, which he was later to describe as probably the best, for its time, of any that he worked with. The sextet was a stomping band – so good, that it even passed the acid jazz-club test: the waitresses dug it. They used to dance between the tables.

'Freddie Green and I got something going with Lonnie's band . . . long before the new rhythmic approach to playing drums was noticed,' Kenny told *Down Beat*'s Burt Korall in a December 1963 interview. 'We'd come to the job early – at least forty-five minutes before the other players – and work out patterns. The results were swinging; you could tell. Even the waitresses enjoyed what we were doing.'

Kenny always claimed that the Lonnie Simmons rhythm section was the basic inspiration behind the characteristic sound and pulse of the famous Basie section of the Count, Green, Walter Page and Jo Jones. Certainly Basie spent a great deal of time at the Black Cat enjoying the band. Said Kenny in a 1965 interview with French jazz writer François Postif: 'Basie was knocked out at the way the rhythm section was jumping and I'm convinced that he changed his piano style after hearing "Fats" Atkins. When Basie first came up from Kansas City, he was playing great, two-fisted piano, just like James P. Johnson and Fats Waller.'

In fact, Kenny remembered hearing Basie play this way at the Roseland Ballroom. He, 'Fats' Atkins and Freddie Green would take advantage of a long intermission or a night off to check out the Basie band. 'Basie, Lester Young, Herschel Evans and Jo Jones already had big reputations,' Kenny said. 'And I'll never forget Basie's shouting version of "Prince Albert". He'd play it for me every time I walked in.'

Another personality who enjoyed the music of the Lonnie Simmons Sextet was the producer and jazz patron John Hammond, who registered his approval tangibly by paying the fifty-four-dollar fee to give the Black Cat the status of a union house, approved by the American Federation of Musicians.

The link between the Count Basie and the Lonnie Simmons rhythm sections offers a basis for fascinating speculation about the way in which the characteristic Basie sound developed.

Freddie Green was, of course, a common denominator – but it seems logical to suppose that Kenny Clarke, as well as Jo Jones, played a role in the section's evolution. In fact, Kenny and Basie became good friends and, after Freddie Green had joined Basie, Klook would sometimes go on the road with the band and Papa Jo would occasionally invite him to take over on drums at some of the gigs. Later, in May 1941, Kenny was to record a couple of tracks with the Basie band for the OKeh label.

What the Simmons and Basie rhythm sections most decidedly had in common was the even, four-beat feel which was steadily replacing the old 'boom-chick' rhythmic pattern. Basie's bass player, Walter Page, was one of the first to play four straight beats in the bar and, quite independently, Kenny Clarke had moved in the same direction, transferring the pulse from the bass drum to the top cymbal and producing what the French call a *son continu*. As the distinguished German critic, producer and jazz historian Joachim Ernst Berendt has pointed out, 'Kenny was the first drummer to produce the *son continu* – keeping the cymbals and the hi-hat ringing and punctuating the sound with "bombs" from the bass drum and accents on the snare drum.' And Freddie Green was one of the pioneers of using four even down-strokes on guitar in playing rhythm backing.

Basie, who was essentially a stride pianist, certainly modified his piano style to accommodate to this new approach. As James Lincoln Collier points out in *The Making of Jazz*:

> He developed a simple, very spare manner of playing, which is today instantly recognizable. His choice in both solos and when accompanying the band was to neglect the left hand on the presumption that the other members of the rhythm section would carry the beat; with his right hand he comped sporadically, just throwing in enough precisely-timed notes or figures to keep the music going. Properly placed, these fragments helped to spur the band on.

And the function of Basie's right hand in this context can be compared with the function of Kenny Clarke's left hand and right foot. The beat placement may have been different, but the effect was similar: heightening and sparking the rhythmic pulse. Just how much Basie was influenced or inspired by 'Fats' Atkins is difficult to determine, but Kenny Clarke always insisted that 'Fats' played 'in exactly the way that Basie later became famous for'.

Kenny also told Postif that Freddie Green had a big influence on the way the Simmons rhythm section sounded. Kenny said,

> I was very much impressed by his great rhythmic qualities. Between Freddie, 'Fats' and me, we introduced a new lightness to the rhythm section. And long before we hit New York, Frank and I had spent a lot of time experimenting with new ways of integrating the bass and drums and making them more complementary to one another. Frank had bought a record of a Duke Ellington session featuring Jimmy Blanton and we listened to it over and over and agreed that drumming had to change to accommodate the new bass style. It all came together in that Black Cat band and it was a great shame that we never got the chance to make any records. That was the best rhythm section of my whole career.

The much-acclaimed Black Cat combo broke up when Lonnie Simmons took a job playing solo Hammond organ at a club in Chicago. He was one of the pioneers of the instrument. Freddie Green and Bobby Moore were recruited by Basie, 'Fats' Atkins went back to Philadelphia and Frank Clarke joined the band of pianist Buddy Johnson. It is likely that the record date the Clarke brothers made for Decca on 1 May 1941, with the Buddy Johnson band, was the last time that they played together.

It appears that Kenny and his brother had little contact with one another after the Lonnie Simmons Sextet disbanded. Frank moved out to California, having become disenchanted with New York, and worked with T-Bone Walker and Jack McVea, among others. He died in 1949.

4
The Days of Hayes and Hill

The next major landmark in Kenny Clarke's career was his joining the Edgar Hayes band in April 1937. Edgar Junius Hayes, from Lexington, Kentucky, had come to New York in 1927 with his Symphonic Harmonists for a long residency at the Alhambra. From 1931 to 1936 he was the pianist and principal arranger of the Mills Blue Rhythm Band, led by Lucky Millinder. When he decided to return to bandleading, he recruited a number of Millinder sidemen, including saxophonist Joe Garland, trumpeter Henry Goodwin and alto saxophonist/clarinettist Rudy Powell.

'Edgar Hayes was like a father to me,' Kenny said later. 'He got me into Local 802 [the New York branch of the American Federation of Musicians] and taught me many tricks of the trade. He was also responsible for my first record date and my first overseas tour.'

Kenny Clarke was still doubling on vibraphone at this time and he played this instrument on the Hayes quintet session for Decca in September 1937 which produced the hit record 'I Know Now', sung by Bill Darnell. Kenny's first record date, however, was with the full fourteen-piece band on 9 March 1937.

Bookings for the Hayes band were handled by Lunceford Artists Inc., the agency operation run by bandleader Jimmie Lunceford in partnership with Harold Oxley. Oxley, according to Kenny, was 'a wonderful guy and just about the only fair agent in the business. That's why he didn't stay.' It was Oxley who decided, in the summer of 1937, that Edgar Hayes should take his band to Europe at the end of the year as a kind of 'pathfinder' operation for a major tour by the Jimmie Lunceford band. Thus it was that in December 1937 an enlarged Edgar Hayes Orchestra sailed from New York headed for Gothenburg, Sweden. It was a bitterly cold day when the musicians disembarked, but their spirits were lifted when they played their first concert that same evening in the newly-constructed Konserthuset. Kenny recalled:

> Never before had we played in a hall with such perfect acoustics. For the first time we were able to hear ourselves without getting the sounds back a split second late as they bounced off ceilings or walls. By comparison, the halls we had been playing in back in the United States were tobacco sheds and gymnasiums. We found much the same conditions throughout the tour. In Stockholm the concert hall was even more impressive.

The tour continued through Finland, Denmark, Holland, Germany and Belgium; audience reaction was enthusiastic. It was as the musicians were about to leave Germany to cross the border into Belgium that an incident occurred which underlined just how unusual a sight a collection of black musicians represented for the European citizenry at this time.

Kenny remembered:

> A few of us had been window-shopping in this border town and, as we turned away to continue down the street, we were suddenly aware of a crowd of people all around us, gaping, pointing and muttering. It was as though we were men from Mars and it was intimidating. There must have been a hundred people there; we were surrounded. Then, suddenly, a little old English lady came on the scene, swinging her umbrella wildly from left to right and yelling, 'Get out of the way! Let them through. Haven't you ever seen a brown man before?' And she cleared a path for us, apologized sweetly on behalf of the crowd and wished us a pleasant trip.

Belgium received the band with wild enthusiasm and the musicians were astonished at how much some of the people knew about jazz. The band was not scheduled to play any dates in France, but while he was in Brussels, Kenny could not pass up the opportunity to make a quick trip to Paris, the city he had dreamed of visiting as a schoolboy in Pittsburgh. During his short stay in Paris he met Django Reinhardt, André Ekyan (the saxophone and clarinet player who worked with

Django and Coleman Hawkins) and tenor saxophonist/clarinettist Alix Combelle. Paris was as seductive to Kenny as he had expected it to be and he wanted to stay longer to soak up more of its special atmosphere. But he had to rejoin the Hayes band for the return voyage to the United States. The band left from Bremen and arrived back in New York in April 1938. It was during this four-month tour that Kenny made the first recording under his own name in Stockholm. The Kenny Clarke Kvintett – Henry Goodwin, Rudy Powell, Edgar Hayes, guitarist Eddie Gibbs, bassist Frank Darling and vocalist James Clay Anderson, with Kenny playing xylophone – made four sides, including 'I Found a New Baby' and 'Sweet Sue'. It is a reflection of the high regard Hayes had for his twenty-four-year-old drummer that he gave him this opportunity.

While the band was in Holland, Kenny had been offered a job by bandleader Bobby Martin, who needed a replacement for Kaiser Marshall. But, even though the prospect of an extended stay in Europe appealed to him, he turned it down. Later he congratulated himself on making the right decision, because when the Hayes band got back to New York it was booked into the Apollo for a date and a very special musician was recruited into the trumpet section – John Birks 'Dizzy' Gillespie, the man who was to become Klook's great friend and musical associate. It was the start of a close relationship and a potent musical symbiosis which, developing and flourishing over almost half a century, was to have an enormous impact on the course of jazz history.

Dizzy had been working with various bands: the Latin outfit of Alberto Socarras, the Savoy Sultans and, most notably, the Teddy Hill Orchestra, one of the most impressive and forward-looking bands of the period. Gillespie had toured Europe with the Hill band just about a year previously and had beaten Kenny into Paris by some months, playing at the famous Moulin Rouge in the Place Blanche.

Dizzy stayed only briefly in the Edgar Hayes band – though he subsequently returned for odd gigs – then he went back to the Teddy Hill band, where Kenny was to join him some months later, after an eight-month spell with Claude Hopkins. Kenny was always concerned to put on record the important contribution the Hayes band made to his musical education. He told Helen Oakley Dance:

> That was a most fantastic outfit. It was the university for me and it was in that band that I first started to write music. Edgar, Joe Garland and Rudy Powell all helped me. Joe Garland used to give me trumpet parts and he'd say, 'Well, you play along with the brass and put accents where you think emphasis is needed.' Joe was a fine tenor and bass saxophonist and a good composer. He wrote 'In the Mood' and we recorded it in 1938, long before Glenn Miller made it a worldwide hit.

Edgar Hayes, quoted in Dizzy Gillespie's autobiography, says of Kenny:

> He was a great one to jump in on open beats; he would jump in where the whole band was playing ensemble work . . . I have some of the records where Kenny used to play with me before Diz. But Kenny started off that beat, drumming like that, Kenny and another drummer named Shadow Wilson. They were great drummers, jumped in there, just like Diz jumped in on other solos. Right between those beats, they would put a stomp beat in there and it would go over nice.

In his excellent, exhaustive and authoritative book *The Swing Era*, Gunther Schuller also pays a handsome tribute to Kenny Clarke's work with the orchestra of Edgar Hayes:

> In some ways the most outstanding player in the Hayes orchestra was drummer Kenny Clarke. Twenty-three years of age when he joined Hayes, Clarke was from the beginning an individual, imaginative percussionist who saw no sense in playing in any of the accepted drumming swing styles, including that of Jo Jones with the Basie band. While most drummers were converting to the ride and sock cymbals by 1937, Clarke, a long-time admirer of Chick Webb, remained loyal to the snare drum and bass drum, using both instruments – at first more the snare than the bass – to evolve a new style of drumming that integrated the drums much more into the arrangements and soloists' work. By participating in the orchestra's rhythmic figures as a full-fledged ensemble instrument, as well as injecting independent snare-drum figures increasingly into the accompaniments to soloists, the result was suddenly a true musical dialogue between drums and orchestra, a discourse lifting the drums (at least partially) out of their limited role as a mere provider of rhythmic substructures (and as an occasional soloist in a 2- or 4-bar break). Clarke's drumming on almost all the Hayes sides is exciting to hear, as he alternates between supporting the band in incisive rhythmic figures and laying down a firm, buoyantly swinging beat. Clarke's timing and sense of balance were superb, especially considering that he was pioneering a whole new concept of big-band drumming. The crispness of his under-

> lying snare-drum accents and occasional counter figures is a delight to experience, especially from the vantage point of nearly fifty years of retrospect. For here we have the beginnings of modern drumming.

Schuller describes Clarke as the Lester Young of the drums in the sense that he veered away from the prevailing mainstream in the late thirties. 'I believe that the bright, positive swing and disciplined ensemble playing of the Hayes band can in large measure be attributed to Clarke's spirited drumming,' he says.

One of the reasons why the Hayes band was so highly regarded was that the leader was a great believer in the axiom that practice makes perfect. Kenny said that before the European tour the band would rehearse almost every day at the Renaissance Casino for a period of months.

> We would rehearse until we became dog-tired – but, you know, no one would ever look at his watch and say, 'Well, that's it.' Never. We just rehearsed and rehearsed. So when someone said, 'Hey, let's go out and get a Coke,' we'd take a break – but we would be back to rehearse again until six or seven in the evening

Very little is recorded about Kenny's spell with Claude Hopkins except that he played vibes as well as drums in the band which, at the time, featured Vic Dickenson – 'the kind of trombone player that I would have wanted to be if I'd stayed with the instrument', said Kenny.

His technique on vibes had improved significantly, thanks to some coaching from Adrian Rollini. 'We used to rehearse together in Bill Mather's drum store,' Kenny told Helen Oakley Dance. 'Adrian and I became real tight, because he'd show me things. I used to have trouble playing real fast on the instrument . . . Sometimes Freddie Green would come in and play guitar with us.'

Kenny had also listened to Lionel Hampton, 'but I liked him better as a drummer. He was a fabulous drummer.'

On one occasion with Hopkins at the Howard Theater, Kenny was playing a rented xylophone, not in its first youth. He was halfway through a solo on an up-tempo version of 'China Boy' and being urged on by the audience, when the instrument started to disintegrate. A critical screw had become loosened and the xylophone finished up in an untidy heap on the stage. Claude Hopkins told him: 'Kenny, pick up your bed and walk.'

It is not entirely clear whether the Hopkins period preceded or followed Kenny's engagement with the Teddy Hill band – he gives two differing accounts. In any case, it was his entry into the Hill band – on the recommendation of Dizzy – that was to have the most significance historically, because it was in that band that the special musical chemistry between Kenny Clarke and Dizzy Gillespie really began to effervesce.

Theodore 'Teddy' Hill was a saxophonist and clarinettist from Birmingham, Alabama who had started out as a drummer. Before forming his own orchestra in 1932, he played with King Oliver, Luis Russell, James P. Johnson and Henry Allen. During its eight years of existence the band featured many fine soloists, including Roy Eldridge (whom Dizzy succeeded), Bill Coleman, Frankie Newton, Dicky Wells and Chu Berry. In *The Making of Jazz* James Lincoln Collier describes it as 'a black swing group that was never more than modestly successful despite some excellent talent'. But Hill's was a critically important band in jazz music's evolutionary process.

With Dizzy in the band – a musician he knew to be warmly responsive to his ideas – Kenny was less inhibited about putting into effect some of the changes he had started to think about seven years earlier. He had been hesitant, in the bands before Hill's, about being too free with his innovatory ideas of style and technique, but now, with the lively encouragement of Dizzy, he felt more confident. 'Diz and I knew we were moving into something,' Kenny said.

He told Helen Oakley Dance:

> Diz used to sit behind me on the stand and I would write out little things and pass them back to him. I'd say, 'Hey, Diz, how do you think this would sound?' He'd say, 'We'll try it.' So I began to play, you know, with my right stick on the top cymbal instead of the sock cymbal. And everyone said, 'Why don't you play the sock cymbal?' But I told them there had to be a better way, because if I used my right hand on the sock cymbal, I couldn't use my left hand.

In *Bird Lives!*, Ross Russell quotes Kenny as saying that he had become tired of playing like Jo Jones, thinking it was time for jazz drummers to move ahead, and he later said that he could never see the advantage of playing the sock cymbal with the right stick. (Interestingly, some five decades later, drummers like Dave Weckl and Joel Rosenblatt solved the 'cross hands' problem by placing the hi-hat on the right-hand side of the kit.)

Kenny told writer Leonard Feather than on the Hill band's arrangement of 'Swanee River' he began 'kicking, playing off-rhythms'. He added, 'Diz was fascinated; it gave him just the right impetus he wanted, and he began to build things around it.'

The essence of the innovations that Kenny was introducing was what he called, many years later, 'co-ordinated independence'. It involved co-ordinating the left hand with the right foot and the right hand with the left foot. And it was the basis of the most important rhythmic revolution in the history of jazz.

A less romantic version of the great drumming apotheosis, as related by Kenny in some interviews, has it that some of the numbers played by the Hill band, such as 'Harlem Twister', were taken at such furious tempi that his right foot would get very tired and, to rest it, he would simply play accents instead of the traditional four beats in the bar. 'Keeping a steady tempo at those speeds would have been impossible drumming the old way,' Kenny said. Fatigue may have been a factor, but I prefer to think that it was an incidental one. Also, it is totally in keeping with Kenny's unassuming nature that he would sometimes use such a banal explanation rather than claim any special inventive ingenuity, simply to save himself from the psychological discomfort that he could experience when talking about himself. Considering his contribution to jazz, he was one of the least arrogant musicians I ever met.

The final outcome of Kenny's experimentations in the Teddy Hill band is one of the most well-worn anecdotes in jazz history. Teddy Hill, who was ready to accept new ideas and rebel against routine, nevertheless preferred not to break completely with the established swing traditions. He would say impatiently to Kenny, 'What is this klook-mop stuff you're playing?' And that is how the new movement was first baptized, before it became rebop, then bebop, then bop. And that is how Kenny Clarke became 'Klook'.

Hill might have tolerated the rhythmic anarchy if it had not been for the growing discontent of some of the more conservative members of the band, the most vocal of whom, apparently, was Henry Woode, the trombone player and an uncle of bassist Jimmy Woode. 'Kenny breaks up the time so much,' Woode complained. 'Why doesn't he play four beats on the bass drum?'

Kenny would respond to the complaints by saying, 'If you are playing, the tempo should be in your head. Don't depend on me. Depend on yourself, because if you are playing music, the tempo you are playing must be in your head. If it isn't, it's no use you being here if you are depending on someone else to keep the tempo for you.'

Heretical stuff – and the twenty-five-year-old heretic from Pittsburgh eventually got fired from the Teddy Hill band. Later, when he worked extensively with Jimmy Woode, he never missed an opportunity to rib him about his reactionary uncle.

Before the crunch came, the Hill band was hired for a long engagement in the Savoy Pavilion for the World's Fair opposite the Chick Webb Orchestra. It was a remorselessly tough schedule of sixteen shows a day and, as well as doing their own programme, the band also backed the celebrated dancing troupe, the Lindy Hoppers.

'Chick Webb's band was on the left bandstand and we were on the right,' Kenny remembered. 'And after we finished playing I would go and sit behind Chick to watch and listen.'

Kenny was still learning – a process that continued until the day he died. For him, Chick Webb was the best drummer in New York at the time and Kenny assimilated a great deal by watching and listening to him at every possible opportunity. 'The guys in the Hill band would say, "Hey, where's Kenny?" – but pretty soon they knew where to look,' Kenny said. 'Chick had a very special conception of drumming which I knew I could never capture, but I learned a lot about technique. And about dedication. Music was his whole life.'

He also received real encouragement from Webb, who

would tell him between sets, 'Hey kid, you're making progress. You're doing fine. Keep it up!'

If Teddy Hill and some of his sidemen were unimpressed by the unconventional drumming of Kenny Clarke, Dizzy Gillespie certainly was not. As he says in his autobiography:

> By far the most important thing that happened to me musically during this period [1938–9] was my friendship and association with the great drummer, Kenny Clarke, who as you can see was hardly considered great by certain people in those days. Kenny was modifying the concept of rhythm in jazz, making it a much more fluid thing, and changing the entire role of the drummer, from just a man who kept time for dancers to a true accompanist who provided accents for soloists and constant inspiration to the jazz band as a whole. Kenny's style of drumming, with 'bombs' and 'klook-mops' in the bass drum and regular rhythm in the cymbals, was ideal for me. It furnished just the right amount of support, push or embellishment I needed. These were important changes. A lotta people didn't like them. Kenny had to suffer a lot to make those changes, but in the end, he turned out to be right.
>
> Kenny initiated a new language into the mainstream of jazz drumming. You know, like you 'infuse'. He infused a new conception, a new language, into the dialogue of the drum, which is now *the* dialogue.

Kenny always regretted that the Teddy Hill band did not make more of a mark in jazz history, besides having been a key stepping stone enabling him and Diz to take their ideas forward. And all jazz lovers must regret that no recordings were made of the band while Klook and Diz were with it. Kenny told François Postif, 'It was the freshest orchestra I ever heard. Out of the rut, full of new ideas but still in the traditional style. It really deserved much more recognition.'

After leaving Teddy Hill, Kenny packed in a wide variety of engagements over the next three or four years, including his epic residency at Minton's Playhouse. In 1939 he played in Arkansas with Sidney Bechet and in February the following year made some Bluebird sides with Bechet in New York. As a result of these dates and Kenny's special adaptability, Bechet hired Kenny for a summer engagement at the Log Cabin in Fonda, NY. Later that year, Kenny recorded with both Mildred Bailey and Billie Holiday.

Klook also joined the band of his fellow Pittsburghian, Roy Eldridge, for engagements at the Arcadia Ballroom on Broadway and at Kelly's Stable on 52nd Street. For a period in 1940,

Kenny became resident drummer at the Apollo – a job in which he revelled because it gave him the chance to accompany all manner of performers, a challenge he had always enjoyed. Daisy Clarke remembers Kenny telling her that on his opening night at the Apollo all the chorus girls came to him at the end of the show and kissed him, because, they said, he'd played so beautifully for them. 'Kenny was so deeply touched that his eyes filled with tears – it was the first time he had cried since the death of his mother,' Daisy told me.

Kenny loved working in stage bands, playing for singers, dancers, acrobats, jugglers, even comics. 'It was a helluva scene,' he told *Jazz Times* writer Bill Quinn in a November 1980 interview. 'We played behind all the top stars of the time. And the drummer's role was the key to everything that went on. You had to hit all the rimshots and bombs right on the money. If you blew it even twice in one night, you could get your hat.' He and Zutty Singleton used to call the drum stool at the Apollo 'the electric chair'.

In the summer of 1941, Kenny got the biggest break of his ten-year career. Big Sid Catlett was leaving the Louis Armstrong Orchestra to join Benny Goodman, and through Big Sid and his old Edgar Hayes colleague Joe Garland, who was in the Armstrong band, Kenny was offered the drum chair. Big Sid told him, 'Hey, Kenny, Pops digs you – you'll be OK.' And to make sure that Kenny had the best possible chance of holding down the job, Catlett took him to the Renaissance Casino, set up his drums and worked steadily through the Armstrong pad.

Said Kenny later:

> Pops had heard me play at the Apollo and Sid had been listening to me at Minton's. He was one of the first to put the word out. He used to say, 'Man, that little cat is playing something out there. You'd better watch out. That little cat out there is mean.'

Kenny had been a great admirer of Big Sid since he first heard him in 1935 and he was hugely gratified and slightly incredulous at the trouble Catlett was taking to prepare him for the Armstrong job. He took him through the book over and over again and by the time the Armstrong band hit the road for a tour, Kenny was ready.

At an early rehearsal on the tour in West Virginia, Satchmo walked in halfway through, listened a while and then said of Kenny, 'Man, that drummer is modern!' And Kenny said afterwards, 'I guess it was a change from what he had been used to – but since Louis was really the first modern jazz musician, he had an ear for innovation. After I heard what he had said I went at what I was doing with much more determination.'

The first date on the itinerary was in the W.C. Handy Theater in Memphis, Tennessee. Louis had taken to calling Kenny 'Little Gizzard' and when they hit the bandstand that night he asked Klook, 'Everything OK, Little Gizzard?'

'Yes, Pops, I'm OK,' Kenny answered.

Louis called 'Skeleton in the Closet' and 'Struttin' with Some Barbecue', and Kenny sailed through the arrangements without a hitch:

> I played them like I'd been playing them for years and Pops couldn't believe it. 'Where did you learn those?' he asked me. 'Doggone it, you sound like you play them all the time.' I told him, 'Thanks, Pops.' Then he reached into the pad and came up with something that he thought I'd never heard before. But I had it down. Of course, I never told him that Big Sid had taken me through everything! That clinched it. From then on I was Satchmo's man. I could wake him up any hour of the night when no one else would dare.

There was an occasion, Kenny recalled, when some of the musicians in the band wanted to get high. They knew Louis had some pot but it was late at night and none of them had the courage to knock on his door. So they put Kenny up to it and he rapped boldly on the door while they hung around apprehensively in the background, ready to run.

'Who's that?' Louis called.

'It's me, Kenny, looking for a smoke.'

'Oh, is that you, Gizzard?'

And when Pops opened the door and put two sticks of pot in Kenny's hand, the other musicians, back in the shadows, were more than a little impressed.

The tour with Louis Armstrong brought Kenny into America's southern states for the first time. Up to that point he had had no first-hand experience of the savage racism and ruthless segregation that prevailed in the South though, of course, he had heard plenty of chilling accounts from southern musicians who had settled in New York.

Kenny told Bill Quinn in a November 1980 interview for *Jazz Times*:

> We'd finished playing, you know, and these cats would come up with their big .45s on their hips and one would say, 'Any of you boys got to go to the toilet, we'll take you. We don't want none of these white folks messing with you in the john.' Those who had to go . . . shit, *all* of us had to go after seeing those looks some of the audience was giving us. Anyway, those of us who had to go would put up our hands. They'd take us and bring us back. Those .45s saved our asses a lot of trouble . . .

Kenny and Satchmo got on together extremely well, it appears. As well as being superlative musicians they also had in common a pronounced partiality to pot smoking. Pops was a prodigious smoker of unbranded cigarettes all his life and Klook was always ready for a joint.

Al Levitt remembers Klook recalling a gig with Louis when, in a rare loss of concentration, Kenny got behind with the beat. He had enjoyed a particularly potent smoke just before going on stage and it took its toll. After the gig, Satchmo came to Kenny's hotel room looking uncharacteristically solemn. Klook waited for the dressing down – but it didn't come. Instead, Pops rolled two massive joints, handed one to Kenny and they then sat smoking away and making general conversation.

Eventually Louis got up, said 'Goodnight' and left the room – but just before closing the door, he put his head round it and said, 'Klook – *after* the gig; not before.'

Kenny felt he was doing fine with Armstrong, but Satchmo's manager, Joe Glaser, didn't approve of Klook's recruitment into the band. Said Kenny,

> He told Pops that he needed a drummer with a bigger name – someone at least approaching the stature of Big Sid. Louis liked what I was doing, but Joe wanted me out. So in the end they brought in O'Neil Spencer, the man who had been working with John Kirby. At that time he had a bigger name than I did – I was just known as 'that little kid who drops bombs – you know, what's-his-name'.

The circumstances of Kenny's dismissal from the Armstrong

Orchestra were pretty disreputable, if Kenny's recollections are correct:

> After we played a date in Waycross, Georgia, the band headed out in the bus to Henderson, Texas. But I was told I wouldn't be needed. I watched the bus pull out, Pops looking out of the window and calling, ''Bye, Gizzard.' And there I was at 1.30 in the morning stranded in Waycross with my drums. Luckily a black cab driver pulled up and asked if I needed a lift. I told him the story, and that I was needing to get back to New York. He put the drums in the cab and drove me to a coloured restaurant that was open all night. He said, 'Leave your drums in the hall, get yourself something to eat and I'll be back in the morning to take you to the train station.' I had a pocketful of money because I'd been paid off, so I got myself some food and then chewed the fat with the restaurant owner all night, telling him about Harlem. Sure enough, at seven o'clock the cab driver arrived and took me to the station, where I got the train to New York.

On the train his good luck held. An attractive young woman came aboard somewhere along the route. She had brought a packed lunch with her and invited Kenny to share it.

> So I had some cold fried chicken and biscuits. And when the train got to her home town, there was a stopover for three hours so she invited me home and gave me a slap-up meal of fried fish. After we'd eaten she took me back to the station, and I went on my way to New York.

Kenny's diminutive stature, his ready smile and his effortless amiability often brought out the Good Samaritan in people. 'The gods really smiled on me that time,' he said. And for Kenny, a smile from the gods more than compensated for a scowl from an artist's manager.

There was a sequel to the Glaser incident some eleven years later, following the formation of the Modern Jazz Quartet. Klook, Milt Jackson, John Lewis and Percy Heath were rehearsing in the Nola recording studios in New York. The telephone rang and Klook answered. A voice said, 'Hello, is Klook there?'

'Speaking. Who is this?'

'Joe. Joe Glaser.'

Kenny put his hand over the mouthpiece and told the other musicians. They knew how Kenny had been fired from the Armstrong band and they told him to put the phone down.

'What's on your mind, Joe?' Kenny asked.

'Well, I'd like you to come down to the office so that maybe we can talk about me handling the quartet.'

'Sorry, Joe – I don't think we're very interested.' And Klook hung up. The management of the MJQ was instead entrusted to Monte Kay.

In the autumn of 1941, on the recommendation of Eddie Barefield, Kenny was hired for a five-week tour with Ella Fitzgerald, who had taken over the Chick Webb Orchestra after the death of the leader in June 1939. Dizzy Gillespie was also in the band – much to Klook's delight – and it was on this tour that the two of them created the immortal 'Salt Peanuts'. (The antecedents of 'Salt Peanuts' offer what Gunther Schuller delightfully terms 'a field day for the inveterate "jazz lick" researcher'. Dizzy, in his autobiography, says he 'set the riff on a record date with Lucky Millinder in 1942, in an arrangement [by Tab Smith] of "Little John Special" '. But Schuller, in *The Swing Era,* points out that the riff can be found on the John Kirby Sextet recording of 'Sweet Georgia Brown', arranged by Charlie Shavers and recorded in 1939. Gillespie says that 'Salt Peanuts' wasn't officially credited as a composition until 1943. He first recorded it with his sextet for the Manor label in January 1945, with Shelly Manne on drums. And he adds, 'I don't recall how the tune got that name, "Salt Peanuts", but as a tune on its own, it became more elaborate than just a riff. Regarding the composition with Kenny, we'd get together and somebody'd think of something to play, and you'd say, "No man, let's try this." And if that didn't work we'd try something else and something else until we'd finally say, "Yeah, man, that's it!" That's how you do it, by common agreement. Kenny and I came to a helluva agreement on "Salt Peanuts".')

Kenny decided he should have a new set of drums for the Ella gig, so he got an advance, bought a set from the store of his good friend Bill Mather and agreed with Ella's road manager, Tim Gale, to have so much deducted each week from his pay.

During the tour Kenny and some of the musicians returned to New York with Ella to make a record date for Decca. Then they headed for Boston, where they were booked at the Coconut Grove. A few days later all the musicians on the recording date received a cheque for the session – except

Kenny. He complained to Gale, who told him, 'You don't get a cheque – the money comes off what you owe for the drums.' Kenny argued that the instalments for the drums were supposed to be deducted from his salary and had nothing to do with the record date. And he dug in his heels, refusing to play that night unless he was given a cheque for the recording session.

Kenny recalled:

> Ella took my side. She said that she wouldn't make the gig unless I played and she told Gale to pay up. The argument went back and forth and then the manager of the Coconut Grove intervened and said, 'Come on guys, the band must go on – it's time.' But I told Ella that I wouldn't play until I got my cheque. The argument went on for thirty minutes and the manager got furious – but I wouldn't budge. Finally Gale gave in, I got my cheque and we went on and played. I really appreciated the way Ella stuck up for me. She saw Gale wasn't being fair.

Kenny didn't stay long with the band after that. Eddie Barefield left, then Dizzy joined Cab Calloway and Klook decided it was time for him to pull out, too. Minton's was waiting.

5
Minton's

The part played by Minton's Playhouse in shaping the course of jazz history has been abundantly documented; but it was such a vital and significant chapter in the personal story of Kenny Clarke, and so central to his role as a key innovator, that I make no apology for recapitulating here one of the revelatory, true stories in jazz – a true story which has become a veritable legend and, like all good legends, has been decorated with a good deal of fanciful and subjective embellishment.

Minton's Playhouse was a shabby, unprepossessing room – part of the Hotel Cecil building – on Harlem's 118th Street between Seventh Avenue and St Nicholas, which, in 1940, did not offer any outward sign of becoming a research and development centre for young musicians intent on taking jazz in dramatically new directions. Yet Minton's was to become the crucible in which many of the elements of the new jazz were fused.

Henry Minton, the man who gave the venue its name, was a former saxophone player who became the first black delegate to Local 802 of the American Federation of Musicians. He was, by all accounts, a diligent representative of the musicians he served, and when he opened the Playhouse, he did it to provide his musician friends with a place to play and a place to eat. Minton loved his food and was no mean cook.

Initially the Playhouse was largely patronized by the more elderly of the neighbourhood's citizens, but when, in 1940, Minton appointed Teddy Hill as manager of the club, a new era began. Hill, who had fronted his own band since 1932, had become disenchanted with bandleading because of the rapacious habits of certain impresarios and he was only too willing to assume the responsibility of booking the musicians for the Playhouse. When he took over, the band in residence was a mainstreamish dixieland outfit led by Albert 'Happy' Caldwell, a tenor saxophonist from Chicago.

Teddy decided to replace Caldwell and, ironically, the man he picked to assemble a new group for the club was the man he had fired from his band a year or so earlier for being a wayward non-conformist: Kenny Clarke. The poetic justice of this was firmly emphasized by Klook when he recounted the story in the ensuing years. Kenny also said, in an interview with François Postif, that it was Dizzy Gillespie who was largely responsible for his being hired by Hill. 'Dizzy liked the way I played and recommended me – and Teddy had a great admiration for Diz.'

Kenny took over the musical direction of Minton's early in 1941:

> It was a great success right from the beginning, because it was the ideal place for us. It had a bar, a back room with veiled lights, a podium for the musicians and little tables for the guests.
>
> To begin with, I put together a quartet. I had wanted to have Dizzy on trumpet, but he was with Cab Calloway's band. So I hired another trumpet player who'd been with us in the Hill band: Joe Guy. He was twenty years old and playing a little bit like Dizzy. In the Hill band Dizzy had played both lead and solos, but when he wanted to save his lip, Joe would take some of his solos and almost unconsciously, I guess, he copied Dizzy's style.

Kenny's first choice for the piano chair was Sonny White – a man he described at the time as his favourite New York piano player and a very close friend.

> I loved Sonny and the way he played and he was such a sweet person. We were so close he used to tell people that we were cousins. But Sonny at the time was Billie Holiday's accompanist and he loved that job so much that he didn't want to leave it. He was a tremendous piano player in the style of his idol, Teddy Wilson.

The man who got the gig on piano was twenty-year-old Thelonious Sphere Monk, who had previously been working with gospel groups on the church circuit. On bass, Kenny hired Nick Fenton, on the recommendation of his friend Joe Guy. Nick, a former violinist, appealed to Kenny because he had a flawless sense of time. 'I thought it was a pretty good combo,' Kenny said, 'and as we started working together it emerged that we all had much the same idea of the direction in which we wanted to take the music.'

Minton's had long been a favourite haunt of musicians and singers because of the twin attractions of its authentic soul food and its policy of welcoming sitters-in, and Kenny felt that the quartet could provide a perfect musical foundation for visiting soloists.

On Monday nights it was Teddy Hill's custom to offer an open-house welcome to members of the cast of the current show at the celebrated Apollo Theatre on nearby 125th Street, and they would come to feast on ham hocks, fried chicken, grits, black-eyed peas, barbecued ribs, hot biscuits and good bonded whiskey. They would also come to listen to the most stimulating and adventurous jazz music to be heard anywhere in New York at that time.

Though Teddy Hill, the bandleader, had been outraged at the unorthodox indiscretions of Dizzy and Klook, Teddy Hill the manager was delighted to make Minton's a nursery for the young lions who wanted to push back the frontiers of jazz.

Ralph Ellison wrote, in a 1959 article for *Esquire*,

> It was Hill who established the Monday Celebrity Nights and who allowed the musicians free rein to play whatever they liked. Perhaps no other club, except Clark Monroe's Uptown House, was so permissive, and with the hospitality extended to musicians of all schools, the news spread swiftly. Minton's became the focal point for musicians all over the country.

At the beginning, musicians dropped in just to listen – because the Kenny Clarke Quartet was pioneering some new ideas. Former members of Teddy Hill's band were regular visitors, as were the musicians from the bands which played the Apollo.

Minton's was open from 10 p.m. until four in the morning and Teddy Hill's open-house policy on Monday nights – an off-day for most musicians – was introduced on the basis that musicians who were allowed to come and eat for nothing would also be ready to play for nothing. And it proved to be a most successful policy. After supper, musicians would go to the bar to drink – paying this time – and listen to the music. And they would go up and jam with the quartet – if they were up to it.

When the Jay McShann band was playing at the Apollo, its twenty-year-old alto saxophonist started to be a regular customer. His name was Charlie Parker. He would come and eat fried chicken and then sit in. Recalling the arrival of Parker on the scene, Kenny Clarke said:

> He was absolutely marvellous. Personally I never heard him play badly. And whenever we had any free moments, Monk and I would go to the Apollo, or to Monroe's Uptown House at 133rd Street and Seventh Avenue, to catch him. He played alto at that time like Lester Young played tenor – and we enjoyed that very much because it was a higher sound, more penetrating. Being in Kansas City, I think Charlie picked up a lot from Lester, particularly in the rhythmic sense – though he went a little further musically.
>
> It was the same with Dizzy and Roy Eldridge. Dizzy had started out as a disciple of Roy's, but he wanted to make the style more musical, to put more music in the rhythm things than Roy did. Monk was also moving in that direction – so we formed a little clique, all working towards the same goals.

Charlie Parker had been jamming regularly at Monroe's Uptown House – working for tips – since he was eighteen. When he returned to his native Kansas City in 1939, he was hired by Jay McShann, with whose band he worked until July 1942. Parker was not a regular at Minton's in the early days of Klook's residency. But he came very much into the picture later – because Klook quickly recognized Bird as a musician of formidable stature with fresh and fearlessly innovative ideas totally concordant with his own.

Talking to Ross Russell about his first impressions of Charlie Parker, Klook said:

> Bird was playing stuff we'd never heard before. He was into figures I thought I'd invented for drums. He was twice as fast as Lester Young and into harmony Lester hadn't touched. Bird was running the same way as we were, but he was way out ahead of us. I don't think he was aware of the changes he had created. It was his way of playing jazz, part of his own experience . . . We laid a few dollars on him and got him to move from Monroe's down to Minton's. Teddy Hill refused to put another man on

the payroll, so we decided to pool our money and give him an allowance. I invited him to the pad I shared with Doc West, another drummer and a good cook. We set him up to meals. He could really eat. He was thin and half-starved. He was trying to live off the kitty at Monroe's.

The revolutionary task force was now complete and it was in the hyper-stimulating atmosphere for which Minton's became famous that, night after night, Kenny Clarke further developed the techniques with which he had started to experiment some ten years earlier.

Charlie Christian had been the first sitter-in to be co-opted into the sanctified inner circle of Minton's. He became a virtual resident of the Playhouse. In a little more than a year, the genius of this self-effacing, soft-spoken guitarist from Oklahoma had propelled him from relative obscurity to stardom with the Benny Goodman band. According to Kenny Clarke, Charlie was crazy about the Minton's rhythm section. The Playhouse provided an atmosphere and a freedom that was a complete contrast to working with the Goodman band and reading arrangements all the time. In that band he wasn't able to play the things he really wanted to play. At Minton's there was nothing written – everything was free and improvised, and Charlie was in his element. He was a very shy person and was not very close to the musicians in Benny's band. He didn't know New York and so he found Minton's a very welcome spot where he could relax and play what he wanted. 'Most of the time he just kept his amplifier in the Playhouse so that he could play with us every chance he got,' Kenny said.

It was Charlie Christian, said Kenny (quoted in Leonard Feather's *From Satchmo to Miles*), who first used the word 'bebop' to describe the musical style that was being fashioned night after night at Minton's. Kenny had an enormously high regard for Christian and he would probably have become a full-time member of the group had he not succumbed to chronic tuberculosis in February 1942 at the tragically young age of twenty-five.

And it was Charlie Christian who helped Kenny Clarke to create one of the first of the bebop originals. Kenny has recalled in several interviews how he and Christian were at the

Douglas Hotel on St Nicholas Avenue one day, visiting a friend who played ukulele.

> I fooled around with the uke for a bit and then Charlie took it out of my hand and showed me how it was possible to make all kinds of chords 'by just stretching your fingers right'. He handed back the ukulele and I started experimenting. I got an idea that sounded good and went up to my room in the hotel and wrote it out. I called it 'Fly Right'. Later Monk helped develop the number and Joe Guy took the manuscript to Cootie Williams. Cootie had Bob McRae make an arrangement of it. Cootie used to play it at the Savoy Ballroom. It became his theme. He recorded it on Columbia.

In *From Satchmo to Miles,* Leonard Feather observes,

> It was typical of the prevailing resistance to change that a recording of 'Fly Right' by Williams's band was not released until almost thirty years later after a researcher discovered it. Meanwhile Clarke had recorded it with a small group of his own in 1946 (for Charles Delaunay's Swing label) under its other title, 'Epistrophy'.

Identifying the precise authorship and evolution of licks, which became lines, which became compositions, is sometimes a complex exercise, as in the case of 'Salt Peanuts'. French pianist Henri Renaud recalls a comparable tangle in connection with another Minton's opus:

> In the early sixties I was playing with Kenny and Jimmy Gourley in the Blue Note. One night I started to play a tune I had heard on an Al Haig Prestige recording – 'Opus Caprice'. After the first few bars Kenny gave a big grin of recognition and said, 'Ah! "Pagin' Doctor Christian"! That was a piece Charlie wrote which we used to play at Minton's.'
>
> Nowadays it is universally known as 'Rhythm-a-ning' and associated with Thelonious Monk. I once asked Al Haig where the tune came from and he said it was a traditional children's song. The first four bars of the song feature in Mary Lou Williams's arrangement of 'Walkin' and Swingin'' for the Andy Kirk orchestra, recorded for Decca in 1936. Mary Lou was one of the first to discover Charlie Christian and it was she who recommended him to John Hammond.
>
> It seems to me very possible that Thelonious Monk, who was the resident pianist at Minton's, used the first four bars of 'Pagin' Doctor Christian' in 'Rhythm-a-ning'. Klook's spontaneous reaction when I played the passage in the Blue Note that night showed that he recognized it as a Charlie Christian theme.

Another indispensable – and irrepressible – sitter-in with the modern-jazz minstrels of Minton's was, of course, John

Birks Gillespie who, in 1941, was relieved of his duties in the Cab Calloway Orchestra after a stormy altercation with the leader – the famous spitball incident which is fully chronicled in Dizzy's autobiography, *To be or not to Bop*.

Dizzy became a regular at Minton's where the nightly jam sessions, as he says, 'were seedbeds for our new, modern style of music'. After acknowledging Thelonious Monk's contribution to the bebop revolution in the harmonic and spiritual areas, Dizzy says:

> It was Kenny Clarke who set the stage for the rhythmic content of our music. He was the first one to make accents on the bass drum at specific points in the music. He'd play 4/4 very softly, but the breaks, and the accents on the bass drum you could hear. Like, we called them dropping bombs.

The Minton's stage was no place for pretenders or fledgling musicians of a nervous disposition, because a most harrowing fate awaited those who failed to measure up: the withering, corrosive scorn of Thelonious Monk (so, at least, the legend has it). The men from Minton's were very much an elite corps who protected themselves against unwelcome sitters-in by working out themes that were too complex and intricate for run-of-the-mill players.

Recalling the Minton's era, Kenny Clarke said,

> We didn't really play bebop then. You know how people in show business always put labels on things – just to sell them more. I can understand that – but we never wanted to be called beboppers, because what we did, we invented tunes and chords so that people we didn't want to play with us just couldn't get up on the bandstand. That's why we did that. Well, we had musicians from all over New York wanting to get in on the act and eighty per cent of them just couldn't play our music. And we sure didn't want to sit and sweat and back up somebody who wasn't doing anything to inspire us. It was important to our enjoyment of the music – and its development – only to have people playing with us who fitted in with what we were doing. So when we had unwelcome sitters-in we used to play different chords and things to discourage them.
>
> Now, in the blues, they would maybe play four chords; Monk would play twenty chords and completely lose them. Sometimes he would say to them, 'Man, get off the stand – you're not playing right.' So the guy would say, 'But I thought we were playing the blues' – and Monk would scowl and say, 'That's not the way we play the blues here; we changed all that.' Monk could be very snide when he wanted to be – nothing fazed him. He'd say anything to anybody if he thought it right. So people were

always excusing him – because he could be very outspoken. That's the way he was. If he had got his face broken every time he did something like that he would have been dead at twenty-one. Sometimes he was just plain insulting. 'Oh, man,' he'd say in disgust, 'you just can't play.' That was the way he would eliminate them. It was really a joke.

And quoted by Ross Russell in *Bird Lives!*, Kenny explained:

Pretty soon Minton's got to be a bad place for older cats. Dizzy began coming up regularly and that gave us the four key instruments – trumpet, alto, piano and drums. That, plus a good bass, was the band of the future. One night, after weeks of trying, Dizzy cut Roy Eldridge. It was one night out of many, but it meant a great deal. We closed ranks after that. To make things tough for outsiders, we invented difficult riffs. Some of our tunes used the 'A' part of one tune, like 'I Got Rhythm', but the channel came from something else, say 'Honeysuckle Rose'. The swing guys would be completely hung up on the channel. They'd have to stop playing.

Illinois Jacquet has recalled how Monk used to play in fiendish keys to discourage the less gifted musicians from staying too long on the stand, and it seems more than likely that such devices were employed in order to keep the music on a high and innovative level. In a 1968 interview with *Crescendo* contributor Les Tomkins, Kenny Clarke said:

Sometimes when we kept other players off the stand by deviating from the bar lines and so forth, it was done purposely and maliciously, I must say. But things like that must be done in order to accomplish a purpose you believe in. A great change had to be brought about. Jazz had undoubtedly reached stagnation point and it needed to move on to something more valuable and worthwhile – something comprehensive, but technically complicated – to raise standards of musicianship. That was the purpose entirely.

Reading the stories about the unceremonious treatment meted out to visiting musicians who couldn't quite cut it, it always seemed to me that this was somewhat out of character for Kenny Clarke, whose concern was always to help and encourage musicians to develop and to build their confidence. I have heard many stories about the way in which he gave young players and singers a chance to sit in with him, sometimes in the teeth of militant opposition from his fellow musicians.

And in an interview with Burt Korall, published in the

5 December 1963 issue of *Down Beat*, Kenny said, 'There's no truth to the story that we purposely played weird things to keep musicians outside the clique off the stand. All we asked was that the musician be able to handle himself. When he got up on that stand, he had to know . . . '

Contrast this statement with one Kenny gave to Leonard Feather: 'We'd play "Epistrophy" or "I've Got My Love to Keep Me Warm" just to keep the other guys off the stand, because we knew they couldn't make those chord changes. We kept the riffraff out and built our clique on new chords.'

The apparent inconsistency in Kenny's recollections is, I believe, not too difficult to explain. Such conflicting statements occur from time to time in Kenny Clarke interviews and, though partly explained by memory lapses are, in my view, more properly attributable to an inherent, deep-rooted desire in Kenny's psyche to emphasize the good-natured and wholesome side of life – just as he would do when recalling his childhood. I'm certain that, had it been left only to him – rather than to the abrasively critical Thelonious – there would not have been such a high casualty rate on the Minton's bandstand. The negative interpretation of Kenny's allowing Monk to do what he himself probably shrank from doing would be that Klook was wanting in moral courage. But anyone who knew Kenny Clarke would immediately torpedo that theory. It is simply that he had genuine compassion – and when recalling the Minton's days to Korall, he was almost certainly expressing a personal, not a collective, point of view.

On the other hand, many of the musicians I have talked to about Klook have indicated that he didn't suffer musical fools, impostors or incompetents gladly – not in any show of arrogance, but simply because of his total commitment to professionalism and his lifelong conviction that the customers were entitled to expect musicians to set themselves the highest standards of performance.

At all events, whatever the hazards that faced would-be sitters-in, there was no shortage of musicians eager to prove that they could hold their own with New York's jazz elite. Sometimes on the small Minton's stage there would be as many as twenty musicians jamming together.

The members of the clique were no respecters of reputations. Sitters-in had to put up or shut up – and they included Chu Berry, Benny Carter, Coleman Hawkins, Johnny Hodges, Willie 'The Lion' Smith, Lucky Thompson, Ben Webster and Lester Young; Harry James, Hot Lips Page, Charlie Shavers and Cootie Williams – and the sixteen-year-old Miles Dewey Davis Jr, who was studying at Juilliard at the time; and Clyde Hart, Jess Stacy, Art Tatum, Mary Lou Williams and Tadd Dameron.

As Kenny Clarke told Leonard Feather many years later, 'Tadd was one of the first pianists playing eighth-note sequences in the new legato manner. I heard him playing flatted fifths in 1940 and it sounded very odd to me at first.'

The Minton's stage was certainly no place for fainthearts, but such was the wildfire excitement that the new music generated that even illustrious bandleaders put their reputations at risk by sitting in with the resident clique – among them Duke, Count Basie, Andy Kirk, Artie Shaw and even Charlie Christian's boss, Benny Goodman.

One of the most persistent sitters-in at the Playhouse was a black saxophone player known simply as 'the Demon', whose principal claim to fame was that he was quite extraordinarily awful. Trumpeter Joe Wilder remembers the Demon:

> He was the worst player ever to enter Minton's. He was horrible. When I used to go there, Eddie 'Lockjaw' Davis was more or less in charge of the band. The group would be playing away like mad and the Demon would take out his horn and stand sort of menacingly in front of the stage until, ultimately, one of the guys would say wearily, 'OK, Demon, come on up and play.' And the Demon would take the stage. But he didn't play one chorus. He played fifteen. Finally, Jaws would go in search of Teddy Hill who would hurry to the stand, stand in front of it with his arms folded and holler, 'Get off my goddam bandstand, Demon!' It became a standing joke.

Thelonious Monk's style of playing put a great deal of emphasis on accents and dynamics and this caused Kenny Clarke to modify his drumming approach:

> I had to change my style to play with this clique. Monk's using accents and things made me play accents more myself, on the bass drum. And I needed to play lighter because we weren't using a straight beat. I couldn't play brushes all the time, so naturally I played the top cymbal and used

the bass drum for punctuations. When people came into Minton's they'd say, 'Hey, listen to that drummer's accents on the bass drum; man, I never heard that before!'

Those formative years, it was a pattern that had to be perfected like anything else. But our unity of style came from our association; that was an unconscious thing. I have always believed that three or four musicians cannot play together if they dislike one another. But for us, we were great friends, we began to learn from each other. We developed a style and a co-ordination that had never previously existed. At Minton's we played traditional tunes like 'How High the Moon', 'Stomping at the Savoy', and things like that – they were popular in those days. But Monk was also composing a lot of pieces, and he made us play them. He would start out the tune and we had to follow. But he always liked to explain just what he was doing – he would run through the chords and melody with us.

The musicians we most liked to play with at Minton's were guys like Don Byas, Lester, Hot Lips Page, Diz, Bird, Freddie Webster, Tadd Dameron and Miles. Most of the musicians who played there were young – I was one of the oldest and I was still under thirty. You know, we hadn't really set out with the idea of developing any particular style of jazz. It just happened like that. When you think back, you tend to say, 'Well, those guys were really doing something!' But it was really unconscious.

Occasionally Kenny would take a break from the drums and play a set on vibraphone while Jack 'The Bear' Parker or Kansas Fields sat in. 'But,' he said later, 'I gave up vibraphone after I heard Milt Jackson in 1945.'

Unhappily, very little of the potent music from those epic Minton's days was captured on record. While many of the visiting musicians recorded individually, away from the Playhouse, the great spontaneous sessions themselves went largely unpreserved for posterity. However, in May 1941, as Ross Russell notes in *Bird Lives!*, a recording enthusiast, Jerry Newman, using a portable turntable, glass-based acetate discs and a cumbersome amplifier, began recording sessions at Minton's and Monroe's.

Writing of one of the tracks, 'Down on Teddy's Hill', Russell says, 'That Clarke was indeed the founder of the new percussion style is evident. One hears a forcing beat, a delicious complexity of polyrhythms, and an unusual awareness of the needs of the soloist.'

Some of the Minton's and Monroe's recordings were later issued on the Xanadu and Everest labels and feature, as well as the club regulars, Kermit Scott, Don Byas, Joe Guy, Hot Lips Page, Rudy Williams, Al Sears and Roy Eldridge. The repertoire is predominantly standard material – 'Sweet Georgia Brown', 'Stompin' at the Savoy', 'Indiana', 'The Sheik of Araby', 'Mean to Me', and so on – but there are also a couple of takes of 'Epistrophy'.

Of that whole band of rebels, renegades and kickers-over of musical traces, the most assiduously eccentric, without doubt, was Thelonious Sphere Monk. Talking about his memories of Minton's many years later, Kenny recalled:

> After we finished work, Monk and I would head for the same subway station. He was living downtown on 61st Street and I was living uptown on 146th Street – so we took trains going in different directions. But it was torture for me every night because Monk would be very, very drunk. He would wait with me on my platform talking away for a few minutes, then he would cross the rails to catch his train on the opposite platform. And I was always afraid that he was going to connect with the electric rail and electrocute himself. But I guess God must look after drunken musicians, because Monk made it safely every night!

Although Minton's was, in Ross Russell's phrase, 'the bebop laboratory', its redoubtable regulars were not the only pioneers of the new music. Bud Powell and Max Roach made signal contributions, as did Fats Navarro. And when Charlie Parker was asked in 1953 to name the key founders of the new school he added Don Byas and Ben Webster. But unquestionably the most important of these was Bud Powell, even though he was not a participant in the early Minton's sessions. Dizzy Gillespie, in his autobiography, asserts categorically that Bud never played at Minton's – though Illinois Jacquet, in the same book, says he did. Kenny himself couldn't remember Bud at the Playhouse in the early days, but he recalled playing there with him in 1947. Certainly, Bud was a major contributor to the bebop revolution.

Without diminishing in any way the indispensable creative imput to the new movement made by Charlie Parker, Charlie Christian, Dizzy Gillespie and Thelonious Monk, I believe it is fair to say that the parts played by Kenny Clarke and Bud Powell have been consistently underestimated by jazz writers. In the case of Bud Powell, his psychological problems were undoubtedly a major factor in his failing to achieve his due measure of recognition from writers and from the jazz public at large – although he was massively revered by his peers. In an interview with Francis Paudras in Paris in 1984, Kenny Clarke said, 'Bud and Charlie Parker were on the same level. Bud was as strong on his instrument as Charlie was on his – and after a while there was a sort of quarrel because Bud knew more about harmony than Bird. Charlie was always a little bit jealous of Bud.' And Arthur Taylor, who worked with Bud Powell in 1952, told me in 1966:

> Bud and Bird played a couple of two-week engagements at Birdland and they were always getting at each other. Bird would cut off Bud's solos and take the tune out, so Bud would hit back by only half-playing behind Bird. But Bud was the greatest ever as far as I am concerned . . . It's hard to play jazz piano without playing something Bud played; and if you don't play something he played, well you're not really playing jazz piano.

Paudras, admittedly a dedicated champion of Bud Powell, quotes musicians such as Sonny Stitt, Sonny Rollins, Paul Bley and Bill Evans as regarding Bud as a master – and Allen Eager as having been more impressed by Bud than Charlie Parker.

In Kenny Clarke's case, he had first of all to contend with the fact that drummers are popularly regarded as peripheral contributors to the evolution of jazz. The old line about a band consisting of 'fifteen musicians and a drummer' still has a disreputable currency. Kenny was additionally handicapped by his own modesty and humility which, though estimable human virtues, tend to militate against achieving a just level of celebrity. And both Kenny and Bud, having exiled themselves in Europe in the late fifties, were certainly victims of the 'out of sight, out of mind' rule.

According to Dizzy Gillespie, Kenny's role 'was just as important a contribution as mine or Charlie Parker's or Monk's'.

The last word on the subject I will leave to Kansas Fields, a contemporary of Kenny Clarke's and a one-time fellow exile in Paris, who recalled in a March 1986 interview published in *Cadence* magazine:

> I used to tell Klook when they were bopping at Minton's, I said, 'Man, I'm waiting for you to make a mistake, 'cause it sounds like you're going to make a mistake – but you always come out.' He said, 'That's bop for you, man, that's bebop!' They call him the father of bebop drums, and he was.

6
Conversion to Islam

The seeds sown at Minton's Playhouse were to flower in profusion on 52nd Street, where the proliferating clubs along the world's most celebrated jazz thoroughfare increasingly reverberated to the new music. It was in the clubs on 52nd Street that the adventurous jazz strain which had been propagated in Harlem's Minton's and Monroe's began to garner a wider audience.

According to Dizzy Gillespie, quoted in Arnold Shaw's *The Street that Never Slept*, it was bebop that really gave 52nd Street its identity. 'By the time we came down,' Dizzy said, 'our ideas were beginning to be accepted. Oh, it took some time – but 52nd Street gave us the room to play and the audiences.'

In the space of one block on this street of Victorian brownstone buildings, between Fifth and Sixth Avenues, were such legendary rooms as the Onyx Club, Kelly's Stable, the Famous Door, the Three Deuces, the Hickory House and Jimmy Ryan's. 'In several hours,' as Marian McPartland once observed, 'nursing a few drinks, you could travel musically from New Orleans up to Harlem and bop.'

The new music did not, however, elicit a positive response from all of the Street's habitués. As Arnold Shaw notes, sportswriter Jimmy Cannon likened bebop to a hardware store in an earthquake; and John Hammond characterized it as 'a collection of nauseating clichés'.

But at least four clubs on the street were prepared to give house room to bebop – the Spotlite, the Three Deuces, the Onyx and Kelly's Stable. And it was to Kelly's Stable, run by

Ralph Watkins, that Kenny Clarke took a group after leaving Minton's. The band included his old Playhouse cohorts, Monk and Nick Fenton, plus Roy Nelson on trumpet and Ike Quebec on tenor saxophone. The ensemble was known for some inscrutable reason as Kenny Clarke's Kansas City Six. It was in Kelly's, according to Leonard Feather, that Quebec and Klook developed the theme 'Mop Mop' on the 'I Got Rhythm' changes, which was subsequently recorded – and appropriated – by Coleman Hawkins, who later played with Kenny at the club. Ross Russell, on the other hand, maintains that the theme was created by Charlie Parker under the title 'Red Cross' during a September 1944 recording session.

Klook also played at Kelly's with a most eclectic Benny Carter Septet consisting of Dizzy Gillespie, guitarist John Collins, clarinettist Al Gibson, bassist Charlie Drayton and pianist Sonny White. The band was something of a microcosm of the different strains of jazz to be heard in the fabulous Street during this great transitional period. The graceful, polished fluency of Benny Carter, with his silky legato, and the decorative, Wilsonian piano of White must have contrasted intriguingly with the brazen, hectoring trumpet of Gillespie and the bebop drumming of Clarke, with its unpredictable placement of snare- and bass-drum accents.

In his autobiography, Dizzy recalls, 'We were playing all kinds of music. We played a lot of Benny Carter's music, but my music, too, Al Gibson's music, John Collins's music.'

Benny was playing alto and tenor saxophones and trumpet at this period – though he laid aside his trumpet when Diz was in the group. He was a most accommodating leader, who gave Gillespie and Clarke the freedom to play in their own style.

Henry 'Red' Allen came in to hear the band one night, was immediately impressed with Kenny and invited him to join his band. Soon afterwards Kenny left to join Allen for dates in Chicago – at the Downbeat Room and the Garrick Stage Lounge in the Loop district – and in Boston. Allen's band included trombonist J.C. Higginbotham, alto saxophonist Don Stovall and bassist Clarence 'Benny' Moten.

Kenny spent more than a year with Allen, but was obliged to terminate the association in mid-1943 when he was drafted into the US Army. He was despatched to a camp in Alabama for his basic training, after which he was assigned to a chemical-warfare company specializing in laying down smokescreens and deploying bombs of a far more lethal nature than those he'd dropped at Minton's.

By this time Kenny had developed a close relationship with a beautiful girl he'd met soon after her graduation from high school. Her name was Carmen McRae. She had been studying piano for five years and was thinking of using her pianistic and songwriting abilities to build a career in show business, which had a powerful attraction for her. She and Klook had been introduced by Eddie West, a tapdancer with a group called the Chocolateers.

Carmen recalls:

> I must have been eighteen years old. We met in New York and I was immediately impressed because he was such a likeable man. Eddie West's wife, Pauline, had been at high school with me, so we became a sort of foursome. And then I heard Kenny play – and I couldn't believe it. I thought he was absolutely fantastic. We became very close and after a while he told me that he was in love with me and that one day we would get married. I told him he was crazy.

But crazy or not, Klook was certainly determined. He was twenty-nine years old and Carmen was the first woman he'd met of whom he was fond enough to wish to develop a lasting relationship.

Kenny had discovered that the wives of servicemen posted overseas qualified for a regular allowance and, as he had no family, he wanted Carmen to have the money. 'I told her,' he recalled to Helen Oakley Dance, 'that since we loved each other and had known each other for so long, we ought to get married.'

So, some time in the summer of 1944, Technical Sergeant Kenneth Clarke Spearman invited Carmen McRae to visit him at the US Army training camp – Camp Seibert in Alabama – and they were married in nearby Gadsden.

However, army life did not have an irresistible appeal for Klook, and although the Camp Seibert unit had a jazz group with which he could keep his hand in, he missed the excitement of working in clubs, concert venues and studios with his fellow musicians and indulging in the time-honoured jazz musician's pursuit of hanging out. So he escaped again – went AWOL for 107 days – and managed, in that time, to fit in spells of playing with Cootie Williams and Dinah Washington. Then the army reclaimed him, and it was as *Private* Spearman that he was shipped overseas at the end of September 1944. He was told that he could either be posted abroad or transferred with the unit band to Jackson, Mississippi – and, on the basis that the unknown devil was preferable to the known one, Klook opted for foreign shores.

Kenny Clarke landed in Liverpool in late September 1944 and was stationed at Tetworth, the marshalling point from which American troops were flown to augment the Allied Forces in their post-D Day push through Western Europe. He soon involved himself in music by forming a vocal quartet and teaching its members the melodies and harmonies of some of the hymns he had played on the organ of his home in Lower Hill, Pittsburgh. The camp chaplain was, seemingly, so impressed with Kenny's evangelical enthusiasm that he contrived to keep him at Tetworth and away from the front line for some weeks. 'Each time my name got called,' Kenny said, 'the priest would say, "No, no – I need Private Spearman here to play the harmonium."'

This holy dispensation was not to endure, however, and in October Kenny was transferred, via Le Havre, to the 13th Special Service unit near Rouen in Normandy where he spent some of his time learning how to lay down smokescreens. He also found time to continue enriching the musical life of his army colleagues. He formed a twelve-strong choir, coached and rehearsed them, and set off on tours of the active-service units, regaling them with renderings of such bop-free compositions as 'Deep Purple', 'A Sleepy Lagoon' and 'Sentimental Journey'.

It was while he was in Rouen that he met up once again with his old leader, Teddy Hill – a fellow draftee – who told Klook that he would be welcome to take a group into Minton's at any time when they got back to the States.

Kenny had given up playing drums in the army, partly because the army equipment was less than exemplary and partly because he just didn't want to carry drums around. Instead he returned to the trombone to accompany the choir, along with an alto-saxophone player, trumpeter, pianist, bassist and a drummer who, taught by Kenny from scratch, had become remarkably proficient in a very short space of time.

The choir and band played various bases in Germany and Belgium and, much to Kenny's satisfaction, also visited Paris, among other French cities, from time to time. Paris was even more attractive to Kenny at this time than he remembered it from his brief visit in 1938 during the Edgar Hayes tour. He told Michael Haggerty in a 1982 interview:

> I took the opportunity to renew my acquaintance with some of the musicians I'd met in my previous visit, and I promised myself that I would return as a civilian some day and spend some time there. In fact, the whole European way of life appealed to me. The tempo of life is slow and easy, and the people are not so superficial.

One Paris engagement was for a four-day spell at the Théâtre de la Madeleine whose audience included Gertrude Stein and Alice B. Toklas. After the performance, Miss Stein said to Kenny, 'My God, what beautiful music! How on earth can you find time to play and sing so wonderfully with this terrible war going on?'

It was also on this visit to Paris that Klook first made the acquaintance of Charles Delaunay, the distinguished French writer, producer and critic who, twelve years earlier, had been the co-founder, with Hugues Panassié, of the Hot Club de France. It was Delaunay's championing of bebop that caused a most acrimonious schism among the Hot Club hierarchy, with the Panassié school arguing that the new music was a travesty of the real jazz. Out of Klook's meeting with Delaunay would come, some two years later, the first bebop records to be issued in France.

Back in Rouen, Kenny discovered that another musician had been posted to the base – a certain John Aaron Lewis, from Albuquerque, New Mexico. He, too, had taken up trombone 'because there were too many pianists about'.

With Lewis, Kenny assembled a larger band and began writing arrangements for it. Lewis also contributed some scores, among them an original called 'Bright Lights' which later became a key chart in the library of the legendary Dizzy Gillespie Big Band as 'Two Bass Hit'.

After Rouen, Klook was posted to a base near Heidelberg in southern Germany, where he was involved in a Special Services propaganda unit that was educating German youth about the American way of life, using films and music programmes. But before he left Rouen, he told John Lewis that he had good connections in New York and gave him his telephone number. 'If you need some introductions after you get out of the army, call me,' he said.

From Heidelberg, Kenny was transferred to a unit in Mannheim and then finally, early in 1946, back to the United States for demobilization. It was in Fort Dix, New Jersey, during the demobilization process, that Kenny met a saxophone player from Savannah, Georgia, who made a great impression on him: James Moody. Also there, waiting to be discharged from army service, was tenor saxophonist Joe Gayles. None of the three knew it at the time, but they were all to meet up again very shortly in the Dizzy Gillespie Big Band.

It took ten days for Klook to go through the demobilization process at Fort Dix. Then he headed straight for New York. It was April 1946. He'd been away from the scene less than three years – yet he was aware, as he made the rounds, that the jazz world can have a disturbingly short memory. He had been, to some extent, forgotten – a mild foretaste of what was to happen a decade later when he moved permanently to France.

There was a joyous reunion with Carmen, who was beginning to win recognition as a most accomplished singer, appearing with Kenny's former boss, Benny Carter, and with the Count Basie Orchestra. Although Kenny was never very forthcoming about his romantic life, many of his close friends of the time testify that he and Carmen had a most loving relationship.

'He really adored her,' Annie Ross remembers, 'and he would talk about her a lot. I'm sure they were very much in love with each other.'

Carmen herself recalls:

We were actually together for about three years after he came out of the army. We separated just before he went off to Europe with Dizzy's band at the end of 1948. Somehow the relationship just came to an end – and I don't even remember the reason.

We lived together in my mother and father's house in Brooklyn. They were upset at first that I'd gone off to Alabama to marry him because they hadn't even met him. 'Why do you have to get married, Carmen?' they asked me. 'We don't know anything about this guy.' But I told them, 'Well, I'm the one who is going to be living with him.' After they met Kenny, though, they really loved him. I did, too. I was impressed with his charming, dignified manner from the first time I saw him. He always talked softly and made sense. And I never saw him really mad – not about anything. He could get his point across without raising his voice – and he would never say anything bad about anybody. He was a very sweet, gentle man.

We never really got mad at each other. Of course, our married life had its ups and downs, like any other – but we were always good friends. In fact, after we separated he took an apartment in Brooklyn because he said he wanted to be near me.

But even when we were living together, Kenny was always off somewhere. He didn't take me with him, and I told myself that I had to have a life of my own. I guess we never really should have gotten married, even though we liked each other so much – at least, not then. We should have waited. But he was the one who really wanted to get married; and I agreed because I wanted to get out of the house – although we finished up staying there anyway.

But, still, we never had a harsh word. It was just that he was gone most of the time and I was bored without him . . .

If the marriage between Carmen and Kenny died from a sort of mutual neglect, certainly the friendship survived and flourished for the rest of Klook's life. Carmen still keeps a picture of Kenny on the dresser of her Beverley Hills home. 'It was one Dizzy gave me – Klook sitting there smoking a joint and laughing away. It was very typical of him. Our relationship was always good – always. The marriage didn't work out, but, when it was sweet, it was sweet.'

It was shortly after completing his army service that Kenny became a convert to the Muslim religion, taking the name Liaquat Ali Salaam. It was a period when many black musicians turned to Islam for reasons that were generally a composite of frustration at the racial injustice that existed in the so-called Christian world, a genuine search for spiritual enlightenment and fulfilment and a wish to identify politically with the Black Muslim movement. Another, more pragmatic reason was advanced by writer Mike Zwerin, who pointed out that, on their police cards, black musicians could be designated as 'Muslim', instead of 'coloured', and this could persuade some owners of segregated hotels that they were visiting Arab dignitaries.

Although Klook was certainly angry and bitter about the insidious racial discrimination that existed in the States, it is doubtful whether his commitment to Islam extended to complete sympathy with the militant Black Muslims. He explained his conversion in rather more practical and uncompromising terms to Ursula Broschke Davis. It was, he said, 'because Islam brings people together. That's what Islam is. But Christians – shit, they don't allow black people in the church even. What kind of religion is that?'

I believe Ursula Davis is right when she claims that Kenny became involved with Islam in order to make a statement against Christianity, not really to embrace another religion. 'Kenny was against any organized religion; to him religion was something highly personal,' she says, and goes on to quote Klook as saying:

> Organized, institutionalized religion is worse than opium, because opium makes your body a slave, while religion makes your mind a slave. Once your mind is taken, you are no longer yourself, you are lost. Religions keep people down . . . I am still searching for the truth within myself . . . If you find peace within yourself, you are at peace with the world – with everyone else.

It is difficult to visualize Kenny Clarke, for all his hatred of prejudice, as a true supporter of Malcolm X, even though he had some very positive things to say about the Black Muslim leader in an August 1971 interview with Arthur Taylor, published in Taylor's book *Notes and Tones*: 'He had a message, a very open, down-to-earth message, which everyone could understand. A lot of people today are living by his words. There's a lot of truth in everything he said as far as black people are concerned, and that's why he's not with us today – because he had too much to say.'

It is interesting – though perhaps not significant – that in the original transcript of that interview was an added comment that what Malcolm X said was '99 per cent truth'. The removal of this may simply have been a piece of editing for stylistic reasons. But whether this was the case or not, there is no doubt that Kenny talked differently about certain topics at different stages of his life (as do most people) and according to the person he was addressing. In that same Taylor interview are a number of outspoken and immoderate comments which are inconsistent with the Kenny Clarke I knew.

Another example of inconsistency is in the view of the Black Panthers he gave in the Arthur Taylor interview and what he said on the same subject in a January 1981 interview. He told Taylor, 'The Black Panthers . . . that's gangsterism, it's not real. Making foolhardy mistakes, lack of organization, lack of individualism . . .' But in 1981 he said, 'This is a great period for black emancipation. Malcolm X, Martin Luther King, the Soledad Brothers, Angela Davis and the Black Panthers have achieved some fantastic things – they have awakened a feeling of solidarity among blacks.'

Whatever else he may have been, Kenny Clarke was not, in any sense, a fanatical Muslim. He remained true to the faith for the rest of his life, but he rarely went to the mosque, preferring solitary prayer to public worship. He had stopped attending the Baptist church in his Pittsburgh neighbourhood when he was twelve years old and, thereafter, prayed in the privacy of his home.

'I'd just invent prayers and I'd say them over and over again until they became like a mould,' he told Helen Oakley Dance. 'I never called God, "God". I always called Him "my Creator".'

According to some accounts, it was Idrees Sulieman (the former Leonard Graham) and Sahib Shihab (the former Edmund Gregory) who helped persuade Kenny Clarke to embrace the Muslim faith. But Kenny declined, unlike some of his peers, to wear his new religion as a badge. He kept relatively quiet about his conversion – possibly because his was rather a personalized version of the Muslim faith.

'My religion is mine,' he once said. 'It's a private thing and I don't share it with anyone.'

Daisy Clarke is emphatic that he was never a Black Muslim supporter. She says:

I think he became a Muslim because it was closest to what he believed in. He went to the mosque for a couple of years but it was far away and he told me that he didn't need anyone between him and his Creator. So he prayed for half an hour every day before going to bed. Even when he was in the hospital after his first heart attack in 1975 he still said his prayers regularly – silently, in Arabic. He must have learned the words in the United States because he was already saying the prayers when I first met him.

British musician Mike Carr had a UK concert tour with Kenny Clarke in the mid-seventies and, for the dates around London, Kenny stayed at Carr's house. 'I remember him kneeling at the side of the bed and saying his prayers every night,' Carr says.

Army service had interrupted Kenny Clarke's career at a particularly crucial point – just when the new music was getting into its stride. Had he not been drafted, Klook would certainly have been much involved in the vital developments that were happening on 52nd Street in 1944 and 1945. It would surely have been Kenny on drums in the Gillespie–Pettiford group at the Onyx, in the first Gillespie Big Band and in Dizzy and Bird's famous Three Deuces quintet. As it happened, Kenny's loss was his protégé Max Roach's gain.

His spell in the US Army had left Kenny Clarke somewhat disorientated and considerably disenchanted. He had not held a pair of drumsticks for almost two years and he found it hard to get back into the swing of the effervescing New York jazz scene. At this time, in the spring of 1946, 52nd Street was still jumping but, in a curious way, this added to Klook's feeling of alienation. He was experiencing the perfectly human reaction of disappointment about not, apparently, having been missed during his two and a half years away.

He told Arthur Taylor in *Notes and Tones* that the army had been a hectic experience for him:

And I was a very bad soldier. Unhappily, I stayed in it for three years, two of them in Europe . . . I met a lot of wonderful people during my soldiering days. Fortunately, just before coming home in 1945, I started to form groups and play the trombone, which was very nice. I began by concentrating on the trombone. This was about four or five months before I was discharged.

But when he got home, he told Taylor, he was ready to quit playing music 'because I was kind of disgusted with everything at that time. I guess a lot of soldiers felt that way on returning home to start a new life.'

What Kenny did not, of course, know at that point in his life, was that there were some pretty apocalyptic Things to Come.

7
The World's Greatest Big Band

While Kenny Clarke was undergoing his army service, his great buddy and fellow Mintonian, Dizzy Gillespie, continued to build a formidable reputation as one of the foremost exponents of the new jazz. He joined the Earl Hines Orchestra in late 1942, had a short and fairly unhappy stint with Duke Ellington in 1943, and then returned to 52nd Street to work at the Aquarium with the John Kirby Sextet before joining Billy Eckstine's band for a seven-month spell.

When he left Eckstine, it was back to 52nd Street again to co-lead a band at the Onyx with bassist Oscar Pettiford, which included George Wallington on piano, Max Roach on drums and, later, Don Byas on tenor saxophone. 'We really wanted Charlie Parker,' Dizzy recalls in his autobiography, 'and we sent him a telegram, but he didn't get it.' In another version of the story, as told to Robert Reisner, Dizzy said that Bird was unable to make the gig because he didn't have a union card.

The Onyx date ended when Dizzy and Oscar had a falling-out and Gillespie moved across the Street to the Downbeat – formerly the Famous Door – working with Budd Johnson, Clyde Hart, Leonard Gaskin and Max Roach.

The first Dizzy Gillespie Big Band was assembled at the behest, and courtesy of the bankroll, of Billy Shaw, the man who managed the Billy Eckstine Band. Shaw's son, Milt, then became Dizzy's manager. The band was put together for a roadshow whose execrable title should have signalled instantly to all concerned that it was a concrete airship. It was called 'Hepsations 1945', and featured Dizzy's band with the dancing

Nicholas Brothers, plus a comedy double act, a singer, a shake dancer and a chorus line. It toured the South playing to somewhat perplexed audiences who were struggling to find a way of dancing to bebop. Personnel-wise, the band was incredible: Charlie Parker, Leo Parker, Charlie Rouse, Max Roach, Freddie Webster, Kenny Dorham, Miles Davis and Fats Navarro were all in the line-up at one time or another. But the people didn't react too enthusiastically to the music. As Walter Fuller recalls in Dizzy's autobiography, one customer in Bluefield, West Virginia was heard to holler, 'Can't you nigguhs play no blues?'

When the tour ended, Dizzy broke up the band and returned to 52nd Street, working in a legendary quintet that consisted of Charlie Parker, Bud Powell (later Al Haig), Curly Russell (later Ray Brown) and Max Roach (later Stan Levey). Then in the autumn of 1945, the Parker–Gillespie All Stars made the trek West for the historic, turbulent two-month booking at Billy Berg's club in Hollywood. It was after returning to New York from this engagement in February 1946 that Dizzy Gillespie began to think about assembling another big band.

The new Dizzy Gillespie Big Band exploded on the jazz scene in May 1946, and it was Clark Monroe, owner of the Uptown House, who really lit the fuse. Monroe was also the owner of the Spotlite, the club at 56 West 52nd Street which, in its two years of existence, regularly featured Dizzy, as well as Billie Holiday, Coleman Hawkins, Harry 'The Hipster' Gibson and Billy Daniels. Monroe suggested to Dizzy that he should bring a small group into the club for an eight-week engagement, then build the combo into a big band to play a further eight weeks. Dizzy put together a sextet consisting of Milt Jackson, Al Haig, Ray Brown, Stan Levey and a lightning-fast twenty-two-year-old saxophone player from Boston, Edward 'Sonny' Stitt. And with arranger Walter Fuller, he began assembling his second big band around the nucleus of the sextet. Initially the rhythm section was Bud Powell, Ray Brown and Max Roach; but with Bud tending to behave in what Dizzy called 'a super-erratic' way, he was soon replaced by Thelonious Monk. The band rehearsed in the Spotlite and at Nola's studios, running down charts by Tadd Dameron, borrowed from the Billy Eckstine book, and new compositions by Walter Fuller and Dizzy.

The rehearsals got under way in April 1946, and one morning Dizzy received a telephone call from an ex-private in the US Army: 'Hey, Diz. It's Klook. I made it! I'm back.'

The reunion with the ebullient and infectiously enthusiastic Dizzy Gillespie provided a considerable boost to Klook's severely depleted morale. He was still half-decided to abandon his career as a musician – but Gillespie wasn't about to let that happen. It was thanks to Dizzy that, fortunately for jazz, the two main men from Minton's started making music together once more.

'It was Dizzy who talked me into playing again,' Kenny told Art Taylor in *Notes and Tones.* And thus it was, in May 1946, that Kenny replaced Max Roach in a fabulous line-up that included Kenny Dorham and Dave Burns on trumpets; Howard Johnson, Sonny Stitt, Ray Abrams and Leo Parker on saxophones; Milt Jackson, Monk and Ray Brown. Kenny also took the drum chair for the memorable Gillespie Sextet recording session of 15 May 1946, which produced such classics as 'Oop Bop Sh'Bam' and 'That's Earl, Brother', with Stitt, Jackson, Haig and Brown.

At this time, Max Roach who, as a teenager and unable to enter Minton's, had stood at the door listening in awe to the drumming of Kenny Clarke, had become a superlative drummer, widely considered as the number-two man in the bebop drum hierarchy. Kenny had taken a keen interest in Max's development ever since he saw him, as a seventeen-year-old, playing with Charlie Parker in Monroe's Uptown House. He remembered Max

> because he would always whistle while he was playing. He couldn't seem to play without whistling, regardless of what Bird was playing. At that time he confined himself to brushes and when I asked him why, he told me he hadn't learned to use sticks yet. 'I'm just beginning,' he said, 'and I'd like you to show me some things.'

And Kenny did just that. 'I often went to see him on 30th Street where he had his drums set up in a cellar. And I persuaded him to study at Juilliard so that he could acquire the knowledge to become an all-round musician and do studio work and everything,' Klook said later. While Kenny was in the army, Max studied and practised hard. He was a hugely dedicated musician and Klook was his great inspiration.

'He was an almost mythological person to me,' Max told me when I talked to him in his New York apartment in October 1985.

> And what really interested me about him was that he wasn't only a drummer, but a man who composed and played other instruments. I didn't really know him until he came out of the army, but after that we became very close. Where he lived with Carmen, in Brooklyn, was not too far from where I lived, where I was raised – and that was marvellous because it meant he was always accessible. I got a lot out of Klook while he was in New York. I must have driven him crazy with my eagerness. But he was always ready to sit down with me and talk drums.

It was a very different Max Roach in 1946 from the timid, whistling, apprentice drummer who had worked at Monroe's with Charlie Parker. Kenny told me:

> Dizzy helped Max a lot in his approach to style, and Max wasted no time in organizing what he learned. When I was at Minton's after the war, Max came in often and played with an unbelievable control and technique – and he had developed a superb left hand. He really had himself together. Knowing Max was an enriching experience. He was a drummer of the new generation, very concerned with technique, but he was also very musical.

It says much for Klook's humility and complete lack of 'big time' attitude that he added, 'I wanted to assimilate Max's style and be capable of playing some of the things he was doing that, so far, had escaped me.'

One morning in June 1946, while getting ready to make a rehearsal with the big band at Nola's studios, Kenny had a telephone call from John Lewis, taking him up on the offer he had made at the army base in Rouen. Lewis had been in New York since Christmas 1945 and was studying at the Manhattan School of Music. Kenny invited John to the Gillespie band rehearsal and told him, 'Bring that piece we used to play in the army – "Bright Lights".'

Klook was certain that Gillespie would be impressed by the

chart because he and Lewis were always being asked to play it in their army days. So, during a break in rehearsal later that day, Klook introduced Lewis to Dizzy. 'He's a wonderful pianist and arranger and he's brought some music with him,' Kenny said.

'OK,' said Dizzy. 'Let's hear it.'

Kenny passed out the parts and the band was only a few bars into the piece when Dizzy cut the music and shouted across to Lewis, 'You want to work with us?'

Lewis, slightly awed and totally unprepared for such a lightning judgement, stammered, 'Well, er, yeah – you know. I mean . . . absolutely!'

'OK. You're hired.'

So Lewis was taken on to share arranging duties with Gillespie and Fuller and 'Bright Lights' became 'Two Bass Hit' – an ingeniously titled sequel to the Ray Brown feature, 'One Bass Hit', written by Dizzy, Fuller and Brown.

The band was rehearsing at Nola's, preparatory to an engagement at the Apollo Theatre, and it was during the run of this gig that Lewis took over the piano chair from Monk. Klook recalled the sequence of events in an interview in Paris in 1967:

> One day Monk and I were hanging out in the Braddock Bar near the Apollo with some friends, talking about old times. It was the kind of musicians' conversation where one anecdote leads to another and everyone tries to top everyone else's story. After quite a few tastes had gone down, I looked casually at my watch and realized with a shock that the show had started and the band must already have hit. 'My God,' I shouted to Monk. 'Come on, we're late!'
>
> We raced back to the theatre and ran right into the manager, who was furious. Dizzy wasn't too thrilled, either. He was striding about on stage and peering into the wings, looking for us. Milt Jackson had taken over on drums, but there was a conspicuous absence of a piano player.
>
> Having been house drummer at the Apollo some years before, I knew the theatre layout very well, so I sneaked around backstage, slipped through the curtains, nudged Bags, took the sticks from him and slid on to the drum stool as he slid off. Dizzy looked over, did a double take, and said, 'How in hell did you get up there?' I said, 'Don't worry about it – I'm here, I'm playing and that's what counts.' We had only missed the opening theme music, but Dizzy was still mad, and poor Monk got the brunt of it. There was no way he could get to the piano without being seen by Dizzy – and when he tiptoed out from the wings, Diz was waiting

> for him. He pointed his finger accusingly at Monk and told him right there, in front of the audience: 'You're fired!' And that was the end of Monk's career with Dizzy. John Lewis was in the wings listening to the band. Dizzy beckoned him on stage and he stayed on as both pianist and arranger after that.

If Kenny had retained any lingering doubts about the wisdom of resuming his career as a professional musician, that stint with the second edition of the Dizzy Gillespie Big Band completely dispelled them. Kenny loved nothing better than to be working with Dizzy, and he rated that big band as the most exciting ensemble he had ever played with in his life. In a *Melody Maker* interview, published in November 1964, Kenny told me:

> Dizzy is without doubt the greatest living musician. Bird was great in his time – he was a creative genius. But Diz was an instructor as well as a creator in those early days. With Diz you learn to do everything the right way. You can see the difference between Bird and Diz in the men they recorded with. Bird didn't worry much who was on the set, but Diz hand-picked his men. Diz had started the bop thing long before Bird came East. He'd recorded 'Down Under' with Woody Herman, and 'Night in Tunisia' before Bird showed. Of course, they both played their part – with Bud and Charlie Christian. But it was Diz who really started the new harmonic structure.
>
> I get very nostalgic for that Dizzy big band. Dozens of bands have tried to sound like that since – but they never made it. I've never heard another band play like that one.

And when I recalled this interview in conversation with Dizzy Gillespie in November 1988, he looked at me with solemn eyes and said, 'It was the best goddam band I ever played in, too!'

The impact of this extravagant, electrifying, erratic, enthralling and explosively energetic band on the jazz community was seismic in magnitude. Just as with the astonishingly precocious Armstrong Hot Five and Hot Seven of two decades earlier, the dynamic potency of the Gillespie Big Band's music left the jazz world both shaken and stirred.

John Lewis could scarcely believe his luck in having replaced Monk in the band and for some time he tried to find a tangible way to express his gratitude to Kenny. But, typically, Klook said, 'You don't owe me anything, man. It's *your* talent, you know. I just happened to find a niche for it. So make the most of it.'

Kenny worked pretty consistently with the Gillespie Big Band over the next couple of years, but then, once again, the feet began to itch. Klook could not have been playing in more compatible and stimulating musical company, but something – and he appears not to have been totally sure himself as to just what that 'something' was – caused him to quit the Gillespie band and return to small-group jazz.

In one of his interviews with Helen Oakley Dance in the mid-seventies, Kenny recalled: 'I hadn't been in the band quite a year, but something came up. I don't know what it was. I wasn't mad with Diz or anything like that. It was just something I wanted to do. So I left Diz and joined Tadd Dameron who was working at the Royal Roost.'

During this period Klook recorded a number of sides with pianist Sammy Price – including sessions with Sister Rosetta Tharpe and Monette Moore – and also made his first date – for Savoy – with Tadd Dameron, a revered colleague from the Minton days, in a quintet completed by Fats Navarro, Ernie Henry and Curly Russell.

Klook was replaced in the Gillespie band by fellow Pittsburghian Joe Harris, but Kenny was still available to make the 9 July Prestige date which produced 'Ray's Idea', another version of 'Things to Come' and the supremely forgettable 'He Beeped When He Shoulda Bopped'.

Two months later Kenny's friend Charles Delaunay arrived in New York to record some sides for the Swing label which he had co-founded with Hugues Panassié in 1937. Delaunay was now one of Europe's leading jazz advocates and a staunch champion of the new music. He was also a firm devotee of Kenny Clarke. Delaunay records in his book *Delaunay's Dilemma* that, up to 1946, he had played drums in a semi-professional way under the pseudonym H.P. Chadel. 'But when I heard Kenny Clarke play, I decided it was time to bring H.P. Chadel's drumming career to a close!'

With sidemen mostly drawn from the Dizzy Gillespie Big Band, Kenny Clarke's 52nd Street Boys comprised Stitt, Dorham, Ray Abrams, Ed de Verteuil, Bud Powell, John

Collins and Al Hall. The octet recorded four Walter Fuller arrangements: 'Epistrophy', 'Oop Bop Sh'Bam', '52nd Street Theme' and 'Rue Chaptal'. The last title was named by Kenny after the Montmartre street in which the headquarters of Delaunay's *Jazz Hot* magazine were located. It is another one of those 'multiple ownership' jazz themes, also known as 'Royal Roost' and, as credited to Sonny Rollins, 'Tenor Madness'.

Those four sides for Swing were the first bebop recordings to be released in Europe and they were to cause the aforementioned irreparable rift among the hierarchy of the Hot Club de France. Hugues Panassié, whose iconoclastic pronouncements on jazz had earned him the title of 'the jazz pope', was militantly anti-bebop. He regarded the new music as anti-jazz – largely, Delaunay always maintained, because he had not managed to be the first French jazz authority to discover it. As it happened, Delaunay had been one of the first French writers to hear the new jazz because he had been sent copies of Dizzy Gillespie's 1945 recordings for the Guild label. Panassié was to remain implacably opposed to Delaunay over the bebop issue for the rest of his life.

Kenny went back with Dizzy for a further long spell in December 1947 when the band made a record date for Victor. Chano Pozo, the great Cuban percussionist, had now been added to the personnel and this session produced such classics as 'Cubana Be, Cubana Bop', 'Algo Bueno' and 'Manteca'.

Klook's return to the band was made possible because Dizzy had fired Joe Harris, following a dispute over Joe's demand for extra pay for what he claimed was overtime after Dizzy had turned up two hours late for rehearsal. It was a blow to Harris, but a real break for Klook because he came back to the fold just before the band was due to make its momentous tour of Europe – a tour that left a trail of ecstatic astonishment wherever the band played.

Yet despite his increasingly devoted attachment to Europe, Kenny was reluctant to commit himself to the tour because he was only too aware that his prolonged absences from the family home while on the road were really damaging his marriage. 'I really wanted to stay home and spend some time with Carmen,' he told me.

> I didn't like turning Diz down – but I told him I didn't feel good about going to Europe. I'd been away from home too much. Besides that, I guess I was somehow still associating Europe with army life, and that kind of cut across the happier memories I had accumulated. Diz tried hard to make me change my mind, but I told him 'No'. In the end, he got his wife Lorraine to talk to me. She said it was important to make the trip because the band were ambassadors for our music and Dizzy really needed me to be there. Well, Dizzy's no fool. He knew that I loved him and Lorraine so much that I wouldn't be able to hold out for long. So in the end I said, 'OK, I'll go.'

Apart from having to endure a turbulent sea crossing during which almost everyone in the band got ferociously seasick, Kenny never had any regrets about changing his mind. He considered that particular band the greatest that Dizzy ever had. Its line-up was Dizzy Gillespie, Benny Bailey, Dave Burns, Lamar Wright, Elmon Wright (trumpets); Ted Kelly, Bill Shepherd (trombones); Howard Johnson, John Brown (altos); Joe Gayles, George 'Big Nick' Nicholas (tenors); Cecil Payne (baritone); John Lewis (piano); Al McKibbon (bass); Kenny Clarke (drums); Chano Pozo (congas) and Kenny Hagood (vocals).

The trip had unpropitious beginnings unconnected with the weather: the accommodation on board the SS *Drottningholm* was not what the musicians had been led to expect. The Billy Shaw office had assured the band that the Swedish promoter, Harold Lundquist, was paying for first-class cabins on the ship – and the musicians trustingly assumed that these were what they had been assigned. But then Kenny Clarke recognized a steward who had been on the boat when he came over with Edgar Hayes in 1938.

'Well, Hans,' said Klook. 'I see they've moved you up into first class.'

Hans shook his head. 'No, I'm still in third class,' he replied.

It was altogether too much for Kenny. A man normally noted for his geniality and general imperturbability, he exploded into a rage of rare intensity. He stormed into Dizzy's cabin and said, 'You better look at your contract, Diz. We're supposed to be in first class, but they've put us in third!' Dizzy checked the contract and found that, sure enough, first-class travel was stipulated. Kenny was now threatening to beat up Milt Shaw and Dizzy had to intervene to prevent them coming to blows.

Kenny told me later, 'I was really furious because to me it was just another example of exploitation. They figured that steerage was good enough for black musicians.'

The incident brought about a dramatic change in Kenny's frame of mind. 'It finally made me realize that I didn't belong in the States,' he said. He was convinced that the Shaw office had received the money for first-class travel from Lundquist but had bought steerage tickets and pocketed the difference – not an altogether unknown practice among booking agents.

On the other hand, Dizzy, in his autobiography, maintains that the real villain of the piece was Lundquist – who did, in fact, turn out to be an unreconstructed crook. Whatever the sordid intricacies of the story, the shabby treatment provided another strand of reinforcement for Kenny's growing affinity to the social, cultural and economic climate of Europe.

Altogether the crossing was exceptionally eventful. In the course of his extensive interviews with Helen Oakley Dance, Kenny relates a most bizarre sequel to his quarrel with Milt Shaw which, were it not of his telling, would certainly seem to be highly suspect. He was still convinced that the Shaw office was robbing the band comprehensively and it didn't lessen his suspicions when Milt Shaw told him that he was going to buy a brand new Oldsmobile after he got back from the tour. Kenny recalled:

> When we arrived at Gothenburg, we went inshore on a tender with all the instruments, because the boat had anchored a mile out. While we were riding in, I was standing on the edge of the boat, looking out to sea and recalling my visit ten years before, when Milt came up and tried to push me off the boat. Al McKibbon was sitting beside me and he said, 'Look out, Kenny!' and he grabbed Milt. I said, 'What are you trying to do, man – are you crazy?' And Milt looked at me and said, 'I'll kill you!' But Al McKibbon said, 'No you won't, either. You must be crazy, are you kidding?' Milt was mad because I had exposed the whole thing. He was very angry about it.

After that incident Kenny told Dizzy's wife, Lorraine, that she should take over from Milt Shaw as Dizzy's manager, which she did when she got back to the States. She's managed him ever since.

The band played about a dozen concerts in Sweden and Denmark between 6 January and 9 February and received vigorous acclaim everywhere. On one occasion, recalled by Mike Zwerin, it was swinging so hard that Dizzy jumped up on the piano. But the Scandinavian tour came to an unhappy end when Billy Shaw, who had arrived from New York to deal with the growing problems caused by the Swedish promoter's unorthodox financial inclinations, was arrested, 'for trying to kick Lundquist in the balls', to quote Dizzy's version of the event. Later, Dizzy records, Lundquist himself was arrested 'and we got some of our money'.

The band travelled south to play dates in Belgium, sponsored by the Hot Club of Brussels, and from this point on, responsibility for promoting the remainder of the tour was graciously assumed by Charles Delaunay.

If the reception for the band in Scandinavia and Belgium had been tumultuous, the Parisian response when Dizzy and his men took the stage at the Salle Pleyel on 20 February 1948 was a kind of ecstatic incredulity, mixed with a leavening of outrage from the Panassié disciples. And just to complete the tour's improbable chapter of accidents, all the charts had gone missing on the day of the Paris concert. Dizzy had said, 'Don't worry, cats. We'll make it without the music!'

And Kenny said afterwards,

> If I hadn't seen it with my own eyes, I wouldn't have believed it. The band, to a man, played all of the parts correctly for the entire programme. And, mind you, it had been together for less than a year.
>
> I remember saying to Benny Bailey, when I heard about the missing music, 'What the hell are we gonna do now?' And Benny said, 'No trouble – we just hit! We've been playing that same music for a month already now. We know it ass backwards.' And that's what made it great. We played without music stands. Everybody stood up and the people just couldn't understand how we could play like that without music.
>
> It was a marvellous idea – and, of course, it was Dizzy's way of doing things, which I think is fantastic. It was the most fantastic thing that I've ever witnessed. You know, playing the same music every night. I've never done that – and the more we played it, the better it got.

French bassist Pierre Michelot, who was to work extensively with Klook in later years, was present at that Salle Pleyel concert – as was practically every other musician in Paris. It was, Michelot says, 'stupefying'. 'How,' he asked himself, 'is it possible for musicians to be able to play like that?' Michelot was especially fascinated by Kenny Clarke 'because I had never before seen a big-band drummer play the way he did. *C'était un bouleversement complet de tout ce que l'on avait l'habitude d'entendre. C'était fabuleux . . . somptueux!'*

Charles Delaunay's reaction was identical. 'I had already heard the orchestra in the United States,' he wrote in *Delaunay's Dilemma*, 'but I couldn't resist joining in the general euphoria. People had heard nothing like it before. The general astonishment was such that, after the first number, the public completely forgot to applaud, as if stunned by the violence and stridency of the orchestra.'

In contrast, Hugues Panassié is said to have observed, as he was leaving the Salle Pleyel, 'I love jazz – but that's not jazz . . . ' Boris Vian, however, writing in *Combat* on 21 February, said, 'Bebop . . . has conquered Paris. Thanks to Dizzy Gillespie.'

In 1973, Disques Vogue released an album of the Gillespie Paris concerts and, in a delicately understated tribute to the brass section, the anonymous liner-note writer observed, 'The attack is of such unforgettable brutality that it can only be described as a punch in the face.'

Certainly the echoes of that unforgettable opening concert, when Paris heard, for the first time, galvanizing live performances of big-band bebop classics like 'Things to Come', 'Good Bait' and 'Two Bass Hit' have still to subside. As long as seventeen years after the band delivered its Parisian *coup de poing*, French pianist/composer/bandleader Jeff Gilson wrote and recorded a composition called, 'I Still Remember Dizzy Gillespie's Big Band in 1948'.

The band played two more sell-out concerts at the Salle Pleyel, did a few dates in the provinces, and then returned to Paris for performances at the Club des Champs-Elysées, Les Ambassadeurs and a cinema in the Place Clichy which, the musicians were delighted to discover, was called the Apollo.

Al McKibbon, quoted in Dizzy's autobiography, says, 'On that 1948 tour the band was about two feet off the ground all of the time.' And in conversations with me in the sixties, Kenny often recalled that epic bebop odyssey.

> Every musician in Paris came to see what was going on – and they were dumbfounded. The reception every night was tremendous. We played 'Cubana Be, Cubana Bop', 'Algo Bueno', 'Manteca', 'Round Midnight' – with Howard Johnson featured on alto – and, of course, 'Things to Come'. I think John Lewis was at his greatest then. He was the swingingest piano player I ever played with – not counting Bud.

When the Gillespie band went back to the States on the French ship the *De Grasse*, Klook's drums went with them – but their owner stayed behind to spend the spring and most of the summer in a city for which he had now developed a really strong affinity. John Lewis also stayed over to study with the mother of bandleader Tony Proteau, who was a concert pianist. 'The French stole Kenny from me,' Dizzy wrote in his autobiography. 'A Frenchman offered to set Kenny up as a teacher because the weakest thing in the bands over there was the drumming and the rhythm sections. The European musicians had started learning our music from records, and with Kenny over there in France, they'd quickly learn much more.'

Kenny did, in fact, do some teaching during his five months in Paris. He opened a drum school for drum manufacturer Marcel Faivre in Vincennes. But he was also very much in demand for club work, concerts and record dates. He played for a month in the great Rex dancehall with the band of Charlie Lewis, a pianist who had settled in Paris after arriving in the late twenties with the Noble Sissle Orchestra. Later Kenny worked in the newly opened Club St Germain with Boris Vian who, as well as being a fashionable and quirky writer about jazz, was a trumpet player of dixieland inclinations and average accomplishment.

One of the most energetic and enterprising persons on the Paris jazz scene at this time was Nicole Barclay, wife of Eddie Barclay, flamboyant impresario, bandleader and founder of Disques Barclay, a major independent French record company. Madame Barclay had a passion for jazz and she and Kenny Clarke became firm friends. Encouraged by the huge success of the Gillespie band in Paris and of France's first international jazz festival, staged in Nice at about the same time as the Gillespie concerts, Nicole Barclay was making plans to organize an international jazz festival in Paris in the spring of 1949.

And she was determined that Klook should have a key role in the event.

Meanwhile Kenny was busy freelancing around Paris, spending the largest part of his time in the orchestra of Tony Proteau and playing in what he described as 'some pretty chic places'. In that band was trumpet player Roger Guérin, who became a close friend and a regular musical associate of Kenny's when he finally settled permanently in Paris in 1956.

Klook made at least eight record dates during his five-month Paris stay. The first, immediately after the Gillespie band's concerts, reunited him with pianist Sammy Price and the second, on 2 March, was a Prestige date with Benny Bailey and other Gillespie sidemen, plus French pianist Ralph Shecroun (later to metamorphose into Errol Parker and always thereafter referred to by Art Taylor as 'Duke Basie'). He also did four more sessions for Charles Delaunay's Swing label with, among others, Michel de Villers (alto), Hubert Fol (alto), Dick Collins (trumpet), André Persiany (piano) and Jean-Claude Fohrenbach (tenor). But the most important recording of this period was a 14 May date for Prestige in an octet which included Howard McGhee, Jimmy Heath, John Lewis, John Collins and Percy Heath.

When Kenny returned to New York in August 1948, it was to re-establish contact with pianist, composer and arranger Tadd Dameron and once again to play a key role in an important evolutionary development: the birth of the cool.

The Vogue album of the historic Salle Pleyel concert was Kenny's last record date with the Dizzy Gillespie Big Band. In fact, he was not to record again with Dizzy until 1963.

The Tadd Dameron band was at this time enjoying a nine-month residency at the Royal Roost (widely known now as the Metropolitan Bopera House), playing either as a quintet or a sextet and drawing its members from a stellar pool of musicians, including Fats Navarro, Allen Eager, Wardell Gray, Miles Davis, Curly Russell and a lofty twenty-six-year-old tenor saxophonist from Los Angeles called Dexter Gordon.

Kenny had retained a high regard for Dameron ever since their Minton's days. He said that Tadd's music enabled him to pursue the evolution of the drums because the arrangements were more modern, more complex, than the music he had played in Dizzy's band.

Writing on Kenny's contribution to the Dameron group, critic Ira Gitler said:

> . . . he helped to spark the pianist's sextet at the Roost. His steady cymbal beat can be heard, rather than just felt, on the Fats Navarro LPs for Blue Note. Engineering techniques had improved enough by this time to bring into focus the cymbal sound, which previously had been reduced almost to the level of surface noise. Clarke's relaxed, loose but never sloppy, and innately swinging style stands out in the Dameron sextet as a truly modern extension of the feeling that Jo Jones had achieved in the Basie band.

Between August 1948 and April 1949, Kenny was involved in a series of superb recordings with Tadd Dameron, featuring such outstanding talents as Navarro, Eager, Wardell Gray, Ernie Henry, Curly Russell, Milt Jackson, Kai Winding, Dexter Gordon, Sahib Shihab, Cecil Payne, James Moody, J.J. Johnson and Miles Davis. Those sides represent for me some of the most inspired and imaginative small-group performances on record. Kenny was also in the Dameron trio that made some sides with Anita O'Day.

It was early in 1949 that a new jazz venue – the Clique, later to become Birdland – opened on Broadway's East Side, between 52nd and 53rd Street. Billie Holiday was the first artist to play the club. She was followed by what Kenny Clarke described as 'a dream band – musically speaking!' Oscar Pettiford was the leader and the personnel was a potent one in terms not only of talent but also artistic temperament: Miles Davis, Fats Navarro, Kai Winding, Lucky Thompson, Dexter Gordon, Bud Powell and Klook.

In recollections he committed to paper in the seventies, Kenny observed:

> The clubowners, Al Martin and Dicky Wells, were good friends of ours. They were sympathetic to our wishes. But with that collection of personalities, there was little or no discipline. There were some fantastic moments when the full band was hitting, but after intermission, it was almost impossible to get the whole band back on stage at the same time. Oscar would become impatient, and we'd often start the set as a trio. One by one, the rest of the cats would wander in from the bar to join us . . . *if* they

> liked what we were playing. Finally Dicky asked me if I would take on the job of rounding up the band after the break. 'Yeah, Kenny,' Oscar agreed only too readily, 'you get them on to the stand.' But I didn't want to take the responsibility. In the end, Lucky Thompson became the effective bandleader because the musicians had a bit more respect for him than they had for Oscar. But even his attempts to get the band into some sort of order were abortive and so the gig came to an end. Dicky Wells came to us after the last set one night and said, 'OK, guys. All you get is . . . get lost!' And that was the end of the dream band.

Oscar and Kenny, however, remained at the Clique and they brought in George Shearing, recently arrived from London, on piano. As well as working at the club, the trio also had a daily 6 p.m. radio gig backing Sarah Vaughan. At one stage in the Clique, the Shearing Trio was working opposite a band led by Buddy Rich. One night, when the trio took the stand after Buddy's set, George gave Kenny what had become a regular drum feature. Kenny was playing brushes, as only he could, and, unusually for him, he went on at some length. He'd just learned to swivel a brush with his left hand and was enjoying giving the technique an extended workout. In the audience that night was Denzil Best – the drummer who was later to replace Kenny with Shearing – and, at the end of the number, he jumped up, applauding wildly, and shouted, 'Kenny, you did more with your left hand than Buddy did all night long!'

Kenny said later, 'He really embarrassed me. It made me feel very uncomfortable because Buddy was always one of my favourites and a drummer for whom I have every respect. That's the reason I had been playing brushes – I didn't want to make a drum contest out of it. I wanted to play quiet and leave Buddy to make all the noise.'

Drummer Al Levitt remembers Klook at the Clique in 1949. Al was sixteen years old and attending a school on 65th Street and Broadway.

> After school, instead of going home, I would head downtown, where there were lots of rehearsal studios, to listen to the bands. I remember going to the Clique one afternoon and checking out Kenny's drums. He was the first drummer I ever knew who had a tympani head on the beater side of his bass drum. I used to sneak into the club from time to time after that and play his drums. I was already familiar with what they called 'modern drumming' because I'd heard Max and Art Blakey and Roy Haynes. But what I didn't know at the time – back in '44 and '45 – was that

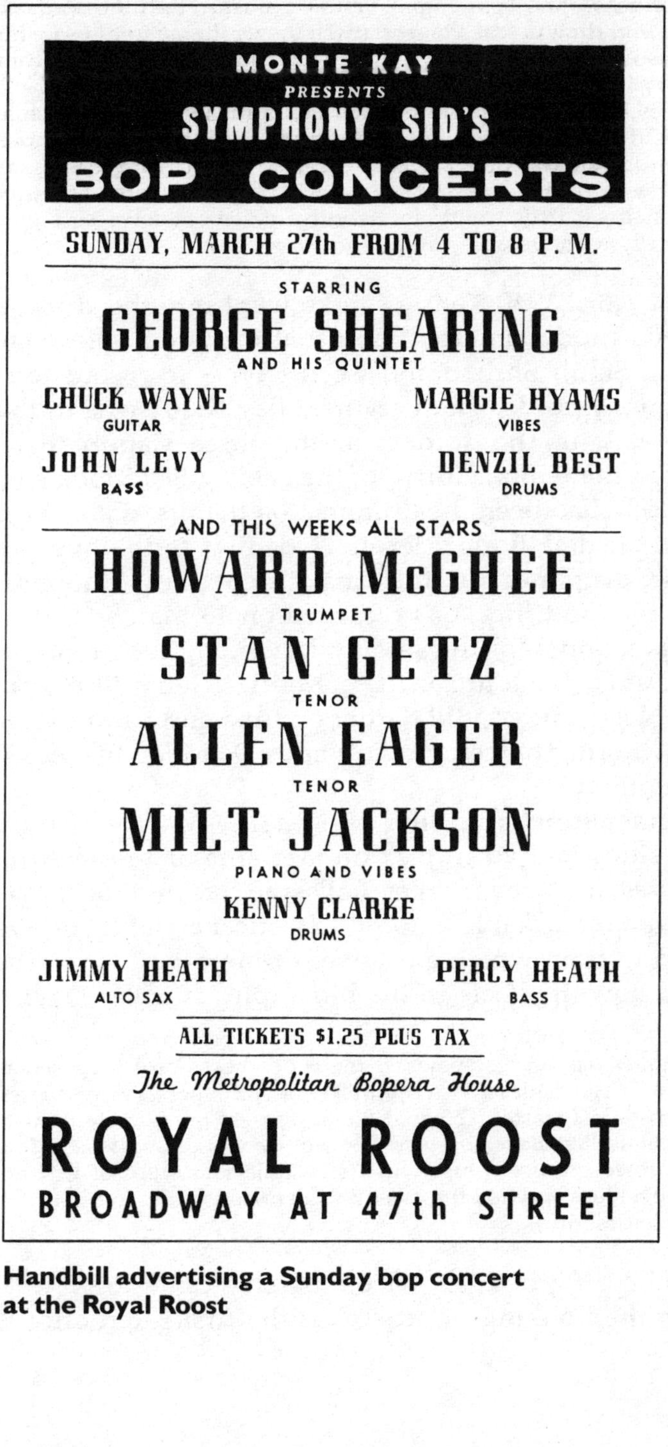

Handbill advertising a Sunday bop concert at the Royal Roost

> Max and Roy had learnt from Kenny. He wasn't on the scene then, but they were. He was just a legendary character for me until I saw him at the Clique. And when I saw him in person, I was able to see how he was the roots to these guys.
>
> Really, the thing that impressed me most about him was his cymbal beat – I fell in love with that, and with the way he played brushes. What also struck me was how perfectly together he was with the bass player. It was like a team, a marriage – much more so than with most other drummers. Kenny could do it with just about any bass player, but especially with Oscar Pettiford and Percy Heath.

On 21 April 1949 Kenny Clarke went into the studio with a ten-piece Tadd Dameron band that included Miles Davis, J.J. Johnson, Sahib Shihab and Cecil Payne, to record four sides for Capitol records. The very next day Klook was in the same studio making the second of the three Capitol dates that produced the famous 'birth of the cool' sides. Klook's protégé, Max Roach, had been the drummer on the first date – 21 January – which yielded 'Budo', 'Jeru', 'Godchild' and 'Move', and was also the drummer for the final three titles ('Moondreams', 'Deception' and 'Rocker') recorded on 13 March 1950.

The personnel for the session in which Klook took part was Miles Davis, J.J. Johnson, Lee Konitz, Gerry Mulligan, John Lewis, Nelson Boyd, Bill Barber on tuba and Sandy Siegelstein on flugelhorn. They recorded 'Venus De Milo', 'Israel', 'Rouge' and 'Boplicity'.

As James Lincoln Collier says in *The Making of Jazz*, these eleven sides had an impact on jazz similar to the Armstrong Hot Fives and the Parker–Gillespie records of 1945. They received a remarkable amount of critical acclaim and were the wellspring from which a number of important jazz tributaries were to flow. Ian Carr in his biography of Miles Davis, says:

> The nonet recordings spawned the cool 'West Coast Jazz' school of the 1950s . . . From Miles's own seminal band, John Lewis went off to form the Modern Jazz Quartet, Gerry Mulligan formed his pianoless quartet with trumpeter Chet Baker . . . and Lee Konitz worked with Lennie Tristano and formed groups of his own. These musicians were all at the centre of the movement and had the essential talent and vision to create something really valid.

In the spring of 1949, Nicole Barclay came to New York to arrange the booking of artists for the first international Paris

Jazz Festival which she was organizing with Charles Delaunay – and Kenny Clarke was at the top of her list. According to Kenny, she told the booking agents that any musicians she picked would be subject to Kenny's approval. Kenny had no problem okaying the ultimate line-up: Miles, Bird, Max Roach, Tadd Dameron, Al Haig, James Moody, Don Byas, Kenny Dorham and bassists Tommy Potter and Barney Spieler; and, representing the pre-bop segment of the jazz spectrum, Hot Lips Page, Jimmy McPartland, Pete Johnson, Sidney Bechet and Big Chief Russell Moore.

Kenny Clarke prepared to make his fourth trip to Paris – the city which was to be his base for the next two years.

8
Paris in the Swing

News of the illustrious company of jazz musicians that were to take part in the Paris Jazz Festival was received in British jazz circles with impotent frustration. The opposition of the British Musicians' Union to performances in the UK by American jazz musicians, unless reciprocal work opportunities were offered in the US to British players, ruled out any possibility of these jazz legends appearing in Britain – just as, in the previous year, the Gillespie band had been unable to arrange any British dates. Some British jazz fans managed to find the money to make the trip to Paris; the rest had to be content with trying to catch the French radio broadcasts on palaeolithic wireless sets which offered plenty of snap and crackle but not much bop.

The Paris Festival in May 1949 carried on where Dizzy had left off and, once again, Paris jazz audiences were left in a state of euphoric trance. To be able to see and hear legends like Miles, Max, Klook, Bird and Tadd in the flesh was, indeed, an unforgettable, exhilarating experience.

As Ross Russell wrote in *Bird Lives!*, distinguished jazz aficionados like Charles Delaunay and André Hodeir treated the musicians with the respect due to major artists.

> The reception given jazzmen in Europe was far different from that prevailing in America. The critics who covered the festival for the Paris papers were the same critics who reviewed important recitals, symphony concerts and operas. New jazz records were reviewed with the same seriousness as new books. In Europe, dark skins were a mark of distinction rather than a cause for suspicion and contempt.

Most of his observations are apt – but the last sentence is, of course, a palpable absurdity – as any West Indian in Britain, Algerian in France or Turk in West Germany will testify. Racism operates everywhere – and an effective defence against it is to have exceptional talent. But even that does not afford 100 per cent protection. After the Gillespie concert in 1948, Boris Vian recorded in *Combat* that certain spectators urged the musicians to go back to Timbuktu, and shouted at Dizzy, 'Why don't you learn French, dirty nigger.'

By and large, however, there was indeed less discrimination against the black US musicians in Europe than they suffered at home. And, without question, their music was much more revered and respected, and accorded cultural status.

The Paris Festival was a resounding success and Klook's contribution to it was singled out for special praise by French jazz pianist Henri Renaud: 'Kenny Clarke made each beat of each bar swing like Harlem's Savoy in its heyday, in a stupendous exhibition of that bebop polyrhythmic drumming to which his name is forever linked. Klook . . . was one of the major attractions of the festival.'

After the Festival some of the musicians, including Klook, Bird, Miles and Tommy Potter, went to Zurich for a concert date. In the packed audience for that performance was a thirty-one-year-old jazz enthusiast called Gigi Campi who, twelve years later, was to create the magnificent Clarke–Boland Big Band.

Back in Paris, Kenny was in his element. By now he had scores of good friends and hordes of devoted fans and he was in absolutely no hurry to return to New York. His old colleague from the Gillespie big band, James Moody, was already living in Paris at this time with his Uncle Louis, who was on the staff of the US Embassy. Moody had been despatched to Paris by his mother to 'cool off' after taking an overdose of benzedrine. 'I was sick and kind of depressed,' Moody told me. 'So I thought I'd go over for a few weeks. I ended up staying for three years.'

Also living in Paris at that time was eighteen-year-old Annabelle Macaulay Allen Short, who was embarking on a career as a singer using the name Annie Ross. Born into a

Scottish theatrical family, Annie was brought up from the age of three in Los Angeles by her aunt, the singer Ella Logan. Hardly surprisingly, as she grew up, she became stagestruck. As Anne O'Neal she appeared in some of the 'Our Gang' films and at the age of twelve she played Judy Garland's sister in *Presenting Lily Mars.* Later she studied acting at the American Academy of Dramatic Arts in New York, but her principal goal was to become a singer. At seventeen she left the States to visit her family in Scotland. Later she came to London and while there received an offer to do cabaret work in Paris with Hugh Martin. The partnership did not last long but Annie stayed in Paris, working as a singer with bands led by Bernard Hilda, Jack Diéval and Emil Stern.

In the summer of 1949 she met Kenny Clarke – an encounter that was to change both of their lives quite dramatically.

It was very soon after the Paris Jazz Festival that Kenny Clarke and French bassist Pierre Michelot first made contact. Michelot, twenty-one, had been a professional musician for three years and had developed a great affinity for bebop after working in American bases and listening to some of the great, modern US jazz musicians on V discs.

> I remember the first time I met Kenny was at a rehearsal in the home of Hubert Fol, the French saxophone player. We met in the lift. I had my bass with me. We exchanged *'Bonjours'* and I remember he was smiling and very friendly. When we rehearsed I found that playing with him was an absolute joy. It seemed so simple – and it was Kenny who made it simple.

Michelot was in the band that Kenny put together with James Moody to play in Frisco's, a club in the ninth arondissement's rue Notre Dame de Lorette, run by a black American whom everyone knew as Frisco and whose son, Josh, was later to be host at the Living Room, the piano bar in the rue du Colisée which became a favourite haunt of jazz musicians.

Kenny recalled the Frisco's band to me in a 1967 interview:

> We had Moody and Don Byas on saxophones, Bill Coleman on trumpet, Nat Peck on trombone, Henri Aspar on baritone saxophone, Jean-Paul Mengeon on piano and Michelot on bass, and we played Tadd Dameron arrangements. Annie Ross and Ernest 'Lobo' Nocho used to sing with the band – things like 'Baby It's Cold Outside' – and the place was packed

Handbills announcing the opening of the short-lived Frisco's, where Klook played with a 'dream band'

every night. But the gig only lasted a week because Frisco had some problems with the *syndicat* of the cabaret owners. That was a great disappointment because it really was a dream band.

That summer Kenny worked once again with the Tony Proteau Band, playing at the Pavillon d'Armenonville, and he later went on a Belgian tour with the big band of pianist Bernard Peiffer. He also played a gig in Tunis with a band that included James Moody, French trombonist Benny Vasseur and singers Annie Ross and Al 'Fats' Edwards.

During this two-year spell in Paris, Kenny made a number of record dates for the Vogue and Swing labels, including one on 20 October 1949 with Sidney Bechet, with whom Klook had first recorded ten years earlier. Bill Coleman, from Paris, Kentucky, who had settled in the European Paris the previous year, was on trumpet, Frank 'Big Boy' Goudie on tenor saxophone, Charlie Lewis on piano and Pierre Michelot on bass. Michelot remembers the date well:

> We did half a dozen tunes; one of them was called 'American Rhythm (Klook Klux Klan)'. I was really amazed because when I heard that Kenny was to record with Bechet I just didn't think it could work. I told myself that New Orleans and bebop couldn't mix. But Kenny, of course, played superbly. He didn't play in the conventional dixieland style – but what he played fitted perfectly, and that's what counts.

In the winter of 1949, Kenny put together a band for an extensive European tour with Coleman Hawkins. The line-up was James Moody, Nat Peck, Hubert Fol, Jean-Paul Mengeon and Pierre Michelot and there were dates in Switzerland, Italy, Belgium and Germany. Moody remembers that, en route to Germany, Hawkins mislaid his passport – 'but the guy at the immigration desk let him in because he recognized him. Can you imagine that?'

This may be evidence in support of Ross Russell's claim that dark skins bring out the best in Europeans; or it may be that German immigration officials are given compulsory courses in jazz-celebrity recognition. But a rather more likely explanation, I suspect, was that the immigration official concerned had a fair collection of Hawkins records at home.

The United Kingdom was included on the itinerary of the Hawkins tour but the proposed London date was highly problematical because there was no possibility of obtaining work permits for the musicians. What London promoters Tony Hughes and Bix Curtis planned to do was to get the band through the immigration formalities as tourists and then endeavour to find some way to get them on to the stage of the Winter Garden Theatre. In an interview published in the 29 November issue of *Melody Maker*, Tony Hughes, rather incautiously, explained that his idea was for Hawkins to be invited over to act as godfather to his recently born son. 'Then I thought, what a thrill it would be if I could get permission for

Handbill for a Coleman Hawkins concert in Berne, Switzerland, during the winter tour of 1949

him to appear while he was on English soil, as guest of honour at a concert . . . flanked by some of our leading British musicians.'

For some reason, Pierre Michelot remembers, only Hawk and the rhythm section made it to London on 4 December 1949 and by now the venue had been switched to the Princess Theatre. Despite the fact that Hughes had signed an undertaking that Hawkins would not appear in public during the visit, the promoters were determined to get him to play. Michelot recalls:

> What happened was that they sat us in different parts of the theatre and had the compère announce, 'By chance, we happen to have in the audience tonight the great Coleman Hawkins and some of his musicians. I am sure, if you applaud loudly enough, we'll be able to persuade Mr Hawkins to come up on stage and play a couple of numbers for us.' So we went up on stage, played a few numbers, and everybody was happy. Well, everybody except the Musicians' Union. I believe they came down very hard on the promoters afterwards.

Hughes and Curtis were, in fact, later charged with aiding and abetting the illegal entry into Britain of Coleman Hawkins and his men and were each fined £100 with forty guineas costs.

Before returning to the continent on the day after the concert, Kenny learned that a big band, led by drummer Leon Roy, was rehearsing not far from his hotel. 'Kenny and I went along,' Michelot recalls. 'The band was playing some Dizzy Gillespie arrangements and Kenny and I had fun sitting in for a couple of numbers. Then we had to leave for the airport to catch a flight to Brussels where we rejoined the other members of the group to continue the tour.'

At the end of the tour the band returned to Paris and, minus Moody, went into the Vogue studio on 21 December to record six sides.

A couple of months earlier, Moody had left Paris for a visit to Sweden and it was while on this trip that he made his most celebrated recording – the session with his Swedish Crowns which produced that imperishable solo on 'I'm in the Mood for Love'. The date was for the Swedish Metronome label and as soon as Moody got some copies of the record he gave one to Klook. After playing the 'I'm in the Mood for Love' side, Kenny told Moody, 'This is going to be a big success for you.' And it was Kenny who persuaded Prestige in America to acquire the tapes from Sweden.

Throughout 1950 Kenny kept reasonably busy, playing in the Club St Germain and other Paris jazz rooms and making record dates with Hubert Fol, John Lewis, Jack Diéval, Gerald Wiggins, Roy Eldridge and Zoot Sims. It is quite probable that Klook was considering settling permanently in

Kenny Clarke's student card – in his Muslim name of Liaquat Ali Salaam – issued to him when he attended the Ecole Normale de Musique in Paris in 1950

France at this point. Certainly he had made it widely known to his friends – both those in Paris and those visiting from time to time from the States – that New York held absolutely no attraction for him any more. He was becoming increasingly adjusted to the French way of life, assimilating the conventions and slowly coming to grips with the language. And while he was earning considerably less money than he could have made in New York, the lack of pressures and the more leisurely pace of life in France were substantial compensations.

But his relationship with Annie Ross had developed, early in 1950, into a love affair and, though it was to be a shortlived liaison, it was to lead to a situation which made Kenny decide to return once more to the United States.

9
The Trials of Toby

The disturbed and desolate childhood of Kenny Clarke in the twenties had some sad echoes three decades later when Kenny's first son was born. Kenny Clarke Junior was – to use the current terminology of tabloid newspapers – the 'love child' of Kenny and British singer Annie Ross. But a more accurate description would be that he was the unplanned result of nineteen-year-old Annie's infatuation with a legendary jazz musician, and Kenny's succumbing to the gratifying adulation of a pretty girl – hardly a novel experience for a jazz musician.

Annie Ross first met Kenny when she was engaged to sing with a band in which he was working:

> I can't recall all the details. It's very vague in my mind how I got to know him. But I did, and of course I was in awe of him. I was star-struck. Here I was, a young girl in Paris among people that I adored and admired who accepted me as an artist. My God, those were golden years.

At the time of the relationship between Annie and Kenny, he was still married to Carmen McRae and, according to Annie, was extremely fond of her. 'I don't think that Kenny and I were really meant to be together – ours was not a real loving relationship. Kenny found that much later in life when he met Daisy.'

Certainly the liaison between Kenny and Annie Ross was not viewed with enthusiasm by either family. According to Toby, his foster parents were much more attached to Carmen McRae than to Annie Ross, whom they hardly knew. He says:

They really wanted Carmen to be my mother, rather than Annie. And Annie's family didn't approve of her relationship with my Dad. They were real ritzy, noble people and they didn't welcome a mixed relationship – and particularly one which produced an illegitimate child. Though later, when I was nineteen and I had a chance to meet the family in Britain, they were really cool. There were a couple who acted like they didn't approve of me, but basically the majority of the family finally accepted me.

The fragile affair between Annie and Kenny really began to decline when Annie discovered she was pregnant. Kenny's reaction, she says, with eloquent understatement, was 'not great'. He was supportive, but perhaps a little irked – particularly because money was short and they had no home of their own. Annie recalls:

At the time Kenny was sharing an apartment off the Etoile with Ernest 'Lobo' Nocho, the singer, and his wife. I moved in there for a while, then we moved to a place in Montparnasse until the baby was born – and then to an attic flat belonging to Henri Guisgand, the French clarinet player. I had a great admiration for Kenny but I feel that his commitment to me was prompted more by moral obligation than by real affection. I don't think we were ever really in love.

Kenny, at this time, was not an easy man to live with. He was still extremely bitter about the exploitation of black musicians by white people, he detested the rampant racism in the United States and he was smarting over the fact that America had not given him the recognition he deserved. This, at any rate, is how Annie Ross remembers the situation.

There were no real arguments between us – I wasn't really in a position to argue. But he was a very moody man – and sometimes he would explode. I really didn't know how to cope with that. Kenny wasn't always the perfect gentleman – but that, I believe, is because he was very frustrated at this time; and my getting pregnant didn't help. It wasn't that he didn't want a son – or that I didn't – but the pregnancy wasn't planned. It was just something that happened and we had to come to terms with it.

I really couldn't believe it when I found I was pregnant, but once I'd adjusted to the idea, I really wanted to have the baby, even though the circumstances weren't ideal. We had big money problems. But there were some great moments, some real joy – though not nearly enough to sustain a relationship.

In November 1950 Kenny got word that Charlie Parker, who

had been on tour in Sweden, was planning to visit Paris before heading home. Kenny had a gig in northern France on the day Bird was due to arrive from Stockholm, so he gave Annie a note for Parker and asked her to meet him at the airport. Thus, on 26 November, a heavily pregnant Annie Ross accompanied Charles Delaunay to Le Bourget to greet Parker. Delaunay had arranged hotel accommodation for Bird, but when he got the note from Annie, Charlie said, 'No, I'm gonna stay with Annie and Klook.' And he moved into the shared flat, staying for three weeks.

In *Bird Lives!* Ross Russell records how Kenny tried to persuade Parker to leave the United States and join the growing community of expatriate jazz musicians in Paris. Klook had already urged the move the previous year, after the Paris Jazz Festival, when he had said, 'Bird, you are slowly and surely committing suicide over there. Come over here and *live* . . . You may never make a hundred thousand a year, but you'll be around a long time and people will appreciate your music. Over here you will be treated like an artist.'

But it was not to be. Charlie Parker returned to New York. It was not long after Bird said goodbye to Annie and Klook that Kenny Clarke Jr was born in the Marignan Clinic – on 24 December 1950.

Klook had already determined that there was no possibility of a settled, secure life for the child in France with both Annie and himself having to pursue their musical careers in order to survive. It was thus arranged that, as soon as it was practicable, the baby would be given into the care of Kenny's brother Chuck and his wife Evelyn, back in Pittsburgh.

It was Kenny's firm belief that he was acting in the best interests of his son, but, sadly, it was not to turn out that way.

Kenny Clarke Jr, otherwise Liaquat Ali Salaam Jr, but generally known, inexplicably, as Toby, recalls: 'I think the reason my Dad brought me to Pittsburgh in 1951, when I was not yet a year old, was because he and my mother were working at night all the time and he wanted me to have the security of being in a proper home environment.'

Another factor which decided Kenny to take his son to Pittsburgh was undoubtedly an economic one. He told me in an interview I did for *Melody Maker* in November 1964 that at this time he was badly in need of money.

Toby went to live with his Aunt Evelyn and Uncle Chuck in a project house in the Hill district of Pittsburgh – on Elmore Square. He says:

> My earliest memories are of the excitement that was created when famous musicians like Max Roach, Thelonious Monk and John Lewis would come to the house. And I remember my Dad arriving once in a 1955 Cadillac. I must have been about five at the time. I also recall Max Roach driving one of the very first Lincolns.

Cars were a subject of some fascination to Toby and it was a preoccupation that was to cause him a considerable amount of trouble later on.

'For years after that visit by my Dad in 1955, I didn't see a great deal of him – but we corresponded quite a lot. I saw my mother more often because she came to the States quite regularly.'

The young Toby was raised with fondness and care by his foster parents – but then, as a tragic sequel to the early death of Kenny Clarke's mother, Toby's Aunt Evelyn died when he was ten years old. 'That threw me for a complete loop,' Toby says. 'She had been like a mother to me.'

The death of his aunt certainly dealt Toby a severe psychological blow whose repercussions persisted into his teenage years. He was taken into the home of his aunt's son, Samuel 'Speedy' Spearman, and his wife Tony. They both had a great admiration for Toby's father and they did their best to give the boy the sense of security and orientation that he badly needed.

But Toby felt cheated and frustrated at being isolated from his mother and father. He recalls:

> My mother would come to town from time to time to see me – but when it was time for her to leave she would just cry and cry. It was such a sad scene – it would tear me up. She has told me a lot about it. Dad took me away from her – which was probably beneficial at the time, but she later regretted the way it went down.

The effect on Toby was traumatic. He was confused, hurt and resentful – and he started to take it out on society. He began by stealing cars as a teenager and by the time he was fourteen he was doing a spell in a juvenile detention centre. Speaking about his drift into crime, Toby says,

> I think it represented some kind of protest on my part. When I had psychoanalysis later, it came out that I was jealous of people who had had a better deal from life than I had had. I guess I could have dealt with it by trying to seek a more fulfilling life for myself in a respectable way – but instead I chose rebellion and anti-social behaviour.

Kenny's reaction to his son's delinquency was, predictably, one of anger and dismay. He told Toby: 'If I were there I would beat your ass! If you really needed a car, I'd have bought you one when you were old enough to drive.' Yet, despite the psychological damage that Toby had clearly suffered, Kenny persisted in the view that it was better for his son to grow up in the ghetto of Pittsburgh's Hill district so that he could learn some 'street values'. 'I could bring you over to Paris and raise you here,' he told Toby, 'but Pittsburgh is a better place to develop your character.'

This, unhappily, did not prove to be a sound prediction. In an effort to straighten out his life and get away from the more malevolent ghetto influences, Toby joined the US Army at the age of seventeen. But, like his father, he did not take readily to the rigours and discipline of army life. After two years of military service, he was discharged, having refused to be posted to Vietnam.

After leaving the army, Toby decided to follow in his father's footsteps and become a professional percussionist. He moved to New York and worked for a while in the kitchen of the Village Vanguard. And he also became involved in drugs – both as a user and a seller.

Drummers Jimmy Hopps, Beaver Harris and Max Roach helped and encouraged Toby to develop his musical skills. Max took him on the road for a couple of dates and invited him up on stage to sit in at a gig in Chicago. 'I'd been practising quite a bit at Beaver Harris's house and I felt that I really had a gift – I was ready to come out of the closet. But when I went up and played with Max I really didn't make it, and I was very embarrassed,' says Toby.

Later Beaver Harris told him that if he was going to be a drummer, using the name Kenny Clarke Jr, he would have to accept that there would be invidious comparisons made between him and his father. 'You'll be expected to play like him,' Harris said. 'And you can't. No one can.' That observation convinced Toby that he should concentrate on playing congas and assorted percussion. Jimmy Hopps got him a job with Roland Kirk for six months and he spent a year with Archie Shepp's group.

But his career was brutally interrupted when he was convicted of drug trafficking and sent to serve one year in a penitentiary. On his release, he was given a job by George Wein on the production staff of the Newport Jazz Festival – and it was at this festival that Toby met Kenny's first wife, Carmen McRae, for the first time. Carmen introduced Toby to Esther Phillips, a singer with a history of drug addiction – and this was the start of an association between Toby and Esther that lasted for more than three years.

Carmen invited Toby out to her home in Beverly Hills for a spell – because she felt sorry for him. She recalls:

> He was calling me 'Mama' and I had to tell him, 'I'm not your mother, I'm your friend.' But he said to me, 'Yes, but you could have been.'
>
> He was in New York with hardly a place to live, and no money, and I said if he wanted to come and work with my group maybe he could be the bandboy or something, so he'd get some money. He told me he couldn't afford to live in LA, so I said he could live in my house and take care of it. I must have been crazy!

When Toby began bringing Esther Phillips to Carmen's home, the arrangement broke down irretrievably. 'If you're using drugs that's fine with me,' Carmen told them, 'but you're not going to do it in my house.' And she invited them, not too graciously, to leave.

Toby says,

> When Esther and I first hooked up, though we were both prone to addiction, we were drug-free. We kept checks on each other – and we were OK for about three and a half years. But then we started going downhill. We were on the road for eight months of the year and this took its toll. When people know you have used drugs they just keep coming up to you unasked and saying, 'Here's an ounce.' Things started going backward, so we broke up.

But the damage was done and it was not long before Toby found himself severely hooked.

> In 1969 I was really strung out on drugs and I called Max Roach in the middle of the night asking for help – he's been like an uncle to me all my life. He told me to get to the airport the next morning and there would be a ticket to New York waiting for me. He put me in a hospital costing $500 a week. He'd called my Dad to tell him about the situation and my Dad told him, 'Do what you can, Max. I'll repay you.'

But, as far as Max Roach was concerned, Kenny had already repaid the debt in advance. Because eighteen years earlier, when Max was desperately strung out on heroin, it was Kenny Clarke who helped him straighten out. Max told me,

> When Kenny came back to the States from Paris in 1951, I was just wasting away and would probably have committed suicide. I had joined everything and I was involved in everything. I was going downhill fast. I was freelancing at this time and working on 52nd Street – with Charlie Parker, Dizzy or maybe Coleman Hawkins – I can't remember. Anyway, Kenny had got word that I was in bad shape. One night he arrived at the club during intermission. I was outside getting some air with some of the guys. As soon as he saw me, he came over, grabbed me with one hand and jacked me up against the wall. I was much taller than him – but his anger gave him remarkable strength. He cussed me out and said, 'You dumb mother, you can't even take care of yourself. Why are you throwing away your life? Get yourself together!' I was angry, being made a fool of like that in front of the other cats – but I think that was the turning point for me. I didn't want to get caught like that again; so I became a healthy human being again. I stopped messing with drugs and booze after that.

Toby was in hospital for about six weeks – then Max got him a passport to go to Europe. 'Meanwhile,' says Toby, 'the hospital wrote a summary of my drug history and sent it to my father. This gave him a little more insight into my problems.'

After discharge from hospital, Toby flew to Paris to visit his father. By this time Kenny had married Daisy Dina Wallbach and they had a five-year-old son, Laurent. At the time of Toby's arrival, Kenny was away from Paris, on the road, and Max Roach – then on tour in the French capital – had to go with Daisy and Laurent to Orly to meet Toby because they didn't know what he looked like.

Toby recalls:

My Dad returned from the tour two or three days later. He knew that I was really confused about a lot of things but at first we really didn't know how to talk to each other. So in the end, he rolled a couple of joints and we started smoking together. After that I just started running off at the mouth. We developed a good level of communication finally. I spent a month in my Dad's house and we scarcely went out. We'd just sit around all day and talk.

Toby and Kenny also spent many hours working on the practice pads with father showing son rudiments and saying, 'Don't forget the one!' (the first beat in the bar which is the 'anchor', the focal point of jazz rhythm).

From Paris, Toby travelled to London to spend some time with his mother, who had moved back there in 1955. He intended to say for a couple of weeks – but the visit extended to a whole year. 'We had a lot of fun together,' he says. He suported himself by playing drums and percussion in a local band – and his most unnerving experience was playing in the Upstairs Room at Ronnie Scott's Club with a band called Noir and seeing his father in the audience.

He was unblinking, unsmiling – just staring straight at me. And after the set he said to me, 'You've got a problem with that *one*, boy.' He was right – I had a habit of getting away from the one. My syncopation was no good. Probably with some straight training I could have got it together – but I'd realized by then that I wasn't really a 'sit-down' drummer.

During his time on the road with Esther Phillips, Toby had made a lot of contacts and after he returned to the States from London he worked with a number of different bands, notably with the group of Chaka Khan for a year and a half.

It was in 1979, at the end of Toby's eighteen-month spell with Chaka Khan, that Kenny Clarke returned to his native Pittsburgh to act as visiting professor in the music department of Pittsburgh University for one full term while his friend Nathan Davis took a sabbatical.

In this period, father and son came closer together than they had ever been. Kenny converted Toby to the Islamic religion, gave him a Koran and told him of his profound regret that he had not been able to give him a good upbringing and to impose what he considered to be a proper sense of values.

Toby says:

I was still messing around with drugs at the time. He detested that because he had seen so many people destroy themselves with drugs. And he knew all about hard drugs because he'd used them himself.

He recognized that I had been confused, jealous and upset because I felt that I had missed out on a lot of things and he accepted that. We talked a lot together and he was very understanding – he really gave me a new outlook on life at that time. He was proud that I was involved in music, but he told me that he had really wanted me to get into a profession which wouldn't impose on me the pressure of being his son. He was proud that I was a member of the American Society of Composers, Authors and Publishers (ASCAP) – he took the certificate home with him and put it on the wall of his home. And he was really happy when my first record came out.

But he said he had really been badly hurt by my troubles with the law. He could understand my frustration, but he couldn't understand why I had allowed it to drive me in that wrong direction.

One day during Kenny's eight-month stay in Pittsburgh, he and Toby were out for a walk and Kenny was noticeably limping.

'What's wrong, man?' Toby asked him.

'This arthritis,' Kenny winced. 'It's slowing me up.'

'Come on, man, I'll race you to the burger joint,' Toby said.

Kenny stopped, regarded his son with massive disdain and said: 'I'm not racing anywhere – and if you run past me, I'm gonna trip you.'

Says Toby, 'On other occasions when I said something out of line, he'd tell me, "Go on, act funny with me and I'll send your brother over to whip your ass."'

The last time that father and son met was in Pittsburgh in September 1984. For years Toby had had problems with citizenship due to the fact that the authorities had had difficulty in finding the birth records of Kenny Clarke, because he had been born at home. Toby was threatened with deportation on three occasions, pending proof that his father was an American citizen. Kenny kept urging his son to 'get his papers together' – but the mills of bureaucracy grind exceedingly slow. Says Toby:

He told me he was pleased that, at last, I seemed to be getting my life together. He was overjoyed that I now had a daughter. She was born in 1980 and it was Kenny who came up with her name: Batima Shahida Salaam. He was really proud of his granddaughter. But he kept telling me to get my papers in order. I had a funny feeling that he felt he was not going to be around much longer.

I think he wanted me to come back with him to Paris and spend some time over there. The night before he left I cried, because I got the feeling that I had seen my Dad for the last time. I really regret that life didn't permit me to spend more time with him. All the people who knew him had a great respect for him, not only as a musician but as a human being. He was a father figure to many of them and he knew how to handle a situation, not only in the musical sense but in terms of human problems and conflicts.

I never heard anyone say anything bad about my Dad. He tried to help as many people as possible. That was his philosophy, his *karma*. If he saw a young artist, trying to make it, and he knew he or she was serious, then he would contribute his knowledge and technique to help the artist along.

He was also a very shrewd student of human nature. If I asked him a question, he could look inside me and find the question *behind* the question. You couldn't fool him or lie to him. He would stop me in mid-sentence and say, 'Don't lie to me.' At other times he'd just look at me in a certain way and his eyes would give me the same warning. He had another way of looking at you that told you it was time to shut up.

He had an aura about him that commanded respect. But, as a musician, he never got the recognition he deserved – except from his peers. Nobody made a more important contribution to the development of bebop than he did. But perhaps one reason why he didn't receive the acclaim he should have had was that he never really cared about publicity or self-promotion. He felt more comfortable in the background than he did up front.

As Nathan Davis says, my Dad was not one for showing off; all he wanted to do was to keep time and make the cats swing. That was how he perceived the drummer's role.

10
The Battle of the MJQ

If the brass section of the Dizzy Gillespie Big Band had not had to cope with such a lip-bruising library, it is conceivable that the Modern Jazz Quartet might not have existed. The group started life as a quartet within the Gillespie band, featured to give the brass a break – John Lewis (piano), Milt Jackson (vibes), Ray Brown (bass) and Kenny Clarke (drums). When the Gillespie band broke up, the combo continued as the Milt Jackson Quartet, with Percy Heath replacing Ray Brown after the latter's marriage to Ella Fitzgerald and departure to the West Coast. Then, in 1952, it became the Modern Jazz Quartet, making its recording début for Prestige in December of that year. Today, scores of records and a few farewell tours later, the MJQ continues to be a major jazz force, largely because its musical director, John Lewis, systematically converted what was a freewheeling, extrovert, loose-limbed bebop combo into a formalized jazz chamber ensemble whose discreet, charming, well-mannered music had an appeal which went far beyond the community of hard-core jazz enthusiasts.

And therein lay the source of much tension and contention. Both Kenny Clarke and Milt Jackson recognized that by allowing Lewis to take control of the musical identity and direction of the quartet, its chances of commercial success would be enhanced; but the price they might have to pay was the sacrifice of some of their cherished musical principles.

It was soon after his return to New York from Paris in April 1951 that Kenny Clarke had teamed up with Milt Jackson again. Dizzy Gillespie founded his short-lived Dee Gee record label in this year. Kenny had made four tracks for the label, just before leaving Paris, with trumpeter Dick Collins, Jean-Claude Fohrenbach (tenor), André Persiany (piano) and Pierre Michelot (bass), of which only the appositely titled 'Klook Returns' was issued.

As soon as Kenny arrived in New York he got word that Dizzy Gillespie was in the studios recording some sides with a small group that included J.J. Johnson, Budd Johnson, Milt Jackson, Percy Heath and Art Blakey. It was the session that produced 'The Champ'. 'I headed straight for the studio,' Kenny said later, 'walked right in and everybody fell out. "You mean you're back?" they shouted. And they gave me a big welcome home.'

On 8 August 1951, Charlie Parker, now at the peak of his career, put together a quintet to record some sides for Norman Granz's Verve label. Klook was on this date, together with Red Rodney, John Lewis and Ray Brown, and it proved to be a vintage recording. Red Rodney recalled, 'It was the only date I ever did with Klook and it was a great experience for me. We did some memorable sides – "Swedish Schnapps", "Blues for Alice" and "Loverman" – and it was one of the most stimulating record sessions I have ever been involved in.'

Kenny Clarke, as it happened, was very nearly *not* involved in it himself. He told me,

> At this particular time in New York I needed money badly and Bird knew it. Originally another drummer was supposed to do the session, but Bird told me, 'Bring your drums, Klook. I don't know what drummer they've got on the date – but he won't be when you get there.' I did the date – and it was a great session. We really cooked.

About two weeks after this date the Milt Jackson Quartet made its recording début for the Dee Gee label with John Lewis on piano and Ray Brown on bass. Later Milt and Kenny took a quartet into Minton's Playhouse, with Percy Heath on bass. As John Lewis was studying at the Manhattan School of Music, Kenny hired Gildo Mahones, a twenty-two-year-old New Yorker, on piano. Sometimes Horace Silver or Jimmy Foreman subbed for Mahones, and Lou Donaldson played with the group for a while. Donaldson was also a guest soloist on the second date of the Milt Jackson Quartet in April 1952 – this time for Blue Note. By this time, however, John Lewis had already discussed the idea of forming a co-operative band with Klook, Milt and Percy and calling it the Modern Jazz Quartet.

It was as the Modern Jazz Quartet that they made four sides for the Prestige label in December 1952. But the MJQ remained purely a recording group until late in 1954 when John Lewis completed his music studies. Sonny Rollins and trumpeter Jesse Drakes also worked with the group at different times, Rollins recording with them in October 1953. And in the summer of 1954 the MJQ, with Horace Silver on piano, played the first Newport Jazz Festival.

Response to the Modern Jazz Quartet albums was encouraging, and with Lewis now available to tour, it was decided to take the group on the road. Milt Jackson recalls the first public performance being at a club called the Chantilly on West 4th Street in Greenwich Village – but the first major booking was at Birdland on the East side of Broadway between 52nd and 53rd Streets. Reviewing the quartet's performance, writer Nat Hentoff observed, 'If the success of the Modern Jazz Quartet depended only on the support of jazz musicians, this could be the most in-demand unit in the country.'

After a highly successful three weeks at Birdland, the MJQ played two weeks at the High Hat in Boston, three weeks at the Black Hawk in San Francisco and followed with dates at Sardi's in Los Angeles, Town Hall and Carnegie Hall New York, Symphony Hall Philadelphia – and a return four-week engagement at Birdland. Public and critical reaction was tremendously positive. But Kenny Clarke was already beginning to have reservations about his involvement with the group.

> By the time we got back to Birdland for the second time, the style of music had completely changed. We had become a chamber group. But I wanted to play music my way. John told me that *his* way was the best way to make money and I replied that, sure, I was interested in making money, but I was becoming afraid that I wouldn't be able to play the drums my way again after four or five years of playing eighteenth-century drawing-room jazz.
>
> John wanted to be responsible for all of the music, and when I told him that Bags [Milt Jackson] and I were composers, too, he said that he was musical director and that was the way it had to be.

Milt Jackson and Percy Heath, Klook always contended, were also unhappy about the musical direction, but they were perhaps concerned not to forgo the financial security that the success of the MJQ seemed to guarantee.

A further cause for disagreement developed on the day when John Lewis announced that there would be a fifth and equal member of the co-operative: Monte Kay, who would be managing the MJQ. Said Kenny, 'I told John that no manager deserved to get twenty per cent of a band's income. But he said the deal had been done. I was very unhappy about this.'

The motivation for Kenny's decision to quit the MJQ early in 1955, at a time when the group was really winning a high level of public approbation, was probably compounded of a number of elements. And, as was not unusual, he offered different explanations at different times.

He told Helen Oakley Dance that after his disagreement with Lewis over the introduction of Monte Kay into the co-operative, he believed that Lewis mentioned the matter to John Hammond, one of whose children was receiving piano lessons from Lewis at the time.

> I think Hammond's response was that, since I seemed to be a trouble-maker, it would be best if they got rid of me. Anyway, there was a strange atmosphere when I came to work the next evening. The next day the band was leaving for Washington for a date in the Howard Theater. I went home and thought about it – and I decided not to go. I felt that if John was prepared to fire me on the advice of an outsider, then I really didn't want to go on working with the quartet. So I quit.

In an interview with *Crescendo*'s Les Tomkins, published in August 1968, Kenny said that when John Lewis first outlined his policy for the group to follow, he agreed with some of his ideas – but not all.

> I eventually left, not because I felt restricted, but because I couldn't accept the overall conception. It should have leaned more towards folklore than to classical music; it would probably have been more agreeable to the public that way, too. I think jazz forms are more suitable to improvise on than classical forms. Happily, they've succeeded commercially. But I have no regrets about leaving them. None at all. Probably, if I'd stayed they wouldn't have been a success!

John Lewis told me that his understanding of Kenny Clarke's reason for leaving the MJQ was that he wanted to return to Paris.

> He was going back to Paris and that was it. He had an opportunity over there and he took it. He always did things like that. I remember in 1937 he was supposed to go with Fletcher Henderson – but instead he took the job with Edgar Hayes, who was not in the same league as Henderson. But I guess he wanted to go to Europe, so that's what he did. Certainly he didn't leave because of the music. He was happy with the music.

Milt Jackson, on the other hand, says that Kenny left the MJQ 'because he was unhappy about the way musicians were treated in New York'. He said Kenny had happy recollections of Europe and wanted to return. (Milt himself left the group for a spell in the mid-fifties because 'even though we were successful musically, and were making a major contribution, it wasn't as financially rewarding as it should have been'. He had another break from the quartet in 1974 when, according to notes left by Kenny, he told him, 'After twenty years I finally got out. The only thing I have against you is that you didn't take me with you when you left.')

In an interview with French writer François Postif, Kenny said he left the MJQ 'because John Lewis thought of nothing but making money. He wanted to become commercial and pander to the public. I didn't agree.' And he told the *International Herald Tribune*'s Mike Zwerin that he didn't regret 'leaving the gold mine just before it panned out. Not for one minute. I've thought about that; someone said, "Klook, you should have stayed here and made all that money." But money's only good when you need it.'

In most interviews about the MJQ, Kenny refrained from raising the more disputatious matters that he referred to in the conversation with Helen Oakley Dance. And he told her, true to his general tendency to sidestep controversy for the sake of tranquillity, 'When people ask me why I left, I always say, well, it just wasn't the way I like to play.'

In a December 1963 *Down Beat* interview Kenny told Burt Korall: 'As for John, his music is a bit too bland and pretentious for me. I fell asleep the last time I heard the MJQ in person.'

On another occasion Kenny recalled an incident at an MJQ rehearsal which, for him, must have been the ultimate heresy. John interrupted the tune they were doing and said to Klook, 'Hey, Kenny, this is not supposed to swing.' And Kenny replied with a mirthless chuckle, 'Yeah? What's it supposed to do then?'

Bassist Red Mitchell also recalls an incident towards the end of Kenny Clarke's time with the MJQ which would seem to confirm the view that the conflict between Klook and John Lewis over the musical direction the quartet was taking was more than a touch acrimonious.

> I was walking on Broadway one day, heading downtown towards the Alvin Hotel which was just across the street from Birdland. As I got to about half a block away from the hotel I heard voices raised in a heated argument. There, on the corner, were Milt Jackson, Percy Heath and Kenny Clarke – and I caught Kenny shouting at the top of his voice, 'Well, let that motherfucker get his own band!'
>
> I'm quite certain that Kenny objected strongly to what John Lewis was doing to the MJQ. And it seems ironic to me that, in the end, Kenny went to France to pursue playing jazz the American way, while John Lewis stayed in the States and Europeanized the music of the Modern Jazz Quartet.

My own view is that the primary cause of Kenny's leaving the MJQ was his increasing dissatisfaction with the musical path that Lewis was following – a factor which, for Kenny, far outweighed any consideration of enhanced financial rewards. However, I am quite sure that Kenny totally misread the attitude of John Lewis when he believed that he was preparing to fire him. Neither was it the case that Klook left the MJQ because he wanted to return to Paris. He didn't leave New York until some eighteen months after parting from the quartet. The most likely explanation is that he found the Lewis repertoire restricting and not in accord with his musical ideals, and he genuinely didn't want to become trapped by the MJQ's commercial success and the obligations that that would impose. It was yet another escape act for Kenny, and I am absolutely certain that, as he told Zwerin, he never regretted it for one moment.

He told me once,

> I stuck it for a while and everybody tried to convince me how much it would mean to me financially – but I tried to think a little ahead, and I realized that it would all add up to being the same. I knew I could get more satisfaction and enjoyment from playing *my* way.

Among the papers Kenny left behind is an interview transcript with a handwritten note on the bottom, which reads:

> I always knew the MJQ would make it because the musicians are sincere and talented, plus John Lewis had a formula for success and a businesslike attitude. Seeing their success, I'm not sorry I left. I'm completely happy with the way things have turned out because I like doing the things I do.

It was signed, 'Kenny "Klook" Clarke, drummer, Paris, France, 1968'.

Now the most sought-after drummer in New York, Kenny Clarke had no difficulty in maintaining a regular schedule of work after leaving the MJQ. He became resident at the Café Bohemia in Greenwich Village and got to play once again with the great bassist, Oscar Pettiford, with either Duke Jordan or Dick Katz on piano and various horn players, including Stan Getz.

He was also busy in the recording studios, making a dozen albums for Prestige and working extensively with Horace Silver and Percy Heath as his regular rhythm section. Among the musicians who had the benefit of Klook's educated, eloquent, sensitive and unfailingly swinging drumming behind them on their Prestige record dates were Miles, King Pleasure, Art Farmer, J.J. Johnson and Kai Winding. For other labels, between April 1952 and April 1954, Klook recorded with Charles Mingus, Kenny Dorham, Stan Getz, Mat Mathews, trumpeter Hal Mitchell and Annie Ross. Annie's date, on 1 April 1952, was for Dee Gee, and with Klook were Milt Jackson, Blossom Dearie on piano and Percy Heath.

The date with Mat Mathews, the Dutch-born accordion player, was the first record session for Herbert Jay Solomon, a twenty-three-year-old flute player who had just finished army service and was using the professional name Herbie Mann. Herbie remembers his first meeting with Klook:

> One day in front of the Union on 52nd Street, Kenny, trying to help out a young musician, said to me, 'You know, I think the flute is good for Latin music but I don't think it's a jazz instrument.' I thought for a moment and said, 'Kenny, when you got out of the army and were playing all that new blip-bop, blip-bop style of drums, while all the others were still playing swing, and they said to you you weren't playing jazz, what did you tell them?' And Kenny answered, 'I said thanks for your interest – but fuck you, that's the way *I* play jazz!' So I said to Kenny, 'Thanks for your interest – but fuck you, that's the way *I* play jazz!' But Kenny really helped me out in those early days and truthfully, that first rhythm section with Klook and Percy Heath was the best I've ever played with.

Mat Mathews and Herbie Mann were, some eighteen months later, to be featured on the first sides Carmen McRae made with Klook. The date was for the Bethlehem label – and, apart from a rather forgettable session made earlier with Mercer Ellington, when Carmen was calling herself by her married name, Carmen Clarke, it was her recording début. With Klook in the rhythm section were Wendell Marshall and guitarist Mundell Lowe. The result was an outstanding album which gave a considerable boost to Carmen's career. She recalls:

> It was Mat Mathews who really gave me the chance to record. He was crazy about my talent and when the Bethlehem A&R man offered Mat the date, Mat told him he wouldn't do it unless I sang on it. So that's how it happened. I did 'Easy to Love', 'If I'm Lucky', 'Old Devil Moon' and a tune that Mat and his wife had written, 'Tiptoe Gently'. When the A&R guy heard me he flipped and he decided to give me a contract – but I read it and never signed it because he would have ended up owning me from head to toe, body and soul.

In a way, Carmen had developed as a singer out of a feeling of frustration because she got bored sitting at home while Klook was on the road, and out of a feeling of defiance because Kenny hadn't given her too much encouragement to sing professionally. Carmen told me:

> When Kenny was with Dizzy and they needed a singer, I really wanted to try for the job. But I guess Kenny didn't want me around because it would have restricted his freedom. That turned me off – it was really what made me want to get away from him. I thought, 'Either he thinks I can't sing or he doesn't want me – or both.' So I found a job by myself in a club, rented a piano and stayed for seventeen weeks. When I started, I hardly knew ten

> songs – so I'd turn on the radio every day so that I could learn new material. I did that altogether for three and a half years – and that was valuable experience. I thank Klook for that because, if he had been cool with me, I would probably be nothing.

Kenny may not have given Carmen much encouragement to pursue a singing career, but he did help her out with a bass player while she was working in a Brooklyn club in 1950. Jimmy Woode remembers coming to New York from Boston to get his 802 Union card and making contact with Klook.

> I had met Kenny earlier through my Uncle Henry who worked with Klook in the Teddy Hill band. Kenny asked me – or, rather, instructed me – to go over to Brooklyn and play with this lady singer and pianist. I paid my cab fare over and made the gig. I played for a week and took a taxi back to my hotel every night. The lady was Carmen McRae. I never did get paid.

Of all the many record dates that Kenny Clarke did between 1951 and 1956, perhaps the most eminent and indispensable were those he recorded with Miles Davis in 1954. In his biography of Miles, Ian Carr describes the 29 April Prestige session, which featured J.J. Johnson, Lucky Thompson, Heath and Silver, as Davis's 'first full-scale masterpiece'. This date produced outstanding, on-the-spot head arrangements of 'Walkin' ' and 'Blue 'n' Boogie' and, commenting on Clarke's role in the former piece, Carr says, 'Kenny Clarke's immensely sensitive and subtle use of the hi-hat cymbal which he opens and closes to point up the rhythms of the theme . . . intensifies the drama.'

Exactly two months later, on 29 June, Kenny made another Prestige date with Miles and the same rhythm section, plus Sonny Rollins. This date yielded four more superlative cuts – 'But not for Me', 'Oleo', 'Doxy' and 'Airegin' and, in his analysis of the music, Carr describes the rhythm section as a 'marvellous unit'. He adds, 'One of the reasons why Heath and Clarke functioned so well together was because they were a regular unit in a working band. Miles's use of them as his studio rhythm section for most of that year suited everybody; musically they were perfect for him at the time.'

The final key Miles date of 1954 was the Christmas Eve session with Milt Jackson, Thelonious Monk and Percy Heath,

Contract Blank

Associated Musicians of Greater New York

LOCAL 802, AMERICAN FEDERATION OF MUSICIANS

NEW YORK 19, N. Y.

THIS CONTRACT for the personal services of musicians, made this 7 day of FEB, 1955 between the undersigned employer (hereinafter called the employer) and 6 (including Leader) musicians (hereinafter called employees) represented by the undersigned representative.

WITNESSETH, That the employer employs the personal services of the employees, as musicians severally, and the employees severally, through their representative, agree to render collectively to the employer services as musicians in the orchestra under the leadership of KENNY CLARKE, according to the following terms and conditions:

Name and Address of Place of Engagement RUDY VAN GELDERS

Date(s) of Employment FEB. 7 - 1955

Hours of Employment 4:00 - 7:00 PM

The employer is hereby given an option to extend this agreement for a period of ______ weeks beyond the original term thereof. Said option can be made effective only by written notice from the employer to the employees not later than ______ days prior to the expiration of said original term that he claims and exercises said option.

PRICE AGREED UPON $ SCALE
(Terms and Amount)

To be paid ______
(Specify When Payments Are to Be Made)

The employer shall at all times have complete control of the services which the employees will render under the specifications of this contract. On behalf of the employer the Leader will distribute the amount received from the employer to the employees, including himself, as indicated on the opposite side of this contract, or in place thereof on separate memorandum supplied to the employer at or before the commencement of the employment hereunder and take and turn over to the employer receipts therefor from each employee, including himself. The amount paid to the Leader includes the cost of transportation, which will be reported by the Leader to the employer. The employer hereby authorizes the Leader on his behalf to replace any employee who by illness, absence, or for any other reason does not perform any or all of the services provided for under this contract. The agreement of the employees to perform is subject to proven detention by sickness, accidents, or accidents to means of transportation, riots, strikes, epidemics, acts of God, or any other legitimate conditions beyond the control of the employees. The employer agrees that the Business Representative of the Musicians' Local in whose jurisdiction the musicians are playing, shall have access to the premises in which the musicians perform (except in private residences) for the purpose of conferring with the musicians. The musicians performing services under this contract must be members of the American Federation of Musicians and nothing in this contract shall ever be so construed as to interfere with any obligation which they may owe to the American Federation of Musicians.

It is agreed that all the rules, laws and regulations of the American Federation of Musicians, and all the rules, laws and regulations of the Local in whose jurisdiction the musicians perform, insofar as they are not in conflict with those of the Federation, are made part of this contract.

Any member or members who are parties to or affected by this contract, whose services thereunder or covered thereby, are prevented, suspended or stopped by reason of any strike, ban, unfair list order or requirement of the Federation shall be free to accept and engage in other employment of the same or similar character, or otherwise, for other employers or persons without any restraint, hindrance, penalty, obligation or liability whatever, any other provisions of this contract to the contrary notwithstanding.

If this contract requires or contemplates the recording, transmission or reproduction of any music by any mechanical means, then it shall not become effective unless and until it shall be approved by the International Executive Board of the American Federation of Musicians.

The employer represents that there does not exist against him, in favor of any employee-member of the American Federation of Musicians, any claim of any kind arising out of musical services rendered for any such employer. It is agreed that no employee-member of the American Federation of Musicians will be required to perform any provisions of this contract or to render any services for said employer as long as any such claim in unsatisfied or unpaid, in whole or in part. The employer in signing this contract himself, or having same signed by a representative, acknowledges his (her or their) authority to do so and hereby assumes liability for the amount stated herein.

Name of Employer SAVOY RECORD CO
Street Address 58 MARKET ST
City or State NEWARK, N. J.
Phone MA-3-7470

Accepted by Employer O. Cadena
Accepted Kenny Clarke (Orchestra Leader) Membership Card No. 5-568
By ______
(Representatives of Employees)

9/15/44 FORM B 44 Printed in U.S.A.

Contract between Klook and Savoy's Ozzie Cadena for a Kenny Clarke All Stars date

producing 'Bags' Groove', 'Bemsha Swing', 'Swing Spring' and 'The Man I Love'. Again the rapport between drummer and bassist contributed significantly to these classic tracks. 'The propulsive rhythm section of Heath and Clarke give these performances great dynamism,' says Carr. These Miles Davis sessions are yet further examples of the dedicated, selfless and hugely supportive way in which Kenny Clarke approached his craft as a drummer.

By now, Klook was beginning to work more and more for Savoy, the record company owned by Herman Lubinsky. He had been invited by Ozzie Cadena, the A&R man of Savoy, to be a kind of talent scout and more or less the resident drummer for the Newark, New Jersey-based label. Cadena had joined the Savoy company, succeeding Teddy Reig, the previous year and was anxious to build up the label's jazz repertoire at a time when Savoy was going through a lean period and established jazz artists were not falling over themselves to record for the company. Cadena was a great admirer of Clarke's ability to drive a rhythm section and he also knew that few jazz players had better connections with top musicians in New York than Klook.

Kenny agreed to work with Cadena for a salary of $7,000 a year plus session fees for all the record dates he would be called upon to do. Over the next couple of years Kenny Clarke brought Horace Silver and Bobby Jaspar, the fine Belgian tenor saxophonist and flautist, to the Savoy label, plus a Detroit contingent including Pepper Adams, Paul Chambers, Donald Byrd and Tommy Flanagan. But his most dramatic find was Julian 'Cannonball' Adderley, a music teacher from Tampa, Florida, and an alto saxophonist of real virtuosity.

Cannonball and his brother Nat, a cornet player, were taking a few days of vacation in New York in the summer of 1955 and one evening they looked in to the Café Bohemia. Kenny Clarke recalled,

> Someone introduced me to this guy from Florida and told me that he was a fine alto player, so I invited him up to sit in. I suggested playing 'Bohemia After Dark', but Oscar Pettiford said, 'He won't know that – I only just wrote it.' Well, I told Cannon to listen to a couple of choruses first and then blow – which he did. And he played with such brilliant

assurance that, at the end, Oscar came over and hugged him. This guy just ate up the changes.

Drummer Al Levitt was in the Café Bohemia audience that night with Jackie McLean and he remembers the astonishing impact that Adderley made, particularly on 'I'll Remember April'.

> People were running around the street saying, 'Hurry up and get in there – there's a guy called Cannonball who's playing his ass off!' They were talking about a new Charlie Parker. Miles was in the club, too, and I happened to overhear him say to Jackie, 'Yeah, he plays good, this guy – but he doesn't peck.' Pecking was a word that was used to describe a certain rhythmical way of phrasing. Jackie used it a lot – I think he got it from Bird – like short, rhythmical phrases that sort of reminded everybody of the pecking of a chicken. The funny thing was that although Miles was more or less telling Jackie that Cannon wasn't really hip, it was Cannon he hired a couple of years later.

If Cannonball hadn't mastered the art of pecking, it apparently presented no problems to Kenny Clarke. In his autobiography, *Miles,* Davis himself gives this description of pecking: 'You divided the riffs, like a chichi riff, broke them up and darted in and out of the rhythm. You could do this real well when you had a great drummer. We had Kenny Clarke and couldn't nobody play that kind of shit better than Klook.'

Talking after the set, Adderley told Klook that he and Nat were planning to return home the next day because they were running short of money. Klook told him to wait until midday before deciding to leave. He had something in mind. That night he called Herman Lubinsky and sang Cannonball's praises so effectively that Lubinsky said, 'OK. Tell him to be at the studio at two tomorrow afternoon.' The next day at noon, Klook called Adderley and told him of the session. Cannonball asked if he could bring Nat along with him, Klook agreed, and the result was *Bohemia After Dark*, the recording début of Cannonball and Nat Adderley, made in the distinguished company of Donald Byrd, Jerome Richardson, Horace Silver, Paul Chambers and Klook.

Meanwhile the word about Cannonball's stunning performance at the Café Bohemia and his date for Savoy had sped through the New York jazz grapevine at whirlwind pace.

Lubinsky called Kenny and told him to offer Cannonball a recording contract with Savoy. There was a counter-bid from Mercury, for whom Quincy Jones was writing arrangements and working as a sort of consultant A&R man at the time.

Adderley decided to return to Florida to resign from his teaching post and become a full-time musician, but he asked Klook's advice as to which offer he should accept. Klook told him to go back to Tampa, put his affairs in order and then take a decision on his return to New York. In the end Kenny, who could have strengthened his own situation with Savoy by capturing this new jazz sensation for the label, characteristically put the interests of his protégé first and recommended Adderley to sign with Mercury, because, he said, Savoy did not have a good distribution set-up. He told Cannonball to ask for a $10,000 fee. Adderley was staggered – but he asked for it anyway. 'I think,' Kenny remembered, 'they finally gave him six or seven thousand – but that was a very healthy sum in those days.'

Cannon recorded another album for Savoy – *Spontaneous Combustion* – on 14 July, with his brother, Hank Jones, Paul Chambers and Klook, then a week later he made his début for Mercury and, needless to add, Klook was on that date, too.

Klook worked for Savoy through to August 1956, making many albums with what became the house rhythm section: himself, Wendell Marshall (bass) and Hank Jones (piano). He worked with Gigi Gryce, Ernie Wilkins, Oscar Pettiford, Nat Adderley, Horace Silver, Lucky Thompson, Hank Mobley, Frank Foster, Kenny Burrell and Joe Wilder. The album with Wilder, made on 19 February 1956, is one of the unsung gems of the Savoy collection. It is full of graceful, lyrical, swinging music – the kind of jazz that Kenny completely revelled in.

As well as working for Savoy, Kenny became increasingly in demand by other labels. He told Jean-Louis Ginibre of *Jazz Magazine* in 1968 that at this time he was recording for MGM, Atlantic, Prestige, Savoy, Mercury, MGM and Riverside. 'In the States,' he said, 'you can't say no. If you turn work down, they stop calling you. I was sometimes working up to twenty hours a day.'

Kenny played some memorable dates during the 1952–6

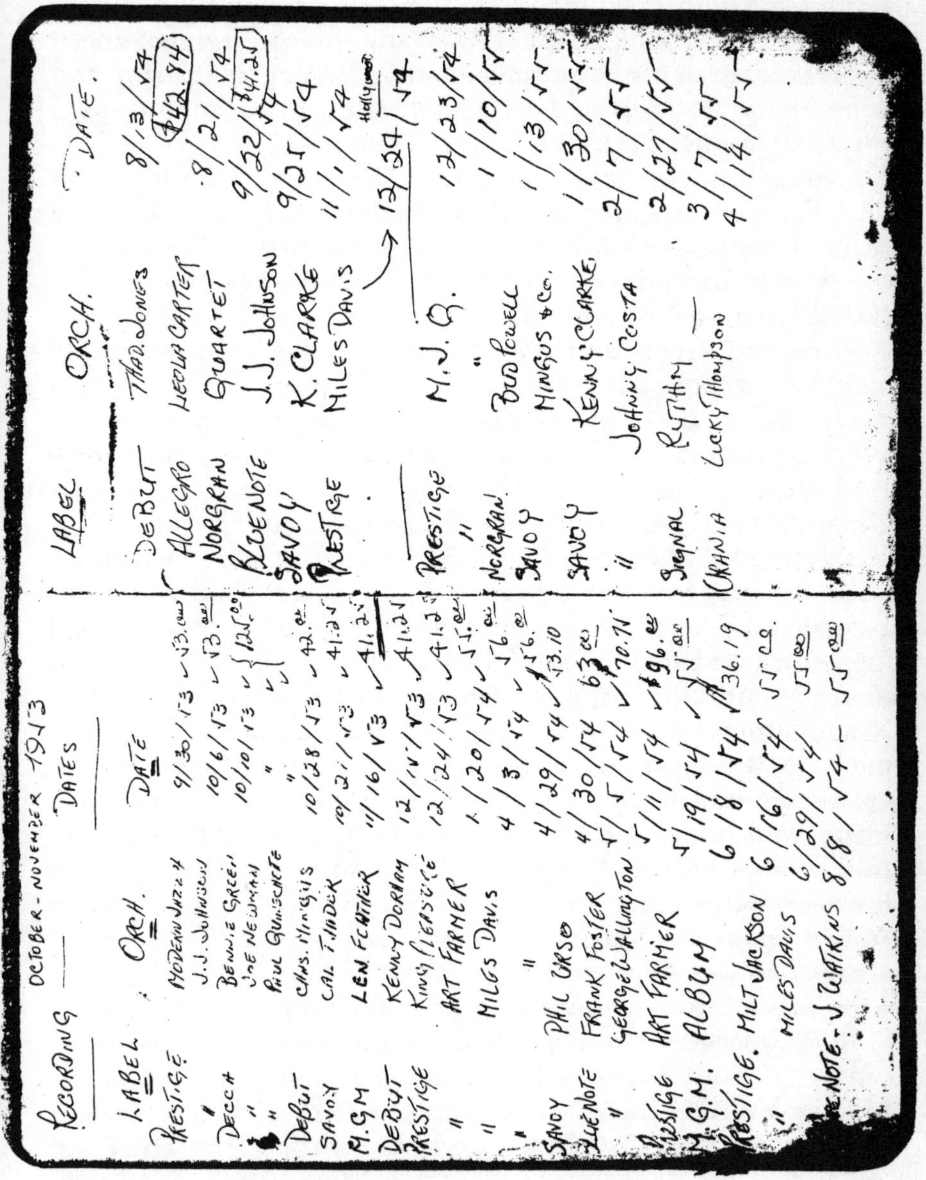

RECORDING — OCTOBER - NOVEMBER 1953 DATES

LABEL	ORCH.	DATE	
PRESTIGE	MODERN JAZZ 4	9/30/53	53.00
"	J.J. JOHNSON	10/6/53	53.00
DECCA	BENNIE GREEN	10/10/53	125.00
"	JOE NEWMAN	"	
"	PAUL QUINICHETTE	"	
DEBUT	CHAS. MINGUS	10/28/53	42.00
SAVOY	CAL TJADER	10/21/53	41.25
M.G.M	LEN FEATHER	11/16/53	41.25
DEBUT	KENNY DORHAM	12/15/53	41.25
PRESTIGE	KING PLEASURE	12/24/53	41.25
"	ART FARMER	1/20/54	55.00
"	MILES DAVIS	4/3/54	56.00
"	"		56.00
SAVOY	PHIL URSO	4/29/54	53.10
BLUENOTE	FRANK FOSTER	4/30/54	63.00
"	GEORGE WALLINGTON	5/5/54	70.71
PRESTIGE	ART FARMER	5/11/54	$96.00
M.G.M.	ALBUM	5/19/54	55.00
PRESTIGE.	MILT JACKSON	6/8/54	36.19
"	MILES DAVIS	6/16/54	55.00
		6/29/54	55.00
BLUENOTE	J. WATKINS	8/8/54	55.00

LABEL	ORCH.	DATE.
DEBUT	THAD. JONES	8/13/54 ($42.84)
ALLEGRO	LEOLA CARTER	
NORGRAN	QUARTET	8/21/54
BLUENOTE	J.J. JOHNSON	9/22/54 ($41.25)
SAVOY	K. CLARKE	9/25/54
PRESTIGE	MILES DAVIS	11/1/54
	→	12/24/54 Hollywood
PRESTIGE	M.J.Q.	12/23/54
"	"	1/10/55
NORGRAN	BUD POWELL	
SAVOY	MINGUS & Co.	1/13/55
SAVOY	KENNY CLARKE	1/30/55
"	JOHNNY COSTA	2/7/55
		2/27/55
SIGNAL	RYTHM —	
URANIA	LUCKY THOMPSON	3/7/55
		4/14/55

Pages from Kenny Clarke's address book of the fifties listing his record dates

period, including two more sessions with Carmen McRae, the *Monk Plays Ellington* sides for Riverside, Milt Jackson's *Opus de Funk* with Frank Wess and Hank Jones, and a superb Atlantic date with Phineas Newborn. Altogether he made more than 130 record dates, often doing two in one day, between August 1951 and August 1956.

Looking back on this phase of his life in the interview with Ginibre, Kenny said they were incontestably the best five years of his career – but also the most exhausting.

Towards the end of this period Kenny was living in a ground-floor apartment on 77th Street between West End Avenue and Riverside Drive. Carmen McRae, from whom he had been separated from more than three years, had formed an attachment to an impressionist named George Kirby and had left New York to go with him to Chicago. It was in Chicago, in 1956, that through alto saxophonist-turned-lawyer Scoops Carey, Carmen obtained a divorce from Kenny Clarke.

It seemed that everybody in the New York jazz community knew the way to Klook's apartment at this time and whenever a musician needed Kenny for a gig or a record date, he would just knock on the window. Klook became so much in demand that he would often tell the janitor to say he was out, or else would slip out of the back entrance and hide in the yard until the coast was clear. In a city where jazz musicians have always vastly outnumbered gigs, the mental picture of a jazzman hiding out lest he be offered work is irresistibly bizarre. But this is what he told Ginibre in 1968 and he repeated it some fourteen years later in an interview with the *International Herald Tribune*'s Mike Zwerin. Zwerin reported, 'Clarke knew something was seriously wrong when he found himself hiding from Miles Davis who was offering him work. Klook told me, "Miles knocked on my door, so I told the little girl I was with to tell him I'm out. He just kept knocking and said, 'Klook, Klook, I know you're in there.' I just didn't feel like going on that gig. I'd been recording for Savoy Records almost every day. I was tired." '

Kenny Clarke, after five years back in New York, was getting ready to escape again.

11
Groovin' High

Along with the hip talk, the goatees and berets, the new melodic, harmonic and rhythmic vocabulary and the eccentric vocalese of the bop movement went, unhappily, an addiction to hard drugs on a much greater scale than had previously been the case in the jazz community. Jazz and drugs – particularly the alcoholic variety – were associated from the very beginnings of the music, and reefer smoking had been a popular way of getting high long before the first flattened fifth chord was heard in Harlem. As James Lincoln Collier observes in *The Making of Jazz*, 'Jazz has never been without the taint of narcotics. Cocaine was sold freely in Storyville, and without question many of the early players sampled it. Marijuana was virtually endemic to jazz from the beginning.'

For hundreds of years, all over the world, drugs of one kind or another have been used as an escape route from the harsh realities of life; and it's quite certain that jazz musicians used marijuana and alcohol to bring them soporific relief from economic hardship, frustration and discrimination. There is, however, not the slightest doubt that jazz musicians also used drugs simply because they enjoyed getting high. Sometimes the attempts to dignify addiction by ascribing it to oppression, squalor or – more improbably – the fact that 'people don't dig my music, man' are, though well-intended, absurdly naïve. Collier says that it is hard to know why exactly the bop movement 'was so saturated with heroin'. I would opt for the very simple explanation that once it was known that a few of the key players in the jazz revolution were shooting heroin, the drug became the badge of the new movement. It was not so much that musicians really believed it made Charlie Parker play better – all the evidence is to the contrary – though there may have been a few, particularly outside the United States, who thought this to be the case. What is much more likely is that heroin was deemed to be hip, and the rapid spread of the habit was much more attributable to musicians not wishing to be seen as square, than to any conviction that you couldn't really play bebop without it.

It was in the late forties that hard drugs began to supplement joints in the bop musicians' pharmacopoeia. When Charlie Parker moved from Kansas City to New York in 1942 he brought with him a heroin habit acquired in his teens. In the words of his biographer, Ross Russell, heroin had become his staff of life. Unwittingly, Bird was surely responsible for turning a lot of musicians on to hard drugs.

Exactly when and why Kenny Clarke first used heroin is hard to determine. Apart from the fact that many of the musicians who were close to him when he had the habit have an understandable reluctance to talk about it, there is also the fact that Kenny appears to have been an elaborately discreet user. It is most likely that he tried heroin for the first time in 1948 or 1949 – the period when the use of hard drugs was gaining a fearful momentum in the modern-jazz community. Certainly by this time many of the musicians who played record dates and club gigs with Klook were hooked.

During the sixties I talked to two major jazz figures about their involvement with drugs, and their responses cast some considerable light on the nature of the junk epidemic. Howard McGhee got hooked in 1950 – a year after he'd been voted America's top trumpet player in a jazz-magazine poll. In an interview in October 1964 he told me:

> When I was voted top trumpet player in 1949, I figured that I might get to working regular. But I didn't. So I hung around with the other cats and got bored. Then someone would say, 'Come on, man, let's get high.' So we got high. And that's how it started.
>
> But, believe me, junk don't make you play better. You just think you're playing better. I'm clean now, and I'm playing better than I've ever played in my whole life. It was six years ago when I quit using the stuff. I'd been

on it for seven years. I was spending a hundred dollars a day, every day. It was insane.

So I quit. I said to myself one day, 'McGhee, you're no good to yourself, no good to your family. Either you quit now or you die. And if you die, you're no help to your wife and kids. You gotta live.' I was broke; I had no place to go. I had sold my home, my furniture, a big record collection that went way back. So I made up my mind. I spent four days locked in a friend's room – no food, no drink, no sleep, no stuff. I walked the floor. I puked. It took time to clean out my whole system. Then I had to fight myself for two weeks. It was hell – but I knew there was a worse hell waiting if I didn't stick it. So I stuck it. For two weeks I didn't sleep. Then one night as I was watching TV, I went off to sleep. It was 9 p.m. I woke up at 9.30 the next morning and I knew I had the thing kicked. I was straight.

In July 1966 I talked to Dexter Gordon about his addiction. Dexter took his first shot of heroin when he was just twenty-two. Two decades later he was still trying to kick the habit.

I started using it around 1945 when just about all the big names were. But it was the most terrible mistake I ever made in my life. It destroys you eventually unless you fight it. I have been off it twice for more than two years at a time and then it's no real fight. When you are working regularly, playing and rehearsing, it just doesn't come up. But when things are slow, you get bored and idle and depressed and the pushers start coming round – before you know it, you are back on again. Boy, those pushers really made a believer out of me.

I got to a stage where I told myself I just couldn't go on. I was spending up to 200 dollars a day on junk, my kids were getting their father's addiction flung in their faces. So I fought it and went clean. But I was getting phone calls every day from pushers, and they were approaching me in the street: 'Aw, come on Dexter, let's swing . . .' I had to tell them over and over again that I was determined to kick it.

In an interview with *Down Beat* writer Bill Quinn in February 1969, alto saxophonist Lou Donaldson painted a grim picture of the jazz scene that greeted him when he arrived in New York in the early fifties: 'When I came on the scene, the junkies had everything and the recording studios had the junkies. If you weren't strung out, you couldn't get a record date. I didn't get high, so I was kind of an outsider at first.'

Kenny Clarke was certainly on heroin by the time he joined the Modern Jazz Quartet; and certainly, at this stage of his career, he was earning enough money to support the habit.

'I remember he was using when he was in the quartet,' says John Lewis, 'but it may have started some time before then. I can remember occasions when we were playing and something seemed to be wrong. He wasn't really able to function properly.' And Carmen McRae says that Kenny was using hard drugs from 1951 right through to the sixties. 'This was after we separated. Everybody was into something or other – would take or do something. Kenny was on heroin, but later, in France, he straightened up. He was tremendously discreet about his habit – I only saw him really out of it on one occasion. He controlled it very well. Usually, those cats, you know how they get – but not Kenny.'

Addiction to illicit drugs inescapably imposes a high degree of discretion on the user, but Kenny Clarke was evidently an exceptionally unostentatious junkie. 'He handled it with an amazing amount of skill and unobtrusiveness,' says Annie Ross. 'For a long time I didn't know that he was hooked. He certainly wasn't a typical junkie. He was always very dignified, very cool. He kept it well under control – maybe because of that kind of "closed-in" thing in his nature that was his protection against the world.'

Another musician who fought a long battle against hard drug addiction is Kenny Drew, a resident at the Paris Blue Note in the early sixties. Kenny first met Kenny Clarke in New York in 1951.

> We'd meet at Al's Luncheonette on Sugar Hill at 148th and St Nicholas – it was a hang-out for musicians. We'd go in for coffee and do-nuts and plan the next jam session. And Kenny and I would get high together. When I came to the Blue Note some years later I discovered he was still using. I saw him nod occasionally – but mostly he was in total control.

Al Levitt, another musician who contracted and ultimately, after fifteen years, kicked the habit, was sometimes with Klook when he bought drugs in Paris. 'I never actually witnessed him fixing – I don't know if he injected, snorted, or what he did. But he never gave the impression of somebody who was really high. Sometimes he would nod off a little bit, but unless you knew that he'd had a fix, you could easily believe that he was just sleepy.'

Pierre Michelot only discovered that Kenny had a habit when they were on an Italian tour together with Stéphane Grappelli, Martial Solal and Lucky Thompson.

> It was in the late fifties and I remember we arrived in Sicily and Kenny had problems. We had to call a doctor because he was very sick. I don't know if he had taken an overdose or what. But he had to return to Paris and we had to bring in Daniel Humair as a replacement. Up to that point I'd never been aware of Kenny being under the influence of drugs. I'd seen other musicians affected, like Chet Baker and Dexter Gordon, but Kenny never. I was astonished to discover that he had this habit – he must really have had it under control.

Drugs started to become a significant problem in France in the early sixties when the whole 'French Connection' narcotics sensation exploded on to the front pages. France was the laboratory for the drug industry, where raw opium was converted into morphine and heroin before being shipped to the United States. America was the prime market, but increasing amounts of hard drugs were now finding their way on to the streets of the main French cities. Kenny Drew remembers:

> It happened around the end of 1962 and the beginning of 1963. The French police and the FBI's anti-narcotics bureau mounted a big offensive looking for the drug factory in the south of France and the repercussions reached as far as the Blue Note. A whole lot of people got busted over a period of three days, including Klook and myself. At that time I was taking enough heroin to kill a horse – around five grains a day. We didn't know it then, but the Blue Note had been under surveillance for months.

Kenny Drew spent a month in the infirmary of the Santé prison for his sins. 'Fortunately,' he told me in an October 1977 interview, 'the French have a very humane attitude to the drug problem. They regard it as a sickness – which it is, of course – and they treat it as such. So I went to the infirmary for one month to get straight.'

After his discharge he left Paris to settle in Copenhagen – the result of an earlier meeting at the Blue Note with Marian, an SAS air hostess who was the daughter of Danish jazz pianist Leo Mathisen. She later became Mrs Drew.

> I was tired of Paris, so I was happy when she suggested a move to Copenhagen. Once there, she helped me to kick the habit – cold turkey. You know, it's a lot easier to turn off dope if you have someone in your corner who really digs you and wants to see you do well – then you kind of *have* to change your ways. You say to yourself, 'Damn! I just can't hurt this person by going on the way I have been.' And so you kick. Marrying that lady was the best thing I ever did. I think if I had stayed in Paris I

would have wound up going back to the States and, with my condition at that time, I don't know what might have happened.

Kenny Clarke managed somehow to escape prosecution after the Blue Note raid. Says Jimmy Gourley, 'The law was very lenient with Kenny. He had a good reputation here and I think he must have had a few good friends in important places.'

Gourley can remember only one occasion when Kenny's hard-drug habit threatened to jeopardize the music.

> We were making a record date in Germany in 1963 and Kenny's 'goodies' didn't show up. Kenny was in bad shape and it looked as if the gig was going to go out of the window. But then the connection came and everything went off fine. It was unbelievable. Here's a man who looks as if he's about to die – and then five minutes later he's in his shirtsleeves behind the drums and shouting, 'OK, let's go!'
>
> But most of the time you could never really tell when Kenny was under the influence. He never let it interfere with the music.

Gigi Campi remembers a time in September 1964 when a small group from the Clarke–Boland Big Band played a concert in the old Rolandseck railway station between Cologne and Koblenz:

> Well, *we* were all in the *bahnhof*, but Kenny was somewhere else! I mean, he was out of it. He was making a loud snoring noise while he was playing – but he was playing tremendously well. I was a little bit embarrassed because I was afraid that everybody would realize that he was high. I remember Francy Boland saying to me, 'I don't know what he's been using, but, My God, I love him when he plays like that!' I said, 'Come on, man, Kenny is really wrecked.' But Francy just smiled and said, 'But he's playing like mad!'

On the way back to Cologne at 5 a.m. Klook was sitting in Campi's Mercedes receiving a benevolent admonition from the boss. 'Kenny, you'd better get yourself together. You have to choose between that stuff and all the things that are really important to you – your family, your music, your health. It's not worth it, man.'

Says Campi,

> Kenny gave me that special glance and said nothing. He could have been

saying 'Get off my back,' or he could have been thinking that I was only telling him what he knew already. But, whatever, he started to use less after that and he finally kicked it altogether – I'd say around 1965. He'd been injecting heroin on and off for fifteen years, but he controlled it fantastically. He was physically very strong – and that time in Rolandseck was the only occasion when I saw him really affected.

Al Levitt came to Paris with the Lionel Hampton band in 1967 and saw Kenny at the Blue Note.

I went up to him and said hello – and I saw at once that he had stopped using. I was surprised and amazed because at that time I was pretty involved myself and I considered him as a confirmed addict. But he had great strength of character and I guess once he'd made up his mind to do something, he went ahead and did it.

Says Carmen McRae, 'Kenny certainly had tremendous self-control. I mean, he just made up his mind and straightened himself out. And anyone who's been hooked on heroin for a number of years will tell you what a nightmare experience that can be. But Kenny was so strong that he could do it, or he could leave it alone.'

Needless to say Kenny hardly ever talked about hard drugs and certainly would not be drawn on the subject of his own habit. But he did make a bitter comment in his 1971 interview with Art Taylor, published in *Notes and Tones*. Asked what he thought about the publicity given to musicians because of their use of drugs, Kenny answered, 'It's all a plan to destroy something in people, to destroy their dignity, their moral content. Drugs is a very well-planned operation, and like Malcolm X once said, if the authorities wanted to stop the flow of drugs in Harlem, they could do it overnight, but I see it's still flowing, so there's your answer.'

12
The French Connection

'Why France?' Michael Haggerty asked Kenny Clarke when he interviewed him on 26 August 1982. Kenny replied:

> The French have always felt that jazz was an extension of their culture. It goes back to New Orleans and to the Creoles and Cajuns. They speak French all the time . . . It's kind of an old French; it goes back, I guess, to the seventeenth century. They still speak French and they feel they belong to France, just as Normans and Bretons do. All those people come from France and still stick to their old traditions. That's why, when you have dixieland or New Orleans jazz, which most of the Creoles were playing at the time, they use a sort of French attack. It was very easy for the French to understand the music. And then the Africans began to play it and made certain changes that were very good, but difficult to understand at the time. You know, like King Oliver, Louis Armstrong, Sidney Bechet, Albert Nicholas and all those guys got a hold of it and turned it around in their fashion. It lost all the French flavour. Before that, Jelly Roll Morton and others were playing music like French *rondes* with classical attack that didn't appeal much to the Africans – so they changed it around, their way. And that's the way we play it today. But the French still feel attached to it, because they had something to do with the makings of the music.

Just as surely as New Orleans, Chicago, Kansas City and New York were the great jazz cities of the United States, so Paris, after the Second World War, became the jazz capital of Europe. As French publisher and jazz enthusiast Daniel Filipacchi has observed, 'France was without doubt the first country in the world to offer official acknowledgement to jazz as a genuine art form, rather than a mere novelty.' And in *Jazz: Its Evolution and Essence*, a highly influential study written in 1954, André Hodeir urged the recognition of jazz as a complement to European culture. Writers like Sartre, Anouilh and

Cocteau were unashamed enthusiasts of the music, as were composers Darius Milhaud, Maurice Ravel, Arthur Honegger and concert pianist Samson François.

Post-war Paris was the beachhead for the jazz invasion of Europe. With American musicians banned from playing in Britain because of the dispute between the American Federation of Musicians and the British Musicians' Union – which went unresolved until 1961 – Paris became the logical jumping-off point for jazz musicians eager to find audiences which might accord them more respect and appreciation than they were able to find in the United States. Some musicians had already enjoyed a foretaste of Europe through military service; others had caught tantalizing glimpses of the old world as they travelled the road with visiting bands and musical shows.

As James Lincoln Collier notes in *The Making of Jazz*, the initial penetration of American jazz into Europe came in the First World War when the military bands of the American Expeditionary Force included some jazz or ragtime players. One of the most prominent was the band of the 369th Infantry Regiment whose drum major was the legendary dancer, Bojangles Robinson. And an ensemble called the Scrap Iron Jazz Band made some recordings in Paris in 1919. In the same year Louis Mitchell's orchestra played the Casino de Paris with Mistinguett. It was also in this year that Will Marion Cook brought his Southern Syncopators across the Atlantic. The line-up included a certain Sidney Joseph Bechet. He left Cook in Paris to join a breakaway unit led by drummer Benny Peyton for a few months. Bechet was to return regularly to France after that, eventually settling there permanently in 1951.

Between the wars a number of American bands and revues made tours of Europe. New Orleans clarinettist Albert Nicholas came to Paris in October 1925 with Josephine Baker's *Revue Nègre* in a band led by Claude Hopkins – a leader for whom Kenny Clarke was to work some fourteen years later. Another US musician to settle in Paris was bandleader Sam Wooding, who had completed a European tour with the Chocolate Kiddies. Wooding put together a band from that show which included Tommy Ladnier, Willie Lewis and Gene Sedric. In

1929, Mezz Mezzrow led a quartet at l'Ermitage Muscovite in Paris; violinist Eddie South was a temporary Parisian from 1929 to 1930; in 1935 Willie Lewis was leading a band at Chez Florence which included Benny Carter; Bill Coleman was playing in Freddie Taylor's band at the Villa d'Este. And, successively in the thirties, the bands of Duke Ellington, Cab Calloway, Louis Armstrong, Edgar Hayes and Teddy Hill made European tours which, indispensably, included Paris. France in general, and Paris in particular, were developing a marked affinity for America's primary indigenous art form. One of Europe's first jazz magazines was a monthly, *La Revue de Jazz*, inaugurated in July 1929 by musicians in one of the popular bands of the time, Grégor and his Grégoriens. It was followed, in February 1934, by the first issue of *Jazz Hot*, a product of the Hot Club de France which had been founded in December 1932 by two Paris students. The Hot Club de France was the first organization in the world to have as its *raison d'être* the promotion and popularization of jazz. It was also in 1934 that the celebrated Quintette du Hot Club de France, with Django Reinhardt and Stéphane Grappelli, made its début.

But it was really after the Second World War that jazz made its most significant and substantial impact. In February 1948, France staged Europe's first major jazz festival in Nice – and it was from this point on that the jazz crusade really got under way. The festival featured Louis Armstrong, Jack Teagarden, Barney Bigard, Sid Catlett and Mezz Mezzrow's band with Bob Wilber, Baby Dodds, Sammy Price, Pops Foster, Henry Goodwin and Jimmy Archey.

In an interview I had with Mezzrow in Paris in 1967, he told me, 'The musicians were treated like kings. We played concerts in about twenty towns. In Orleans we played in a great big barn and the mayor made a speech afterwards and kissed me about ten times. He said it was the first time he'd seen his people so happy since before the war.'

At the time of this interview Mezzrow, who had first come to France in 1929, had been living in Paris for nearly twenty years and was a confirmed francophile. 'In France,' he said, 'people treat you as an artist and not as a bum.'

In *The Making of Jazz*, Collier speaks of two myths which

have sprung up about European attitudes towards jazz – one that there is no racial prejudice in Europe and, two, that Europeans have always been more sensitive and receptive to jazz than Americans. He admits that there is sufficient truth in both myths to give them 'a surface plausibility'. But from my own personal experience of five years in Paris in the sixties, during which I talked to many black jazz expatriates, I would argue that the truth content of the two 'myths' is much more than superficial. Of course there was, and is, racial prejudice in Europe – but it is invariably a selective strain. I recall that the same Parisian who would treat Algerians as subhuman would be positively overawed and deferential in the presence of Duke Ellington or Miles Davis. Black American musicians in the fifties and sixties certainly did encounter prejudice in Europe, but the vast majority assured me that it existed on nothing like the same scale as in the United States.

Equally, there was almost universal acknowledgement among musicians that Europeans – particularly in France, Italy, Germany and Scandinavia – tended to be more knowledgeable about the history and development of jazz, and certainly had a greater respect for the musicians than did their fellow Americans. They valued jazz as an important, vital and unique art form – they did not dismiss it as inconsequential musical wallpaper for whorehouses and speakeasies.

As Johnny Griffin, a French resident for more than twenty years, observed, 'Europeans taught me how to relax. In the States I'd been on a treadmill, running all the time and going no place. The French had this *doucement* attitude – at first it exasperated me. But then I saw how much people were enjoying life. So I slowed down and started enjoying life, too.' And, talking of Sidney Bechet's assimilation of the French way of life, French jazzman Claude Luter said, 'Bechet taught us what he knew, and we taught him to live like the French – to be a bit more relaxed and not to have his mind 100% on the job.'

A relaxed and civilized environment where *doucement* was the order of the day was exactly what Kenny Clarke was in need of in the summer of 1956. Klook, the recording-studio refugee, was tired and debilitated by the unrelenting materialism and pressure-cooker atmosphere of New York. He wanted out. Now free of emotional attachments, and with his five-year-old son safely installed with his aunt and uncle in Pittsburgh, Kenny was eager to go as soon as the chance offered.

The opportunity came in March 1956 when Kenny was working with Phineas Newborn and Oscar Pettiford at Basin Street West. Quite by chance, while relaxing in his apartment one afternoon, Kenny turned on the television set. The channel was showing a Maurice Chevalier spectacular and the orchestra was being conducted in a rather energetic way by a man in a white suit. 'I know that guy!' Kenny said to himself, trying to put a name to the conductor's dorsal elevation. Then the cameras caught a frontal view – and revealed the conductor to be French pianist and composer Michel Legrand, who had flown over to work as musical director of the show.

Kenny knew Legrand from his Paris days and so, after the programme, he telephoned the CBS studios, got through to a backstage extension and said, 'This is Kenny Clarke. I'd like to speak to Michel Legrand. It's important.' Legrand came to the phone. He was delighted to hear from his old friend, and arranged to see Klook that night at Basin Street West. It was a joyful reunion, with Legrand sitting in on piano and singing some numbers with the trio.

Just before he left the club, Legrand asked a question that was *douce* music to Klook's ears: 'Listen, Kenny, would you like to come back to Paris?'

'Are you kidding?' Kenny said his face lighting up with that special Klook grin. 'I'd love nothing better.'

'Well, my uncle, Jacques Hélian, is putting a big orchestra together to play nothing but jazz. It would be fantastic if you could be in it. Do you think you can make it?'

'I'll make it.'

'Do I have your word on that?'

'You have my word, Michel.'

Two weeks later, a one-year contract arrived in the mail and, in August, Kenny received an envelope from Paris containing a one-way, first-class ticket to Le Havre on the SS *Liberté*. On 7 September Kenny embarked for the voyage back to France and Paris – this time for good.

The ship was only two days out when Klook was paged by the purser. When he learned that Hélian had cabled him $200 spending money he could hardly believe it. Some days later, when the boat train pulled into Paris, a band of friends was there on the platform to greet and serenade him. Kenny Clarke, aka Klook, aka Liaquat Ali Salaam, freemason, unorthodox Ahmedea Muslim and the finest jazz drummer in the world, was back in Paris. He grinned serenely. He was forty-two, he had a lot of music ahead of him and he was exactly where he wanted to be.

Among the expatriate musicians in Paris at this time was saxophonist Allen Eager, who had been with Klook in the Tadd Dameron band at the Royal Roost. Very soon after Kenny's arrival in Paris, he and Eager teamed up, together with trombonist Billy Byers, British trumpet player Jimmy Deuchar, Algiers-born French pianist Martial Solal, and Belgian bassist Benoît Quersin for a Jazz International session released on the Vogue label.

The French record companies – notably Vogue, Pathé-Marconi (with Delaunay's Swing label), Barclay and Philips – were not slow to exploit the opportunity of recording some of the American expatriates in Paris, and Klook soon found himself engaged in studio work. The twelve sides he made for Philips in November 1956 – *Kenny Clarke Plays André Hodeir* – with Byers, René Urtreger or Solal, Michelot or Jean Warland, Hubert Rostaing (alto) and Armand Migiani (baritone), won the Grand Prix du Disque of the Académie Charles Cros and the Prix Jazz Hot in 1958.

The record presented André Hodeir arrangements of jazz standards like 'Round Midnight', 'Jeru', 'The Squirrel' and 'When Lights are Low' and in his liner note Hodeir, who incidentally saw his role of arranger as being 'the stowaway on the jazz ship', commented:

> When they listen to this record the American public will appreciate that Paris has become a great international jazz centre and that very good jazz musicians are no longer as rare here as they used to be. As for the rhythm sections which enliven the solos and ensembles, rarely have we heard, here on the old continent, any quite so stimulating – thanks to the key

member, the prestigious drummer who needs no eulogies because this LP, after so many others (and better than most of them, we hope) testifies so eloquently to his pre-eminence – Kenny Clarke.

By now, the American pilgrimage to Paris was in full swing, even gaining momentum, and the French capital was becoming, incontestably, the jazz Mecca of Europe. Sidney Bechet was playing with Claude Luter at the Vieux Colombier, and Don Byas (since 1946), Albert Nicholas (1935), Joe Turner (1949), Art Simmons (1949), Benny Waters (1953) and Bill Coleman (1948) were all Paris residents. The year 1956 had seen concerts by Kid Ory, Miles Davis, Lester Young, the Modern Jazz Quartet, Stan Getz and Stan Kenton. Gerry Mulligan's Septet played a fifteen-day engagement at the Olympia Theatre, Chet Baker made three records for Barclay, and Lucky Thompson recorded with Martial Solal and Henri Renaud.

Kenny worked for seven months with the Jacques Hélian Orchestra, an eighteen-piece outfit which played variety shows and society gigs and made tours with various singers. The personnel included two Belgian musicians who were later to join Klook in the Clarke–Boland Big Band – bassist Jean Warland and vibraphonist/bongo player Fats Sadi. Los Angeles-born Ernie Royal led the trumpet section at one time, and the more notable French players included Raymond Fonseque (trombone) and Bob Garcia and Jean-Louis Chautemps (reeds).

When Jacques Hélian became ill in March 1957, however, he had to break up the band and Klook was obliged to look elsewhere for regular work. Some years afterwards French writer François Postif told Kenny that he remembered seeing the Hélian band at the Mutualité in Paris and getting the impression that Klook was less than elated with the music. 'Well,' Kenny replied with a rueful smile, 'it wasn't quite the same as playing with Dizzy's band.'

After Hélian, Kenny did a two-week season at the Olympia Theatre with pianist Hazel Scott and then became house drummer at the Club St Germain, working with pianist Martial Solal and Pierre Michelot on bass and backing various French musicians, plus, from time to time, visiting American jazzmen.

When Solal was otherwise engaged, either Maurice Vander or René Urtreger would replace him. And when Kenny was away on the road, Al Levitt, who had arrived in Paris at about the same time as Kenny, took over on drums. He remembers:

> Between 1956 and 1958 Kenny and I became very close. Every night, when I didn't have a gig, I would go to see him, whenever he was appearing. This period was one of the high points of his playing. He was really great. I'd spend time with him during the day. We never practised together but we did a lot of talking and I learned a lot from him – both as a musician and a man.

In May 1957, twenty-four-year-old Quincy Jones arrived in Paris, armed with a contract to work as A&R director for Disques Barclay. Already a gifted and prolific composer and arranger, Quincy was concerned to develop his talents by studying composition with the eminent teacher, Nadia Boulanger. He was also concerned about the lack of working opportunities in the States. He told me: 'Just look at the scene in New York: 40,000 musicians in Local 802 and 2,000 jobs!'

Like Klook, Quincy had developed a fondness for the French way of life some years earlier. He had come to Europe with the

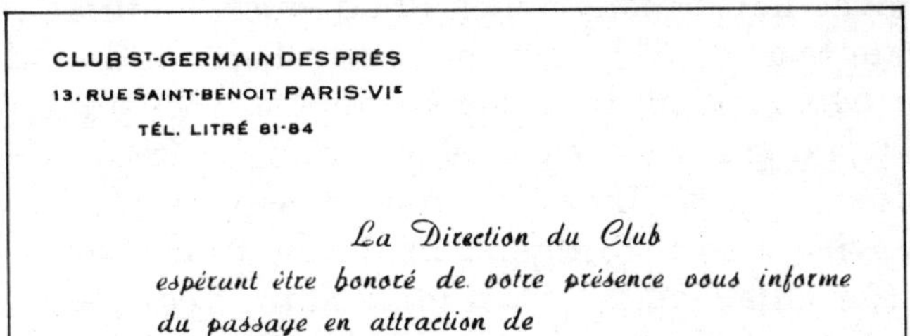

CLUB S^{T}-GERMAIN DES PRÉS
13, RUE SAINT-BENOIT PARIS-VI^{E}
TÉL. LITRÉ 81-84

La Direction du Club
espérant être honoré de votre présence vous informe
du passage en attraction de

BUD POWELL
et
KENNY CLARKE

du 30 Octobre au 14 Novembre 1957
Tous les soirs de 22 heures à 3 heures du matin
quarante minutes de prestation par heure
en trio avec : PIERRE MICHELOT
en quartet avec : BARNEY WILEN

Publicity leaflet from what Klook described as 'the great days' of the Club St Germain

Lionel Hampton band in 1953 – when Annie Ross was the featured vocalist. As he told British writer Raymond Horricks, 'The atmosphere in Paris is so relaxed that it makes work easy. How can I describe all I feel for this city? Life doesn't seem the rat race that it is in America, and yet really you are working just as hard.'

British pianist John Hawkins was working in Paris at this time as a studio musician and remembers that, although Quincy Jones was recording mostly middle-of-the-road music, he would use Klook on drums whenever he could. One of the first sessions Kenny did for Jones was with the Eddie Barclay Orchestra. It was called the Eddie Barclay Orchestra not because Monsieur Barclay actually played in it – although he was a modestly gifted pianist – but because he owned the record company. The orchestra included Stéphane Grappelli and Lucky Thompson and the pianist was Art Simmons, an underrated musician who was very active on the Paris scene in the fifties and sixties.

Simmons, from Glen White, West Virginia, had come to Europe in the US Army and had been in the same Special Service Corps as Kenny Clarke and John Lewis. After the war he'd stayed in Germany and studied music for three years with a private teacher. He then moved to Paris and studied for a further two years at the Ecole Normale de Musique. When he started working as a professional musician, his first club gig was at Chez Inez, run by Inez Cavanaugh, where he shared piano duties with Aaron Bridgers. Bridgers, from Winston-Salem, North Carolina, had been a student at the Teddy Wilson music school in New York and had also been a pupil of Art Tatum. He and Art Simmons were to work opposite each other for many years in Paris, notably at the Living Room. They and Joe Turner, who began a long residency at La Calavados in 1962, were thus continuing a piano tradition that had been established in the thirties by Herman Chittison, Garland Wilson and Garnett Clark.

Despite being away from New York, the jazz epicentre, Kenny Clarke continued to become involved in significant jazz developments, and one of the most important of these was the use of jazz for the soundtracks of major feature films. Director

Henri-Georges Clouzot had Kenny Clarke playing drums for his outstanding short feature, *The Picasso Mystery*, in 1956. In August 1957, the Modern Jazz Quartet made the soundtrack for *Sait-on Jamais* (*No Sun in Venice*), for which John Lewis had written the score. But the most innovative blending of the cinematographic and jazz arts occurred when Louis Malle engaged Miles Davis to provide the soundtrack for his thriller, *Ascenseur pour l'Echafaud* (*Lift to the Scaffold*) in December 1957.

Miles Davis had come to Paris in November to play a concert at the Olympia Theatre and to work for a three-week spell at the Club St Germain which, by this time, was unquestionably the major jazz venue in Paris. Miles put together a quintet, with Kenny, the twenty-year-old Nice-born tenor saxophonist Barney Wilen, René Urtreger on piano and Pierre Michelot on bass.

Louis Malle was a dedicated Miles fan. When he learned that Davis was about to arrive in Paris, he went to the airport to meet him and asked him if he would agree to provide the background music for the film. Miles accepted and, a couple of weeks later, another little bit of jazz history was made. For the first time, totally improvised jazz music was used to provide the score for a feature film – and, as *Jazz Magazine*'s Jean-Louis Ginibre observed some four years later, the music made what would otherwise have been a minor film into a much more impressive piece of work.

Miles, who earlier that year had made the magnificent *Miles Ahead* album with Gil Evans, was in excellent form. Exhibiting that same remarkable flair for spontaneous arranging that had characterized the 'Walkin' ' date, he created the background music on the spot while the film was projected on to a screen. 'He would just shout: "OK, D minor," count us in and that was all the direction we got,' Michelot says. 'But somehow it worked!' Although the fragments of improvisation which make up the soundtrack were inspired by the plot developments of the film, the music has an independent validity. Miles's trumpet sound has that mournful, wistful quality of his work on *Miles Ahead* – and if there hadn't been a film already in existence for his extemporized music, then one would certainly have had to be created.

Klook's drumming is, as ever, beautifully poised and sensitive – particularly his brushwork on 'Sur l'Autoroute', one of the two up-tempo pieces of the suite.

Recalling the way in which Miles created the music while the film was being shown, Kenny told Michael Haggerty,

> That was fabulous. He said, 'Wait a minute, right here! Stop! Right here.' And he'd say, 'We play this, and this right here' – 'cause this seemed to go with the scene and it was really well thought out. And we did the music to the film right then and there . . . It turned out beautiful. Miles really put it together wonderfully. And, I mean, it all happened on the spur of the moment, you know. After about three hours, it was over . . .'

The session finished in the early hours of the morning and Louis Malle was ecstatic. The experiment had succeeded beyond his most sanguine expectations. The soundtrack album was later released by Philips.

Just before coming to Paris, Miles had been working at the Café Bohemia in New York with a group that included drummer Philly Joe Jones. There was a particular number in which Miles and Philly Joe had developed a certain call-and-response phrase and Al Levitt recalls the slight contretemps that arose at the Club St Germain when Miles played the phrase but got no response from Kenny Clarke.

> Miles turned around to Kenny and rasped in that sandpaper whisper of his, 'Kenny, how many mother-fucking times do I have to tell you – when I go *bap*, you go *bap-da-bap-da-bap*!' Kenny glared back, said nothing – but his eyes answered, 'Aw, come on, man, that's ridiculous – when you play with Kenny Clarke, don't expect to hear Philly Joe.' I don't think Kenny would have played that phrase even if his life had depended on it.

Just about a year after Miles had pioneered the instant jazz soundtrack, French director Edouard Molinaro engaged Art Blakey's Jazz Messengers to provide the score for his film on white slavery, *Des Femmes Disparaissent*. Although the Messengers actually adapted existing compositions – by Benny Golson – to create the score, it is interesting to note how similar is their approach to that adopted by Miles. The instrumentation is the same, Lee Morgan's trumpet hauntingly atmospheric – both open and muted – and the timbre and mood of Golson's tenor saxophone is remarkably close to that of Barney Wilen.

Wilen was contracted, both as composer and leader, for another Edouard Molinaro film, *Un Témoin dans la Ville*, in April 1959, for which he engaged Kenny Clarke, Kenny Dorham (trumpet), Duke Jordan (piano) and bassist Paul Rovère, a brother of Gilbert. More and more directors on both sides of the Atlantic were now making use of jazz for background scores – as opposed to featuring jazz artists in the films themselves. In 1958 Robert Wise had Gerry Mulligan play the soundtrack for the Susan Hayward film, *I Want to Live*, and, the following year, the Duke Ellington Orchestra provided the score for the Otto Preminger film, *Anatomy of a Murder*. In 1959 the MJQ made the soundtrack for Robert Wise's *Odds Against Tomorrow* and Roger Vadim used a quintet led by Duke Jordan to provide the music for his adaptation of the eighteenth-century Laclos novel, *Les Liaisons Dangéreuses*.

Kenny Clarke was involved in providing the music for a number of other films over the next few years, including *Château en Suède* with a big band led by Hubert Rostaing; *Le Glaive et la Balance*, with organist Lou Bennett; and *A Bout de Souffle* with a big band led by Martial Solal. He wrote the music for *On n'Enterre pas le Dimanche* and, with Lucky Thompson, Maurice Vander and Michelot, Klook appeared in a short nightclub sequence in *Aimez-vous Brahms*, the film adaptation of the Françoise Sagan novel starring Ingrid Bergman and Anthony Perkins. In 1965 with Martial Solal, a prolific writer of film music at this time, Kenny Clarke took part in the Marcel Carné film, *Three Rooms in Manhattan*.

By the late fifties Kenny was becoming increasingly busy in the recording studios, making sides with French pianist Henri Renaud, Sidney Bechet, Stéphane Grappelli, Lucky Thompson, Milt Jackson, Bobby Jaspar, Stan Getz, Joe Turner, Chet Baker, Lester Young and, under the direction of Quincy Jones, dates with the Eddie Barclay Orchestra, Sarah Vaughan and the former Andy Kirk and Cab Calloway singer, June Richmond. At this period he was in the studios almost every day and it is probable that he was incognito on a lot of the dates. For Quincy, Klook was the number-one choice as drummer, whatever the project. In his 1982 interview with Michael Haggerty,

Klook refers to a date with the Michel Legrand Orchestra accompanying singer Jack Jones (November 1970) and he also records how he had a hard time with Quincy whenever he was obliged to miss a studio date.

> I remember in 1958 I had to go to Cannes for the film festival and couldn't do a date for Quincy. You'd have thought the world had come to an end. 'Man, what do you have to go to Cannes for?' Quincy asked me. But I got Kansas Fields to do the date – and Quincy was happy with that because Kansas had a good conception and was a good reader. So it worked out.

Quincy Jones's work for Disques Barclay was astonishingly prolific. He told Raymond Horricks that he wrote an estimated 250 recording dates for the label, and he used Kenny Clarke whenever he could.

Another recording remembered by Klook in that Haggerty interview was the one for Mercury with Sarah Vaughan on 7 July 1958 – the session that produced 'Misty'. Zoot Sims, Ronnell Bright and Richard Davis were on the date and there was a full string section. 'When she finished the song,' Kenny recalled, 'all the string players stood up and applauded. I've never seen anything like that in my life. Sarah just bowed and backed right out.'

Meanwhile Kenny continued in residency at the Club St Germain. In October 1957, J.J. Johnson guested at the club – and it was on the thirtieth of that month that Klook was reunited with the great Bud Powell.

Bud had come to Paris exactly one year earlier as part of a tour package, 'Birdland 1956', promoted by Disques Barclay and Morris Levy and featuring, among others, the Modern Jazz Quartet, Lester Young and – with a rhythm section consisting of René Urtreger, Michelot and Christian Garros – Miles Davis. Bud was now booked to play a three-week engagement at the Club St Germain, working with Klook and Michelot – a booking subsequently reduced to two weeks in commercial deference to the demands of the jiving segment of the Left Bank *noctambules* who found bebop difficult to dance to. This engagement for the Powell–Clarke–Michelot combo was the precursor to a long residency at the celebrated Blue Note club, where the trio were to become known as the Three Bosses.

In December 1957, guitarist James Pasco 'Jimmy' Gourley Jr, originally from St Louis, Mo, returned to Paris from Chicago to take up residence once again. He had first come as an ex-marine in 1951, courtesy of the GI Bill, after having worked in the bands of Jay Burkhart and Vido Musso and in the quintet of Jackie Cain and Roy Kral. At this time one of the main jazz centres on the right bank was the Mars Club at 6, rue Robert Etienne, a rather prim-looking cul-de-sac near the Champs-Elysées. The club, which at various times featured Annie Ross, Blossom Dearie, Billie Holiday, Nancy Holloway and Carmen McRae, was then run by another former member of the US armed forces, Ben Benjamin.

Jimmy Gourley had been resident at the Mars Club for a time during his first sojourn in Paris. He went back to work there again for most of 1958 with Art Simmons and French bassist Michel Gaudry. But by this time, Ben Benjamin had sold the club and it was now managed by a genial Canadian called Pete Rice. In August, Benjamin called Gourley and told him he was planning to open a new club – the Blue Note – at 27, rue d'Artois, a quiet back street on the other side of the Champs-Elysées. He wanted Gourley to bring his group into the club.

Originally a milliner's shop, the Blue Note was the logical replacement for a club called the Ringside which had enjoyed a certain vogue as *the* jazz venue for *le tout Paris*. Established first on the Champs-Elysées and later in the rue Thérèse near the Opéra, the Ringside had Art Simmons as the resident pianist there for three and a half years, during which time he had played for Don Byas, Hot Lips Page, Sacha Distel, Eartha Kitt and Ella Fitzgerald. But then, exhibiting the familiar jazz-club vulnerability to life's vicissitudes and to the inconstancy of seekers after night-time distraction, the Ringside closed its doors.

The Blue Note opened in the autumn of 1958 with Zoot Sims as the star attraction, backed by a multinational rhythm section: Dutch pianist Nico Buninck, Canadian bassist Lloyd Thompson and American drummer Al Levitt. As a matter of fact, Levitt missed the first set for some reason, so Jimmy Gourley sat in on drums. Benjamin had originally invited

Gourley to bring his Mars Club trio to the Blue Note, but Gourley says, 'Art Simmons didn't want to switch because he didn't get on too well with Ben. I did take the gig, though, and it was one of my better moves.'

Gourley became resident at the club in November 1958, after Al Levitt had returned to the States. He led a quartet with which he had worked at the Tabou Club – Henri Renaud on piano, Jean-Marie Ingrand on bass and Jean-Louis Viale on drums. 'But,' says Gourley, 'business was slow. The club was too new and our names weren't too well-known. So we spoke to Ben Benjamin and told him that if he wanted business to pick up, he would have to start hiring some major jazz stars on a regular basis.'

What the Blue Note really needed was to secure the most revered jazz name in Paris as resident attraction; the man who, at the time, was in his third year at the Club St Germain. A man called Kenny Clarke.

13
Paris: *La Décade d'Or*

To gain access to the Blue Note on most evenings it was necessary to circumnavigate the 240-pound bulk of its manager, Ben Benjamin, who spent much of his time standing in the entrance, welcoming guests and chain-smoking furiously. Prior to his army service Ben had been a salesman and had worked in a booking agency – but his ambition had always been to run a jazz club. He enjoyed the company of musicians and singers, was a big vaudeville fan, loved Cole Porter, worshipped Judy Garland and Lena Horne and was reputed to know the bridge of almost every popular song ever written. He was adept at that throwaway, wise-cracking, self-deprecating strain of Jewish humour and he treated musicians well in every respect – except for the rather crucial one of remuneration. Jimmy Gourley remembers receiving between seventy and eighty francs a night – which in the early sixties was worth between £5 and £6. If he had been required to pay normal bar prices, a moderately indulgent musician would have had some difficulty in getting stoned at the Blue Note because a scotch would have set him back seventeen and a half francs. Maybe this is what Benjamin figured.

But, truth to tell, it wasn't really Ben's fault that the pay was so wretched. Ben wasn't actually the owner of the club – he was only married to her. She was Polish, she had the money, a rebarbative temperament and a low opinion of musicians. Her name was Etla; but Bud Powell, not her biggest fan, preferred to call her Hitler. In his exhaustive book on Bud Powell, *La Danse des Infidèles*, Francis Paudras recalls that she had 'eyes cold as razorblades'.

The Blue Note was a long, narrow room with chairs and tables on either side, and a small stage at the far end with a miniature dancefloor immediately in front of it. The bar occupied half of the right-hand side of the room and was in the charge of Jacques, brother of Etla, who watched over the takings with Argus-eyed vigilance. He was said to be able to detect a fiddling waiter at fifty paces.

For over-indulgent revellers, one comforting aspect of the establishment was that you could always tell where you were because a big sign above the stage said 'Blue Note'.

For the last week of 1958 Stan Getz, then living in Copenhagen, was the guest attraction of the club. Benjamin had by now contacted Kenny Clarke and persuaded him to become the Blue Note's resident drummer. Ben had hoped he would be able to start on 31 December, but Klook had a

Handbill announcing Lester Young's engagement at the Blue Note early in 1949, just a few weeks before he died

long-standing commitment to play at the Club St Germain on New Year's Eve.

'Kenny wouldn't break his promise,' Jimmy Gourley remembers, 'so for New Year's Eve we had to work without a drummer. For the first set I played on some borrowed drums and when we came back onstage after the intermission, Stan said, "Jimmy – get back on the guitar!" '

It was on 1 January 1959 that Kenny Clarke began a residency at the Blue Note which, with some breaks, was to last until November 1966. Henri Renaud had been succeeded in the rhythm section by a young pianist called Jean-Pierre Gigand. But he, too, left after two weeks to do army service and was replaced by René Urtreger. And after two or three different bass players, Pierre Michelot joined the group. 'And then,' says Jimmy Gourley, 'we had a beautiful rhythm section. We played four forty-five-minute sets a night, between 10 p.m. and 4 a.m., alternating with a solo pianist.'

Among the artists featured at the Blue Note in the first months of its existence was Lester Young, who made a series of guest appearances between January and March 1959. They were to be his last engagements. Young was a very sick man. Ill health had dogged him since his discharge from the US Army in 1945 after a traumatic, nine-month spell of military service. His condition was aggravated by an over-indulgence in alcohol and a progressive indisposition to eat. During his final engagement at the Blue Note in March, Lester made his last record date – for the Verve label. Except that George Joyner (Jamil Nasser) was on bass, the other musicians on the date were the Blue Note team: Klook, Gourley and Urtreger.

Writing of the session in *Into Jazz* in April 1974, Graham Colombe says, 'The rhythm section is dominated by the magnificent drumming of Kenny Clarke, who fills the gaps in Lester's lines with intelligence and swing.'

Just about two weeks after this date, Lester Young suffered a fatal heart attack in New York's Alvin Hotel. He died, aged forty-nine, on 15 March 1959. That same month saw the return to Paris of the man who, with Klook, was to establish the Blue Note's reputation as the premier jazz club in Europe: Bud Powell.

(These two tormented geniuses – Lester Young and Bud Powell – provided the inspiration for Bertrand Tavernier's 1987 film *Round Midnight* which revolves around the Blue Note club. It was as a result of conversations with Francis Paudras, the French commercial artist who became a close friend and benefactor of Bud Powell in the sixties, that Tavernier produced the shooting script for the film. The central character, Dale Turner, was conceived as a composite of Lester Young and Bud Powell and, in playing the part, Dexter Gordon managed a near-perfect portrayal of Dexter Gordon.)

The Blue Note did not become an overnight success, despite Ben Benjamin's acceptance of the need to feature big-name guest artists. Pierre Michelot recalls occasions in the early days when there were more people on the stage than in the audience. 'I remember the first time Lester played in the club we had an audience of eight people,' he told me.

But the regular presence of Bud Powell and Kenny Clarke, two giants of the bebop era, and the booking of more and more jazz stars as guest artists, soon had Ben Benjamin cutting down his cigarette consumption to sixty a day. When Jimmy Gourley learned that Bud was to be given a residency at the club, he got ready to pack his guitar case because he was convinced that Benjamin wouldn't be needing him any more. But not so. Ben appreciated that Jimmy had got the club started and he assured Gourley that his job was safe.

At the beginning, the Three Bosses – Bud, Klook and Michelot – formed the main resident group, and Gourley would work opposite with a backing group for the visiting celebrity. 'I really appreciated Ben keeping me on because I didn't have much of a name,' Gourley says. 'But Ben was a great guy and he really took care of me. I got to play with just about everyone over the next four years as a result of that.'

The list of Blue Note guests was impressive indeed. They included Chet Baker, Don Byas, Charlie Byrd, Donald Byrd, Sonny Criss, Booker Ervin, Victor Feldman, Stan Getz, Jimmy Giuffre, Dexter Gordon, Johnny Griffin, J.J. Johnson, Elvin Jones, Lee Konitz, Brew Moore, Pony Poindexter, Sonny Rollins, Sahib Shihab, Zoot Sims, Lucky Thompson, Mal Waldron and Ben Webster. And there were long-spell engagements for

Kenny Drew, Nathan Davis, Lou Bennett and René Thomas. Says Jimmy Gourley,

> It was Kenny who was really the driving force. Musicians in the States were always happy to come over and play there knowing that Kenny would be in the rhythm section. Because Klook didn't play with Bud all the time. In 1960, when Lou Bennett came in on Hammond organ, he worked with Kenny and me and Bud used a French rhythm section of Jean-Marie Ingrand on bass and Jean Guérin on drums. The line-up switched around all the time.

Bud Powell's first engagement at the Blue Note lasted for a couple of months, and during this time, in April, Benjamin hired a German, George Shearing-style quintet led by Manfred Burzlaff to play opposite the Three Bosses. In that band the drummer was Joe Nay, for whom Kenny Clarke had long been an idol. 'Imagine how I felt,' he told me later. 'I had only been playing drums for a year – I was a very raw musician; now here I was working opposite the greatest jazz drummer in the world.'

True to character, Kenny took an interest in Joe and gave him much help and encouragement. The quintet's engagement at the Blue Note lasted for eight months and during that time Nay watched Klook play on every possible occasion.

> I thought it good for me, as an inexperienced drummer, to study Kenny's technique, try to copy it as best I could, and then try to develop my own style from that. What I loved about Kenny, apart from this superb time and his feeling, was that he was very much a team musician. He worked for the band he was in – he was not an egotistical artist. He was a tremendously musical drummer and he had unbelievable technique. He was the professor.

Nay studied the drumming of Kenny Clarke so assiduously that he really began to sound like him; and, some years later, when the two met in Frankfurt, where Joe was working in a club with the trio of Austrian pianist Fritz Pauer, Klook told him, 'OK, Joe. Now it's time you developed your own style of playing.' And it is reported by Norwegian jazz writer, Randi Hultin, that when Miles Davis heard a record on which Joe was playing, he said, 'Who is that drummer? He sounds exactly like Klook.'

Joe actually had two precious lessons with Kenny Clarke. 'And,' he says, 'I learned more about playing drums from those two lessons than I could have learned from all the drum tutors in the world.'

Nay was an apt and eager pupil and Kenny's guidance and inspiration were major factors in his career development. In 1964, when Joe Boyd was putting together a European tour with Pee Wee Russell, Ruby Braff, Bud Freeman, George Wein and Jimmy Woode, he wrote to Joe asking if he could make the tour and said, 'Kenny Clarke has other commitments, but he told us you were the best man in Europe for the job.' That letter remains one of Joe Nay's proudest possessions.

At this time a regular visitor to the Blue Note was a pretty twenty-year-old Jewish girl from The Hague, Holland – Daisy Dina Wallbach – who came to Paris to take a beautician's course at the school run by the hairdresser Antoine in the rue St Didier. She had first met Kenny through mutual friends a year earlier and they had immediately experienced a strong mutual attraction. Kenny invited Daisy to dinner and the relationship developed very rapidly into a loving one. But towards the end of 1958, Daisy decided that she was tired of 'learning how to make up old ladies' and left Paris to work in a children's home in Caux, Switzerland.

Kenny had been living in the Grand Balcon, a hotel in the Left Bank's rue Dauphine, whose twenty rooms were almost exclusively occupied by musicians. But after he met Daisy, he began to think in terms of a more settled life and a place of his own, so he started to look for an apartment. He finally found one on the fifth floor of a building at 23 rue Marsoulan in the 12th arondissement, near the Nation. It was offered at about £50 a month – so he wrote to Daisy and asked her to come to Paris and set up home with him. At this time Kenny was making a determined attempt to kick his drug habit and he needed Daisy to take care of him and give him moral support. She recalls:

> So I came back after only six weeks in Switzerland and we moved into the apartment. It was expensive for what it was. It was poorly furnished and consisted of a bedroom, living room, kitchen and bathroom. It was a very old building with minimal amenities, but at least it was better than living

in a hotel or a hostel. However, we soon started to have neighbour problems because Kenny would get home from the Blue Note at four in the morning and, what with his rather heavy step and the noise of the antique elevator – well, the people in the other apartments complained. Kenny told them he had a right to work at night, he was a musician by profession and he had to work unsocial hours. The neighbours suggested that he should take off his shoes when he came in at night – but there was no way that Kenny was going to do that.

So the *ascenseur* went on whirring and groaning at four in the morning, the floorboards continued to squeak and creak under Kenny's 160 pounds and the neighbours became progressively less civil. Daisy and Kenny determined to try to find a little house in the *banlieue* where they could come and go as they pleased, but there was a daunting gap between that determination and its realization. Kenny was earning 150 francs a night at the Blue Note – worth about £11 at the time – and even with the additional income he got from studio work, he was not a wealthy man. The possibility of finding a house within his means seemed pretty remote, but he and Daisy lived in hope.

Using the Blue Note as a sort of base camp, Kenny continued to play concert and tour dates throughout Europe, as well as in North Africa and Senegal, and also kept busy in the recording studios. Early in 1960 he made an extensive tour with Coleman Hawkins, Bud Powell and Oscar Pettiford which included dates in Italy, France, Switzerland and Germany. On 2 April, the quartet took part in the Essen Jazz Festival and, happily, this concert was recorded. As I observed in the liner note of the Sonet release of the tracks, this tour was a momentous meeting of four great, iconoclastic jazz figures.

It was a historic, magical moment when Coleman Hawkins, Bud Powell, Oscar Pettiford and Kenny Clarke came together on the stage of the Grugahalle in Essen . . . and played for an audidence of some 8,000 people. That audience was uniquely privileged, because it was to witness the performance of some of the most inspirational spontaneous music from a quartet of jazz masters who were, unhappily, destined never to play together again.

During 1960 Quincy Jones returned to Paris with an all-star nineteen-piece big band in the ill-starred Harold Arlen blues opera *Free and Easy*. It had a disastrous European tour, losing

Jones $67,000. While in Paris Quincy went into the recording studios to make an album with a revolutionary new vocal group led by Mimi Perrin – the Double Six. This group – so called because, with each member of the sextet overdubbing, it could produce the sound of a twelve-piece ensemble – had grown out of another vocal combo, the Blue Stars, founded by singer/pianist Blossom Dearie in the mid-fifties and named after the label for which it recorded. Key members of the Double Six were, in addition to Mimi Perrin, Christiane Legrand (sister of Michel) and Ward Swingle, an American singer who was later to create the Swingle Singers.

Quincy Jones was intrigued by the Double Six concept and he contributed seven originals to the session which was released later on Capitol in the States as *The Double Six Meet Quincy Jones*. Kenny Clarke played on three of the tracks, with Art Simmons on piano and Pierre Michelot on bass.

The year 1960 also saw the arrival in Paris of Lou Bennett, a Hammond organ player from Philadelphia who had worked at Minton's and Smalls' Paradise in New York and who had been recommended to Ben Benjamin by Babs Gonzales. Lou joined Klook and Jimmy Gourley at the Blue Note to play opposite the Bud Powell Trio, and this was the beginning of an association that lasted for twenty-five years. In July, Bennett made an album *Amen* for the RCA label with Klook, Gourley and bassist Jean-Marie Ingrand which earned him considerable recognition.

The following year, 1961, the jazz scene in Paris continued to flourish as more jazzmen arrived from the States – some to play and pass on, some, including Kenny Drew, to settle for a time. Jackie McLean played an engagement at Le Chat Qui Pèche, Peanuts Holland guested at the Trois Mailletz, and featured attractions at the Blue Note included Stan Getz, Dutch pianist Pim Jacobs and singer Rita Reys, J.J. Johnson, Brew Moore and Lucky Thompson. It was a landmark year for Kenny Clarke in terms of recording because it produced the very first Clarke–Boland album – an eight-piece session made in Cologne in May and released on Blue Note under the title *The Golden Eight*. Although Klook had recorded earlier with Boland – on a Don Byas date in February 1960 – this was the first recording under their joint names. It also immortalized the telephone number of Klook's Paris apartment, 'Dorian 0437', the title of one of Boland's originals.

Throughout 1962 Kenny worked at the Blue Note with Lou Bennett and either Jimmy Gourley or, when Gourley left the club for a period to work at the Blues Bar, with Belgian guitarist René Thomas. There were concerts in Paris by the John Coltrane Quartet, the Jazz Messengers, Ella Fitzgerald, Count Basie, Horace Silver and Gerry Mulligan, and among the guests at the Blue Note that year were Zoot Sims and Sonny Criss.

Kenny's tenure at the Blue Note was not without its tribulations. He had developed something of a love-hate relationship with the club – because although it furnished a steady, if meagre, income, it could also be an unrelenting slog. He had the opportunity to play with a lot of great musicians – but there were also times, as with all resident engagements, when the gig just became a chore. Furthermore, there were regular fights about money. Kenny told Michael Haggerty,

> I stayed at the Blue Note, you know, for connections, because a lot of universities and conservatories would write to me because they wanted to have some jazz teaching in their establishments, so they could always contact me at the Blue Note. I got a lot of jobs that way. It was like an office for me, you know. Whenever I worked with the big band (Clarke–Boland) I would put someone in my place and tell them when I'd be back. Sometimes I'd be gone two or three weeks, but they knew I'd always be back.

Actually Kenny spent a good deal more time at the Blue Note than did Bud Powell who, between his arrival there in March 1959 and his return to New York in August 1964, travelled a great deal through Europe on concert and club engagements, as well as appearing for spells in other Paris jazz clubs. Because of Bud Powell's psychological and medical problems, the Blue Note staff were under orders to refuse him alcohol – but he would constantly try to outwit them by inviting strangers to buy him a drink. Sometimes when the cashier, Jacques, served Bud a Coca Cola, he would pick up the rum bottle and make out that he was adding a shot – just for Bud's benefit. On one such occasion, at a time when the Three Bosses were working together, Kenny approached Bud at the bar and made as if to take the drink away from him. Bud resisted fiercely and Kenny, evincing mock anger, adopted a boxing stance and delivered a right hand punch which stopped just short of Bud's chin. Bud was stupefied. He genuinely thought that Klook had intended to floor him.

Francis Paudras relates this incident in *La Danse des Infidèles* and says that Bud was so offended by Kenny's behaviour that he refused to play the next set with Klook and told Paudras to take him home. The following morning he told Paudras: 'I'm not playing with Kenny Clarke again. You have to do something about him – I want you to hit him like he tried to hit me.' Paudras tried to play the incident down, explaining that Kenny had been fooling – but Bud wouldn't listen. He wanted revenge. Paudras had a business appointment that afternoon, but to pacify Bud he told him that he would go to see Kenny and would settle the matter. Later he called Kenny from a café and explained the situation. 'Bud really believes you meant to hurt him,' Paudras said. 'So I have told him that I will pay you back. When you next see Bud, please tell him that when I saw you we had an argument, I got angry and punched you on the jaw.' Kenny cheerfully agreed. When Paudras returned home, Bud asked him anxiously, 'Did you see him? You did it, you did it?' Paudras nodded affirmation. That evening Bud couldn't wait to get to the Blue Note to see what damage Paudras had inflicted on Klook. He went right up to Kenny and peered closely at his chin. Kenny played the game – rubbed his chin ruefully and said to Bud, 'Man, that Paudras really packs a punch!' Bud responded with an expression that mixed satisfaction with embarrassment and concern and then went to the bandstand to play the first set. But, says Paudras, despite the 'revenge', Bud remained troubled by the incident – believing that Klook had really meant to hurt him.

Paudras remembers another Blue Note incident when Kenny Clarke's anger was all too genuine – and it was French drummer Daniel Humair who was the target.

> I came to the Blue Note one night, and there was a heated argument in progress outside the club. It seems that Humair had said something about

Kenny in a jazz magazine interview which made him quite furious. I heard Kenny tell Humair, with icy calm, 'When people ask me who is the best drummer around today, I say Daniel Humair. Take my advice, as you are a drummer, speak with your sticks and your drums and leave criticism to the professional critics. If you want to say something, say it with your instrument.' Then he turned around and strode into the club.

It was in the spring of 1962, when they were taking a taxi home from the Blue Note, that Daisy and Kenny saw a notice in the front of the cab offering a house for rent or sale in the suburb of Montreuil-sous-Bois, east of Paris. The house belonged to the cab driver's mother. Kenny was not unfamiliar with Montreuil – he'd been there first in 1949 to visit a friend. The following Sunday he and Daisy went to look over the house – and on 1 April 1962 they moved into 142 bis rue de Rosny. The following month, on 26 May, Liaquat Ali Salaam and Daisy Dina Wallbach were married in the *mairie* of the 12th arondissement with Lou Bennett and his wife Sonia as witnesses. 'Lou and Kenny came home from the Blue Note and stayed up all night,' Daisy recalls. 'Lou said it was the quickest wedding he ever saw.'

Towards the end of 1962, when Kenny was again working with Jimmy Gourley and Lou Bennett, he was involved in a bitter argument with the highly disagreeable Etla which resulted in his being fired from the club. She had 'fired' him a few times before, but on this occasion it was for real. The argument developed, ostensibly, because Kenny was late starting his set after Kenny Drew had played. The reason was that Drew's drummer, Larry Ritchie, was left-handed, so Klook had to rearrange the kit each time he went up to play. Kenny was meticulous in these matters. He would never start to play until everything was set up exactly the way he wanted it. Etla began shouting at Kenny, hurling insults at him. Finally she told him to get out.

'She was totally obnoxious,' says Jimmy Gourley. 'Really objectionable and vindictive; but she was the boss, she had the money. Well, when she fired Kenny, I left, too. I really couldn't stand the way she talked to him.'

The whole scene had been watched, not completely inscrutably, by a party of four Japanese tourists. Obviously pained to see the great Kenny Clarke humiliated in public, they invited him for a consoling drink. One drink led to another, and another, and when Kansas Fields arrived to give Kenny a lift home, Klook – who was never a big drinker – was comprehensively plastered. 'It was the one and only time I saw him drunk,' Daisy says. 'When he told me he'd been fired, I was used to that so I didn't take it seriously. Later I learned that it was really true.' The Blue Note's loss was to be the Club St Germain's gain. But considerable compensation for Ben Benjamin after the departure of Kenny Clarke was the arrival in Paris of Johnny Griffin, the little giant from Chicago, who'd been making a name for himself in New York – notably at Birdland – in tough-tenor partnership with Eddie 'Lockjaw' Davis. Griffin opened at the Blue Note in December 1962 and stayed, on and off, for about a year. Griffin recalls:

> I had never met Kenny Clarke, but before I left New York I ran into Max Roach outside my apartment building and told him I was heading for Paris. He said to me, 'When you see Klook, tell him the guys here are still trying to play what he laid down years ago.' Some days later I met Klook outside the Blue Note – he wouldn't come in because of his falling-out with the management. But I gave him Max's message and I could see that it meant a lot to him.

At this time Kenny Clarke was making increasingly frequent trips to Germany for concerts and record dates, not only with the Clarke–Boland Big Band but also for events organized by German jazz producer and writer Joachim Berendt whom he had first met in 1949 during the Paris Jazz Festival. Klook became a fairly regular commuter on the 7.43 a.m. Trans-Europe Express from Paris to Cologne. In January 1963, Berendt organized an Americans in Europe concert in Koblenz, assembling an all-star cast that included Sonny Criss, Herb Geller, Don Byas, Sahib Shihab, Benny Bailey, Idrees Sulieman and a rhythm section of Lou Bennett, Jimmy Woode and Kenny Clarke. Bud Powell also appeared in the concert, working with Woode, drummer Joe Harris and Sulieman. Lucky Thompson was also supposed to be on the date but, for some reason, could not be contacted. So Benny Bailey recommended as a replacement a twenty-four-year-old saxophonist from Kansas City – Nathan Davis – who was doing his army service and was stationed in Berlin with the 298th Army band.

Nathan was duly hired and his musicianship and affable personality made a most favourable impression on Kenny Clarke. Davis remembers:

> I played in the section and took a few solos. Afterwards, Klook told me he liked the way I played. He said he wanted to stay in touch because something might be coming up in Paris and he took my address. I didn't really expect to hear from him – it was all just a little bit too good to be true; me, a completely unknown musician getting a chance to work with the greatest jazz drummer in the world. I had worshipped Klook ever since I started playing jazz in Kansas City in the fifties and had been really inspired by those Savoy recordings he made with Horace Silver and Oscar Pettiford.

When Kenny returned from Koblenz to Paris he started putting together a group for the Club St Germain. He hired his long-time Blue Note partner Jimmy Gourley, pianist René Urtreger and bassist Michel Gaudry. Originally Kenny planned to book Sonny Criss, who had now settled in Paris, but there was some disagreement – so Kenny wrote to Nathan Davis in Berlin and asked him to join the group. A few days later Nathan arrived in Paris with his German-born wife, Ursula, very little money, no French, and one telephone number – Avron 1853. Klook's number.

Nathan recalls:

> Kenny was like an uncle to me. I was nervous as hell because I looked up to this man so much. But he took care of me. I went out to his house and he fixed me bacon and eggs. I'll never forget the sight of Klook, my hero, cooking breakfast and washing the dishes. I thought to myself, 'What a beautiful cat this guy is!' He was so warm – he made me feel like family. He installed us in the Crystal Hotel, right across the street from the Club St Germain. Then he had to go out of town for a couple of days on a gig. By this time I had developed a heavy cold and was feeling terrible – but Daisy took care of me. She got me some medicine for my cold – I didn't even know how to ask for it.

As soon as he got back to Paris, Kenny set up rehearsals at the club and then he took Nathan around Paris introducing him to Pierre Michelot, Albert Nicholas, jazz critic Maurice Cullaz and many others in his circle. 'He really made me feel comfortable,' Nathan says, 'and he told the guys to look after me when he had to go out of town. "He's my new tenor player," he would say. "He's a bad little cat."'

A few days after opening at the Club St Germain the band left Paris for a TV date in Italy. Jimmy Woode was the bass player on this occasion. Nathan Davis says:

> It was on this date that I found out what a humane guy Kenny really was. We played this Horace Silver number, 'No Smoking' – and I screwed up on the melody, right on TV. I managed to get it together after a few more bars, but I was really depressed about having goofed and let Klook down. I mentioned it to Jimmy Woode and Jimmy said to Kenny, 'Hey, Klook. What did you do to this cat? He is scared stiff!' And Klook came over to me and said, 'Nat, don't worry about it. That's OK. Nobody would have noticed it.' And he put a consoling arm around my shoulder.

The Kenny Clarke Quintet was supposed to play the Club St Germain, seven nights a week, for three months. But the engagement lasted for the best part of 1963, with Raymond Fol replacing Urtreger on piano. Just as he had done at the Blue Note, Klook proved to be a powerful magnet for all the US jazzmen passing through Paris. When Miles Davis was in town he would come to the club every night to see Kenny – though he could never be persuaded to sit in.

Nathan Davis remembers:

> But Dizzy Gillespie sat in. One night I found myself playing alongside Dexter Gordon, Johnny Griffin and Sonny Criss. My God, that was really a baptism of fire. I hadn't developed a big sound at that time, so Klook said to me, 'Hey, Nat – you go first, because if you follow Dexter and Griff, your sound is so small that it will be an anti-climax.' He would always give me little bits of advice like that.

Art Blakey's Jazz Messengers – a strong team, with Freddie Hubbard, Wayne Shorter, Cedar Walton and Reggie Workman – played opposite Klook's quintet at one point. Nathan Davis says:

> It was the battle of the bands. The Messengers really made us play at the top of our game and the place was packed every night. People would be standing in line, three and four deep, waiting for the club to open. Klook and Blakey – the two great drummers from Pittsburgh. Kenny came to me after one set and said, 'Hey, Nat, we've got to play a little harder because Blakey's guys are really burning.' And in the next set Klook jumped on

> Michel Gaudry for not playing strong enough. 'Hey, Michel, can't you play harder?'
> Michel said, 'Kenny, I'm playing as hard as I can.'
> And Kenny said, 'Don't you ever feel you want to pull the bass apart and break your strings?'
> Michel said, 'No', and Kenny said, 'Well, you're fired.' He really got mad because he didn't want to be upstaged by Blakey's band.

Kenny Clarke's presence at the Club St Germain not only drew musicians to the room but also attracted a host of celebrities, among them Elizabeth Taylor, Charlton Heston, Anthony Perkins and the heroine of the Left Bank, Juliette Greco. 'Klook was the main attraction,' says Davis. 'Wherever he would be playing, that's where the people would go. He was not only a superb musician but he had a very appealing personality. People loved him.'

The quintet worked extensively abroad throughout 1963, making visits to Spain, Morocco and Sicily and also to Tunisia where it took part in the very first Carthage jazz festival.

In the summer of 1963 the Three Bosses were booked for a second record date with the Double Six – this time a collection of the bebop compositions associated with Dizzy Gillespie for which Mimi Perrin had written some ingenious and imaginative lyrics. The recording involved a complex logistical arrangement, with Dizzy coming to Paris to lay down the instrumental tracks for ten of the numbers and the vocal tracks being overdubbed later. Two further tracks were added in the States with a different rhythm section – Kenny Barron (piano), Chris White (bass) and Rudy Collins (drums), plus James Moody on tenor saxophone. The Double Six for this date were actually seven-strong, because Eddie Louiss, later to work extensively with Klook on organ, managed to get leave from the French Army to rejoin the group for the session.

In a newspaper interview at the time, Kenny said, 'Originally the rhythm section was supposed to do the tracks in Paris, with Dizzy overdubbing in New York. But to my great surprise and satisfaction, Dizzy took the trouble to fly over to Paris so that we could work together. I really appreciated that.'

The engagement at the Club St Germain came to an end in the autumn of 1963 when the club changed hands and the new owner decided it would make a more salutary contribution to the Paris cultural scene as a discotheque called the Bilboquet. Kenny was invited back to the Blue Note by Ben Benjamin, who was anxious to atone for the abominable behaviour of his wife. Klook didn't take up the offer immediately, but when Johnny Griffin left the club early in 1964, and Benjamin badly needed a big name, Kenny consented to return, teaming up again with Lou Bennett and Jimmy Gourley, with Jimmy Woode coming in on bass. By this time the expatriate colony had been augmented first by multi-instrumentalist Eric Dolphy, who had stayed on after a Charles Mingus tour, and Donald Byrd; later by two brilliant young musicians from New Jersey, organist Larry Young and trumpeter Woody Shaw; and finally by New York drummer Art Taylor.

After the Club St Germain suffered its grisly transformation, Nathan Davis worked and recorded with Dolphy, played with Dolphy and Donald Byrd at the Chat Qui Pèche and later, at the same venue, with Woody Shaw, Larry Young, French bassist Jacky Samson and another son of New Jersey, drummer Billy Brooks. Shaw had come to Paris with the intention of joining Dolphy, but the saxophonist died suddenly of diabetes, coupled with a heart attack, while on a visit to Berlin, on 29 June 1964.

Throughout the rest of 1964 Klook worked at the Blue Note with his group, sometimes with René Thomas replacing Jimmy Gourley. Bud Powell, after a long lay-off through illness, returned to the club, working with Michel Gaudry and Larry Ritchie, and guest attractions included Sonny Stitt, Victor Feldman, Joe Harris, Mal Waldron, Sonny Criss and Pony Poindexter who, in his autobiography, wrote, 'Playing with Klook was like riding in a Cadillac. We burned!'

In August the Clarke–Boland Sextet made its Blue Note début – Klook being joined by Sahib Shihab, Fats Sadi, Francy Boland, Jimmy Woode, Joe Harris and singer Bobbi Parker. And to supplement the thriving club scene, there was, again, an abundance of jazz concerts in Paris, with visits from Thelonious Monk, Mingus, Max Roach, Duke Ellington, the Modern Jazz Quartet, Ella Fitzgerald, Muddy Waters, Lightnin' Hopkins and Dexter Gordon. The 'Newport in Paris' concert organized by George Wein in October featured Miles Davis (with Herbie Hancock, Wayne Shorter, Tony Williams and Ron Carter), Pee Wee Russell, Bud Freeman, George Russell, Harry Edison, Sir Charles Thompson, Jo Jones, Jimmy Woode, Coleman Hawkins, Roland Kirk and Sonny Stitt.

But for Daisy and Kenny Clarke the most momentous event of 1964 occurred at 4.10 a.m. on 4 August, when their only son, Laurent, was born.

* * *

In a two-part article on Kenny Clarke for the *Melody Maker* in the autumn of 1964, I wrote the following introduction:

> Klook arrived an hour late for the rehearsal at the Blue Note that misty November afternoon in Paris. He began setting up his kit with weary, unhurried assurance. He was tired after a long round of one-night stands. Organist Lou Bennett and guitarist René Thomas stood watching the measured, methodical process in almost reverent silence. There was no question of hurrying Klook. He would take his time. When Kenny Clarke sets the tempo, nobody argues. He took fifteen minutes to select his sticks. Then he lowered himself on to his stool, played a few crisp rolls, and looked up, waiting for Bennett to feed him four bars of intro. It was 'Our Delight' by Tadd Dameron. And suddenly Klook came alive. He grinned. His arms moved with loose, effortless fluency. And, of course, he swung. I was listening to what countless musicians regard as one of the most therapeutic sounds in the world, Klook playing drums.
>
> He played for an hour – relaxed, masterful, unerring in time. He didn't beat the kit to death. He coaxed it into vibrant life.

As Jimmy Gourley says, 'Kenny Clarke had a way of playing that never required him to warm up. It was 1,2,3,4 – *bam!* And you're off and running. He was just so consistently good – such tremendous attack; and he could hold a tempo from beginning to end. That was one of his great qualities.'

This was Kenny's eighth year in Paris and he had now become something of an institution. He was the most revered and respected of the Paris community of expatriate American musicians – a colony which was growing substantially as word filtered back to the United States that there was a greater respect for the music and its practitioners in Europe than existed in jazz's homeland.

Art Taylor said, 'Although there aren't the same working opportunities here as there are in the States – there are lots of compensations. For one thing, I can go and hear Kenny Clarke any night at the Blue Note and learn something.'

And Kenny Clarke said, when I asked him if he didn't find it a problem being so far away, for so long, from the source of modern jazz, 'If Diz or Bird had come to settle in Europe, would they have missed the States? No, the States would have missed them.' If that reply had come from another musician, it might have sounded arrogant. From Klook, it sounded just logical.

The decade between 1959 and 1968 was certainly the golden age of jazz in Paris and the presence of Kenny Clarke and Bud Powell at the Blue Note for most of this period was unquestionably a key factor in the high level of jazz activity in the French capital.

In the 'Where and When' feature of its issue of 10 September 1964, *Down Beat* listed some of the attractions at the major Paris jazz clubs:

Blue Note: Kenny Clarke, Sahib Shihab, Fats Sadi, Francy Boland, Jimmy Woode, Bobbi Parker
Blues Bar: Mae Mercer, Sonny Criss, Champion Jack Dupree
Calavados: Joe Turner
Caméléon: Nathan Davis
Caveau de la Huchette: Maxim Saury
Chat Qui Pèche: Woody Shaw, Freddy Meyer
Cigale: Jack Butler
Ladybird: Kansas Fields
Living Room: Stuart da Silva, Aaron Bridgers
Riverboat: Robert Husson, Mowgli Jospin
Slow Club: Claude Luter, Marc Laférrière
Trois Mailletz: Memphis Slim

Not only was there a busy club scene but there was a constant succession of jazz concerts, prolific programming of jazz on radio (Europe No. 1's *Pour Ceux qui Aiment le Jazz* presented by Daniel Filipacchi and Frank Ténot featured two hours of jazz, five nights a week) and much recording studio activity.

I spent five years of this period in Paris as a foreign correspondent for the old *Daily Herald* (later to become, God help it, the *Sun*). I was also contributing jazz interviews, reviews and comments during this time to *Melody Maker, Down Beat* and *Crescendo*.

There was so much jazz activity to cover that there was never a copy-flow problem. For a jazz lover, coming from a country which locked out American musicians, the experience was unforgettably fulfilling.

And at the centre of all this activity was Kenny Clarke – by common consent the spiritual leader of the Paris jazz community. He became unofficial consul and counsellor to American musicians on the subject of working conditions and the assimilation of French culture, customs and social conventions.

At one stage during this golden decade I jotted down a list of all the American jazzmen who, at that time, were resident in Paris. It read: Lou Bennett, Eddie Boyd, Aaron Bridgers, Jack Butler, Skeeter Camera, Kenny Clarke, Bill Coleman, Nathan Davis, Jimmy Gourley, Johnny Griffin, Ron Jefferson, Mezz Mezzrow, Albert Nicholas, Art Simmons, Hal Singer, Memphis Slim, Art Taylor, Benny Waters and Phil Woods. One-time Paris residents Don Cherry, Kenny Drew and Dexter Gordon were at that period in Denmark; Don Byas was in Holland and Jimmy Woode in Austria.

But easily my most cherished memory of those years in Paris was one November night in the Living Room, the club in the rue du Colisée which was the preferred hang-out of off-duty jazz musicians – and of some notable show-business celebrities, too. Names in its visitors book included Dame Margot Fonteyn, Sidney Poitier, Ava Gardner, Jacques Tati, Orson Welles, Joe Louis, Peter Ustinov and Omar Sharif. But on the night in question it was thronged with a rare collection of jazz celebrities.

Writing for *Crescendo* magazine and using (for contractual reasons) the name of my long-time lady companion, Jean Elliott, I recorded the event as follows:

> The scene: the Living Room, the most comfortable and intimate jazz club in Paris where the Art Simmons Trio and solo pianist Aaron Bridgers are in residence.
>
> The time: around 6.30 a.m.
>
> The cast: just about the most incredible collection of jazz talent ever seen in one club.
>
> Let's start with pianists. In addition to residents Simmons and Brid-

> gers, there were Jaki Byard, Joe 'Stride' Turner, France's Martial Solal, Teddy Wilson, Earl 'Fatha' Hines and Hazel Scott.
>
> Not a bad sax team, either: Ben Webster, Don Byas, Nathan Davis and Johnny Griffin.
>
> Also in evidence: Art Blakey, Connie Kay, Art Taylor, Freddie Hubbard, Lou Bennett, René Thomas, Percy Heath, Mae Mercer and Milt Jackson.

The reason for so many jazz musicians being in Paris at that time was that the Paris Jazz Festival was in full swing and the MJQ had just played a concert in a French provincial town. But at that period such a meeting could only have occurred in the Living Room. As I concluded at the time, 'It's a sobering thought that a jazz summit meeting such as this will probably never happen again.' And by 7 a.m., when it all broke up, I was badly in need of a sobering thought.

For the most part, Paris's jazz musicians welcomed the presence in their midst of so many American jazz celebrities. They got the opportunity to play with artists they had admired for years and to improve their musicianship. But there were some dissenting voices. As the Paris colony of self-exiled American jazzmen began to expand, working opportunities for French musicians – particularly the modern-jazz players – became increasingly restricted. Professional musicians in France were not nearly as well-organized as their British counterparts but, towards the end of 1965, there was some pressure exerted on clubowners by the Paris branch of the musicians' *syndicat* to accept some sort of quota with regard to the employment of foreign musicians. Vice president of the Paris union at the time was saxophonist Guy Lafitte, a fine musician and a totally amiable and charming man, completely innocent of xenophobia, who nevertheless felt that the union should defend the interests of its members. Whereas in 1930 there had been 7,000 professional musicians working in the Paris region, the number had dwindled to less than 2,000, many of whom were without regular work.

The campaign began with a letter to twenty-five clubowners in Paris asking their co-operation in giving a better share of available work to native musicians. Although hardly anyone seemed aware of it, it had been the law in France since 1933 that the percentage of foreign musicians in any group should not exceed ten. This meant that practically every jazz club in Paris was in breach of the law. At this time Kenny Clarke's group at the Blue Note was 25% French (René Urtreger) and 75% American (Klook, Jimmy Woode and Jimmy Gourley). To comply with the law, Ben Benjamin would have had to hire another twenty-six Frenchmen. Lafitte said to me at the time:

> It's a tremendously difficult and delicate operation. But we have to start somewhere. For too long, good French musicians have suffered because of the foreign influx. A good 50% of jazz musicians in Paris are unable to work regularly. In this way they don't develop to the full extent of their capabilities; they therefore go unnoticed by the critics, who are, in any case, always likely to prefer the exotic to the home-produced talent.

Catch 22.

Needless to say, the union move was not too well received by the Americans. 'So now it's "Yanks go home!"' said singer Big Jones. 'But where is the French tenor player who's going to pull in the people like Johnny Griffin?' And another expatriate said, 'They've been trying this for years. They know if they take us out of the clubs, they'll just close down. Then there'll be no work for anyone.'

French pianist Georges Arvanitas observed at the time that too great a concentration of expatriate jazzmen in Paris was not, in the end, in their own best interests. 'There can never be too many from a musical point of view, but from a financial and economic view, the money was good when only a few came over. Now, there are more good players, but they are no longer stars, but a commonplace.'

In the autumn of 1965 American jazz musicians were certainly predominant in the Paris jazz clubs. Jack Butler and Benny Waters were at the Cigale; Don Cherry at the Chat Qui Pèche, to be succeeded by Steve Lacy; Johnny Griffin and Arthur Taylor at Jazzland; Art Simmons and Aaron Bridgers at the Living Room; Mae Mercer and Stuff Smith at the Trois Mailletz; and Klook and his men at the Blue Note, sometimes featuring Nathan Davis. The Caméléon had Jean-Luc Ponty, later Guy Lafitte and the Caveau de la Huchette, Maxim Saury – but, otherwise, it was not too positive a scene for French jazz musicians.

It was a virtually insoluble problem, because the arguments of both sides had merits. Certainly if the letter of the law had been observed, the jazz-club scene would have been decimated. But the union did make some progress; it secured an agreement with the organizers of the second Paris Jazz Festival in November 1965 that the all-French big band of Jean-Claude Naude would be added to the bill. This was followed by the addition of the Jean-Luc Ponty Quartet to two Jimmy Smith–Dizzy Gillespie concerts at the Olympia Theatre.

Kenny Clarke was featured in the 1965 Paris Jazz Festival, playing with a group of all stars that included Don Byas, Stuff Smith, Roy Eldridge and Earl Hines and it was during this set that a fierce musical argument developed between Klook and Hines – a conflict which provided a vivid illustration of one aspect of Kenny's character. Klook was quite unforgiving in the matter of time, because his own was unfailingly impeccable – perfectly poised between metronomic accuracy and that over-eager tendency to gain, which many drummers confuse with swing. Kenny swung superbly while keeping the time exactly right. He was, to be sure, a listening drummer – but he was also very much a listened-to drummer, because the section men could always comfortably take their tempo cue from him. And soloists got great stimulation from his backing.

Klook's commitment to holding the tempo was severely challenged, however, when he and Jimmy Woode backed Hines in a trio number. Earl played 'Boogie Woogie on the St Louis Blues' and, as I reported in *Down Beat* at the time, 'a dispute between Hines and Clarke as to where the beat lay nearly wrecked the proceedings . . . only the timely and authoritative intervention of Eldridge's forceful trumpet restored order. Hines's jagged and unorthodox piano style does not blend easily with the drumming of Clarke, whose time is beyond reproach.'

Kenny knew, as always, exactly where 'one' was and he was utterly implacable about it. Hines, as he was sometimes inclined to do, got across the beat – but Kenny simply refused to go with him. As Fatha went blithely on with his florid improvisation, Kenny raised the volume and gave rimshot emphasis to the backbeat with explosive power. But there was no response from the piano – until Eldridge came in on Kenny's time and compelled Hines to change. It was one of the most fascinating musical contretemps I have ever witnessed.

A similar situation occurred fifteen years later at the 1980 Berlin Jazz Festival when Klook played with Warne Marsh, Eddie Gomez and Sal Mosca in a tribute to Lennie Tristano. When Mosca soloed on 'It's You or No One', he dragged the beat terribly – but Kenny kept the time exactly where it was supposed to be and would not relent. He wedged the tip of his tongue in the corner of his mouth, looked slightly murderous and continued to play the time according to Klook.

Klook's residency at the Blue Note continued through 1966, working at first with Nathan Davis, Urtreger and Gaudry opposite Martial Solal, bassist Gilbert Rovère and drummer Charles Bellonzi – very much a Klook protégé – and later with René Thomas and Lou Bennett. Bud Powell had returned to the States the previous August. In April Dexter Gordon played a four-week engagement.

In January 1966 I filed a review of a night at the Blue Note for *Down Beat* magazine:

> For some years now the indomitable Kenny Clarke has been the rhythmic backbone of the Blue Note, Paris's most celebrated jazz club. Leading a trio completed by Lou Bennett (organ) and Belgian guitarist René Thomas, Kenny, now fifty-one, has been laying down an unflagging beat with the faultless time that has kept him for so long among the great drummers of our time.
>
> With the departure of René Thomas and the temporary absence of Lou Bennett (playing a month at Ronnie Scott's club in London), Blue Note boss Ben Benjamin teamed tenorist Nathan Davis with Kenny Clarke, and, with a nod in the direction of the Paris Musicians' Union, brought in France's Martial Solal Trio for a month's stay.
>
> Kenny Clarke, immaculate and inscrutable behind his drums, is probably the least exciting drummer in the world – visually. But he is as good to listen to as he ever was. Experience, and the taste and discretion that go with it, are writ large on everything he does. 'And,' says Nathan Davis, 'he can still go. We sometimes play "Salt Peanuts" real fast – and Kenny is right in there, playing a storm.'

But if, after ten years in Paris, Kenny Clarke continued to be held in highest esteem by his peers, exile in France did nothing to enhance his rating with the American jazz public and critics – at least judged on the admittedly suspect basis of

Down Beat poll ratings. Most American musicians who based themselves in Europe seemed to suffer from this 'out of sight, out of mind' syndrome – but none more than Kenny Clarke. It is possible that patriotic Americans nursed some resentment towards him for having abandoned the country of his birth to immerse himself in garlic and Gauloises and for his having expressed some fairly trenchant views about America's social shortcomings. Between 1964 and 1970 Klook was unplaced in the drum section of the *Down Beat* readers' poll – though it sometimes ran to twenty-six places (and actually had Keith Moon in fourteenth place in 1970). In the critics' poll in the same period he managed eleventh place in 1966 and ninth place in 1970 – otherwise, nothing. While this says a lot more about polls than about Kenny Clarke, it is none the less surprising that a musician who made such an immense contribution to jazz could be so comprehensively ignored.

By the middle of 1966, with the increasing activity of the Clarke–Boland Big Band, Kenny was getting physically and spiritually tired of the demanding Blue Note gig – particularly since he gave 100% every time he played; he never permitted himself to coast. He told me that summer, 'I'm trying to keep jazz going. All the musicians tell me I have to stay at the Blue Note because it is good for drummers and good for jazz. But I'm tired, and working at the Blue Note is really something of a sacrifice.'

Matters came to a head in November 1966 – once again in a dispute about money. Considering his stature, Kenny was miserably paid – though the dismal economics of jazz clubs certainly militated against any top-class jazz musician being adequately remunerated for a resident engagement. Jimmy Woode, who was with Kenny on his final night at the club, recalls that Kenny had become impatient with the union-inspired infiltration into the club of more and more French musicians. The two causes were, in any case, linked in Kenny's eyes because he felt that the French quota system would cause attendances to decline, making the prospect of getting better money even more remote. Woode told me,

There was a big argument about this with Jacques, the cashier. I have never seen Kenny so angry. He really blew his top. And, at the end, he did a most un-Klooklike thing: he spat at Jacques. Then he turned to me and said, 'Come on, baby boy, that's it. I quit.' And he stormed out of the club. That was Klook's last night at the Blue Note.

And the end of another epic era in the extraordinarily eventful musical life of Kenny Clarke.

14
The Clarke–Boland Big Band

Almost everything about the Clarke–Boland Big Band was improbable. It was invented, nurtured, nourished, fussed over, financed, promoted and absolutely adored by a German-born Italian socialist whose qualifications for band management were that he was a trained architect and owner of a flourishing coffee bar in Cologne's Hohestrasse. Its leaders were two musicians who competed with each other in the art of staying in the background and maintaining a low profile. Its roster of members over the years embraced more than a dozen nationalities, half a dozen religions and a daunting assortment of egos, most of them on the large side. To bring the band together for rehearsal, record dates and concerts involved a formidable complexity of travel arrangements and much intricate juggling with the musicians' individual work schedules. Despite all of this, plus the inevitable, multiple frustrations, financial Everests, outbreaks of pique, petulance and pig-headedness, and that well-known capacity of airlines to deliver a bass player to Cologne and his bass to Caracas, the band not only survived for eleven years but developed into a unit of surpassing excellence, becoming an important – and genuinely significant – part of jazz history. It was by far the finest jazz orchestra ever assembled outside the United States.

And Pier-Luigi 'Gigi' Campi, the man who made it all happen, is quite emphatic that the band simply could not have existed without Kenny Clarke. 'We needed his magic touch,' he told me.

As a teenager in Italy during the Second World War, Campi

used to listen under the blankets in a Jesuit college to jazz broadcasts from the American Forces Network. He listened to Louis Armstrong, Jimmie Lunceford, Roy Eldridge and Duke Ellington and among his circle of friends, jazz records were more highly prized than black-market coffee.

But it was when Campi heard a Charlie Parker record in 1948 that he started to become a real jazz devotee. In 1949 he attended an international meeting of young socialists from all over Europe and, as he alighted from the train in Zurich, he saw a poster announcing a concert that evening by Django Reinhardt. A record by the Quintette du Hot Club de France was among those he had heard clandestinely in college and he couldn't resist the opportunity to see and hear Django in person. So he decided to skip the scheduled briefing for the political meeting that evening and attend the concert instead.

Gigi recalls:

> There was another group mentioned on the poster but the names meant nothing to me. Django played the first half and I was really excited by the music. But in the second half, this group of black musicians played – and the music sounded strange, but wonderful. I remember coming out of that concert feeling absolutely exhilarated. I was telling myself, 'Django was fine – but those black musicians, they were really fantastic.' Three years later, James Moody and his group were touring Germany. My wife and I were passing through Munich on the way to a ski resort and we discovered that Moody's group was playing in town that evening. We went to the concert and as soon as the band took the stage, I said to my wife, 'I've seen that drummer before.'

The drummer, of course, was Kenny Clarke, who'd been a member of the band that had played the second half of the Django concert in 1949. And Gigi discovered that the men with Kenny at that time had been Miles Davis, Charlie Parker, Tommy Potter and Tadd Dameron, fresh from the historic first Paris Jazz Festival.

'I went backstage after the concert,' Gigi says, 'and had my first close-up of what you later called "the thousand-candle-power grin". Kenny impressed me enormously, not only as a drummer but as a person.'

The success of his coffee bar enabled Gigi Campi to indulge his love of jazz by organizing concert tours and producing jazz records. He set up a tour for the Chet Baker Quartet and recorded Lars Gullin, Lee Konitz and Hans Koller for his Mod label. His enthusiasm, however, outstripped his entrepreneurial flair as a jazz promoter. He lost $10,000 on a 1956 Lee Konitz tour.

> But I learned something from being on the road with Lee. My friends and I were big fans of cool jazz at that time, but Lee would always be singing Lester Young solos on the train. I think that tuned me in again to the swing-band era. He also said that the next time he came on tour, I should make a point of hiring Kenny Clarke to play drums. But, after this tour had flopped, I decided to cut my losses and quit the jazz business. However, I remembered Kenny Clarke, of course, and I resolved that if I decided to get involved with jazz production and promotion again, the first thing I would make sure of was that I had a good rhythm section.

At the time that Campi was beating a retreat from jazz promotion, François 'Francy' Boland, a twenty-six-year-old pianist, composer and arranger from Namur, Belgium, was in the United States writing arrangements for Benny Goodman and Count Basie, having been recommended by Mary Lou Williams. Boland, a largely self-taught musician, had studied music for a few years at the local conservatory and had taken piano and harmony courses at the Liège Royal Conservatory. A great admirer of the swing bands, particularly those of Les Brown, Basie and Artie Shaw, he wrote his first big-band arrangements in 1942 when he was thirteen years old.

Francy had also written arrangements for the German orchestras of Kurt Edelhagen and Werner Muller and it was through Edelhagen that Gigi Campi first became aware of his arranging skills. Kurt Edelhagen was the leader of one of Germany's most successful big jazz bands, a multi-national outfit which he assembled in 1957 and which, though a touch bombastic and lacking in subtlety, was one of the most impressive large jazz ensembles of its time in Europe and boasted some fine soloists – including, at various times, Dusko Gojkovic, Jiggs Whigham, Carl Drevo, Peter Trunk, Jimmy Deuchar, Shake Keane, Ronnie Stephenson, Wilton Gaynair, Ferdinand Povel, Benny Bailey, Peter Herbolzheimer, Derek Humble and Ken Wray.

Edelhagen had a contract with the West Deutsche Rundfunk in Cologne, whose studios were opposite the office of Gigi

Campi, and musicians from the band were always in the coffee shop. Campi used to go across the street to listen to the band rehearse, and on one of these occasions he heard a most arresting version of the Rodgers and Hart standard 'Johnny One Note'. He asked who'd done the arrangement and Chris Kellens, a Belgian who played trombone in the Edelhagen band said, 'That's one by the maestro, Francy Boland.' Campi told Edelhagen that if he really wanted to develop the style and character of his band, he should give more arranging commissions to Boland.

Said Campi,

> Francy was sending all the arrangements he was writing for Basie to Edelhagen as well, including 'Major's Groove', which later became 'Griff's Groove', a feature for Johnny Griffin. I had met Francy in 1955 when he was working with Chet Baker after the death of Chet's pianist, Dick Twardzik, and I remember enjoying his piano playing. Now, having listened to some of his arrangements, an idea was forming in my mind.

Later Francy, who had returned from the States after some disagreement over payment for the Basie arrangements, came to Cologne to look up some of his friends in the Edelhagen band, and Gigi told him that he was plannning to put together a big band to play Boland's arrangements. They then spent an hour or so discussing the personnel for the band. At this time Gigi had returned to working as a jazz promoter, at least to the extent of featuring live jazz in his coffee house, so he had some musicians in mind. Campi made a point, in particular, of putting on jazz at the time of the annual *fasching*, the German mardi gras carnival, as a kind of antidote to what he called the 'traditional junk carnival music'. At carnival time in February 1960, Campi booked tenor saxophonist Don Byas and assembled in support Francy Boland, Kenny Clarke and a group of musicians from the Edelhagen band: Chris Kellens (trombone), Eddie Busnello (alto), Fats Sadi (vibes) and Jean Warland (bass). Recordings by this group were later issued by the German Electrola Company as *Don Wails with Kenny*.

The first real Clarke–Boland recording, however, was made in Cologne a year later, in May 1961. It featured Kenny and Francy with Raymond Droz on alto horn, Chris Kellens on baritone horn, Britain's Derek Humble on alto, Austria's Carl Drevo on tenor and Jimmy Woode on bass. That was the first manifestation of what was to become the regular rhythm section of the Clarke–Boland band. Campi sent the tape to Alfred Lion of Blue Note who hailed it as 'fantastic' and released it under the title *The Golden Eight*.

Both the Electrola and the Blue Note albums had been recorded by a brilliant engineer, Wolfgang Hirschmann, who was to become *the* engineer of the CBBB over the next decade. Campi, Boland and Clarke all had the highest regard for Hirschmann. Kenny once said that the three sound engineers he really respected were Hirschmann, Rudy van Gelder and a German technician at the old Paris Barclay studios called Gérard Eilert, because they all used just one mike above the drums to capture his sound. 'Sometimes they would use extra mikes for the hi-hat and snare drum, but I preferred just one,' Kenny said – which is another illustration of his belief in the efficacy of simplicity.

It was seven months later, in December 1961, that the Clarke–Boland Big Band came into being in the Electrola Studios in Cologne – and its recording début was fortuitous. The session had originally been a date for Billie Poole, who was playing at the Storyville Club in Cologne at the time with Klook, Jimmy Gourley and Lou Bennett. Campi was arranging to record Billie for Riverside and had decided, with Kenny and Francy, to assemble 'a little big band' for the date. Francy wrote the arrangements and the line-up was Benny Bailey, Roger Guérin, Jimmy Deuchar and Ahmed Muvaffak Falay (trumpets); Nat Peck, Ake Persson (trombones); Carl Drevo, Zoot Sims (tenors), Derek Humble (alto), Sahib Shihab (baritone), Francy Boland (piano), Jimmy Woode (bass) and Kenny Clarke (drums).

France's Roger Guérin had worked often with Klook since 1956. Shihab had come to Europe in 1959 with the Quincy Jones band and had stayed over, settling in Stockholm. Zoot was on tour, and Persson, another former Quincy Jones sideman, was now based in Berlin and freelancing. Falay had come to Europe from Turkey, and although some people thought he had acquired his middle name after mortally offending a none-too-literate fellow musician, it seems that it really was genuine. Benny Bailey, yet another former Quincy Jones alumnus, was living in Berlin and working in the Sender Freies Berlin radio orchestra, and Nat Peck, a Paris-based American, had chalked up a great deal of big-band experience with Glenn Miller, Don Redman, Duke Ellington and – needless to add – Quincy Jones.

All was set for the record date, when, one week before the musicians were due to assemble in Cologne, Billie Poole had to return to the States because of a bereavement in the family. Rather than cancel the date, Campi had Francy Boland write seven new arrangements at breakneck speed and the session became the first date for the Clarke–Boland Big Band. It was released by Atlantic, and aptly titled *Jazz is Universal.*

Campi told me,

> The opening track on that album, 'Box 703, Washington DC', was like an explosion. I remember Ake Persson coming into the control room to hear the playback and saying, 'Gigi, put this band on the road for six weeks and we'll scare the shit out of everybody!' The spirit among the musicians was tremendous – everyone knew that we had a sensational band together. The feeling was electric. I remember Ake came into the office after we'd finished recording late one night and I told him I had some extra money to give him. He shook his head and said, 'No, we don't have to speak about money.'
>
> I said, 'You mean you're not happy with the fee? You want more?'
>
> 'No. I mean that I should be paying you for the privilege of playing in a motherfucking band like this after all these years.'
>
> And that was the kind of spirit that developed – the music and the feeling became more important than the money – a really remarkable thing when you consider how hard musicians sometimes have to fight to get paid, or to get paid adequately.

What was especially important about *Jazz is Universal* was that it proved beyond a doubt that jazz was no longer the exclusive preserve of American musicians. 'The thoroughly integrated sound that emerged from this band,' wrote 'Voice of America' producer and presenter Willis Conover in the liner note for the album, 'is convincing evidence that international boundaries have no meaning at all to the practising jazz musician.'

Seven of the thirteen musicians in the band were European and their ability to hold their own with their American colleagues did no damage at all to the cause of winning a just measure of appreciation and recognition for some of the excellent European jazz musicians who were emerging. An indication of how the band's enthusiasm for the music was as abundant as its musicianship is the fact that the album was recorded in just four hours!

It was always Campi's goal, with the CBBB, to create a band which had an immediately recognizable identity – which was why he wanted Francy Boland to write all the band's arrangements. Boland's very special concept of arranging helped to achieve this aim, and the brilliant solo and section work of a band whose members loved to play together and who developed such a great personal and musical rapport, did the rest.

The key elements, according to Campi, were first of all the rhythm section: 'I knew when I heard Kenny, Francy and Jimmy play together for the first time that I simply had to build a big band around them.' A second crucial element was the magnificent lead trumpet and solo work of Benny Bailey – a musician for whom both Dizzy Gillespie and Thad Jones expressed admiration tinged with awe. The third was the immaculate lead alto saxophone and brilliant, serpentine solo work of Derek Humble. And a fourth was the massive loyalty and surging enthusiasm of the big Swede, Ake Persson, who was an indefatigable champion of the band. Ake was also a formidable trombonist. Nat Peck once said, 'Every time I sit down with him it's like I'm hearing him for the first time. Thrilling! I've never worked with *anyone* who has stimulated me so much.'

Encouraged by the success of the *Universal* album, Gigi Campi decided to assemble an even bigger band for the next record date on 25, 26 and 27 January 1963. Two albums resulted from this session made with a twenty-one-piece orchestra – six trumpets, five trombones, five saxophones and an augmented rhythm section with Joe Harris on percussion – *Now Hear Our Meanin'* released on CBS, and *Handle with Care*, released on the Atlantic label. Britain's Ronnie Scott came into the band for the first time, as did Idrees Sulieman and Austrian trombonist Erich Kleinschuster. And, in the absence of Zoot Sims, Campi flew in Billy Mitchell from the United States as principal tenor-saxophone soloist. Also in the line-up – through a misunderstanding more worthy of fiction than fact – was trombonist Keg Johnson, direct from New York.

The band needed a bass trombonist – and nobody seemed to be able to come up with a suitable candidate. Then Ake Persson came to see Nat Peck, clutching an album. 'I've got him,' he said. 'Listen to this.' And he played a track from the Gil Evans album, *Out of the Cool*. Nat was impressed. Persson pointed out the name on the sleeve and they called Campi in Cologne. 'You must get Keg for this date,' they said. Campi, always responsive to enthusiasm, agreed to bring Johnson in from New York.

During the session Keg did a pretty good job, but somehow, Peck and Persson thought, he wasn't quite matching his playing on the Evans album. After the first day's recording was over, Persson and Peck had drinks with Johnson. They told him how they'd heard him on the Gil Evans album. 'Some of the best bass-trombone playing I ever heard in my life,' said Nat Peck. 'Absolutely fantastic,' confirmed Persson.

'Well, thanks,' said Keg. 'But actually, that wasn't me. I didn't play bass trombone on that album. As a matter of fact, I'm not really a bass-trombone player at all. I had to borrow the instrument for this date.'

The bass-trombone player was actually Tony Studd. But Ake and Nat took a year to break the news to Campi.

Talking to me about the album in November 1966 when I was preparing an article on the band for *Down Beat*, Kenny Clarke said it was one of the most satisfying dates of his career. He said:

> The record is proof positive that there are as good musicians in Europe as there are in the States. I have never felt that the standard in Europe was much lower than in America. In Germany, it is just as high, even higher. I've worked around the studios in the States and I really think that music here in Europe is on a higher plane.

When I asked Klook how the Clarke–Boland compared with the big band of Dizzy Gillespie, he smiled the inimitable Klook smile and said, 'There is no comparison. That was the greatest band I ever played with in my life. I have never played in a band that was so inspirational and dynamic. It will never happen again in my lifetime. But we can come pretty close.'

It was not until May 1966 that the Clarke–Boland Band played its first live concert – in Mainz, West Germany – which was broadcast in the regular jazz programme of jazz producer and critic Joachim Ernst Berendt for the Sudwestfunk, Baden-Baden. Reviewing the concert, the critic of the *Mainzer Zeitung* wrote:

> The Clarke–Boland Band showed that musically and technically they are masters of their craft. The compositions and arrangements were excellent and the solos displayed a combination of vitality, a beautiful smoothness and command of musical range . . . What strikes one after close listening is the classic harmony of the brilliant *soli* and *tutti* passages, played with elegance and confidence and distinguishing the band from all other big jazz ensembles.

Boland's arranging style did indeed make excellent use of the *soli* and *tutti* devices, and they became something of a CBBB hallmark. He used them in 'Get Out of Town' on the *Handle with Care* album, and they were dramatically in evidence on the Clarke–Boland Band's third album, recorded in Cologne on 18 June 1967 for the Saba (later MPS) label of Hans Georg Brunner-Schwer. For this album, which featured Eddie 'Lockjaw' Davis as guest soloist, Boland wrote an arrangement based on 'Chinatown' and called 'Sax no End'. It was a masterpiece of saxophone scoring – and it needed a saxophone team of the calibre of Derek Humble, Carl Drevo, Johnny Griffin, Ronnie Scott and Sahib Shihab to do it justice. After Eddie Davis solos over four choruses with just the rhythm section and Fats Sadi's bongos, the saxophone section, masterfully piloted by Humble, plays three complex and intricate *soli* choruses with fine precision, co-ordination and compatibility. Two roaring *tutti* choruses follow. Saxophonist Kenny Graham, reviewing the *Sax no End* album in *Crescendo* in May 1968, said:

> One particular bit did my old ears a power of good – a saxophone chorus, brilliantly led by Derek Humble. I just love hearing saxophones having a chance to play a well-written chorus instead of riffs, figures and the boosting-up-the-brass chores that they usually find themselves doing.

> Maybe that's what Francy Boland is really all about. Nobody does saxophone choruses these days – they're not on. F.B., oblivious of trends etc., bungs 'em in. This and similar notions of his come off a treat because he *believes* in them.

'Sax no End' was a major landmark in the band's progress towards its ultimate corporate identity and it was followed by a number of other arrangements featuring saxophone *soli*, such as 'All the Things You Are', 'When Your Lover Has Gone', 'You Stepped out of a Dream', and many more. Ronnie Scott remembers those *soli* passages only too well. He says of 'Sax no End', characteristically self-critical,

> They were very difficult to play – in fact, I never really got 'Sax no End' down. But they were beautifully written and sounded marvellous. Derek was the navigator in chief – and, of course, Shihab was a great anchor man. After about the first four times, he never had to look at the part.

Certainly the arrangement made a big impression and was always a favourite at live performances. Oscar Peterson was so taken with the chart that he actually recorded a trio version for his MPS album *Travellin' On*. But perhaps the most remarkable thing about the *Sax no End* album was that all seven titles were recorded in seven hours.

'It was almost always a first-take affair when the band recorded,' Gigi Campi says. 'We hardly ever played anything more than three times – and then we usually found that the first take was the best.'

In between the big-band dates Clarke and Boland made a number of sessions with smaller groups featuring different members of the band – Johnny Griffin, Fats Sadi, Sahib Shihab – and an octet album with singer Mark Murphy. The band also began to make more live appearances, playing festivals and concerts in Germany, Switzerland, Austria, Italy, Holland, Belgium, France, Hungary, Finland, Denmark, Sweden, Yugoslavia, Czechoslovakia and Britain.

Campi worked tirelessly to project and promote the band and, recognizing early on the importance of getting airplay for the CBBB's music, he concluded an agreement in 1967 to sell a monthly half-hour programme by the band to radio stations in Helsinki, Stockholm, Copenhagen, Hilversum, Brussels,

Vienna, Zurich, Baden-Baden, Munich, Stuttgart, Frankfurt, Saarbrucken, Hamburg, Berlin and Cologne.

Between 1967 and 1969 the CBBB recorded a series of fine albums, including *Faces, Latin Kaleidoscope* (with Phil Woods), *Fellini 7½* and *Off Limits* for the MPS label which were excellent showcases for the arranging and compositional talents of Francy Boland and for the band's exceptional 'togetherness'.

The vintage year of the Clarke–Boland Band was 1969 and by common consent the peak performances of the band's career were heard – and, happily, recorded – during an unforgettable two-week engagement at Ronnie Scott's Club in London from 17 February to 1 March. As I wrote at the time, if there has to be one set of recordings, from all of the band's repertoire on disc, selected to stand as a monument to the finest jazz ensemble to come out of Europe, then it has to be the thirteen tracks and two albums from that 1969 Ronnie Scott's Club date.

The band broke attendance records at the club and, says Campi, only then did the musicians really feel the full extent of the power of which they were capable. To have the opportunity of playing together night after night for two weeks made it possible to achieve a rapport and a mutuality of feeling that even this intuitively integrated band had not equalled hitherto.

By this time the CBBB had an additional drummer. Recruiting a second drummer for a band that has Kenny Clarke in its rhythm section would seem to be setting a new standard in futility. But it worked. British drummer Kenny Clare, a noted session musician, with excellent technique and good reading ability, had first come into the band as a sub when Klook had other commitments. He handled the job so well that he was taken on the 'permanent staff'. There are various explanations as to why this happened and, in all probability – as is usually the case – there is an element of truth in most of them.

Whenever it was suggested to Klook there was one drummer too many in the band, he vigorously disagreed. Two drumheads, he argued, are better than one. He told Max Jones in a *Melody Maker* interview published on 15 March 1968:

> It came about because of my teaching. From my experience with students

I thought that maybe drummers can play together without being noisy or confusing. So I tried it out at the Selmer school in Paris and found it worked well.

Between the two of us, I think that Kenny and I can play anything in the world . . . He is someone who thinks exactly the same way I do about drumming. He's one of the most intelligent drummers I've ever met . . . We're two soul brothers.

I would suggest that this may be another example of Kenny's tendency to retrospective rationalization. Ronnie Scott's recollection is that Kenny Clare's presence in the band was intended to take some of the pressure off Klook, 'who wasn't the greatest reader in the world. The arrangement allowed Kenny Clarke to coast from time to time – and it worked because they were so compatible. It would have been disastrous otherwise.' And in best Ronnie Scott style he instanced the massive all-star band organized by Charlie Watts in 1987 which had not two drummers but three. 'Someone asked the vibraphone player what he thought of the tempo of a piece the band was rehearsing. "Fine," he said, "I liked all three of them."'

Kenny Clare recalled his first gig with the band when he talked to *Crescendo*'s Tony Brown in May 1968. He had made a good impression and was asked by Gigi Campi to play alongside Klook on the next date.

They gave me a couple of notes on vibraphone which I invariably played wrongly – well, they figured that I'd always be available to do anything that Klook wouldn't be free to do. I could do sundry percussion. Then one number was a Turkish march thing and I played snare drum. When it was played back it sounded very much together, like one drummer. They talked it over. Next time I came, would I bring my drums as well? See if we could make it with both of us playing. It worked – and it's been like that ever since.

There is no doubt that driving the CBBB took a lot of energy and endurance and the addition of Clare not only added to the rhythmic foundation but also spread the heavy percussion load.

Playing along with the greatest drummer in the world was a pretty intimidating experience for Clare. He once told me of the first gig with Klook in Ostend in 1967 when the dual-drumming exercise became a nightmare. 'Try as I would at rehearsal, I just couldn't get it together. The drums were fighting each other.'

He left the theatre after the rehearsal full of gloom and depression and decided that the best thing to do for the sake of the band would be to slip silently away. He went to book a flight back to London – but there wasn't one. He shrugged resignedly, walked around the town for a couple of hours, then finally made his way back to the theatre for the concert.

'I started the first number full of apprehension – but from the very first beat, it all came together miraculously. I just couldn't believe it!'

And that was the beginning of a beautiful percussion friendship. From then on, Clare became an integral part of the rhythm section and missed only one gig with the band. Strangely enough, Clare said he was never able to play the same away from the band. 'There are many drummers who would love to get the same springy kind of beat that Klook gets. I'm one of them. When I'm with him, I can play that way without even thinking about it. As soon as I'm away from him, I can't do it any more.'

True to character, Klook gave every encouragement to Kenny Clare and undoubtedly one of the important reasons why they worked so well together was that they had such a warm relationship off the stage, as well as on.

British drummer Frank King, reviewing the two Polydor albums that resulted from the Scott engagement, wrote in *Crescendo*: 'The perception and telepathy between Kenny Clarke and Kenny Clare is magnificent. They have such a fantastic togetherness that in places it is miraculous.'

With Jimmy Woode unavailable, Ronnie Scott's bassist, Ron Mathewson, was brought in for the club engagement and with Clare, Scott, Tony Coe (on tenor and clarinet), Humble and Tony Fisher (trumpet, depping for Jimmy Deuchar), the British contingent in the band was as big as the American. Yugoslavia's Dusko Gojkovic was recruited into the trumpet section.

Gigi Campi had to miss the first week of the engagement, but when he walked into the club on the Monday of the second week, Johnny Griffin told him, 'Gigi, you're gonna hear some shit tonight!' Campi sat at a table with writer Bob Houston, my wife and myself and beamed as his 'family' took the stage. ('Italians,' he'd explained to me once, 'always try to wrap everything up in a sense of family – and that's how I regard the band.') Campi had heard practically every note the band had played since its début. But when it hit, with a high-voltage version of 'Box 703', Campi turned to us wide-eyed and said, 'Wow!' Later he told me: 'I couldn't believe how good the band sounded. When they played the *tutti* in "Now Hear My Meanin' " I got goose pimples all over.'

For Ronnie Scott those two weeks were undoubtedly one of the major highlights in the history of the club, as well as being musically inspirational. 'It was marvellous. People used to applaud in the middle of the arrangements – showing their appreciation of some of the *tutti* or *soli* passages. It was really one of the greatest musical experiences of my life.'

The year 1969 was certainly a banner one for the Clarke–Boland Big Band. It played the Pori Festival in Finland that summer and Lars Lystedt, *Down Beat*'s Scandinavian correspondent, described the condition of the audience as 'spellbound'. In September the band shared the bill at Rotterdam's De Doelen concert hall with the mighty Thad Jones–Mel Lewis Orchestra, and reporting for Britain's *Melody Maker*, Jan van Setten told of 1,780 people 'exploding into thunderous acclaim after the four-and-a-half-hour marathon concert'. It was a real battle of the bands, he said. 'Who won? Music.'

At the Prague Jazz Festival in October, the CBBB 'totally eclipsed' the Duke Ellington band, according to *Melody Maker's* Jack Hutton. 'This year's Prague Festival proved one thing conclusively to me – the Kenny Clarke–Francy Boland Big Band is the finest big band in existence,' he wrote.

And after a Paris concert in that same month, Jacques B. Hess of *Le Monde* wrote:

> The CBBB is a triumph, at the highest level of talent and professionalism. The warmth, the commitment and the enthusiasm of the musicians is refreshing and a marked change from the lacklustre and blasé performances of the Ellington and Basie bands which we have become used to over the last few years.

In October 1970 the CBBB was back in Britain for a three-week engagement at Ronnie Scott's and at this time Carmen McRae came to London to record with the band in the Lansdowne Studios. With a minimum of rehearsal time, the superbly professional ex-Mrs Clarke managed astonishingly well with some difficult scores, especially considering that six of the eight tunes recorded were new to her. The whole session was completed in eight hours. It was named after a Boland–Jimmy Woode song on the album, 'November Girl'.

There followed a three-week European tour which had Dizzy Gillespie as special guest and which culminated in an appearance at the Berlin Jazz Festival. But the tour was not a great success musically because the band had to submerge its own personality to play a programme that was more closely associated with Dizzy.

In fact there were now signs that the band was beginning to run out of steam and, no doubt, one of the factors which undermined its momentum was Campi's failure to conclude an agreement to take the band to the United States. It was a great disappointment for Kenny Clarke – and for all concerned with the CBBB. But, for a variety of reasons – predominantly financial – plans to have the band appear at the Village Gate in New York, followed by concerts in Boston and Chicago, an appearance at the 1970 Newport Jazz Festival and a tour of Canada, did not come to fruition.

'I'd really love to take the band on the road in the States,' Kenny Clarke told me in 1967, 'just to prove the point about the high standard of European musicians.' But it was not to be.

What finally caused Kenny Clarke to acknowledge that the days of the CBBB were numbered, however, was the untimely death of Derek Humble on 2 February 1971 at the age of thirty-nine. 'The band was never the same without Derek,' Kenny said, voicing a sentiment that was shared by the whole CBBB family.

In June 1971 the band made its last recording, *Change of Scenes*, with Stan Getz as guest soloist and, in March 1972 in Nuremberg, played its last concert date when, according to Gigi Campi, 'it was a sorry shadow of its former self'. He went on:

Johnny Griffin came to me after the concert, and virtually read the funeral service. The following morning I had a long discussion with Francy and Klook to see if we could keep the band going. I still thought there might be a possibility of pulling off an extensive tour of the USA which could have regenerated the spirit of the band. So some days later I went on a round trip of Europe to try to put the band together again. I called on Idrees, Nat Peck, Tony Coe and Johnny Griffin and finished up in Montreuil with Francy, Klook and Benny Bailey. And finally I realized that it wasn't going to happen . . .

And that's when even Campi's apparently unquenchable enthusiasm gave out. It was April 1972 and the Clarke–Boland Big Band had breathed its last.

But, as Bob Houston, who was closely associated with the band through most of its lifetime, wrote afterwards, though the demise was a matter for regret, that the band had existed at all was a matter for celebration – 'as with all phenomena which survive on excellence against the tides of current fads and fashions . . . The CBBB was one of the most enjoyable manifestations of the last decade in jazz. Be grateful that it happened at all, and that we have it on record to enjoy.'

And Kenny Clarke said, 'It was a fantastic, unique experience from which I learned a lot. It was not only a great band, it was a community, a congregation of friends – and one of the happiest bands I've ever worked with.'

The Clarke–Boland Big Band left a rich legacy of its repertoire on record. In the eleven years of its existence it recorded thirty-nine albums.

Kenny Clarke's role in the CBBB was not only the obvious one of being the rhythmic dynamo; he was important as a co-leader in his own reserved and unobtrusive way. He led by example; he had the total respect of all the musicians who ever played in the band, and that respect, coupled with respect for one another, was what kept the band so tight and its musical standards so high.

Says Johnny Griffin,

The CBBB couldn't have lasted with a Benny Goodman or a Buddy Rich leading it – because there were too many bandleaders in the band. It wouldn't have worked if the leaders had been dictators. I mean, the vibrations from the egos! My God, imagine – three trumpet players all Leos: Idrees Sulieman, Benny Bailey and Art Farmer. It was like an armed truce. It was amazing with all those different characters and the strength in each one. And it would mesh! There was no one on the band that you could pick on! It was really like a zoo, with tigers, lions and gorillas in it!

'I never met anyone who stayed so calm,' Kenny Clare said of Klook in an interview with *Crescendo*'s Tony Brown. 'You should come along to a recording session. All pandemonium let loose, everybody talking or blowing like a bunch of madmen. Kenny never raises his voice or gets excited. He is a wonder.'

Ronnie Scott confesses that he was always a little bit in awe of Kenny Clarke. 'But he was always so amiable and pleasant. He didn't come on like your typical extrovert bandleader. He just sat there, and played – and that was enough.'

Gigi Campi remembers times when Kenny would arrive late for rehearsal or recording due to plane or train delays. 'We would all be waiting in the studio – and as soon as Kenny walked in you were aware that there was suddenly more power in the room. His presence – quiet, dignified and calm – was such a positive force.'

Jimmy Woode says that it was simply not Klook's way to get out in front of the band and pep-talk the musicians. 'He might speak quietly to you individually – but his leadership was implicit in his solid integrity. Francy and Klook were not exactly charismatic leaders like Duke.'

Ron Mathewson remembers Klook as a man who commanded respect from all the members of the band without any attempt to pull rank: 'He was really helpful to me when I came into the band for the gig at Ronnie's. He said, to me, very nicely, "Keep a straight four. Let the guys feel you, because you're new. They want to trust the rhythm section. Just play it cool and let it happen."'

Francy Boland's co-leadership consisted entirely of creating the band's inimitable book, writing not for the instruments but for the musicians, and providing support and solos from the keyboard that were consistently streets ahead of his own evaluation of them. Boland carries self-effacement almost to the point of self-erasure. He told me, 'Kenny didn't really have a lot to do with the music. And I wanted it that way because I was the arranger.'

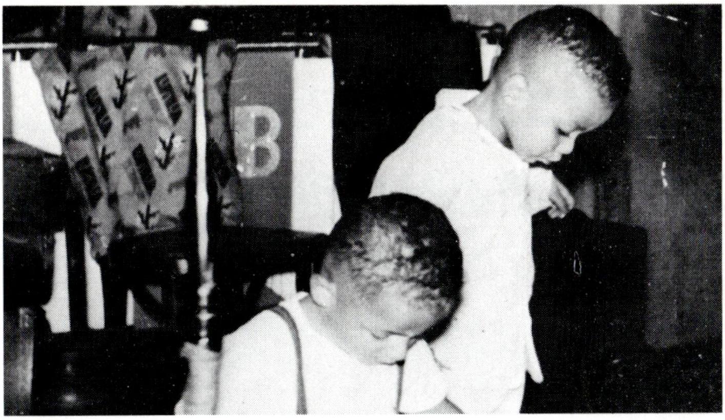

Kenny Clarke (*left*), with elder brother Chuck, Pittsburgh, *c.* 1917

Minton's (*left to right*): Thelonious Monk, Howard McGhee, Roy Eldridge and (possibly) Teddy Hill

Royal Roost 1949 (*left to right*): Miles Davis, Dizzy Gillespie, Max Roach, Kenny Clarke, Chino Pozo and his cousin Chano Pozo

Club St Germain, Paris 1949: Charlie Parker (as), Art Simmons (p), Kenny Clarke (d)

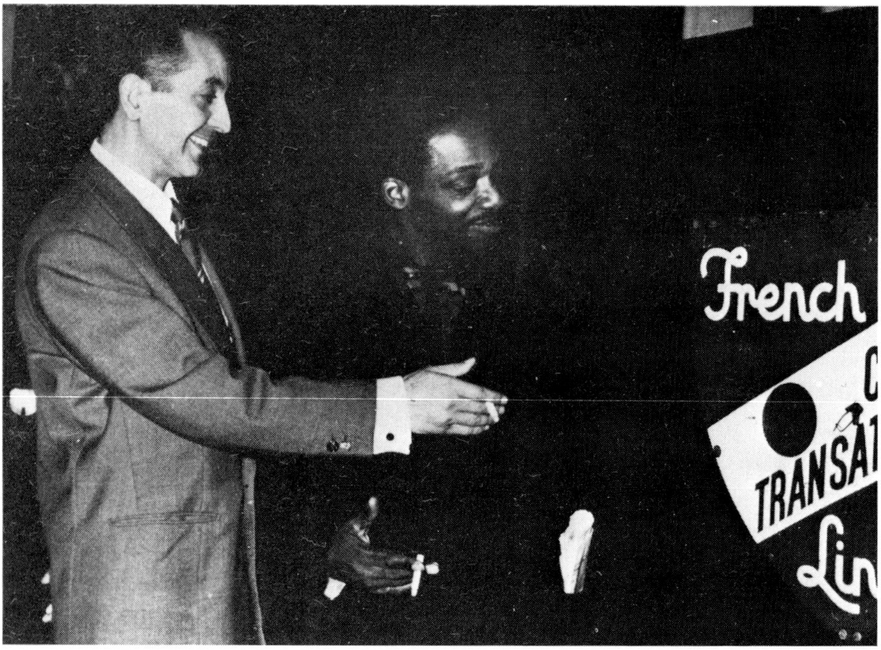

Paris September 1956: Kenny Clarke with French bandleader Jacques Helian (Marc Bicker)

Club St Germain, Paris 1957: Kenny Clarke (d), Sonny Stitt (ts) (André Sas)

Pathé-Marconi record date, Paris 1957: Pierre Michelot (b), Kenny Clarke (d) (Jean-Pierre Leloir)

Club St Germain, Paris 1957: Martial Solal (p), J.J. Johnson (tb), Kenny Clarke (d), Barney Wilen (ts), Pierre Michelot (b, *hidden*) (André Sas)

Club St Germain, Paris 1957: Barney Wilen (ts), Kenny Clarke (d), Miles Davis (tpt) (André Sas)

Olympia, Paris 1958: drum battle with Art Blakey (André Sas)

Cannes 1958: Dizzy Gillespie (tpt), Kenny Clarke (d), Stan Getz (ts), Sacha Distel (g), Barney Wilen (ts) (Jean-Pierre Leloir)

Blue Note, Paris 1959: Kenny Clarke (*left*) with Lester Young (Jean-Pierre Leloir)

Blue Note, Paris 1959: Kenny Clarke with (*left*) Mae Mezzrow and Carmen McRae (Jean-Pierre Leloir)

Essen Jazz Festival, 1960: Bud Powell (p), Oscar Pettiford (b), Kenny Clarke (d) (Hanns E. Haehl)

Dexter Gordon with French drummer Charles Bellonzi outside the Blue Note, Paris 1963 (courtesy of Charles Bellonzi, Francis Paudras Archive)

Club St Germain, Paris 1963: Dizzy Gillespie (tpt), Kenny Clarke (d), Gilbert Rovère (b) (Jean-Pierre Leloir)

Author interviewing Kenny Clarke for *Melody Maker*, Paris 1964 (Bob Lampard)

Ben Benjamin (*right*), manager of the Blue Note, at the Antibes Jazz Festival with (*left*) Woody Herman

Blue Note, Paris 1965: Lou Bennett (org), Jimmy Gourley (g), Kenny Clarke (d) (Jean-Pierre Leloir)

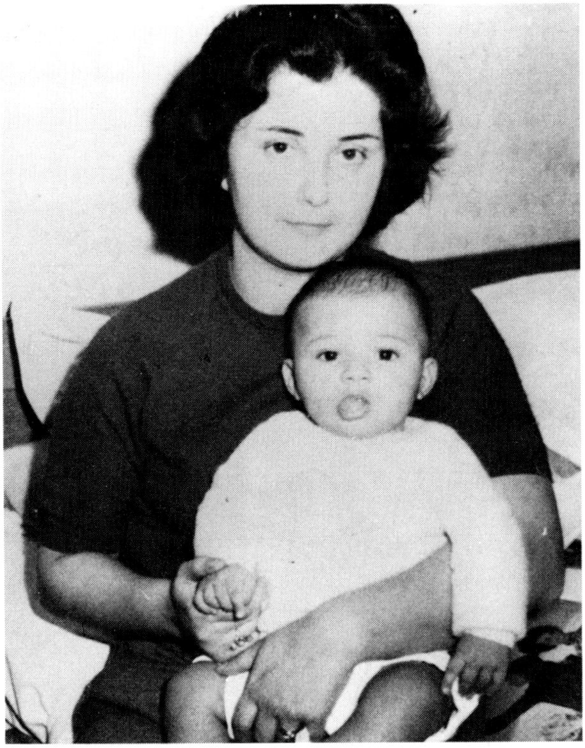

Photo of Daisy Clarke and Laurent, taken in winter 1964 by Kenny Clarke, who wrote on the back: 'Avec maman Daisy. Laurent à trois mois et demi. Beau garçon! Oui!'

Kenny Clarke with Daisy and their son Laurent, Montreuil August 1964

Three mainstays of the Clarke–Boland band (*left to right*): Kenny Clarke, Gigi Campi, Francy Boland

Kenny Clarke with two pupils (*left*, Mezz Mezzrow's son Milton) at the Premier drum school, Paris (Bob Lampard)

Kenny Clarke at the Barclay Studios, Paris, during a Musidisc session with pianist Oscar Peterson, February 1973 (Jean-Pierre Leloir)

Dinner with Diz, Paris February 1984 (Jean-Pierre Leloir)

Pictured with French pianist Henri Renaud in 1963. Kenny Clarke 'radiated goodwill, good nature and affability – an impression reinforced by his predilection for tweed jackets and pipes' (André Gardé)

The terraced house in Montreuil-sous-Bois which was Kenny Clarke's home for more than twenty years.

Kenny Clarke inspecting the pear tree in the garden of his Montreuil home (Jean-Pierre Leloir)

'Toby' – Kenny Clarke Jr – in Pittsburgh at the age of three

Toby in New York (*with dark glasses*) in 1969 with (*left*) Max Roach and (*centre*) Sonny Stitt

Kenny Clarke (François Perol)

And without any apparent awareness of the sublime irony of a Boland being struck by someone else's inclination to maintain a low profile, he added, 'Kenny was a very reserved person and he kept his thoughts to himself. He never expressed enthusiasm when I came in with a new arrangement; though he might give me a compliment – a small compliment – from time to time.'

Clarke and Boland, during their association together, were never in any danger of engulfing one another in explicit mutual admiration. But had it not been there in some abundance, the band simply would not have flourished. Whatever Boland may feel about the measure of respect and appreciation he received from Kenny, Gigi Campi remembers an incident which speaks eloquently of Klook's high regard for his partner.

> The band was rehearsing and swinging like a demon – without a drummer. Kenny was standing out in front, rolling a joint. Suddenly he looked up in mock disbelief and genuine joy, and said, 'This band doesn't need a drummer. That Belgian motherfucker swings it just with his writing, goddam it!

'For Kenny,' Campi adds, 'there were two great arrangers in jazz: Tadd Dameron and Francy Boland.'

15
Interview '73

A little more than a year after the break-up of the Clarke–Boland band, I sat talking to Kenny on the terrace of a café just off the boulevard St Germain. It was a beautiful, sunlit, summer day. The *fermeture annuelle* signs were out in force and Paris was bathed in its magical August tranquillity. Kenny, at fifty-nine, looked spry and relaxed and his conversation was regularly punctuated by the famous Klook grin and that curious, childlike chuckle-cum-giggle. We talked about many things. Kenny was in a philosophical, reflective mood. His was the demeanour of a man who had arrived where he wanted to be, who enjoyed the legacy of his memories and who was content to be making his music on the sidelines of jazz and to have the comfort and security of his home and family. His political and social comments had none of the militancy that had manifested itself in earlier years; Klook had mellowed considerably.

At this particular time he had been rehearsing with his trio – organist Eddie Louiss and guitarist Jimmy Gourley – in the Club St Germain in the nearby rue St Benoît, the club he had first played in a quarter of a century earlier. Klook's trio was in the middle of a three-week engagement and was playing to packed houses.

What follows is a distillation of our conversation, which I opened with a hugely profound remark to the effect that playing with a trio must be a very different proposition from playing in the Clarke–Boland Big Band. I then asked Klook if he was sad that the band no longer existed.

KC Frankly (*characteristic, giggling chuckle*), no. I don't feel sorry it's over. It was good while it lasted, but nothing lasts for ever – and I think the band died when Derek Humble died. Sometimes you don't realize the importance of people until they are gone – then you feel their influence on the band. The moment they are missing, you feel the emptiness. Derek was like that – not only was his playing superb, but he was a great character. He had a beautiful way of doing things. He was the leader – but we didn't realize it until he was gone.

MH Did temperamental clashes play a part in the break-up?

KC No, no. Never. There were no arguments. It was the most friendly band I've ever worked with.

MH Throughout your career you have steered clear of becoming involved in so-called 'free' music. How do you react to people who say that jazz has to become free in order to progress – that you can't keep playing in 4/4 time, for example?

KC They should learn to play 4/4 first. Jazz has become classical music. We try to play some of the old things we used to do good, really *good.* I mean you have Beethoven specialists, people who play Beethoven all their lives, the same pieces over and over again. No one ever says to them, 'Man, why don't you change your repertoire?' So they play Beethoven. OK. I play Charlie Parker. I play Thelonious Monk – and I'll be playing it all my life. The important thing is that it's well done. If you play it good, it's good.

MH Do you think some of these so-called *avant-garde* musicians are faking because, as they don't use conventional chord sequences, you can't really check them out?

KC Whatever they are doing, they are not doing it well (*chuckle*). I don't care what they do, but *do* it! Do it good! Some of them are just making a farce out of the whole thing.

MH Having been away from the source country now for seventeen years, what is your view of the state of jazz at the present time? Is it in better or worse shape than it used to be? Is it still an underprivileged music?

KC Jazz is always there – what they call jazz. In my mind it's American folklore. That's all.

MH Does it get a fair hearing?

KC You hear it all over the world (*chuckle*). What do you *want*? Anywhere on this planet you hear jazz. That's proof enough for me.

MH A lot of jazz musicians would say that they don't get a fair break.

KC Well, they are going into politics. That's not music.

MH But when you read about the way some jazz musicians have been exploited in the past, by record companies, promoters, you can understand why they are a little bitter.

KC Well, Mike, it's a case of every man for himself in a situation like that.

MH Isn't it the case, though, that jazz has always existed in an atmosphere of intolerance and injustice?

KC No. Not really. It is just American folklore. It just grew up with the times – with whatever was going on at the time. You have all this freedom music now because everyone is lax – sexually. Let it all hang out – and the music is taking that form. So whatever happens today, that's the way the music goes, because it's in the people. Music is an integral part of social life – folklore plays a major part in American life.

MH You don't give credibility to the idea of the chain gang as a stimulus to musical creativity?

KC I think it has absolutely nothing to do with it. Some of the greatest composers came from bourgeois families. Duke Ellington came from a wealthy family.

MH But not Louis Armstrong.

KC No, not Louis. But that just proves that musical creativity has no connection with social position. I have never really paid too much attention to the times we live in – we just have to accept the situation and make the best of it. We can't really do anything else. All I'm concerned about is to do what I can for my family and myself. We all have a road to travel – and I really haven't given too much thought to how I arrived on it. But if I can help somebody on the way, then so much the better. And if we get tired of the journey, we can always jump off the train (*chuckle*). The most important thing is to be free – and there are all kinds of freedoms. The most vital one is freedom of thought. You can put me in a cage. OK. Give me my flute, a book or a picture of a nice chick and I'll just sit there – and I am free. But the guy who is guarding me – *he's* not free.

I've never made a lot of money – but I've always been happy, and that's the most important thing. To wake up feeling good – and to try and stay in good health. You've got to die of something, but if you can feel good until the last day, then that's really something – not being sick or infirm and having to depend on others. Live right up until the day you go. And bam! That's what's going to happen eventually. You have to go – I don't care who you are or what you are. You have to leave. You'll never get out of this world alive!

MH You have said on many occasions that you would never go back to live in the United States.

KC The States can't offer me anything. The people over here are working for jazz, trying to do things. Over there they are only working for their pocket books. Here in Europe they really do care about the art form – the Americans don't. I stay here for art's sake, not for the money.

MH You don't have any other reasons for not wishing to go back? Discrimination, for example, or bad working conditions?

KC Let me tell you, Mike, that on my papers they say I'm white . . . whatever that means. That's the way it is. And if I tell you the truth about it, I have never experienced discrimination in the USA – not really.

MH All things being equal, if a more civilized and cultural approach to jazz prevailed in America, would you be tempted to go back?

KC Well (*chuckle*), I've done all that. I've played all the studios – I've had as good a time as any musician in New York, whoever you can think of. Even Fritz Kreisler! It's not that. It's people. There are racists on both sides of the fence. I remember when I first came to New York in the early thirties people in Harlem wouldn't go further than 110th

Street because their part of the city was the most beautiful part of New York. They used to say, 'Well, if I go south, it'll be as far as the South Ferry, but no further.' That's the way they felt about it. Lenox Avenue. Tree-lined streets – fantastic!

MH It's changed a bit since then.

KC Just like everything else.

MH When your old buddies come to Paris they keep trying to persuade you to go back to New York. They can't understand why you live over here. Do you prefer the lifestyle in France?

KC Here I enjoy a few freedoms – and freedom, as I said, is the most precious thing a man can have. Freedom of thought – freedom to do just what I want to do.

MH Do you find yourself thinking wistfully about the old days from time to time?

KC Yeah. Because those days, in the forties and fifties, were incredible. We created a different kind of music. The other musicians couldn't keep up with us. The beboppers were always ahead. We could play our own music and the other guy's music as well. But they couldn't play our stuff. That was the most intelligent jazz I ever heard.

MH Do you feel happy to be regarded as the father of modern jazz drumming?

KC Well, I never considered myself as that. It was just the way I wanted to play – and if they wanted to play along with me, fine.

MH But you pioneered a totally new approach to jazz drumming. It is only fair that you should get credit for it.

KC Listen, it doesn't mean anything, Mike. It's just the fact that there were people there at the time who appreciated what was going on. That's enough. It didn't put any money in the bank for me, but respect from your peers is much more important. The problem with many musicians today is that they are caught up in the rat race of materialism. They are thinking, 'What can I do that will be a hit – that the public will like?' Well, I always set out to give the people what *I* like. To hell with the public! You have to *believe* in what you do.

16
A Different Drummer

'La batterie est l'âme du jazz et le moteur de son évolution.'

Kenny Clarke
September 1963

Montreal, 10 March 1964

Dear Kenny,

I don't know why I should be writing to you as I'm mad as hell with you on account of having played with you again and you have completely ruined, and fucked up my ears. I can't seem to get together with my drummer after having played with the master. It sure brought back old times – I must admit, though, that I had almost forgotten how tasty drums could be until I played with you again – what with *all* of these MFs who call themselves drummers going at them as if they were going in the boxing ring.

I hadn't heard that they were trying to get me for Juan-les-Pins but it would be just great to play with you again – as a matter of fact I would take a 'cut' (but please don't tell them). I don't exactly know just what is going on but if you will tell the organizers to write me personally I'm sure we could work out some deal – these fucking agents are always trying to pressure the promoters into taking the whole package from their office when they want one particular artist (they're still up to their same old shit) . . .

Are you seriously thinking of making a trip back here? I don't know what for because all of the groovy cats eventually come to Europe – tho' I'd be most happy to see you.

I almost left that cymbal with you, since you gassed me so much. But I thought I'd get the 'man' to send you a whole set and you would be cool for a long time . . .

Take care of yourself because you are the 'Last of the Mohicans'. Let me hear from you when you get the chance. I received a letter from Don Byas, what a surprise. I answered it last week.

May God bless you, your man always,

Dizzy

1365, St Nicholas Ave
Apt. 30 – S
NYC, NY
9 November 1964

Hello Klook –

I just want you to know that working with you is the most beautiful experience that I have had in many years.

I do hope that it can happen again soon.

Sincerely,
J.J. Johnson

25 January 1974

Dear Kenny,

I still think you are the greatest drummer in the whole world, and I think of you often. You are sorely missed here. I hope you are well and happy.

I hope to see you one of these days, and hopefully to play with you.

Have a great 1974!

Fondly,
Dick Katz

Kenny,

This is a hell of a way to meet you, but fortunately I met Jerri and now I can get to you. Please keep on doing that thing. Give all of us the pleasure of hearing you. You are the baddest one who ever did it.

You are too much.

Grady Tate

PS. The greatest compliment I've ever received was from J.J., who said, 'Damn, man, you sure sound a lot like Klook!'

These four letters are typical of the feelings of most musicians who played with Kenny Clarke. And their preservation in Kenny's personal archive is consistent with his oft-repeated philosophy that what mattered primarily was not pleasing the critics, nor even the public, but winning the respect and approval of his fellow musicians. It was from that source that he drew the most abiding satisfaction as a musician.

Klook's visiting card read, 'Kenny Clarke – musician', and in a way, that really said it all. He was indeed a consummate musician. But just what was it about Klook's playing that set him apart from other top-ranking jazz drummers? What exactly was it that made him the man who transformed the development of modern jazz drumming? What, in short, made Kenny Clarke a different drummer?

One immediate observation that comes to mind is that I

have never seen anybody quite so poised, composed, effortlessly balanced and so much at home behind a set of drums. As for Kenny's technical approach, Alan Dawson, a highly accomplished drummer himself and a long-time drum teacher, says:

> I would call Kenny the link between the swing era and the bop era – the line runs from Jo Jones straight to Kenny Clarke. I believe his biggest contribution was kind of freeing up the bass drum a little more. Jo Jones had liberated it a little, but actually to incorporate the bass drum as a voice rather than an underlying constant 4/4 type of thing – as was the case with most drummers prior to Kenny – was something that Klook pioneered.
>
> In addition, Kenny's cymbal rhythm was the kind where the emphasis seemed to be right on 1-2-3-4 – he was playing the notes between 2 and 4 and, actually, he was even turning the beat around; but you hardly heard that aspect. There wasn't much emphasis put on those notes between 2 and 4. What you heard was more, 1-2-to3-4 to1-2-to3-4.
>
> Apart from his technical innovations, Kenny was also known, of course, for his tasteful playing behind other people and for his very creative solo approach which was largely snare-drum-orientated. He didn't use tom toms much at all. Most of his solos concentrated on snare drum and bass drum. He was also renowned for that deep, beautiful snare-drum sound he had – I think his snare drum was pretty deep, maybe a 14″ × 7″ or even 14″ × 8″. That was one of the things I was always able to recognize: Kenny Clarke's snare-drum sound. And he had an approach to solos that involved using the rudiments, though in a kind of updated way – not at all march-sounding, but using standard drum rudiments such as the three-stroke ruff, flams and little, short roll patterns.

Roy Haynes endorses Alan Dawson's observation on Klook's cymbal technique: 'Klook would be playing single beats, but you'd get a continuity. You still got the feeling of *ding-ding-da-ding*.' This is what German jazz critic Joachim Berendt has described as *le son continu*.

Al Levitt says:

> Drummers used to keep time on the snare drum and use the cymbals for crashes. Then Jo Jones came along and kind of moved it away from the drum and the bass drum on to the hi-hat, playing the time, the tempo, on this. What Kenny did was to move it again – from the hi-hat to the ride cymbal, using the snare drum and bass drum to play accents.

And, interestingly, in *The Swing Era*, Gunther Schuller establishes an evolutionary link in the cymbal technique of McKinney's Cotton Pickers' drummer Cuba Austin and Klook when he refers to Austin's 'hissing, sizzling cymbal patterns'. Noting that Austin's syncopated accents complemented rather than paralleled the band's figures, Schuller adds: 'Austin, in effect, plays the kind of commenting accents that Kenny Clarke developed in the late thirties and forties. Only what Clarke did on the bass and snare drums, Austin . . . does on the cymbals.'

Kenny himself described his drum approach as co-ordinated independence. In a most felicitous analysis, published in *Jazz Hot*, he said:

> If you play the snare drum with the left hand and the hi-hat with the right, you are obliged to cross arms. Now, it's difficult to play for long in this manner and still keep suppleness. I therefore thought it preferable to maintain the tempo, firmly but lightly, with the right hand on the cymbal. The left hand on the snare (or on one of the tom toms) and the right foot on the bass-drum pedal work in close co-ordination, providing accents and syncopations which keep 'relaunching' the sections or the soloist. The hi-hat is used for making the after beat.
>
> When you play tempo on the cymbal, all is clear. This gives space to the soloist – more freedom to improvise. He can move on this tempo, stimulated by my accents on the snare and bass drum. My role is to get him off the ground fast. Once in the air, it is necessary to keep him at a good altitude and, from time to time, to lift him again. To bring him back to earth, it is necessary to make all the prescribed signals, letting him know in advance with softness and technique – without which he risks going into the stratosphere, never to be seen again!

Pianist Dick Katz, talking of Klook's cymbal sound, once said,

> He had one cymbal; it wasn't very big. We used to call it the magic cymbal because when somebody would sit in on drums and use his set, it would sound like a garbage can. But when he played it, it was like fine crystal. He kept the cymbal level like a plate and played with a short, side-to-side wrist motion. It was a very graceful thing to watch.

Although he used the bass drum a good deal for accents and was generally regarded as a pioneer of the so-called 'bomb-dropping' effect, Kenny invariably played four beats in the bar on the bass drum but, as Al Levitt remarks, 'very lightly and softly, so that it was more felt than actually heard'.

Kenny himself repudiated bomb-dropping. In an introduction to his instruction book, *Kenny Clarke on Drums*, he said:

> Time was when, to be a player in the rhythm section – primarily bass,

piano and drums – was to be regarded as the most self-effacing member of the orchestra, basically that of time-keeper, except in the eyes of other musicians. The rhythm section played a secondary role to the sections and front line. Quite to the contrary, I have found that to be able to speak with succinctness, clarity, consistency in tempo, never intruding . . . knowing that you are sincerely attempting to interpret, complement and enhance all the sections and/or soloists have to say, can be one of the most rewarding of musical experiences.

Under the guise, pretext and illusion that it is 'modern' and 'hip', many drummers commit the crime of meaningless 'bomb-dropping'. Though, to them, they are helping to 'kick' the band, for the most part it is mere intrusion. For foremost in every drummer's mind should be his functioning role: to listen and apply a steady, swinging tempo and beat, and then, with well-chosen consideration, his timely punctuations.

A drummer must use his wits as well as his wrists. Fills should be motivated and related to what is happening in an arrangement and statement – not thrown in haphazardly. Too, they should be executed in good taste, with colour and punctuation, and with concern for what precedes and follows the fill.

. . . I am in complete accord with Max Roach, Jo Jones and the late Denzil Best, among others, all of whom attempt to learn as much as possible about a number, including lyrics and harmonies, before attempting to play it. To have some idea of what a composer had in mind is to afford yourself a more compatible and intelligent reading of the piece, thus making it possible to bring into play all your technical abilities in a most meaningful way.

As I have noted earlier, Kenny's musical innovations were in the process of development long before the Minton's era. He told Les Tomkins in a *Crescendo* interview in August 1968:

At all times I was striving to change drum patterns. I think the drummer plays an integral part in beautifying a musical performance . . . when I took up drums, when I was about seventeen, I felt that musicianship was what was lacking in drumming . . . Drummers were hung up with the feeling that they had to keep a steady 4/4 rhythm going all the time . . . There was a lot that could be done to try to ornament or garnish what was going on with the music, to complement the soloist, and things like that. There's a lot to be done *yet*.

It was a hard job at first. I've been chucked out of more bands than I wish to name! There was quite a bit of opposition to my ideas. It seems to be the history of man. Any innovation fuels opposition.

When I met up with Dizzy, Bird, Monk and Tadd Dameron, and we worked together at Minton's, that was a revelation. Now everything I had been striving towards became possible. Finally, I had found musicians with whom I could play on equal terms.

Undoubtedly Kenny's wealth of experience in the early part

of his career was invaluable in his developing a new vocabulary for drums. He remarked in a *Melody Maker* interview with me in November 1964, 'Youngsters today don't have the chance to get the broad experience I had. Playing for vaudeville is a great training for drummers. You can learn a lot from dancers. But it's a lost art now.'

In the thirties, Kenny also derived inspiration from Fort Worth drummer Ray McKinley when he was with the Dorsey Brothers Orchestra. Klook told Ira Gitler, 'I used to buy all his records. I started copying his things and playing them, little eight-bar phrases and things like that – I'd fit them in. That's when I started the style of playing along with the brass.'

In the same 1964 interview, I asked Kenny Clarke to name the musicians he would choose to record with if he had the pick of the world's talent. This is what he said:

> First I'd pick Diz and make him the leader. Then I'd have John Lewis or Hank Jones on piano. Lewis is one of the funkiest musicians you've ever heard. Some day he's gonna come back and show everyone how funky he is. He has a very deep feeling and I'm sure he has his tongue in his cheek at the moment.
>
> On vibes – Bags. The greatest vibes player who ever touched a mallet. I studied the vibes once – but when I heard Milt Jackson I gave it up. Ray Brown on bass – the greatest – Jimmy Heath on tenor. He's one of the most underrated musicians around. And Sonny Stitt on alto. That would be some band.

On the subject of drumming inspiration, Kenny left these thoughts among his papers:

> The four great drummers I heard when I was coming up were Jo Jones, Big Sid Catlett, Cozy Cole and Walter Johnson – Jo for his devil-may-care attitude, but always correct; Big Sid for his timing and dynamics; Cozy for his easy approach to musical problems and Walter for his sureness.

In particular Kenny thought that Big Sid was 'years ahead of his time'.

In later years he developed a high regard for Woody Herman's drummer, Dave Tough: 'He could really drive a band. He kept tempo and he knew how to be an accompanist.' In various interviews I had with him over the years Klook also had a number of pertinent observations about some other fellow drummers:

Max Roach: Max is one of the few who tries to get a musical sound out of the drums – he's really the only one I know who tries to draw music out of the drums and doesn't get distracted by displays of unnecessary technique. He has the best sound of any drummer I know. He really has a feel for the drums.

Art Blakey: He's from Pittsburgh, too, but five years younger than me. His father was my barber. He'd often come to hear me play and we talked a lot about drums. When he joined the Billy Eckstine band in 1944, that's when he changed his style. Dizzy and Billy taught him to play like me. Dizzy said to him, 'Play like Klook.' So he began to play in my style – but in his own way. Blakey is really unique.

Connie Kay: Before he joined the Modern Jazz Quartet he was one of the best drummers in New York. I can't say the same now, I'm sorry to say. He became a percussionist rather than a drummer.

Baby Dodds: I heard him when I was living in New York, but that was not my idea of playing drums.

Gene Krupa: A wonderful musician. He used to play for the shows – doing the kind of work I like to do – and I've liked him ever since.

Albert Heath: The most studious drummer I know. He does a fine job.

Jo Jones: He's an old master.

Tony Williams: He's too young to know [this was November 1964 – Williams was eighteen]. He can't know. When I was his age I had Big Sid and vaudeville to help me – and I still had a long way to go. Tony has a world of things to learn. Star overnight? That sort of thing does young drummers more harm than good. These guys are getting – I suppose – two or three hundred dollars a week. When I was with Roy Eldridge I would make fifty cents a night – and I'd still be yelled at and scolded. But it gave me the incentive to play better and earn more.

Simplicity was a major virtue in Kenny's eyes. Al Levitt recalls that on the early records Klook made with Miles Davis and Horace Silver, he did not even use a tom tom: 'He just has snare drum, bass drum, ride cymbal and crash cymbal. I don't think he used tom toms until he joined the MJQ.'

One of Kenny's favourite remarks when it came to music was: 'The beauty is in the simplicity.' And in an interview he and Max Roach did for French television, he said that he approached drums by looking always for the simplest solution. That, he said, was a well-established American tradition.

And, of course, swing was paramount. He told Michael Haggerty, 'When I start to play, my concern is to find the way that we can swing the most. Even if the soloist is bad, we still have to swing.'

Kenny used to say that the rhythm section of an orchestra is like the foundations of a house: 'If the foundations are good, the house will stand; if the rhythm section is strong and coherent, the orchestra will have a chance to play well. No band is greater than its drummer – but that doesn't, of course, mean that the drummer has to dominate.'

In *Jazz, Its Evolution and Essence*, André Hodeir wrote:

> There can be no doubt . . . that the rhythmic imagination of Kenny Clarke stimulated the melodic genius of his partners . . . Anyone who has seen someone like Kenny Clarke from close up and in the heat of action, must have realized how carefully the great modern drummers listen to the soloist in order to create for him a rhythmic counterpoint.

'Above all,' as Klook used often to say, '*listen!*' And he took his own good advice. This, plus his gifts of time, swing, sensitivity, technical accomplishment, integrity and dedication made him . . . a different drummer – the perfect jazz drummer.

The last word, though, should go to his great friend Dizzy Gillespie who, in a television tribute to Art Blakey, observed that, in his view, Blakey was the volcano of the drums, Max Roach 'the painter who put the colours together', but Kenny Clarke, quite simply, was the 'godfather of the drums'.

17
Pride and Prejudice

Although he came from a tall family – his brothers and half-brothers were all six-footers – Kenny was small in stature, measuring 5ft 5ins. 'They used to call me the runt,' he would say with a grin. But what he lacked in physical size, he more than made up for in moral stature. And he had undeniable charisma. 'Charm' is a much debased word, but Kenny possessed this quality in its most natural, uncontrived sense. He radiated goodwill, good nature and affability, an impression reinforced by his predilection for tweed jackets and pipes.

He had quite a collection of English Peterson pipes, including a Sherlock Homles-style *meerschaum*. He was also a collector of cigarette lighters and watches. 'He had at least ten watches,' Daisy Clarke recalls, 'and he really treasured them.' The fact that, on an impulse, he gave one of his collection to Quincy Jones is a reflection of Klook's high regard for Quincy.

There is no doubt that his marriage to Daisy, the arrival of his son Laurent, upon whom he doted, and the peaceful security and comfort of his little house in Montreuil-sous-Bois, all contributed to a mellowing process. He became increasingly philosophical as he got older and the bitterness that had driven him into exile was largely dissipated.

He told Gudrun Endress of *Jazz Podium*:

> People like me do not make much money. But I have accepted that. I know what counts in life for me. I know I can be happy and I can have a nice home and enjoy a happy family life without a lot of money. I have everything that is important to me. What more could I buy with money? If

I had to choose between a lot of money and music, I would prefer to stay poor for the rest of my life than be without music.

I have often played with an empty stomach and was still very happy to play. I think it was fate that I have accomplished everything that I wanted and I am very happy and content with the results of my work.

Kenny had long since reconciled himself to the fact that playing jazz drums with commitment, integrity and a determination not to sell out to easy popularity was not likely to make him rich. But it did not prevent him from adopting a tough bargaining stance with promoters and agents. In fact, the exploitation of musicians by the jazz businessmen in the United States was a most important factor in his decision to leave the country and it continued to incense him for many years afterwards. He told Helen Oakley Dance in 1977 that, after the argument with Milt Shaw during the European tour of the Gillespie big band in 1948, the agents said to him, 'You'll never work in New York again.' And Kenny added, 'It's still going on today. Granz and Wein never hire me. But I just laugh at them you know, because I say, "I need you guys like a hole in the head. If you fellows are paying the same wages you're paying in America, I can't use it."'

Kenny recalled playing in the States the previous year and working the Jazz Showcase in Chicago with Al Haig.

I talked things over with the boss of the club and he said, 'Look, Kenny, I can only give you $250 a night.' I said, 'Well, don't worry about it – that's OK.' And after I finished the job at the Showcase, I went to Boston and they offered me $50 a night to play in Storyville. Joe Newman's wife was running the club and when I said 'no' to the money she said to me, 'But Kenny, everybody gets $50 a night.' I told her I wouldn't go round the corner for $50. I said, 'I've been in Paris for twenty years and I've never worked for that kind of money since I've been over there, so I'm not coming back home to work for $50 a night.'

Later I found out that George Wein owned Storyville. So he sees me at the Palais de Chaillot in Paris some time later and he says, 'When you come to New York, I'll give you a job.' I told him, 'I don't want a job, I don't need a job – and please don't offer me a job.' And that was the end of that. They never offered my anything – and I'm glad about it.

Nathan Davis confirms that while Klook was not in the least mercenary and a long way from being financially ambitious, he nevertheless 'knew how to ask for good money'. It was not the money itself that was paramount, but the need to strike a blow for the dignity and self-respect of the jazz musician and, perhaps, to retaliate, to effect a little retribution for the years of exploitation.

Davis recalls an occasion when Kenny showed that he could be a tough negotiator when the need arose.

> At the time I was working with Kenny at the Blue Note. Klook had got to know the Warner Bros chief, Jack Warner, pretty well. His daughter used to come to the club very often. Well, Warner were preparing to make a movie in France and there was a French guy – I can't remember his name – who was hired to put the band together to make the soundtrack. He came to see Kenny in the Blue Note and he said, 'I want you for this film, Kenny. How much is your fee?' Kenny mentioned a figure, and it was too much for the French guy. 'Oh, no,' he said, 'that's far too much. We'll hire a French drummer.' And Klook, completely unruffled, said, 'OK – if that's what you want, that's what you get.'
>
> Some nights later Jack Warner came into the club with a bunch of people. At the break Kenny went over to their table and joined the party. After some general conversation, one of Warner's associates said, 'Oh, Kenny, while I think of it – perhaps you can help me. We have this problem with the music – it just doesn't sound right.' And Kenny said, 'Well, I'm not on the film but if I can help you out I'll be glad to.' At this, Jack Warner intervened and asked, 'What do you mean, you're not on the date?' And he turned to the cat next to him and said, 'How come Kenny isn't on the date? Just tell that French fixer I want Kenny – no wonder the music isn't right!'
>
> The next night the French fixer comes in, looking more than a little sheepish. He sits at a table on his own, orders a Perrier and waits for intermission. Kenny has already spotted him, and he looks up at me with a slow smile and says, 'Nate, I got his ass now.'
>
> At the break the guy approaches Kenny, smiles a wan, sickly smile and says, 'Kenny, I've been thinking it over and, well, we'll pay what you ask.'
>
> 'Uh, uh,' says Kenny, shaking his head. 'Now the fee is double.'
>
> 'But, Kenny, be reasonable – there's no way I can make that.'
>
> 'Double,' Kenny repeated, 'and you better hurry before I double it again.' And, of course, the guy paid up.

Kenny Clarke's was a complex personality and there could be some puzzling inconsistencies in his responses. Nowhere was this apparent ambiguity more in evidence that in his comments on racial questions. He seemed to shift his ground at various times and, again, he would adjust his militancy level according to his audience. I have referred earlier to his identifying much more closely with the Black Power movement when he was interviewed by Arthur Taylor than he did on other occasions.

In the Taylor interview, recorded in August 1971 for *Notes and Tones*, Clarke offered a bleak prognostication for the future of black people. Asked what his future plans were he replied,

> There's very little to be done now because the music has gotten into the wrong hands. Musicians everywhere are sitting home by the telephone waiting for a white man to call them for a gig and I don't see any future in that. I've been playing the drums for forty years and the only future I see in our music is for black people to have their own thing going; otherwise it's no use.

Kenny maintained that in the twenties and thirties musicians had more control over the music. But then, he said,

> The Jewish people bought them out. When I started out, black people had their own publishing companies, their own dancehalls and they did their own booking, because no one wanted to touch jazz. White people thought it was the music of savages and so they didn't want to be bothered with it. The Jews found out it was a goldmine and they took it over, bought the black people out and bought a lot of their souls along with it.
>
> By the late thirties it was all over. That's why fine people like Teddy Hill quit playing music. Teddy quit as a bandleader because Moe Gale, Billy Shaw and all those people wanted to tell him who to have in his band, where he was going to work and why he was going to work. He had nothing to say, so he quit. I'll probably wind up following in Teddy's footsteps. I hope in another five years' time I can say I don't want to play any more.

(Klook echoed this disenchantment with the music business when I interviewed him two years later for *Melody Maker*, the conversation that forms the basis of Chapter 15. He said, 'I think I can go on for another five or six years, then I'll give it up. I want to give it up. I'm tired.')

Kenny told Arthur Taylor that he could see no way that the adverse conditions in which black musicians were obliged to work would be improved:

> You can't backtrack. In the first place, black people haven't got enough money to do it. In the second place, they haven't the leadership they had in those days. To join a band then was like going to school. Nowadays bands don't exist. As far as the black man is concerned, I don't see any future for him in the United States or in any other white country. There's future for a black man only with his own. If some intelligent black Americans went back to Nigeria, Kenya or Ethiopia to form their own record companies, then I could see progress. But there is no future in the white man's world because every black musician today is waiting for the

white man to call him to give him a job. Even if it's a black musician who gives you a job, it's through another white musician or a white manager who hired him to hire you. It's a vicious cycle.

As fast as you create something, white so-called musicians take it away from you and exploit it because they have the money and the means of communication to do it. They have radio, television, records, and they pass off everything you create as their own. They know that if they expose it on television, everyone will think a white man created it, because they'll never let the black man expose the music that he created in the different media of communication they have invented . . . That's why I don't see any future for black musicians in a white world.

Jimmy Gourley recalls a conversation with Kenny over dinner at Kenny's home one evening which testifies to Klook's sensitivity on racial matters.

We got into conversation about what happened to Kenny during his army service. It seems he had had some really bad experiences in the army. I said to him that he would know more about that than me 'because you're black and I'm white'. For some reason he took this as a racist remark – although I was only trying to indicate that I was aware that blacks were discriminated against in the army just as they were in civilian life.

The next day at rehearsal Kenny was real angry and for about three or four days after that he was in a bad mood. He'd seen my remark as a put-down. 'What did you mean by that crack?' he said. I couldn't figure it out, because he'd known me for years by this time and he should have known the way in which the remark was meant. 'OK,' I told him in the end, 'fire me.' But he kept me on. The only thing was that later he gave Eddie Louiss a raise but not me! Mostly, though, he struck me as someone who was always fair on racial issues. But I guess he'd seen hard times in America and that maybe stayed with him and sometimes coloured his open-mindedness.

I have a feeling that he sometimes came down on me a little harder when I goofed musically because I was white. But that was OK – I can accept my failings. And Kenny was a giant.

In an interview published in the *Atlanta Voice*, Kenny made the following observation about the exploitation of the black people by the whites:

In the US the whites try to keep the black man down because they fear the black man and view him as an arch-enemy. In America, black doesn't refer to colour, but to status . . . Europeans are more sure of themselves than American whites, which allows Afro-Americans more freedom to express themselves.

Annie Ross was unequivocal when I asked her what would really make Kenny angry. 'The white race,' she said without hesitation. 'He used to feel that the white people had stolen his music. He was quite militant about it – militant enough to become a Muslim, change his name and get out of the country. He had a very hard time – he'd been ripped off time and time again.'

Among the papers that Kenny left behind was the following handwritten note: 'Ask every so-called "white" musician if he's on the back of a black, and the answer would be so startling that he'd probably throw his horn or his sticks in the East River and run like a thief should.'

The deep-rooted bitterness in all these observations about discrimination and exploitation must be seen in the context of a man who was exposed to racial prejudice and injustice – like the vast majority of black people in the United States – from early childhood.

Kenny has said that one of his early recollections was of going to school in Pittsburgh at the age of twelve with a white girl called Ethel Kramer, the daughter of a German immigré who was a blacksmith. Kenny's grandfather had a couple of mules and Kramer used to shoe them. He treated Kenny with kindness and Kenny just couldn't understand it. He used to ask himself, 'Why is this man so nice to me? Every place else I go, white people are just the opposite.' He was confused. Said Kenny,

> I hadn't met people like Kramer before – everyone else was so hostile. But Kramer taught his daughter to be nice to everyone and not to look down on black people. He was just not capable of being mean. He was a God-fearing man who believed in humanity. Ethel would ask me in to have tea and her father would talk to me and ask how I was getting on in school. I'll always remember his kindness – it stays in my mind because it was a unique experience for a black kid.

It is quite clear that Kenny Clarke tended, when he spoke to white people, to adopt a much less rancorous position on the question of racism. When I asked him about the exploitation of musicians in the 1973 interview, Kenny went out of his way to be non-controversial, contesting my comment that jazz had always existed in an atmosphere of intolerance and injustice.

And in an interview with *Down Beat*'s Burt Korall, published in December 1965, Kenny said:

> Something unhealthy is happening to jazz in America. I hear a lot about Crow Jim, reverse segregation . . . How can any musician in his right mind put down Stan Getz and people like that? It's a bunch of you know what. [In those days editors balked at using the word 'shit' in print – though that is undoubtedly the word Klook used.] One race can learn from another. No one race has everything. This attitude could do jazz a lot of damage.

Korall commented:

> Clarke was angry, no doubt about it. He looked around the café (in Paris, opposite the Club St Germain) and then exploded: 'I may be put down for this . . . but I must admit that I'm not interested in allying myself with causes. I'm a Negro; I know what's happening. I don't turn my back on the realities because I'm 3,000 miles away. I do what *I* can as I move through my life. But . . . as far as I'm concerned, it's the music that's important. That's the legacy we leave behind.'

It would be easy to conclude from these contrasting attitudes that, in his conversations with white journalists, Kenny Clarke was being disingenuous and playing down his disgust at racism and exploitation in order to come across as an easy-going, good-natured moderate. Certainly it has been my experience that, when they are aware that their comments are to be published, many black musicians soft-pedal their antagonism to discrimination. After all, they have to make their living in a white-dominated society and, as a matter of simple expediency, it makes sense not to be perceived as being perpetually consumed with hostility towards white people.

There may have been an element of Machiavellian thinking in Kenny's muted response to questions about racism from white journalists – but it really doesn't square with the frankness with which he spoke to Arthur Taylor, knowing that his comments were to find their way into a book.

My feeling is that Kenny genuinely wanted to spare our feelings, that he was sensitive to the possible discomfort we might feel if he talked about our race and its crimes against black humanity in the same way as he would talk to his fellow blacks. I realize that this may appear to be a naïve interpretation – but such a response is totally in keeping with Kenny's character. And I do not regard it as deceitful or evidence of a lack of moral courage. Some might see the reaction as pusillanimous; but I prefer to regard it as an indication of Kenny

Clarke's well-known consideration for others. I would concede, however, that it could also have had something to do with his tendency to seek the least troublesome solution.

Writer Bob Houston remembers an occasion in Cologne when Hank Mobley was sounding off in fiercely abusive style about the evil proclivities of the white race. Houston, the only white man in a room full of black musicians, was interviewing Kenny at the time. He told me, 'When Mobley started his tirade, Kenny got up from the table, strode across to him, grabbed him by the arm, and gave him a most abrasive talking to. I don't know what he said – but there was not another word from Mobley. I never saw Kenny so angry. Later Mobley apologized to me.'

Except for Houston's presence, Klook might well have applauded Mobley's diatribe – though, of course, if Houston hadn't been there, it would have been somewhat redundant. But I see his response to the incident as being civilized and considerate, not equivocal.

If there was an element of character weakness in Kenny's silencing Mobley while probably endorsing the sentiments, then I would argue with Oliver Goldsmith that 'we must touch his weaknesses with a delicate hand. There are some faults so nearly allied to excellence, that we can scarce weed out the fault without eradicating the virtue.'

For all his genuine hatred of racial discrimination, Kenny Clarke was not completely innocent of racial prejudice himself. His remarks to Arthur Taylor about the Jews taking over the jazz goldmine were not entirely free of prejudice and Nathan Davis, who was close to him for many years, recalls that Kenny – though himself married to a Jewish woman – could sometimes make deprecating remarks 'those old Jew boys'. Of course, prejudice inevitably breeds prejudice, and black people as a whole can hardly be condemned if they harbour resentment towards the white race. What is rather more surprising is Davis's recollection of hearing Kenny, the Muslim, making sotto-voce anti-Arab remarks when the Blue Note was visited by a group of Saudi Arabians. Klook referred to them as 'Goddam camel-drivers'.

Essentially, Kenny Clarke was a man who opted for the quiet life. His main concern throughout his professional career was to be allowed to do what he loved best: to play jazz with musicians he respected and who respected him. He did not seek to make a lot of money from music – though he could be quite fiercely militant if he felt that he or his musicians were being underpaid. Neither did he expect to be a 'big star'. Even though he was universally acknowledged as one of the greatest and most influential drummers in jazz, he never thought of himself as a giant.

As I have noted earlier, Kenny's attitudes, observations and recollections were not always consistent – partly because he certainly mellowed as he grew older and partly because he would talk less candidly to some people than others. But throughout the conversations, interviews and articles I have analysed, and in notes Kenny himself left behind, there is one part of his personal philosophy that is unerringly constant. He played not for the public but for his fellow musicians. He told Gudrun Endress of the German magazine *Jazz Podium* in December 1976:

> I play for the musicians who are standing in front of me. Those are the first people I want to please. If I please them, I am very happy – extremely happy; and the rest of it doesn't count to me. If someone sitting in the audience happens to like what I'm doing, so much the better. But if a trumpet player or a saxophone player likes it, it pleases me much more. When musicians turn around and say, 'Kenny, that was wonderful,' that is the high point of my evening.
>
> It's trying to please the musicians who work with me that has kept me in the profession – not the public . . . The public don't know. They are like a lot of sheep. What the radio and the magazines and the trade papers say, they believe. You can't depend on them – the public are very fickle. I have always thought this way. I never tried to please the public. It's futile . . . It's the same with composition – most audiences are like eight-year-olds; but when a musician sits down to write a piece of music, he doesn't aim at eight-year-olds. First he thinks about the musicians who are going to play the piece – because they must understand the music. If they don't understand the music then there is no point in composing it in the first place.

It is ironic that Kenny Clarke's dedicated professionalism, his serious, assiduous approach to his craft and his quiet dignity actually militated against his enjoying a level of public and critical appreciation consonant with his outstanding musicianship. He did not affect the wilful eccentricities that characterized many of his peers. He was a sober, balanced, calm and unpretentious man without delusions of grandeur. He expected to be treated with respect – he detested exploitation of man by man, especially when it was white exploiting black – but he did not seek the fawning deference that many celebrities seem constantly to need as a reaffirmation of their splendour.

He was a far more humble man than most great jazz musicians. It is difficult to imagine Miles Davis, Dizzy Gillespie or Thelonious Monk settling for the relative obscurity of an eight-year residency at the Paris Blue Note. But as Kenny told François Postif,

> I never tried to become a celebrity. I wanted to be a musician and to please musicians. To be an accompanist – that's my greatest ambition. It is not the role of a drummer to be a star. Drummers who have made concessions to easy popularity with the public have only had fleeting success. If you tell a drummer, 'Man, you're great!' then he tends to forget his proper role and starts to play for the public. He is ruined in advance because there will come a time when the other musicians don't want to play with him any more.

That comment says a great deal about Kenny Clarke and it explains why so many musicians loved to play with him. Later, he was to take Miles Davis and even his great friend Dizzy Gillespie to task because of what he considered to be their unprofessional attitude to the public. He told Michael Haggerty in 1982:

> The last time Miles came over, he kind of let them [the French audiences] down. That hurt me to my heart. You know, he wasn't the Miles who made *'L'Ascenseur pour l'Echafaud'*. He let everyone down. I didn't see him the last time he was here. I'll tell you the truth – I didn't want to be let down either. Because my conception of Miles is something fantastic. I guess it's like seeing someone make a 360-degree change. So I thought it best for me not to listen to him – because it wouldn't be the inventive Miles like the records he made in the fifties. I knew it wouldn't be anything like that.

Kenny said he felt it a shame that Miles couldn't adhere to the integrity of his earlier music – like Dizzy Gillespie had.

It lasted a while, then it faded in Miles. He couldn't keep it, grasp it and hold it. You know, like Diz. I think that if you hear Diz today and you heard him twenty years ago, you can still hear it. Some of the things that you like best that he does and he still does them – which is great. Miles just seemed to fade right out. . . . At the first Paris Jazz Festival, Miles came and he was something unbelievable. Really, to hear him today, you wouldn't believe it. You'd think it was two different people.

Kenny also criticized Miles's 'I don't care' attitude in a later interview with me: 'Miles is not respected now by serious musicians – they don't like him not announcing tune titles and walking off stage when he's not playing.'

And while he always respected Dizzy Gillespie's sterling musicanship, he claimed that Dizzy, too, had lost the respect of his fellow musicians because of his public attitude, his tendency to clown it up on stage and to perpetrate that cynically mischievous Dizzy trick of mimicking the kind of Uncle Tom performance that both he and Kenny despised. Dizzy is, of course, actually delivering a swipe at white prejudice when he Toms on stage – but Klook always felt it was damaging to the music, satire or not.

Kenny Clarke took his music very seriously. He was justly proud to be a custodian of the rich American jazz heritage and he was always at pains to see that jazz was given credit as a vital and esoteric art form. He was not, however, pompous about the music – it was totally foreign to his nature to be bombastic or pretentious. And if he took jazz seriously, he wasn't solemn about it. He believed that music should be fun and should promote joy and happiness in both performer and listener. You had only to watch Klook playing drums to see the exhilaration he derived from making music. And you only had to be with him for a few moments to learn that always, just beneath the serious surface, was a hair-trigger sense of humour. Kenny believed that life was for living and laughing.

Quincy Jones recalls a piquant example of Klook's humour from his sojourn in Paris in the fifties. Kenny, with a lady friend, was in conversation with a group of musicians during intermission at the Club St Germain. Drummer Kansas Fields was making an emphatic point and he used a four-letter word. Kenny grabbed him by the arm, fixed him with a menacing

142 bis, Rue de Rosny
93100 Montreuil
Tél. 287 18-53

BANDS I'VE PLAYED WITH OVER MY [redacted] 40 YEARS OF MUSIC

GENE JENKINS ✓
GEORGE HORNSBY
JACK SPRUCE
ROY ELDRIDGE *
SHADENA WALKER
LEROY BRADLEY *
FRANK STOEFFER
JETER-PILLARS *
LONNIE SIMMONS ✓
EDGAR HAYES *
CLAUDE HOPKINS *
TEDDY HILL *
ELLA FITZGERALD *
LOUIS ARMSTRONG *
BENNY CARTER *
ROGER BOYD
DIZZY GILLESPIE *
QUINCY JONES *
PHINEAS NEWBORN *
CLARKE-BOLAND BAND **

TADD DAMERON *
KAI WINDING *
MILES DAVIS *
COLEMAN HAWKINS *
HARRY EDISON *
STAN GETZ *
RED ALLEN *
LENNIE TRISTANO *
TONY SCOTT ✓
HAZEL SCOTT *
TONY PROTEAU *
BERNARD HILDA *
OSCAR PETTIFORD *
J.J. JOHNSON *
MODERN JAZZ Q' *
CHARLIE MINGUS *
JACQUES HÉLIAN *
LESTER YOUNG

Klook's list of the bands he played with in his long career. The significance of the ticks and asterisks is not known

look and rasped, 'Hey, motherfucker – don't be cursing in front of my bitch!'

Kenny was a methodical keeper of diaries, in which he recorded his gigs and record dates, usually with a note of the fee. After his move from New York to Paris, the entries become progressively more Gallic – evidence that Kenny made a sustained effort to speak, and think in, the language of his adopted country.

Observations in the diaries are few – but sometimes very revealing of Klook's character. On 25 September 1956, just twelve days after his arrival in Paris, Kenny wrote: '*Prend bain chaud au Claridge. Bien fait. Voilà*!'

Among the entries of gigs with the Jacques Hélian Orchestra would be an occasional comment, mostly when the music hadn't pleased him too much. He would simply write, 'Awful!' And on one occasion, stricken with influenza, Kenny wrote in his diary, '*La grippe. Merde*.' When he was sick in Copenhagen in 1959, there was a succession of entries reading, '*malade comme un fou*'.

An entry for 3 June 1958, when he was resident at the Club St Germain, read, 'Jamming with Diz, Sonny Stitt, Richard Davis, Ronnie Bright *et al.* Crazy!!!!!'

Sometimes there were entries like, '*N'oublie pas le Petit Klook*' (a reference to his son, Toby) and, on 20 December 1960, four days before Toby's tenth birthday, Kenny wrote, 'Send money to Petit Klook.'

Kenny was a considerable seeker after knowledge, a prodigious reader and, in his own quiet way, a philosopher. Among his personal papers were many thoughtful and perceptive observations about life. There were papers on which, to broaden his vocabulary, he had noted down definitions of various words: inveigh, profligate, pragmatic, invective, acquisitive.

And there were pages on which he had jotted down random thoughts, sentimental and cynical, about music, life and politics. Here are some of them:

> I am a truly civilized man. If you don't believe me, ask the man who knows me . . . *L'homme est formé par la souffrance* (Suffering makes the man).

European civilization is not original like the African and Asian civilizations. The civilization in Europe is a little of all the great ones. Whereas African and Asian civilizations are unique within themselves.

Atomic bomb? Yes, the Jew discovered it, and the Christian dropped it! That's proof positive.

A Language to Express One's Self

We express ourselves with a language, be it English, French, Swahili or the like. Sometimes we quote philosophers great or small. But, we do not quote the written word every time we speak. Most of the time we try to express ourselves according to our feelings. We may speak in anger, or love, or sorrow, but what we feel is not written. We're improvising. The words just seem to fall into place as we speak. So it is with music. The language of music. Some learn to speak the language by studying the so-called masters – Beethoven, Mozart, Bach and lots of others called masters – and yet some speak the written word every time they speak. There must be some kind of written speech before them, or they cannot speak. Can they not speak as they feel? Have they nothing to say for themselves? Jazz music (improvisation) is the answer. Freedom of speech, in which one can express one's self in his own manner, to say what's in his heart musically. We call this improvisation – on a theme usually, or on a group of chords or chord structures.

Evolutionary Cycles

The cycles in the Spenglerian evolution of a civilization:

A Spring Phase, giving birth to a new religion and world outlook.

A Summer Phase, culminating in philosophical and mathematical conceptualizations.

An Autumn Phase, maturing into 'enlightenment' and rationalism.

A Winter Phase, declining into materialism, a cult of science, and degradation of abstract thinking, leading to senility and death.

Music

As we all know, our music (American jazz) made such intelligent strides in the late thirties through the late fifties. To such an extent that our 'white' rivals were not capable of comprehension. At that time we were coaxed back to a simpler form of music called 'rock and roll', which these people could easily understand. Then after we made this simpler form of music popular, they stepped in and took it with their money. We must be vigilant of these attacks upon our creative ability. In referring to music, I refer to all the sciences, arts and sports. *Take heed!* This is my signal to all our inventors and men of creative ability.

The Piano in Jazz

There are today five jazz pianists, in this order: Hank Jones, Phineas Newborn, Oscar Peterson, Tommy Flanagan, Martial Solal.

All the rest are piano players, of which we have a zillion.

Rehearsals

A piece of music is similar to childbirth or a pregnant woman. It must take time – and a considerable amount of time – before the piece really takes form and comes to life. (To my mind, some of the worst music produced today is in our recording and radio studios, where musicians try to sight-read music as fast as they can without the *moindre* [least] idea of interpretation. This is an abortive music to say the least.)

Our modern jazz orchestras should be well rehearsed weeks before a performance, be it a concert, recording or radio broadcast. In thus rehearsing, the orchestra gives the public its maximum, in every phase of its performance. A performance of ten to twelve pieces should take at least fifteen days' to three weeks' rehearsal time. Or, at least, sixteen hours for each piece. In this manner each musician understands thoroughly his *partition* [part] and, armed with this knowledge, he is capable of giving a justifiable performance. [There must be] section rehearsals, reeds, brass and rhythm alike, each in its turn, until the whole piece comes to life with the entire orchestra. Different ideas on how a passage should be played will be rampant, as it takes time for musicians to agree upon a certain interpretation. Once this is agreed upon, the music will begin to take form and the results will be gratifying.

Philosophy of the Times

Yes, folks, my generation is in power. Yep, we're out there flexing our muscles and strutting about.

And I want to tell the generation out there that's waiting to take over, may God give you the wisdom and intelligence to straighten out this awful mess.

* * *

Stereotypes and discrimination against the people of African heritage should decline with better education and helpful legislation???

It is important to get rid of deep-rooted fallacies about these people because they have deeply damaged a great percentage already. Many have resigned themselves to becoming what everyone thinks they already are. *The Power of Suggestion!*

The Rhythm Section

Speaking in terms of our music (jazz), every country needs a rhythm section, or an inner drive to survive and become great. Take Australia, for instance. It could be a great country, but it has no rhythm section. We are America's Rhythm Section. Duke Ellington saw the need for this and consequently created the world's first rhythm section.

* * *

It's autumn in my life, and when the leaves start falling, I'm not one to run up the tree and glue them back into place; and when the leaves turn brown, don't recolour them green!

* * *

It seems I hurry to do the things I *love*, and *have* to do, so that I will have more time to do nothing about the things I do not love, and don't have to do.

K.C.

18
Twilight in Montreuil

After he left the Blue Note, Kenny divided his time between concerts and record dates with the Clarke–Boland Band, gigs with his trio and teaching. It was very much in character that Klook, the master drummer, was concerned to pass on his skills, his knowledge and his vast, richly varied experience to others – whether they were full-fledged drummers like Max Roach, Roy Haynes, Billy Higgins, Louis Hayes, Al Levitt, Grady Tate and Philly Joe Jones, or complete beginners. Kenny was always ready to advise and encourage aspiring musicians and he brought to the task of teaching drums a real dedication.

In 1967 he began teaching at the St Germain-en-Laye Conservatoire. 'I started with just four pupils, but when I left five years later, we had eighty-nine students each paying $40 a seminar,' Kenny told Michael Haggerty. And, in the year that he started the drum course, Klook told me,

> Schools are really necessary because the standard of drumming today is thirty per cent worse than it was when I became a drummer. The people who teach drumming don't really understand the instrument – they haven't studied it as a whole. There are many rhythm players today who are quite satisfying to hear, but they'd be even more satisfying if they played with a more musical approach. The first principle of drumming is to find your sound then let the technique come. Once technique becomes the master it distorts the sound of the drums, then it's useless.

From the time he settled in France in 1956, Kenny had nurtured an ambition to open his own drum school. On 16 March 1967 he saw that ambition realized when, in collaboration with Dante Agostini and the Premier Drum Com-

ÉCOLE DE JAZZ

DU CONSERVATOIRE MUNICIPAL DE SAINT-GERMAIN-EN-LAYE

Directeur : J.-P. PERRAULT

Professeurs :

Kenny CLARKE — Roger GUÉRIN — Dominique CHANSON
Claude GUILHOT — Dante AGOSTINI — Patrice GALLAS

COURS DE TECHNIQUE - INTERPRÉTATION - IMPROVISATION

le dimanche, de 9 h à 12 h 30, au Conservatoire Municipal
1, rue du Maréchal-Joffre — 78 - Saint-Germain-en Laye
Tél. 963.15.48 (poste 246)

RENSEIGNEMENTS ET INSCRIPTIONS TOUS LES JOURS AUX HEURES OUVRABLES

Advertisement for the Saint-Germain-en-Laye Conservatoire where Kenny taught drums for five years

pany, he inaugurated the Kenny Clarke Drum School at the Selmer premises in Paris. The school provided tuition for students between the ages of six and twenty and one of the first to enrol was Milton Mezzrow, son of Mezz.

Kenny was a patient and painstaking teacher with very well-defined ideas on the essentials of jazz drumming. 'One of the important things to teach is teamwork,' he told me.

> Drums are a gift instrument for egomaniacs – but that is not what drumming is about. So many young drummers learn a couple of technical solos and they want to be a whole band. But at my school, after a drummer reaches a certain level, then we bring in bass and piano so that he can feel the sense of teamwork.
>
> A drummer who just wants to dominate, who ignores the rest of the band, is like a relay captain who keeps running with the baton because he's got the strength. The rest of the team are standing there looking at him and asking, 'Where the hell's he going?'

While he was working at the Blue Note, Kenny would get conservatory percussion students coming up to him and asking about hi-hats and pedals – because they had no bass drum or hi-hat at the conservatory. 'So I taught them,' Kenny said.

> I was teaching *premier prix* percussionists to play drums. They had harmony and composition down, but they wanted to learn rhythm and syncopation. It is very hard to get French musicians to play the last half of the fourth beat. We couldn't get them to do it to save their lives. Then, after a while, they caught it – like I knew they would in time. It's like a catapult, that eighth note. In the end, the director of the conservatoire at St Germain came to me in the class and said, 'Oh, this is wonderful! I'm going to have all the violin and cello players come to your class.' And he did. Pianists, violinists – everyone wanted to learn syncopation.

With his late-night club gigs, work with the Clarke–Boland Band, his classes at St Germain-en-Laye and three days a week at the Premier drum school, Kenny was finding his regular routine rather exhausting, particularly when it came to teaching the youngest members of the class. 'When you get a kid of seven or eight who has never held a pair of drumsticks, it can be pretty tiring,' he said.

> It takes some real hard work – but it's rewarding when you see them making progress. After a while I let the best students start teaching the beginners and I concentrate on the more advanced students. One problem is that when a student is good you have a tendency to spend more time with him than the others.

Kenny's hope for the school was that it would produce three or four really good drummers a year. Whether he achieved that target I don't know, but at least one graduate from the school, Jacques Thollot, went on to achieve some distinction.

In the spring of 1968, Kenny took his trio – Eddie Louiss on organ and Jimmy Gourley on guitar – to Ronnie Scott's Club in London for a four-week engagement. Reviewing the trio in the *Sunday Times*, Derek Jewell observed that Clarke's performance

> has the impact of surprise, the surprise provided by a truly great drummer, maybe the greatest of all, in a small-combo context. He is the inner force, the leader, the soul, without ever detracting from the playing of his companions.
>
> No one lags when Clarke drums. The rhythm flows without effort, the metronomic beat often implied as the patterns shift and shimmer. The top cymbal is still the glittering centrepiece of his work, and all the time Clarke plays as if he has power in reserve. It is a joyous experience.

It was Kenny's first appearance in Britain since 1958, when he had appeared with a Jazz from Carnegie Hall package that included J.J. Johnson, Kai Winding, Zoot Sims and Oscar Pettiford.

During Clarke's stay in the UK, the Premier Drum Company arranged clinics for him in London, Middlesborough and Leeds. For the clinic in the Notre Dame Hall in London there were more than 600 drummers present to hear Kenny's trio and some demonstration drumming by Klook, his Clarke–Boland partner Kenny Clare, Philly Joe Jones and another British drummer, Terry Cox. Kenny's helpful and practical answers to audience questions and a grandstand finale in which Clarke, Clare and Jones were joined by Louiss and Gourley and traded choruses, eights and fours with one another, made the clinic, in the words of *Crescendo* reviewer Frank King, 'a tremendous success'.

A year later, Claude Nobs, artistic director of the Montreux Jazz Festival, invited Kenny Clarke to bring his drum school to the festival as part of a programme of music clinics. There was a trumpet/flugelhorn workshop presented by Clark Terry and Benny Bailey, and a four-day sequence of drum clinics, plus a midnight spectacular, 'A Midsummer Night's Drum',

KENNY CLARKE DRUM CLINICS

Kenny 'Klook' Clarke shows you how

MIDDLESBROUGH
Sunday, February 16—2.30 Little Theatre, The Avenue, tickets from Hamilton Music Store, 45 Corporation Road.

LEEDS
Sunday, February 23—2.30 Great Northern Hotel, Wellington Street, tickets from R. S. Kitchen Ltd., 29-31 Queen Victoria Street.

LONDON
Monday, February 24—5.30 Ronnie Scott's Jazz Club, 47 Frith Street, tickets from any London Premier dealer or

Premier 87 Regent St., London, W1R 7HF.

Advertisement for Klook's drum clinics during his visit to the UK in 1968

featuring Kenny, Dante Agostini and Stuff Combe on drums, with Benny Bailey and Lucky Thompson.

Kenny was supposed to direct the drum school from 3 p.m. to 6 p.m., but on each of the four days the sessions overran because they generated so much interest; the Paris school had become well-known among aspiring drummers. By now, two years after the school had been founded, almost 2,000 students had passed through it and they had spread the word about the drum method which Klook and Agostini had developed.

Reporting on the Montreux event, the British magazine *Crescendo* commented,

> To watch this quietly-spoken, modest and talented man was a lesson in humility and dedication. Here was the almost legendary Kenny Clarke beating out rudiments to eager, fumbling schoolboys – and keeping at it, regardless. We asked him to explain his patience and he looked a little embarrassed. 'To tell the truth,' he said, 'I enjoy it. I learn from them.'

The departure of Kenny Clarke from the Blue Note at the end of 1966 signalled the beginning of the end of the golden age of jazz in Paris. Jazzland, the Left Bank club which Johnny Griffin had opened in the summer of 1965, closed its doors in December 1966.

By 1968 the Blue Note had become a discotheque, offering live music only twice a week; and the Club St Germain jazz room was soon to follow suit, becoming the Bilboquet discotheque.

Klook now had to confront a situation which, sooner or later, all the self-exiled American jazzmen had to face. He told me:

> The problem is, that after you've lived in France for a number of years, you tend to become considered as a French musician and offered the same kind of money. Promoters will bring musicians from the States, on the same level as me, and offer them much more money than they are prepared to pay me – plus transportation.

Don Byas, who had come to Europe with Don Redman in 1946 and stayed in Europe for the rest of his life, had long since reconciled himself to the fact that sustaining star status was a daunting challenge. He told me, 'It's no good expecting to make a lot of money. But if you want to get out of the rat race and live a peaceful, comfortable life without too many headaches, Europe is fine.'

Certainly Kenny Clarke was totally in favour of excluding himself from the rat race and enjoying a peaceful, comfortable life – but the loss of his 'rarity value', plus the fact that the jazz scene in Paris was in a state of chronic decline, made it necessary to look further afield for engagements. The Clarke–Boland Big Band's concert and record dates helped to pay the rent but the income from this fell far short of what Kenny needed to assure a reasonable standard of living for the family.

Kenny told me:

> The sixties were the golden years in Paris. When Miles came over, he was received like a prince. Paris was really turned on to jazz. But then, at the end of the decade, there was a transformation – on the one hand we had the French 'yé-yé' music, which was a peculiarly Gallic form of rock 'n' roll, and on the other hand we had the burgeoning avant-garde and free-jazz movement. Because of these two developments jazz – the jazz I love – really got hurt.

And recalling the transformation to Michael Haggerty, Klook said:

> Our music took a horrible beating. I was listening to Benny Goodman last night on television. Wonderful, wonderful concert. Why can't people get hip and realize where the real thing is? Running around screaming and hollering. I guess it's something the youth have to get off their chests. They know something is wrong and they are trying to unchain themselves.

Towards the end of 1967 the first free-jazz festival was organized in Paris at the Bobino Theatre, with Aldo Romano, Jacques Thollot, Henri Texier and Barney Wilen; and there were visits from Don Cherry, Archie Shepp and Roswell Rudd. Over the next couple of years a substantial avant-garde colony established itself in Paris – Shepp, Burton Greene, Dave Burrell, Alan Silva, Anthony Braxton, Ornette Coleman, Noah Howard, Bobby Few and Frank Wright – all came to perform and record, some to settle for a period, in a city which was becoming increasingly responsive to the new jazz wave. A new record company, Byg, created by Jean-Luc Young and Jean Georgakarakos, began recording free-jazz music at a tempestuous rate. But as the freedom movement gained momentum, the outlook for the mainstream of jazz became steadily bleaker.

Kenny Clarke's response to the new wave was less than ecstatic. He told Haggerty a few years later,

> Man, there was a record company here that would just pay Archie Shepp to stay in the studio all day. And they didn't know what to play, but they would start playing anything. The producer would say, 'Great!' Now he's got all of those records on the racks and he can't give them away. I would tell Archie, 'Man, you should have this music thought out and well done – then it will last. But the way you're doing it, someone hears it once and they'll break the record and throw it in the trash pile.'
>
> There are still a few musicians in Germany who stick with it and refuse to give it up. Well, in the States I knew it wouldn't last any time . . . because if people can't pat their foot to it, then they don't think it's jazz. With the freedom music, you never knew where the beat was. In fact, the players – they didn't know where it was themselves. The drummers are into that freedom bag more than the other musicians. The others are trying to do things together. The drummers keep fucking them up – wanting to do their thing. Not realizing that they have to be the foundation, not the runaway horse. The drummer has to hold the reins and stay there. The rhythm section – the drums, bass, piano – that's the foundation. And then you can build anything you want on that. But it has to have a foundation – and that's what free music didn't have.

Although Kenny was not much impressed by the free-jazz movement, he never closed his mind to new musical directions, to musicians seeking to explore fresh musical paths. On the contrary; he was always receptive to innovation, and in the light of his own musical development, he could scarcely have been otherwise. He told Burt Korall in a *Down Beat* interview, 'I'm out there listening whenever the fellows come through, and there isn't a record of any consequence that I don't play at home. I made sure to hear Eric Dolphy when he was in Paris. I spent my evening-off digging him. I can't say he's my cup of tea, but I was there.' And Francis Paudras remembers that the first time Bill Evans came to France to play a concert, Kenny was in the wings listening. 'Kenny went to all the major concerts,' Paudras says, 'even if they featured a different category of music from his own.'

In an article I wrote in March 1968 for a book called *The Paris Spy*, I pointed out that Paris was in the process of a dramatic transformation with the advent of drugstores, frozen food, canned wine, workable plumbing, credit accounts, supermarkets and self-service restaurants. *'Plus ça change, plus c'est Americain,'* I observed.

> They've even perfumed the Metro and are carting away, one by one, those incomparably pungent street urinals, the *vespasiennes*. The blinding irony in all this is that the one area where Americanization would have been most acceptable – the Paris jazz scene – has not merely remained immune from this invasion but has actively repelled it. As I write there is not a single front-rank American musician playing in any of the Paris jazz clubs.
>
> Kenny Clarke . . . who has been a Paris resident for twelve years, recalling the Paris jazz scene ten years ago, says: 'They were great days. I worked at the Club St Germain for two years and at various times I was playing with Stan Getz, Miles Davis, J.J. Johnson, Art Blakey's Jazz Messengers and the Modern Jazz Quartet. People packed the club to see their jazz idols in the flesh. I can't understand why this sort of thing doesn't happen now.'

The decline in working opportunities in the late sixties was not without its compensations. Kenny enjoyed being able to spend more time at home with Daisy and Laurent, tending his garden and catching up on his reading. Regular record dates with the Clarke–Boland Band, combined with club and concert work with the trio, enabled Kenny to keep his hand in; but after the break-up of the big band, Kenny worked only sporadically. As he observed at the time, 'I play very little in France now because there is nowhere to play. Clubs would book me, but they can't afford me. And things I would like to do I just can't do because the musicians I would like to have with me demand quite a lot of money.'

In the early seventies the Bilboquet remembered its illustrious past and began booking jazz again. Klook and his trio would do a one-month stint there each year, sometimes in August, sometimes in December. In addition Klook would play the occasional festival and make guest appearances at the Montmartre in Copenhagen and the Domicile in Munich.

In October 1972 Kenny set foot again in the United States – the first time in sixteen years – when he went to receive a Duke Ellington Fellowship from Yale University, an accolade which carried with it a gold medal and the opportunity to spend a month on the Yale faculty at full professor's salary. Klook played a concert with his old friend Dizzy Gillespie, but he did not avail himself of the opportunity to spend a month in New Haven. He returned home after a few days – though not before making a pilgrimage to Pittsburgh to see his brother, Chuck. It was their last meeting – Chuck died five years later – and it was not a particularly happy reunion.

In her book, *Paris without Regret*, Ursula Broschke Davis writes of a basic incompatibility between Kenny and Chuck. She points out that Chuck never came to see Kenny in Paris – nor even to New York when Kenny was there. 'When the brothers met after so many years, they still could not communicate,' she says.

> Kenny felt that he understood his brother but that his brother still could not understand him. Kenny remembered that his brother was quite upset that he had stayed in Paris for so many years. He said, 'My brother resented it very much before he died, about my living in Europe. But I explained that it was more profitable for me to live in Europe.'

Davis points out that Kenny gave this explanation because he did not expect his brother to understand his deep-seated objection to the American way of life. It was easier to represent his exile to Europe as a move dictated by materialistic considerations.

Ursula Davis also claims that Kenny's animosity towards America was so great

> that he did not even want his son, Laurent, to visit the place where his father was raised. Laurent wanted to go, but Kenny was not really pleased with the idea. 'They would destroy him in a minute, because he has a big heart, he is kind. They would have him into something right away. So I don't want him to go there. I want him to get his education here (in France) and then, when he becomes a man, he can go there and he can do what he wants then.'

It is more than a little likely that Kenny's resolve to keep Laurent out of the United States was strengthened by the unhappy experience of his elder son, Toby.

* * *

In February 1973, Klook played the first of two congenial

record dates for Musidisc in Paris. Stéphane Grappelli was celebrating his fiftieth year as a professional musician and the record company invited Oscar Peterson to Paris to make two albums with him in the company of Klook and Niels-Henning Orsted Pedersen. The second date, in April, reunited Kenny once again with Dizzy Gillespie, and with two former Blue Note regulars: Johnny Griffin and Kenny Drew. Orsted Pedersen and Humberto Canto, on tumbas, completed the line-up. Dizzy wrote a special tune for the date dedicated to his favourite drummer called, 'Brother K'.

July 1973 saw Kenny Clarke back in Montreux for the jazz festival and playing with Dexter Gordon, Hampton Hawes and Bob Cranshaw on a Prestige night which yielded three albums – *Blues à la Suisse* by the quartet, a Hampton Hawes trio LP, *Playing in the Yard* and a set by Gene Ammons and Friends. But increasingly Kenny was concentrating on work with his own trio, using either René Thomas or Jimmy Gourley on guitar and Eddie Louiss or Lou Bennett on organ. He also worked a good deal with organist Rhoda Scott, with tenorist Hal Singer and French musicians Michel de Villers and Roger Guérin. But as he reached his sixties, the transformation of the Paris jazz scene into a free-jazz playground, coupled with his increasing inclination to take things easier and spend more time at home, resulted in his making fewer public appearances.

Opportunities for studio work also declined. Between 1974 and 1984, Klook made only a dozen record dates. But he was happy to have more time to spend with his family and to read the novels of J.B. Priestley.

Each year the Clarke family would spend a three-week August vacation in Figanières in the South of France with the family of French clarinettist Henri Guisgand. In 1968 Kenny had bought five and a half acres of land in the region with the intention of building a holiday home there. Later he sold half the property to Dizzy Gillespie. Says Daisy Clarke:

> We never did manage to get our holiday home built. Kenny didn't much like vacations. He preferred to sit out in the garden at home. He and Laurent had a very good relationship. In Paris Kenny would take Laurent to the Louvre and to the Musée de la Découverte – they visited all the museums together. The were were really tight – and they used to gang up

against me. If I rebuked Laurent, Kenny would say, 'Leave the boy alone.' And if I had to tell Kenny off, then Laurent would say, '*Mama, laisse Papa tranquille*!' Laurent was very devoted to his father and he would worry about him – particularly about his health as he got older.

Kenny also had more time now to spend in the garden of his little Montreuil home. The garden had been something of a wilderness between 1962 and 1970 when the family had a German shepherd dog called Stella whose habits were incompatible with elegant horticulture. But after the dog died, Kenny called in a student from a local school to put the plot in order and plant roses, of which he was particularly fond.

Though at 190 lbs Kenny was somewhat overweight for a man of 5 feet 4 inches, he was an averagely fit sixty-year-old. He exercised most days and he took very little alcohol. 'He would drink mostly fruit juices, and Coca Cola,' says Daisy. 'He liked port and a Campari-soda now and again, and also an occasional glass of really good white wine. But he didn't drink hard liquor. He never had an alcohol problem because he really didn't like it.

As to diet, Klook avoided the more murderous foods. He enjoyed fried chicken and liver, bacon and onions and, according to Daisy, was apt to demolish a combination plate of fish and bananas with vigorous enthusiasm. When he was working late, he would sleep until at least noon the following day. Generally speaking, he took good care of himself.

He was, however, a fairly heavy smoker and this, with the cumulative stress and strain of working night after late night for so many years, plus the fact that he was carrying a few too many pounds, combined to take an all-too-familiar toll. On 6 December 1975, Kenny suffered a heart attack.

'I got him into hospital very fast and he was in intensive care for eleven days,' says Daisy. 'It was the first time in his life that he'd been in hospital and he hated it. Every day when I visited him he'd say to me, "Daisy, get me out of here."'

After his discharge from hospital Kenny spent a convalescent period at home and, to the relief of Daisy and Laurent, gave up smoking. After a few weeks he was able to resume playing. He played dates with the Dusko Gojkovic band in Germany and with Rhoda Scott in Switzerland.

In September 1976, WTTW Television in Chicago decided to produce a special three-day tribute programme to Dizzy Gillespie and Kenny was invited to take part, along with Al Haig, Milt Jackson, Ray Brown, James Moody, Sarah Vaughan and Joe Carroll. It was a most happy reunion for the alumni of the great Gillespie band which had made its momentous début some three decades earlier.

After the television show Kenny remained in the States, working for a week at the Jazz Showcase in Chicago with Clifford Jordan, Al Haig and Wilbur Ware. He then spent some days in New York – a visit which did absolutely nothing to make him revise his attitude to the city. In a piece I wrote at the time for *Black Echoes*, I observed:

> Kenny found little interest among clubowners there – except for a few who wanted to offer him about one third of the money he earned in the Chicago club. Strange that the founder of modern jazz drumming should encounter such indifference on what was, after all, a rare visit to New York – and it is perhaps a good indication of why Klook has preferred to live in Europe for the past twenty years.

While he was in New York, Kenny met up once again with Walter Fuller, arranger and composer of some of the great Gillespie band charts, and they discussed the possibility of setting up some US recording and concert dates for 1977 with Dizzy, Milt Jackson and Ray Brown. Klook told me then, 'I'd like to go back and work there for a couple of months. I also want to visit Nathan Davis, who runs the jazz studies course in the university of my home town.'

Back in Paris, Kenny Clarke began teaching again, this time at a new school established at the American Center on the Boulevard Raspail, together with his good friends Pierre Michelot and Roger Guérin. And in August, while Laurent went off to summer camp, Klook and Daisy went to Belgium where Kenny had a six-day teaching assignment. Daisy returned to Montreuil two days early but was unable to get into the house because she had forgotten one of the keys. So she called the police who broke a bathroom window to gain access.

Once inside, Daisy discovered that the kitchen light had been left on by mistake. She also found a note on the kitchen table, addressed to Kenny Clarke and written in French. It said, 'There's no point in leaving the kitchen light on because, if I really want to rob you, Mr Clarke, I can.' The intruder – clearly a bebop fan – took nothing. But he made off with a considerable amount of loot from two neighbouring houses.

Kenny's hopes of record dates and concerts in the States with Dizzy, Ray Brown and Milt Jackson were not fulfilled. But in the winter of 1977 he did return to America to take part in Pittsburgh University's seventh annual Jazz Seminar, organized by Nathan Davis, by now an associate professor at the university and co-ordinator of the jazz studies programme. Kenny joined Dexter Gordon, Woody Shaw, Terri Pollard, Mike Longo, Abraham Laboriel and Davis for the three-day event which included workshop sessions and a concert performance on the final night in the Carnegie Music Hall.

'It was Klook's first playing appearance in Pittsburgh for thirty years,' Nathan Davis recalled. Just before the concert Kenny was presented with an inscribed gold plaque by the university in recognition of his signal contribution to jazz music. He was also given the freedom of the city by the Mayor of Pittsburgh.

Not before time, acknowledgement in the form of honours and awards now began to come Kenny Clarke's way. In June he had been made an honorary member of the Mark Twain Society in recognition of 'his outstanding contribution to world peace'. And a year later the New York City department of cultural affairs presented him with the Prez Award 'for the important role you played in the great jazz phenomenon known as "Swing Street" or 52nd Street and in recognition of your superb artistry, creative genius and invaluable contribution to jazz – America's classical music'. A more tangible and beneficial gesture of appreciation of Kenny Clarke's key role in shaping the development of American music came in 1983 when the National Endowment for the Arts awarded him $20,000.

Kenny received numerous other awards during the latter part of his life, some overblown, some slightly shoddy, all well-intentioned. But it remains an enigma why his quintessential influence on the evolution of jazz was not – and has still not been – fully appreciated and understood. It was not in Klook's nature to lose much sleep over this neglect; but there were times – rare times – when he would admit to being a little bit hurt that, compared to his own personal investment in the music, his rewards from it, both in terms of finance and status, were less than adequate. What mattered most to him, of course, was the satisfaction he got from playing with musicians he respected. 'That has always been the primary motivation,' he told me, adding with a characteristic grin and chuckle, 'but I don't have any real deep objection to getting good money.'

In the winter of 1979, Nathan Davis took a one-term sabbatical and invited Klook to Pittsburgh to deputize for him as a visiting professor. Ursula Davis observed seven years later,

> . . . he thus became a professor at the university in his home town where, when he was growing up, there were no black professors and few black students. He stayed with friends in a suburban neighbourhood where, as a youth, he would have been questioned by police for being there. Changes had taken place, but Kenny was not impressed. He did not feel right. The same feeling that he had in his youth crept up on him.

Klook told Davis,

> It's even worse now. They don't want to hear about anything black. It's built up for whites and that's where it is. It's like South Africa; it's the same thing – practically. The more things change, the more they stay the same. The racial suppression is even worse than when I lived there . . . All the black faces don't mean anything. They are so far from the truth.

Kenny brought his wife to Pittsburgh with him, but it was a particularly fierce winter with heavy snowfalls and Daisy returned to France after three weeks. She told me,

> While we were there we looked up some of the family. We went with Toby to see Evelyn's sister, Aunt Margaret, and her husband, Leo – but that was about all. Kenny enjoyed teaching, but he said, 'I can't teach improvisation – you either have it or you don't.' So he solved the problem by forming a nice little band with the students. He wasn't completely comfortable in the job, but he was happy to be helping out his friend, Nathan.

James Johnson, a Pittsburgh graduate with a PhD in ethnomusicology, was a student during the time that Kenny Clarke was teaching at Pittsburgh. He thought that Kenny was a little shy, particularly when it came to taking classes with more than 200 students in attendance. 'But,' he said, 'we learned a lot just by being around him – not only about music but about life. He spoke very quietly and sometimes you really had to strain your ears to catch what he was saying. The students treated him with great respect – he was such an enormously likeable person.'

Don Franklin, another PhD in musicology and a professor at the university, says that his most abiding memory of Kenny Clarke was the easy way in which he played with the students in a campus concert:

> What struck me was the naturalness of his musicianship; the fact that he shared it with everyone without really thinking about it. He was a very warm and modest person and when he directed the band he was really playing with it rather that being the conductor, the leader. He was revered by the students – his youthfulness and his uncomplicated, natural approach made him most effective as a teacher. He wanted to be accepted as a fellow musician – not as a person in authority.

Despite his easy rapport with the students, his missionary feel for teaching and the respect he was accorded by the university, Kenny was not sorry when the term was over and he was able to return to his family in France. He still retained a deep distrust of American society. In an interview with a Norwegian newspaper a few months after his return from Pittsburgh, he said,

> The white Americans are afraid – they are afraid of Communism and afraid of the blacks. They have always been scared of something. They have two things in their head – money, and how to protect their way of life. Racism is the USA's biggest sin. One day the whole thing will explode because the Americans can't understand the tremendous power they have created in the black people by keeping them down.

Yet, perhaps because he was aware, deep down, that his alienation from his country had militated against the complete fulfilment of his ambitions as a musician and that the United States was still the hub of the jazz universe, Kenny still kept alive a glimmer of hope that a triumphal return, much in the manner of Dexter Gordon's in 1976, might yet be attainable. He had hoped it might be accomplished with the superb Clarke–Boland Band; and he tried again in 1976 when he and Walter Fuller discussed the project with Dizzy which never came to fruition.

In 1982, Kenny was asked by Michael Haggerty if he planned to go back to the States again soon. Kenny's answer was appreciably more mellow than on many previous occasions. 'No,' he said. 'Whenever they feel they want me back, you know, then I'll go. I've nothing against the States. But a lot of young people there, you know, they've never heard of me. I imagine they want to. Who is Kenny Clarke? So maybe I'll get a chance to go back soon.' Then he added, sadly, 'There are not too many Americans left here in Paris from the early days. No, no. I feel alone.'

In fact Kenny's next trip to the United States was in July 1980 when he was invited over to play in a Dizzy Gillespie retrospective by the Wolf Trap Foundation for the Performing Arts in Virginia, as part of the Wolf Trap International Jazz Festival. Along with Dizzy, Kenny played with Sonny Stitt, Jackie McLean, Slide Hampton, John Lewis and Ray Brown. Recalling the event later, Jackie McLean said, 'Kenny was getting on in years, but he was still at the top of his game – he showed he could still swing us into bad health!'

Klook made another trip to the States in August 1983 when he paid a visit to Pittsburgh and also spent some time in New York where he recorded *Pieces of Time* for Giovanni Bonandrini's enterprising Soul Note label, with Andrew Cyrille, Milford Graves and Don Moye. Among the compositions for the date was one written by Klook and dedicated to his son, 'Laurent'.

The last time Kenny visited his native country was in June 1984 when he took part in a Night of Percussion concert at the Irving Plaza in New York.

In between the US visits, Kenny continued to play galas and club dates in France with his trio and, occasionally, to get called for festival gigs around Europe with all-star combos. In July 1979 he appeared at the Antibes Jazz Festival with pianist Michel Sardaby and bassist Alby Cullaz; in October 1980 he played the Berlin Jazz Festival with Warne Marsh, Sal Mosca and Eddie Gomez; in 1982 he came to London to make a jazz video at University College with Slim Gaillard, Johnny Griffin and Kai Winding, and the following year he played at the San Remo Festival with the Clarke–Boland Sextet.

For Kenny's seventieth birthday, on 9 January 1984, the French television programme 'Jazz Cocktail' put on a Kenny Clarke special with Jimmy Gourley and a few other musician friends. The St Emilion and the champagne flowed freely and there were special birthday calls from Johnny Griffin in Nice, from Dizzy Gillespie in New York and from Roger Guérin and Charles Bellonzi.

It was in the summer of that year that I began to speculate about the possibility of assembling, under Kenny's leadership, a band of American musicians who had been resident in Paris during the 'golden age' of jazz there. Having spent five years in Paris in that momentous decade, I had retained a deep nostalgia for the period and a fund of recollections of some sublime musical moments.

I first discussed the possibility with Nathan Davis, with whom I had a close friendship going back twenty years. Nathan's respect and affection for Kenny were on a level with my own and almost before I had finished outlining my project, he was working on the personnel. Next I went to see Kenny in Paris – and he, too, was enthusiastic. The plan was to assemble an eight-piece band which would tour the European summer festival circuit in 1985. It was August 1984 and since Klook was now seventy years old, it was decided that drumming duties would be shared between him and another drummer – as in the Clarke–Boland Band – so as to render the playing schedule less physically demanding.

Billy Brooks, a musician based in Berne, Switzerland and a Parisian from 1964 to 1967, was signed up to be the second drummer. The other founder members were Woody Shaw (Paris, 1964 to 1965), Dizzy Reece (Paris, 1968 to 1978), Slide Hampton (Paris, 1968 to 1974), Jimmy Woode (Paris, 1964 to 1968), Johnny Griffin (Paris, 1962 to 1967), Kenny Drew (Paris 1961 to 1964) and Nathan Davis (Paris, 1963 to 1969). The aim of the Paris Reunion Band project was to capture some of the mood and spirit of the Paris jazz scene of the sixties and also to pay tribute to Klook, the man designated to be its leader, who had been an inspiration to all the musicians involved.

Ina Dittke, a young New York-based booking agent from Düsseldorf, took on the job of setting up the Paris Reunion Band's first tour, which involved June and July dates at the North Sea Jazz Festival in The Hague, Montreux, Antibes, San Sebastian, Berlin, Paris, Athens and Tring in the UK. But sadly, Kenny Clarke, the man for whom the band was created, never got to play with his former Paris colleagues. In the early hours of 26 January 1985, Klook suffered a fatal heart attack. It was a little more than nine years after his first attack.

Daisy Clarke recalls,

> It happened so quickly – just after midnight. Ten minutes before, he had been talking on the phone to Lou Bennett and he was fine. We went to bed, he complained of a pain and took a pill. Then suddenly he collapsed. I called the fire service – because they are very quick – and they were at the house within two minutes. I don't know if Kenny was still conscious. He was rushed into intensive care and they massaged his heart. They wouldn't let me stay with him. Then, some minutes later, they came out of the ward and said, 'Your husband has just died.' Just like that. I couldn't believe it. I called the Guérins to tell them, and I called Lou Bennett, but I couldn't bring myself to call Laurent right then. Lou was stunned because he'd been talking to Kenny just a few minutes before.

After the first heart attack in 1975, Kenny had been on anti-coagulants for two years, but then stopped taking medication, apart from analgesics for various aches and pains he suffered from time to time. And six months after giving up smoking, he started again. Daisy said:

> He smoked in secret, because he knew Laurent and I would give him a hard time. He smoked Marlboro cigarettes and sometimes a pipe. He really smoked quite a lot. He used to hide the cigarettes, hoping we wouldn't find out. But, of course, we knew and we kept telling him to give it up. He would say there was nothing wrong with his heart. But musicians never like to admit they're ill. He had been OK up to the end of 1984. But it was a very cold winter so he didn't go out much to get exercise, though the doctors had told him he should.
>
> In December he had been working five days a week with Lou Bennett at Le Petit Opportun and a lot of musicians used to come and sit in because they loved getting a chance to play with Kenny. But it was very tiring for him because the sets would go on much longer – so eventually I called the clubowner and asked him not to let musicians sit in.

> Kenny used to come home exhausted, but there wasn't really much we could do about it because when he wasn't playing he was unhappy. Music was his life. Music came first for him; Laurent was second and I was third. In that order. He couldn't live without music.

There is no doubt that Kenny had been overtaxing himself in order to maintain his connection and commitment to the music that was his lifeblood. Jean-Pierre Leloir, who had been photographing Kenny Clarke over a period of more than thirty years, remembers how much Kenny had aged over the later years of his life. He became a martyr to his muse; he looked grey and weary and, at certain moments, rather melancholy.

Says Gigi Campi:

> The last time I saw him was, I think, in September 1984 when he played in the radio orchestra of Milan with Francy Boland conducting; and I must say he looked tired. Very tired. But he never lost his readiness to smile. On his seventy-first birthday, 9 January 1985, I called him on the phone as usual. I don't remember anybody else's birthday except Klook's. He was laughing and joking over the phone like always. It was beautiful. Nobody would have got me to believe that less than three weeks later he would be dead.

The funeral service took place on 29 January in Montreuil-sous-Bois, and the following day Kenny Clarke was cremated at the Père Lachaise cemetery.

More than 300 mourners joined the funeral procession from 142 bis, rue de Rosny to the Montreuil Centre des Expositions where, in the best jazz tradition, Kenny's musician friends paid him musical tribute. Among the scores of musicians who gathered to pay, and play, their last respects were Herbie Hancock, Johnny Griffin, Steve Lacy, Hal Singer, Bobby Few, Marcel Zanini, Jimmy Gourley, Lou Bennett, Al Levitt, Toni Russo, Roger Guérin, Manu Dibango, Christian Vander and singers Virginia Vee and Nancy Holloway. The truck bearing the coffin was almost totally obscured by a mass of floral tributes and in front was a large photograph of Kenny Clarke doing what he did best and loved to do most: playing the drums.

The French newspapers gave considerable space to the passing of Kenny Clarke. *La Voix de l'Est* headlined its front page, BYE BYE, KENNY – LE JAZZ TE DIT MERCI. And *Libération* devoted an entire page to an obituary and an appreciation of *l'inventeur de la batterie moderne*. In his tribute, published with those of other musicians in *Jazz Hot*, Jimmy Gourley wrote, 'Thanks Kenny. Jazz was lucky to have had you. Amen!'

The *International Herald Tribune* accorded Kenny Clarke's passing eight paragraphs; the *New York Times* and the *New York Daily News* three paragraphs each. The London *Times* manged thirteen column inches, concluding with '. . . Clarke's majestic drumming always made its [the Clarke–Boland Band's] performance fascinating to listen to. Musicianship, not showmanship, was his foremost concern and he eschewed the ostentatious frenzies which lesser men so often substituted for inspiration.'

British jazz writer Alun Morgan described Kenny as 'a dedicated and unselfish player, a team man through and through who was largely responsible for making jazz drumming the art it is today'; and, in a half-page article in the *Village Voice*, Stanley Crouch recalled that after André Malraux died, he had observed that Kenny Clarke was the greatest thinker left in France – a claim that Kenny himself would undoubtedly have greeted with that explosive giggle-cum-chuckle of his.

But on the whole the tributes, outside specialist jazz publications, tended to be ritualistic, inadequate or inaccurate – sometimes all three together. Mostly they showed no appreciation of the fundamental changes that Klook had initiated nor of his status as a musician, nor his dignity, compassion and nobility of spirit as a man.

Had Klook had the opportunity to read his obituaries, their content would have come as absolutely no surprise to a man who spent most of his working life resigned to receiving lower rewards and less recognition than he deserved. What was much more important for Kenny was the intense satisfaction he got from his music, and from the appreciation and respect his fellow musicians had for him. Which is why, in one of many notes he left behind, he wrote: 'I may not have the respect of the public in general, but I have the affection of the greatest musicians on earth, and that's enough honor for me.'

19
We Remember Klook

George Avakian
He was a truly nice guy; a doll; a gentleman. Well-spoken, never got drunk or raised his voice to anyone. Always a pleasure to be around him. Not many left like him. I remember one amusing experience I had with him in June 1940.

It was at the end of my junior year at Yale. Two friends of mine used to run Sunday jam sessions, using pick-up five- or six-piece New York groups, at a bar/restaurant twenty-five miles north of New Haven. They asked me to assemble a group just before the end of the school year. I can't remember all the personnel, but I think Sidney Bechet and Lips Page were the horns. Klook was the drummer. The box office was weak – too late in the season, I guess – and my friends came up short of cash to pay the musicians. A couple of my classmates and I had about $25 between us; not enough. But Kenny volunteered to forgo his share that day so that everyone else could get paid. My friends, the promoters, promised to pay him the following week and I told Kenny I'd come to New York with his share, because next week was graduation and I'd be driving to the city with my belongings. I would stop off at Minton's on my way home. Kenny was a bit down about it – but he trusted me. I can't remember how much he was owed; maybe $35, which was good money in those days. My friends came through with the cash the next week. I tried calling Kenny to reassure him, but he was always out when I called – so I dropped in, unannounced, at Minton's one night. I waved the bread at Kenny, who beamed back from the stand and, at the end of the set, he was ear-to-ear happiness. 'Somehow,' he said, 'I didn't really think you guys would come through; are you sure this isn't your money?' I assured him it wasn't. He said he knew me well enough to know that, if I had to, I'd pay him myself, and that bothered him more than the possibility of not getting paid at all.

'Nothing to worry about,' I reassured him – and, of course, this led to my staying all night. It could have been a very expensive night for me because I had fearlessly parked my Dad's large Dodge sedan – packed to the roof with my books, clothes and King Oliver OKehs, Johnny Dodds Vocalions and Bix Gennetts – just around the corner off Lenox Avenue. Happily, New York was relatively safe then. I never once considered going out to check the car. But at 3.30 a.m. it was untouched, despite the several hundred dollars' worth of merchandise visible through the windows.

Kenny never tired of telling people this story. Even in Paris he would suddenly come out with, 'Let me tell you about this guy – I'd given up ever getting paid for this gig . . . etc, etc.' Which was embarrassing, but I realized what it meant to him: that he must have been stiffed countless times by people he'd trusted.

Benny Bailey

I consider myself extremely fortunate to have worked with Kenny in Dizzy's big band. When I first joined the band in 1947 I didn't realize at first how special he was. I thought that was how all big-band drummers played. But, of course, Kenny had his own inimitable style. He was a neat, clean player and if you hear him on record, you know immediately that it's him. There are not too many drummers who are that identifiable.

The longer I knew Klook – and, of course, I worked with him for years in the Clarke–Boland Band – the more I became aware of his knowledge of music. And he just couldn't help swinging. I listen now to the records we made with the Clarke–Boland Band and I hear the happy feeling that his drumming generated. I guess I didn't notice it quite so much at the time because I was too busy concentrating on reading the parts. The feeling was really wonderful – he made the music very special. The best records Miles ever made were the sides he did with Klook and Monk in 1954.

He was a friendly, adaptable, easygoing person who just loved to play. He wasn't concerned about making a lot of bread. I have this memory of him appreciating the comfort of his nice little house in Paris, smoking his pipe and enjoying a glass of wine. His pet hates were phoney people, and dishonesty – he hated clubowners and agents who ripped off musicians. I guess he was an idealist.

Charles Bellonzi

The drumming of Kenny Clarke hit me like a flash of lightning when I listened to him on record with Miles, Dizzy and Bud. When I went to Paris in September 1960 I saw him play in all the clubs: Tabou, Caméléon, St Germain, Blue Note, Le Chat Qui Pêche. Kenny and Bud Powell had a sort of inner power that was fantastic. They were quite simply masters. I had a lot to learn – I had to try to capture their feeling. My friendship with Kenny gave me the chance of my life. He liked me a lot and became my spiritual father. I realized just how much he had contributed compared with other great drummers. With his perfect equilibrium he introduced a kind of muscular softness with brushes. He was fantastic – no grand gestures, no unnecessary movement. The tempo was suggested rather than expressed . . . with Kenny, you always heard the melody.

(*Jazz Hot*, March 1985)

Lou Bennett

Kenny was a superb catalyst; he always found ways to make music sound better. In twenty-five years of playing with him I had so many beautiful moments. Kenny's main concern was to swing. He would put up with a musician who wasn't the greatest in the world as long as he swung; but if he couldn't play *or* swing, then Kenny wouldn't hide his impatience.

Generally, though, he was an easygoing man who almost never got mad. He'd get more disgusted than mad and would prefer to walk away from a potential argument and go home. One of his favourite sayings was, 'No point in clouding my mind with meaningless things. If it's not important, don't bother me with it.'

I'd say his main sources of frustration were the vultures in the music business. I think that's why he took refuge in Europe. He really hated it when musicians were ripped off, or given lousy hotels and endless bus trips between gigs. Although he was easygoing most of the time, he wouldn't let anyone walk all over him. He stuck very firmly to his principles.

Kenny was like an uncle for me. He helped me in so many ways and our families were close. In Paris he was about the only person that I could really talk with. And I was just about the last person to talk with him. About half an hour before his second heart attack we were talking on the phone and laughing together because we were both watching an American comedy on television. When I got the call that he'd died soon afterwards I just couldn't believe it. Of all the musicians who knew Klook, I'm sure none of them misses him more than I do.

Walter Bishop Jr

Don't know how he got his name . . .
He was a credit to the game.
If I had my druthers,
He, plus some others,
Would be in the drummers' Hall of Fame.

Kenny Clarke had a total commitment to excellence and a profound dislike of bullshit of any kind. He was a consummate professional with style and class, and he was a great role model for many musicians, including myself.

The evolution of the drums, as I heard it, was: Papa Jo, Big Sid Catlett and . . . Klook. And Klook was one of the Big Four of Bebop – along with Diz, Bird and Monk.

A warm, affable, unpretentious and generous man, he had an impeccable demeanour both on and off the bandstand. And when he played he was always supportive. He *listened*, and he knew how to complement what his fellow musicians were doing.

The last time I saw him was on his last visit to New York. We had lunch together and in the evening I went with him to see Dexter Gordon at the Blue Note. I got Carmen McRae to come along, too. That was an evening to remember.

Francy Boland
He was very special.

Ray Brown
I first met Klook when he came out of the army in the mid-forties and joined Dizzy's band at the Spotlite. We were all waiting for him because Dizzy had been talking about him so much. And we weren't disappointed. For Klook, the sound of the drums was a major preoccupation. I remember coming to work early one day and Kenny was wiping down his bass drum with a damp cloth because he said it helped him get a better sound. And he showed me a certain place to stand when I played bass so that the sound sort of went through his bass drum and the drum beats came out sounding like bass notes.

He was a beautiful person; in Dizzy's band he was like a father figure to guys like me and James Moody and Milt. He took good care of us, got us out of trouble and taught us a lot of things. As a drummer he was totally distinctive – you can always recognize Klook immediately; his style and his sound were as personal as a human voice.

Kenny Burrell
I met Kenny for the first time at the Café Bohemia in 1956. I used to sit-in there. At that time Kenny was doing a lot of dates for Prestige and Savoy and he got sessions for me and other musicians from Detroit, like Pepper Adams, Tommy Flanagan and Paul Chambers. I have to thank him for that because he helped get us into the scene. We did quite a few records

together and I got to know him pretty well. I remember all the guys felt that Kenny had such a subtle way of swinging – it was bebop and modern, but it was subtle. That's why I asked him to do my first album as leader for Blue Note in May 1956, with Tommy Flanagan and Paul Chambers and Candido as special guest.

Kenny influenced so many drummers who came after him, especially in terms of accompaniment – he was a supreme accompanist, so sensitive to the needs of the soloist. I remember Louis Hayes – another Detroit musician – used to talk all the time about Kenny's special cymbal beat. It was unique. Some people couldn't figure out just what he was doing. It wasn't just a 4/4 beat – although it sounded like it. It was more subtle.

Kenny was such a beautiful guy – so friendly and warm. And his good nature came out in his playing. He wanted to help make the music happen, to make it swing. He had no use for ego-tripping.

Donald Byrd

Kenny was the bridge between swing and bebop. He was the first bebop drummer. And he was a fantastic musician. No question. He could work with everyone: Bechet, Hawkins, Bird, Armstrong. Everyone. When he played brushes, it was like Papa Jo, but he took it someplace else; when he soloed on the snare drum, he took it someplace else. Kenny was the drummer who turned everything around. And his time was impeccable. I remember one of the first albums I did with him for Savoy – *Byrd's Word* – in 1955. Somebody said to me that if you put the stylus down at any point on any track the time was absolutely constant. You don't find that in too many drummers.

I remember another session we did with John La Porta when Kenny said he'd play an eight-bar intro. He did some really tricky things and, at the end, we were all standing around trying to figure out where 'one' was – he expected us to feel it. And the solo he played on Dizzy's big-band recording of 'Two Bass Hit' is ridiculous. It shows how far advanced he was in comparison with other drummers at the time.

As a person, Kenny was a man who liked the quiet life. If he didn't like something that was happening, he would split – just cut out. Although he became an exile because he had no faith in the American system, he was not really a revolutionary or a rebel. But he had a deep hatred of racial segregation. When he was getting ready to leave the US in 1956, he asked me to come with him. But I had just got married and was just getting started in New York – so I didn't take him up on the offer. Later I had a couple of spells in Paris and after the last one, when I decided to return to the States, Kenny really gave me a lecture. He told me I should stay in Europe because America would never change.

He could never reconcile himself with the racial injustice and intolerance in the US. And I believe he became a Muslim out of disgust for Christianity.

One thing I found out: he really didn't dig Louis Armstrong. He told me some of the things that went down while he was working with Pops which he didn't much appreciate. And he felt that Armstrong was an Uncle Tom.

Of course, he became *the* man in Europe. He had known Paris since the thirties and he had absorbed the culture, the way of life. Despite his exile, he was still king in the late fifties and the sixties. But in the seventies some musicians started putting him down a little bit, and that hurt me – because there's no way that Klook could ever be anything but a king.

Gigi Campi

Father Klook – I called him that because there was always a reassuring, paternal element about his presence. He was so well balanced – both as a man and as a drummer. He became part of the drums when he sat behind them. To me he was, by far, the greatest drummer ever. I don't know anybody who could play the cymbal like he did.

He had a good mind and was knowledgeable about world affairs and philosophy. We'd often sit up until six in the morning talking about everything under the sun. There was a lot of common sense in everything he said. A man with such a complex, organized rhythmic sense must also have his mind together.

Politically (being a Capricorn) Klook was a conservative, but he wasn't a reactionary. He was careful with money and knew how to turn a dollar. But you never had the feeling that money was so important for him – even though he had had a hard life. He could never understand why I was a socialist because he associated socialism with the totalitarian systems of the Eastern Bloc. He believed passionately in racial and religious tolerance and always said that it was wrong to be arrogant towards ignorant people – they needed help, not denigration. He had a great compassion and was always ready to help young musicians.

I remember one time at the Bologna Jazz Festival he and I went down into the basement after the concert where there was a jam session in progress. A young drummer was in the middle of a particularly energetic and noisy solo. I said to Klook, 'Come on, man, let's go; I can't stand this.' Kenny fixed me with his big, cool eyes and said, 'Look, Gison, somebody is playing drums and you'd better listen to him because, if he picks up the sticks, it's because he has something to say. There's always something that one can learn from somebody.'

Nathan Davis

As well as being a complete musician, Kenny Clarke was a complete gentleman. I owe him a great debt of gratitude for all the help and encouragement he gave me after I came out of the army. The experience of working with him and the Club St Germain and the Blue Note in Paris was something beyond my wildest dreams. What an initiation!

Klook had a beautiful sound on drums and he told me once that he always took the trouble to get a good sound on record dates because he figured that, if his drums sounded good on record, musicians would always want to hire him. He also emphasized his belief in the simple approach. 'I listen to Buddy Rich and all those cats,' he said to me, 'but Max and I figured that if you just play simple and swing and make the soloist sound good, then you're going to get hired again.'

Kenny saw no point in working himself up into a lather for the sake of showmanship, expending unnecessary energy on pointless displays of technique.

He was very particular about his appearance and he believed that professional musicians owed it to the public not only to play good but to look good. That is something I pass on to my students now – one of the many things I learned from Kenny.

He deserves so much credit for what he did for the music and for other musicians. And that man paid his dues! I remember he told me once that when he first started in Pittsburgh he had no cases for his drums. He'd walk three miles to a gig, carrying his bass drum under one arm and the snare and cymbals and stands under the other.

When we started the Paris Reunion Band in 1985 we all felt so down that Kenny didn't live to be part of it. But all the musicians wanted the band to come into being as a way of paying tribute to Klook's memory. And that's the way we see it today: as a salute to one of the greatest musicians and nicest people who ever lived.

Kenny Drew

Kenny had a fantastic musical concept and was his own special kind of drummer. His swing and the lightness of his touch were his own. He could make music swing like nobody else and a touch, both with sticks and brushes, and a feel for dynamics that gave a great lift to the music.

Although I met him in New York during the time of Minton's, I never got to play with him until I came to the Blue Note in Paris. It was a delight to work with him of course, not only because of his musicianship but also because of his warm nature. He was a beautiful person, considerate, co-operative and full of humour. He treated all the musicians who worked with him very well – though he was tough on guys who came late to the bandstand or didn't dress properly. He could also be tough with promoters or clubowners who tried to take advantage of him. Kenny had his own quiet but firm way of dealing with that situation.

He was politically and socially committed – not in a protest-marching, banner-waving sense – but he was a staunch defender of his black heritage and of black music. His death represented a great loss to the music scene. He was very helpful to me during my two and a half years in Paris and I will never forget him. We all miss him very much.

Curtis Fuller

To me, Kenny Clarke was the father of bebop. He dropped the first bomb! And he's where Buhaina came from. He was a legend – like Lester Young. And he commanded respect – because he gave it.

I used to sit in with him at the Blue Note in 1959 and 1960 – I stayed in France for a while after Quincy's Free & Easy tour came to an end, and I got to know Kenny pretty well. He was one of the nicest human beings I ever met – so warm; and he helped so many guys. He gave a lot of musicians the chance to get recognition.

Slim Gaillard

I first met Kenny in Birdland in New York and I always remember him as a man who enjoyed life and laughed a lot. He also had high musical standards and expected musicians to play up to the same level – or get off the stand. He was the champ at holding a tempo.

As a man he was quiet, easygoing and he was nice to everybody. But he hated loudmouths.

He recorded with Slam Stewart and me in 1941 and I also played with him much later in the Meridien Hotel in Paris with Dizzy. He was a truly great drummer.

Simone Ginibre

I met Kenny in 1959 when I became house singer at the Blue Note. My name then was Simone Chevalier. I worked opposite Klook at first, with René Urtreger or Georges Arvanitas. Later I worked regularly with Kenny's trio, and one night he said to me, 'Tomorrow afternoon we are going to rehearse.' I asked him, 'Why a rehearsal suddenly?' And he said, 'Because you need it – and if *you* are bad, then I'll be bad, too.'

I was still learning as a singer and Kenny would reduce me to tears sometimes, saying, 'Who do you think you are – Carmen?' That really upset me because Carmen McRae was my favourite singer. But he was doing it for my own good. He made me rehearse a lot in the afternoons and he taught me so much about music.

I worked at the Blue Note, sometimes with Klook, sometimes with Bud Powell, up to 1964 and the last night I played there was with Kenny – plus Sahib Shihab, Francy Boland, Jimmy Woode and Joe Harris, who played percussion.

Kenny was a perfect accompanist for a singer – because he listened. He played *for* you. He would play differently behind me from the way he'd play for Nancy Holloway – because we were different.

As a person, Kenny was beautiful. He was very sweet, very quiet and he had a great sense of humour. He used to laugh a lot and he was very kind to me. As a matter of fact he did me the favour of making me give up my singing career. He said to me one night, 'Look, you're nice, you sing OK – but you're not getting anywhere.' (Which was true.) 'You should get married, settle down and have a kid.' I was thirty-four at the time. I took his advice – and I never regretted it.

Benny Golson

The thing that was outstanding about Kenny Clarke was his ability to swing at any tempo. There are many drummers who are good time-keepers – but it's not the same thing. I can't conceive of Kenny Clarke playing and not swinging. It was an intuitive thing.

I got to play with Kenny in Paris in 1958 when I was there with the Jazz Messengers – it was a first trip to Europe for all of us and we jammed with Klook in the Club St Germain and also played with him at the Olympia Theatre. I had only known Klook superficially in the States but I got to know him much better after he moved to Europe. When I made that first visit to

Paris, Kenny helped me with the language and made a point of coming with me to the hotel so that he could interpret for me. He was so helpful.

I never heard anything negative about him as a man or as a musician. He was a legend. And that cymbal beat! The basic pattern on cymbal is a quarter note and two eighth notes; when it got a little bit hipper you heard the quarter note, a dotted eighth and a sixteenth; but Kenny went a little beyond that, like with a double dotted eighth and almost a thirty-second . . . just tipping the edge. His swing was so buoyant that the players out front could lean back on it and relax. When you have an outstanding drummer like Kenny, you are almost unaware of him because he becomes a part of what you are doing. Not too many drummers have that capability.

Jimmy Gourley

He was the driving force. Musicians wanted to come to the Blue Note just to play with Klook. He was the drummer you judged all the other drummers by. The sound he got from the drums, his beautiful time, his enthusiasm, the lift he gave to soloists, no matter who they were – these were Kenny's great assets. Sometimes we'd have real nothings coming up and sitting in, but Kenny would play just as hard behind them as he'd play with the giants.

Mind you, Kenny didn't have any time for passengers when it came to the regular group. You had to pull your weight. Klook didn't like it if someone lay down on him. He'd soon let them know! But if you were trying your best, then he'd be lenient about your mistakes. It was a great privilege to have known him as a friend and to have worked with him, on and off, for twenty-five years.

Johnny Griffin

When I first came to Paris I didn't hang out with Klook a lot because I worked mostly with Arthur Taylor. Sometimes, though, I'd go out to Kenny's house and cook and then we'd sit in the backyard and talk. I got closer to him when we went on vacation together – we rented a house and brought our families. I talked a lot with Klook then.

He took a great interest in what was going on in the world – he always had his head in newspapers and would listen to the news on radio. He didn't just live in music – he lived in people's sorrows all over the world, and was concerned about them.

He was a man of dignity and actually rather conservative. I wrote a tune while I was in the Clarke–Boland Band called 'The "JAMFs" are Coming'. JAMFs, of course, stands for jive-assed motherfuckers. One night at Ronnie Scott's Kenny announced the tune and somebody shouted, 'What does "JAMFs" mean?' Kenny was really embarrassed. He looked fiercely at me, and then turned back to the mike and said, 'Oh, well . . . it means, er . . . it means, "Just a Mere Friend".'

He was a very positive person, but if something bugged him, he'd let you know about it in no uncertain terms. He would get angry in a very calm way. Like a Sicilian. Never loud, never menacing – but he'd talk through his teeth and you would sense that there was danger ahead.

He took a pride in his appearance. That's the way he was brought up. He came from that generation where you couldn't play in a band unless you dressed neat and had good manners. That stayed with him.

He liked to have a good time, smoke a joint or two, take a drink – never too many – and to enjoy the company of pretty ladies. He was such a pleasant, nice-looking man, always smiling, and a perfect gentleman. His manners were impeccable. He liked to smile, to laugh and to listen to jokes. He was not a loud talker or a braggart, but he was a hell of a musician. With music he was like a kid with toys. He was completely in his element.

Marc Hemmeler

I first met Kenny in Paris in the sixties and we became very firm friends. I played with him a great deal at the Blue Note, on and off for two years, and did many concert dates and recordings with him and Stéphane Grappelli. I love playing ballads and he would always ask me to play 'My One and Only Love'. It was one of his favourite songs. He was a man with a big heart and sometimes his demeanour was as innocent, simple and trusting as a child's. He loved to laugh and he loved to play and he adored his wife and son.

One of my most treasured memories is of a jam session at the Mars Club with Art Simmons on piano, Michel Gaudry on bass, Elek Bacsik on guitar, Les Spann on flute, the Delta Rhythm Boys, Harold Nicholas and Ella Fitzgerald. What a line-up! Klook was there, too – and, since there was no drum set at the club, he took out his brushes and played on a telephone directory resting on the piano.

In the last ten years of his life, after his first heart attack, he didn't play very much. I think he was a little apprehensive about overdoing things. I had a trio at the Bilboquet for part of that time and Klook often used to come and listen to our music. One evening we had a new drummer with us – it was really his first professional gig and he was a little nervous. You can imagine the expression on his face when the door opened and in walked Art Taylor, Max Roach and Kenny Clarke. He must have been terrified. But Kenny was so nice and encouraging to him. That was typical of Klook. He was a very modest man, discreet – not to say a little timid, and he was always ready to help young musicians.

He was a good businessman. He knew how to get good money and he always paid his musicians well. One night in 1975 Kenny, Jimmy Gourley, Jack Sewing and myself were playing in a club outside Paris when a man came up to the bandstand and asked if Kenny would play his drum feature, 'Night in Tunisia', with two extra choruses and dedicate the piece to 'Bernard'. I spoke to Kenny and he agreed. After the number the guy gave me 2,000 francs which I handed over to Klook. He split the money four ways. That was Kenny.

I remember a night in the Blue Note when Elvin Jones came into the club. Kenny played even more magnificently than usual. He was fantastic – and, knowing him, I had a very strong impression that he was saying to Elvin, 'I may be in France, playing nightly in the Blue Note, but I'm still Kenny Clarke.'

Kenny was one of the five great drummers in jazz – and probably the best of all when it came to brushes. His time was impeccable, his swing legendary. He was a perfect accompanist, a very sensitive musician. And he could play on any drumkit. He would take half an hour adjusting it, and then he would play it as if it was his own.

He loved life, and he adapted to the French lifestyle really well – with the exception that he insisted on drinking Coca-Cola with his meals!

Billy Higgins

Most of everything I arrived at as a drummer comes through the masters: Max Roach, Philly Joe Jones and, in particular, Kenny Clarke . . . I really liked the *sound* Kenny Clarke got out of his instrument. He was not only an accompanist, he integrated the drums into the music.

(*Hot House*, February 1990)

Nancy Holloway

Kenny Clarke for me is the greatest drummer ever and the greatest accompanist a singer could wish for. I first met him in 1956 at the Mars Club in Paris. I had just started as a singer and I had a lot to learn; but Kenny took to me right from the beginning. He was one of my best buddies – he gave me so much.

The first time I worked with him was in 1958 at the Blue Note with Jimmy Gourley and Lou Bennett. This was the time when rock was beginning to make an impact and I wanted to do a rock number. I was more of an entertainer than a singer. I had this tune that was a thirteen-bar blues and Lou and Jimmy really didn't want to play it. But Kenny told them, 'Let her sing what she wants, man. She's up there in the front.' And he played rock for me, and it was fabulous.

The incident I will never forget was in 1961 when I had my own club, Chez Nancy Holloway, in the rue St Florentin. Art Simmons was on piano and Arthur Taylor on drums. One night, during intermission, Kenny Clarke came into the club with Oscar Peterson and Ray Brown. Arthur Taylor came up to me and said, 'I ain't playing for you, bitch, because you can't sing.'

I was destroyed. I felt terrible. I went over to Kenny's table to say hello and sat down with him. He asked me what was the matter and I told him Art didn't want to play with me any more. Immediately Kenny said, 'I'll play for you.' And he went up and played the whole show with us. I'll never, never forget that because that was one of the things that helped me so much when my confidence was shattered.

Kenny was a beautiful person. My mother came to visit me in 1958 and she fell in love with him. He took the time and trouble to talk with her and showed interest in what she had to say.

Kenny did so many things for me – big things and little things. For instance, when I was running the Mars Club with Pete Rice in 1958 or 1959, Carmen McRae came over to Paris for a week's vacation. I love Carmen and I wanted her to work at the club, but I didn't dare ask her because I knew we couldn't pay enough money. But it was Kenny who said to her, 'Yes, baby, why don't you do it?' And thanks to Kenny, Carmen did three days at the club.

Kenny has influenced so many other musicians, and through his drum school in Paris he taught hundreds how to play. Wanting to teach, to pass on your knowledge and experience, when you are as great a drummer as he was – I think that's just beautiful.

He was one of the sweetest cats to work with – all that talent and all that kindness, too. He would play for a singer on drums just like a pianist does. I could have sung with only his accompaniment.

After my club closed I went back to the Blue Note and worked with Kenny until 1961. That was the greatest thing for me.

We all loved Kenny. He was one of the great persons that appeared in my life.

Noah Howard

I first met Kenny in the Fall of 1969 at the Chat Qui Pèche in

Paris. Our band had been booked for a week at the club and we were playing what, at the time, was called free jazz. Kenny came down to the club almost every night – sometimes with Memphis Slim. I was about twenty-six at the time and they were sort of father figures for me. I spent a lot of time with Kenny talking about music and his young days, going all the way back to Parker and the MJQ. What Kenny was always saying about music was, 'Learn as much as you can so that you can interpret what you are playing to the fullest extent.'

Our relationship lasted for many years. He was also a friend and a source of inspiration to our drummer, Muhammad Ali. When I approached him in May 1977 to record with my group his immediate response was, 'What took you so long to ask?' The reason I wanted Kenny was for his fluidity of rhythm which fitted very well with the pieces we were recording. We rehearsed the material and then went into the studio to record. After the session I remember him saying to all of us, 'Hey, that was a lot of fun.' And he told me personally, 'I know you are expressing your own personality. Everybody has a right to tell their story.'

Milt Jackson

He was a tremendous person. As a matter of fact, most of my philosophies in life came through a combination of him and Dizzy. They had a very heavy influence on my whole life in every aspect, musically and otherwise. I used to hang out with Kenny a lot in New York, and every time I came to France I'd look him up. We were both thorough Capricorns and we understood each other very well.

His musical philosophy was the same as Dizzy's: Whatever you do, it has to make sense, to have a meaning to it. The music was so great in the forties because it had a definite meaning, a realism attached to it.

After he settled in Paris, a lot of us tried to talk him into coming back to the States, but he didn't like what was happening there. He paid a price, though, because eventually, he started to be considered as a local musician and to be paid accordingly. I think he detested that. I noticed that he didn't get hired for the European festivals – and I think the reason was that he demanded the kind of money that a first-class artist is entitled to expect – and they didn't want to pay it. Occasionally it happened because I demanded that he be hired to play with me.

He was one of the most swinging drummers I ever met. He had a perfect concept of swing – and that's what jazz is all about. When he played behind you it was inspirational – he made you play the best you possibly could.

Philly Joe Jones

Kenny Clarke influenced me enormously. He totally revolutionized the world of the drums. He originated the way we play bass drum today – all those spaces. He taught us so much that we could progress a little further. When I heard him play, I was so knocked out that I didn't sleep at night. When I listened to Kenny I had the impression of being in the presence of the gods; that's how impressed I was when I saw him play.

We lived together in New York for a time and that was a great opportunity for me. Kenny was my mentor. Max Roach and Art Blakey also expressed great feeling on the drums – and there are other great drummers like Elvin Jones and Roy Haynes. Some of them are excellent. But not like Kenny Clarke. Even Max, great as he is, doesn't touch me as much.

(*Jazz Hot*, October 1985)

Quincy Jones

I had so many beautiful moments with Klook while I was living in Paris. I had first met him in New York and immediately got a warm buzz from him.

When I was working for Barclay Records, of course, I hired Kenny every chance I could. He rates triple-A in my book. He was a pioneer, an innovator. He put syncopation into the bass drum. People talk today about hip-hop and go-go – but that all goes back to the movement that was started by Klook and carried on by Max Roach and Art Blakey.

I count myself uniquely fortunate to have been able to call on

Kenny for so many of those record dates in Paris. We developed a great friendship and I still have the watch he gave me in 1960. That touched me very much. He was an earthy, intelligent, warm, sincere and romantic person. I loved him and I miss him very much.

Al Levitt

Kenny was a very profound person, very mature; he was aware of a lot of negative things that existed in the world, and I'm sure it bothered him – but he didn't let it affect his relationship with people he got close to.

As a drummer, what really set him apart from his peers was that he swung so much in a musical way. He was one of the few drummers who could just play with one stick on one cymbal and nothing else would be needed. His cymbal beat was so swinging that it was the whole foundation of the rhythm section.

What was also important was the way he integrated his playing with the bass player's. I only recently found out that Kenny had a brother who was a bass player and they would practise together a lot, looking for an approach that would let the bass come more to the fore – rather than being dominated by the bass drum.

Kenny's experience with piano, vibraphone and trombone helped him to play drums in a musical way – not in the usual drummer's way. And he would play solos on the drums in the same way as a pianist would play a piano solo.

John Lewis

I shared an apartment with Kenny in Queens in the early fifties and I got to know him pretty well. He was a wonderful, wonderful, wonderful person. Very kind-hearted. Everyone who knew him enjoyed being around him. And, of course, as a drummer he was unique. I never heard anybody play drums like Klook. When I first played with him it was so fulfilling because I was able to play exactly what I wanted to play and know that he would be with me. I was used to the normal, conventional way of playing drums. Kenny didn't play that way – he had a special, individual magic. He was one of the most creative drummers I ever heard.

When he played in Dizzy's big band he established a standard that made it hard for the drummers who followed him. They just couldn't do the things he used to do. As a matter of fact, some of the music had to be dropped because the drummers couldn't play it.

Jackie McLean

My earliest recollection of Kenny Clarke was when I was about seventeen or eighteen and would take Bud Powell to his gigs and try to keep him from drinking too much. This was in the late forties after Bud had come out of hospital. It was the biggest thrill of my life when I first got to play with Klook – on a Blue Note record date with Miles in May 1952.

Kenny gave me a lot of encouragement – he urged me to work harder at my music, just as Blakey was to do later.

Another treasured memory I have is the night that Cannonball Adderley burst upon the New York scene at the Café Bohemia. I was in the club, sitting in with Herbie Nichols, and Oscar Pettiford wanted to put me up against Cannonball. So I stayed on the stand when Oscar's band came back. There was Horace Silver, Jerome Richardson, Oscar and Klook, plus Cannonball and Nat Adderley. We played 'I'll Remember April' – and Cannonball was fantastic.

My last memory of Kenny was playing with him at Wolf Trap in 1980 in a band with Dizzy, Slide Hampton, Sonny Stitt, John Lewis and Ray Brown. That was the last time I talked to him and even at this late date he was encouraging me to continue to try to reach the highest possible level of musicianship. I loved him a lot and I was crushed when he passed.

His contribution to jazz cannot be overstated. He was the first to take a step beyond Sid Catlett and Papa Jo. I used to love his cymbal beat. As Miles used to say, it sounded like just one stroke because it had that continuity. He was always one of my idols, one of my mentors, and he was one of the original four – Bird, Dizzy, Monk and Klook. He had a rhythm that nobody else had. He was purely, definitely and exclusively Kenny Clarke.

Shelly Manne
I love Klook, I can always recognize him, in whatever company, just by the sound of his cymbal. A true master.

Pierre Michelot
It was not just drummers whom Kenny Clarke influenced – but bassists, saxophonists, trumpet players, pianists; he influenced them all because drums play such an important part in jazz. I worked with Kenny regularly over a period of fourteen years and obviously became very familiar with his style of playing and with the beautiful way he accompanied. He had a very special sound – I can always recognize it.

When I first began working with him, I was naturally a little bit intimidated. But he didn't attempt to tell me what to do. And he didn't need to – I just listened to him and tried to follow him. And it worked.

He was a very calm person and easy to get along with. I never saw him really angry – but he could become annoyed if musicians weren't playing to the best of their ability. Music was his main passion. He was a total professional and he expected his fellow musicians to be the same. He didn't like dilettantes.

His French friends really appreciated the fact that he made a real effort to speak their language. He really didn't speak it too fluently, but he was better than many of his fellow Americans because he assimilated himself into French society.

Kenny was a man who had no sadness in his spirit. He believed in simplicity both in life and in music, and he was concerned not to poison his life with unnecessary problems. When we played together we achieved a kind of creative complicity that made it so satisfying. He would have this marvellous smile on his face and would give me a little wink from time to time to indicate, '*On est bien, on est heureux; tout va bien.*' Everything I learned about playing time came from Kenny.

Big Nick Nicholas
I had the great good fortune to work with Klook in Dizzy's band for a whole year in 1948. He was the peak of the hierarchy of modern jazz drumming and a big influence on hundreds of drummers. Two of the most memorable musical moments I treasure from that period were the recording of 'Manteca' and 'Cubana Be, Cubana Bop' and our first concert at the Salle Pleyel in Paris. I remember how beautifully, sympathetically Kenny played behind me on my feature, 'Yesterdays'. He had such a good sound.

Kenny was a totally honest man and he hated dishonest people. He always came on to the stand ready to do his best and he expected his fellow musicians to do the same. He had a way of bringing out the best in people.

Francis Paudras
I first met Kenny when he was living in Paris with Annie Ross. I was living right opposite at 64, rue de Clichy. Later, when he was working at the Blue Note, he would sometimes come to the studio where I worked to smoke a joint with Dizzy Reece and myself and listen to records. It was a fantastic experience for me to have this giant of a musician in my studio. And apart from being a musical genius, Kenny had such great human qualities. He was the most discreet and humble of all the musicians I have met. He had such an assured grasp of his importance to the music that he did not go in search of publicity. He combined self-assurance with humility.

He adapted quickly to the French way of life, took the trouble to learn the language, and lived in his little suburban house just like a middle-class Frenchman. He liked peace and tranquillity, was a man of few words and had a most generous disposition. I think no musician was more loved and respected by his peers than Kenny.

Henri Renaud
Kenny Clarke was the most sought-after studio drummer, his lively musical intelligence enabling him to accompany sym-

pathetically soloists of very varied styles. Thus he could record with Sidney Bechet as well as Charlie Parker; with Roy Eldridge as well as Miles Davis; with Coleman Hawkins as well as Dexter Gordon; with Cannonball Adderley as well as Lee Konitz, with the blazing big band of Dizzy Gillespie as well as the sedate Modern Jazz Quartet. One can say without exaggeration that he was the master of masters of modern percussion.

Max Roach

Klook really figured in my life as a friend and counsellor. He was very special and always supportive of the kind of things I was trying to do. I got so much from him. He was always ready to share with me. He had a strong personality, was extremely generous, and I never heard him put anyone down.

He looked after my daughter when she won a scholarship to study in Switzerland and he was an uncle to all five of my children. I felt the same way about his two boys. They always had a home here in the States and *vice versa*. I guess if I had a big brother it would be Kenny Clarke.

When my oldest son was taken ill in Europe with ptomaine poisoning, Kenny did everything for him. He was just marvellous.

He also had a great influence on me as far as my political outlook goes. He left the States because it was so uncomfortable for him and I was always impressed by the way he was treated in Europe.

I would always call on Klook when I was in France. The last time I saw him was when I was playing in Paris as part of a tour that Gaby Kleinschmidt put together for the double quartet. I was at the New Morning and Kenny was there sitting right close to the stage. I was playing on the worst set of drums ever, and when I came off, Klook said, 'You know, Max, there are no bad drummers. Only bad drums!'

As for Klook's playing – well, he had superb co-ordination. All four of his limbs worked together in complete harmony so that one didn't overplay the other. Most drummers are nearly always off balance, but Klook had everything right. He had none of the common faults of other drummers; everything was even. That's why everyone wanted to play with him. We younger guys, Shelly and the others, didn't get a break until he went to Europe!

Once when I was on tour, I was just going on stage and Klook said to me, 'Max – make history.' That was typical of Kenny. He was always ready to give encouragement.

Red Rodney

Kenny Clarke was one of the greatest drummers in the entire history of jazz – the no. 1 bebop innovator. He really laid it down for Max Roach and Roy Haynes. He showed them the direction in which to go – he was the progenitor of all of today's great drummers. But he didn't really get the recognition due to him – I guess because he moved to France. I still get asked about him today by some of the younger cats.

He was a very musical drummer; he knew the form and the structure of the music we were playing. Later in the same mould came Shelly Manne and Mel Lewis. Kenny's musicality was an added bonus to his flawless time.

As a human being, he was without peer. He was a beautiful person. I remember, as a kid of eighteen, coming to New York after leaving Gene Krupa and hanging out on 52nd Street. Kenny gave me a couple of Monday nights at the Downbeat and the Three Deuces. He encouraged me – and I learned just by listening to what he was doing. He had this ability to make you feel good about yourself. He was a sensitive man with a natural dignity and he was an outstanding contributor to our music.

Annie Ross

One of the things I really appreciated about Kenny was that he could be very funny. He had a great sense of humour. He was also a very generous man – although, at the time we were together, he had nothing to be generous with. At that time it was always a fight to get the money. It was frustrating for him, because he had left the States to put the racial problems behind him, had found that jazz musicians were much more respected in France, but he still couldn't really make enough money to live on. Later, of course, things got a great deal better financially for him.

As for his musicianship – it was superb. His time was phenomenal and he played with such authority that it made you feel very secure to have him behind you. I have a great admiration for Kenny, both as a musician and as a person.

Ronnie Scott

I remember Kenny as a placid, pipe-smoking amiable guy with a very stable disposition. I can't ever remember him losing his temper in all the ten years I worked in the Clarke–Boland Big Band.

I was always slightly in awe of Kenny, but it was a great pleasure to work with him. He played with that relaxed, unhurried feel – never dragging, but very laid-back. And it didn't matter what the tempo was, he always swung. He had incredible poise and a marvellous sound. You can always recognize that cymbal beat. I know Kenny Clare got a great kick out of playing with Klook – but Klook also enjoyed having Kenny in the band. They really blended well together. Of course, it might have been different if it had been Buddy Rich.

Klook enjoyed the big band like all of us did and although he was unobtrusive as a co-leader, the way he swung the band was certainly a key factor in its success.

Horace Silver

He was the daddy of the bebop drummers. He started it. He's the inventor of it. He was first and then, I don't know whether Art came second or Max came second. But they came after Kenny Clarke. Max Roach most definitely was influenced by Kenny Clarke.

The first time I played with him was when I started working with Miles in April 1954 after a year with Art Blakey. It was Kenny on drums, Percy Heath on bass and Lucky Thompson on tenor – and it was quite a different experience for me because Kenny was the master drummer. He played a different style, so I had to adjust. After that it was great; with him and Percy I had a ball. It was because we sounded so good with Miles that they called us for record dates. We made sessions with Art Farmer and Gigi Gryce. I consider myself blessed to have played with him.

The last time I saw Klook was in Paris some years before he died. He was playing in a club with Lou Bennett and during the intermission I had a talk with him and I asked him, 'Klook, how did you get your style, the unique way you play? What prompted you to play this way?' And he said, 'Way back, man, when I was living in Pittsburgh, as a young guy I used to practise all the time with this bass player, me and him together. And he always used to tell me to stay out of his way. That's how I developed my style because he was always on my back about staying out of his way.'

Kenny was a beautiful person. I rarely saw him when he wasn't in a good state of mind – he was always smiling, jovial, happy. I only saw him lose his cool once – in a nightclub when he almost got into a fight because this person was bugging him. He took it as long as he could, then he got mad and grabbed the guy by the collar. He was going to punch him and they had to break them up. But he was justified because the guy was bothering him. That was the only time I saw him get violent.

He was really an excellent musician. I remember that on one of the sessions we did with Miles for Prestige – with Davy Schildkraut, Percy, Klook and myself – Kenny unpacked his drums and found he'd forgotten his sock cymbals. I don't know what he did, but when you hear the record you're not aware that the sock cymbals are missing.

Hal Singer

The new music would not have been the same without Kenny Clarke's contribution to the rhythmic concept. His rhythmic ideas were just as important as the lines and the harmony.

I first met Klook in New York in 1943 and as I got to know him I discovered just what a wonderful person he was. He was a proud man who earned the respect of all who knew him and he was a very good friend to me. Throughout his life he helped a lot of musicians achieve wider recognition.

He had a great feeling and respect for our music and he gave so much to it. In practically every drummer you listen to today you can hear Klook's influence.

Grady Tate
I never heard Kenny Clarke play in person – but I've always felt as though I had because I studied him so much and I always tried to emulate his style and his musicianship. I first met him in 1973, and when he came to New York for the last time, he let it be known that he wanted to hook up with me. We met at a place called the China Song and, much to my surprise, he told me just how much he had studied me and the many records I had made. This was a shock because I was in awe of him – I was a dedicated disciple.

But that was one of the beautiful things about Klook – he not only never stopped playing, but he never stopped listening; and that was what kept him fresh. Whatever was happening out there, Kenny was aware of it.

Maybe some drummers won't appreciate my saying this, but, for me, Kenny never was a drummer – his first calling was that of master musician; he was, incidentally, a drummer – as well as being a painter and a poet of our time. What he did made the most complex things sound simple. This was his genius. He was an absolute monster. I loved him to death.

Frank Ténot
Kenny was one of the greatest percussionists in the history of jazz, certainly among the top ten. Most important, he was one of the main inventors, with Max Roach, of the bebop rhythm. I first heard and met him in Paris in February 1948 when he was part of Dizzy Gillespie's Big Band. After he moved to France in 1956, I saw a lot of him, both for professional reasons and as a friend. I often chose him for the radio programmes and recordings which I produced.

Kenny was a very kind person, with a steady, easygoing temperament – a characteristic which distinguished him from other American musicians who tended to be aggressive and assertive, especially where money was concerned. Kenny would play for a small fee if he thought the producer couldn't afford more. He was always trustful and seldom complained. He was always on time, he gave advice to less experienced musicians and he showed respect to the stars (who often didn't have a quarter of his talent). He met all eventualities, even the unpleasant ones, philosophically. In other words, Kenny was always possessed of a great stability – and not only in his playing.

Although Kenny preferred to speak English, he could express himself well in French *argot*, with a Parisian accent. He liked to call his buddies his *potes*. He was also a connoisseur of food and wine and he adapted perfectly to the French way of life. He didn't care much for publicity and interviews. It was hard to get him to tell any anecdotes – he was sensitive about possibly offending people.

It's interesting to trace the path of Kenny's life. He arrived in Paris with a bunch of young lions of the bebop revolution, basking in the title of top percussionist. He ended his days living in bourgeois suburban tranquillity giving drum lessons to people of all backgrounds and ages. One thing is certain: during the almost thirty years he lived in Paris, Kenny Clarke contributed significantly to raising the level of French jazz and improving the quality of French musicians.

Clark Terry

Kenny Clarke was right at the top with the other leaders. An all-time great. I can't remember exactly when I first met him – it seems I always knew him – but I guess it must have been at around the time of the formation of the Modern Jazz Quartet. He was the warmest person you could ever wish to know and lots of fun to hang out with. At a party one night I remember him straightening out some American about how to open a bottle of champagne. You don't pop the cork and let the bubbly spew all over the place. You ease it out gently, almost no noise and no loss of beverage, he told him. 'Don't crush the grape,' he'd say.

As a drummer his greatest assets were time, sensitivity and taste. He influenced many drummers – peers – and the younger ones to follow. I played a gig with him soon after his first heart attack in December 1975, and he was wailing like a brand-new drummer and swinging as ever.

As a human being he was fearless and involved and straight ahead with everyone at all times. You might say, mallets towards none!

Kenny was a proud representative of his race; he was well aware of his heritage but not at all militant – he took it all in his stride, with a big smile.

He was a very tolerant man, but he didn't dig cats who couldn't play.

Joe Wilder

My first memory of Klook would have to have been in 1943. I was playing at the Apollo Theatre and I went to rehearse with Luis Russell's band. Kenny was the drummer. I didn't know him then – but I heard him play and the way he set off the band was just unbelievable. You didn't hear many drummers like that. He was a fantastic band drummer – playing for the guys.

Later I would play with Kenny when I went to Minton's to sit in. They were all there – Tony Scott, Monk and Tiny Grimes – and, of course, the Demon, the world's worst sitter-in!

I also remember recording with Kenny for the Savoy label – we sort of became the house band for a while. I didn't hang out with Kenny much because I don't drink and I never smoked pot – and, you know, you become a sort of annoyance to the guys in this situation. They wanted to do what they wanted to do and they didn't want to be embarrassed by having me hanging around.

The thing that impressed me most about Kenny was that he was one of the first guys I heard play a drum solo in which you could follow the melody; you could hear by what he was doing that he always had the melody in mind, and you could always tell where he was in the tune.

I never actually worked officially with Klook outside the recording studio, but I did sit in with him at the Blue Note in Paris one night while Chet Baker was appearing. Kenny made an enormous contribution to jazz – not only as a musician but, as a clean-cut, neatly dressed guy he did a lot to dispel the stereotype of the lazy, disorganized, irresponsible jazz musician. What he did for the development of our music has not been fully appreciated. There are a lot of drummers around who picked up things from other drummers and are not really aware that it was Kenny who originated them.

One amusing moment comes to mind when I think of Kenny. It was in 1956 and he was about to quit the United States to settle in France. I ran into him in the street and he said to me, 'I hope I'm going to be able to get out of the country.' I asked, 'Why, what's the problem?' And he said, 'I have about twenty-five parking tickets and I bet they're gonna get me at the pier!'

Jimmy Woode

Kenny Clarke was one of the warmest persons I have ever known – he was something of a father figure for me and a great inspiration. I never heard anybody say a bad or negative word about Kenny. Never. He would never give anyone reason to speak negatively about him. he was without question one of the greatest musicians and one of the most beautiful people I ever had the privilege to meet.

Phil Woods

My first playing experience with Klook was in 1960 during the Paris run of Harold Arlen's musical, *Free and Easy*. Ben Benjamin hired me to play the last set with the Bud Powell Trio (Bud, Pierre Michelot and Klook). I would dash from the theatre to the Blue Note and just make the bandstand for the third set. I was green and scared to death. Bud, of course, was an idol. He kept looking at me strangely and was probably wondering, 'Who is this young, ofay alto player and what the hell is he doing on the stand?' I expressed my trepidation to Klook. He took me across the street for a coffee and allayed my fears and told me I was doing fine. His kind of gracious consideration was my first exposure to this man's exemplary human qualities.

In 1968, shortly after moving to Paris, Kenny helped me clarify my newly acquired expatriate status. He even got me a spot on a TV panel show which included himself and Mezz Mezzrow. I was nervous about my jailhouse French, but actually nobody got a word in edgeways because Mezz raved on for the whole thirty minutes advocating legalization of hashish and other nonsense. Klook just sat there smiling, taking it all in. This was my first indication of the remarkable tolerance of this wonderful man.

I loved the Clarke-Boland Band, and when Derek Humble was ill, Klook asked me to fill in for him. Derek, by the way, was my favourite all-round alto player, lead or jazz. He was the best I ever heard. The album the band was doing was *Latin Kaleidoscope*. When Derek heard I was deputizing for him, he recovered miraculously after I had done one tune! Instead of sending me home, Klook paid me in full and I toured a few days with the band and just hung out with the cats.

We all looked up to Klook as the senior expatriate (a word I detest) and he was a great supporter of my European Rhythm Machine – always there in the audience, pipe in hand, smiling his approval. I'll never forget his encouragement during those tough times. *Au revoir*, Klook, *et à bientôt*!

Extract from: *Who's Who in America*

CLARKE, Kenneth Spearman (Kenny Clarke), musician; b.Pitts., Jan. 9, 1914. s.Charles Spearman and Grace (Scott) C.; ed. Ecole Normale de Musique de Paris; m.Daisy Dina Wallbach, May 26, 1962; 1 son, Laurent. Drummer; mem. Leroy Bradley Orch., 1933, Edgar Hayes Orch., 1936–37, Teddy Hill Orch., 1938–39, Louis Armstrong Orch., 1941, Ella Fitzgerald Orch., Minton's Playhouse, Birth of Modern Jazz, 1941–42; has appeared with Dizzy Gillespie, Charlie Parker, Th. Monk, others; prof. percussion Conservatory de St. Germain-en-Laye, France; mem. Clarke–Boland Orch. Served with AUS, 1944–46; ETO. Mason. Research field of percussion; creator modern conception of drumming; co-ordinated independence style for drummers. Home: 142 bis, rue de Rosny, Montreuil s/bois 93 France. Office: 18, rue de la Fontaine au Roy, Paris 11, France.

Bibliography

Berendt, Joachim, *The Jazz Book*, Paladin, London 1976

Carles, Philippe, Clergeat, André & Comolli, Jean-Louis, *Dictionnaire du Jazz*, Robert Laffont, Paris 1988

Carr, Ian, *Miles Davis*, Paladin, London 1984

Chilton, John, *Who's Who of Jazz*, Macmillan, London 1985

Collier, James Lincoln, *The Making of Jazz*, Macmillan, London 1981

Davis, Miles, with Quincy Troup, *Miles Davis: The Autobiography*, Simon & Schuster, New York 1989

Davis, Ursula Broschke, *Paris without Regret*, University of Iowa Press, 1986

Delaunay, Charles, *Delaunay's Dilemma*, Editions W., Macon, France 1985

Feather, Leonard, *The New Encyclopedia of Jazz*, Horizon Press, New York 1960

Feather, Leonard, *The Encyclopedia of Jazz in the Sixties*, Horizon Press, New York 1966

Feather, Leonard & Gitler, Ira, *The Encyclopedia of Jazz in the Seventies*, Horizon Press, New York 1976

Feather, Leonard, *From Satchmo to Miles*, Stein and Day, New York 1972

Gillespie, Dizzy, with Al Fraser, *To be or not to Bop*, Doubleday, New York 1979

Gitler, Ira, *Jazz Masters of the Forties*, Macmillan, New York 1966

Gitler, Ira, *Swing to Bop*, Oxford University Press, New York 1985

Godbolt, Jim, *A History of Jazz in Britain, 1919–50*, Quartet Books, London 1984
Haggerty, Michael, *A Flower for Kenny*, WHRB Jazz Dept, Cambridge, Massachusetts 1985
Hodeir, André, *Jazz: Its Evolution and Essence*, Grove Press, New York 1956
Horricks, Raymond, *Jazzmen d'Aujourd'hui*, Editions Buchet Chastel, Paris 1960
Horricks, Raymond, *Quincy Jones*, Omnibus Press, London 1986
Parker, Chan & Paudras, Francis, *To Bird with Love*, Wizlov, Poitiers, France 1981
Paudras, Francis, *La Danse des Infidelès*, Editions de l'Instant, Paris 1986
Reisner, Robert, *Bird: The Legend of Charlie Parker*, Quartet Books, London 1962
Russell, Ross, *Bird Lives!*, Quartet Books, London 1973
Scheffner, Manfred, *Bielefelder Katalogs* (1977 to 1989), Vereinigte Motor-Verlage, Stuttgart
Schuller, Gunther, *The Swing Era*, Oxford University Press, New York 1989
Shapiro, Nat & Hentoff, Nat, *Hear Me Talkin' to Ya*, Dover, New York 1966
Shaw, Arnold, *The Street that Never Slept*, Coward, McCann & Geoghegan, New York 1971
Taylor, Arthur, *Notes and Tones*, Perigee Books, New York 1982
Zwerin, Mike, *Round About Close to Midnight: The Jazz Writings of Boris Vian*, Quartet Books, London 1988

Kenny Clarke Compositions Registered with the Société des Auteurs, Compositeurs et Éditeurs de Musique in Paris

Algerian Cynicism
A Z Blues
Blues Mood
Cascade
Cat Blues (Blues Kitten)
Dimanche
Epistrophy
Fire Drums
I Don't Want Nothin'
I'll Get You Yet
Jay Jay
Klook Returns
Klook's Report
Laurent
Love Me Pretty Baby
Milk Shake
Nobody Knows
On n'Enterre pas le Dimanche
Pieces of Time
Roll 'Em Bags
Rue Chaptal (Royal Roost)
Salt Peanuts
Sonor
Strollin'
Volcano
Was It a Rose?
Wild Man

Discography

This discography is largely based on that compiled by Michael Haggerty, with assistance from Matthew Annenberg, as part of a tribute to Kenny Clarke – *A Flower for Kenny* – published in May 1985. I would like to express my grateful thanks to Mr Haggerty and Mr Annenberg for permitting me to use their listing as a basis for this discography. I wish also to express my sincere gratitude to Manfred Scheffner, author of the indispensable *Bielefelder Jazz Katalog*, for the enormous amount of time and trouble he took to check, annotate and revise a large number of the entries.

Kenny Clarke recorded so prolifically in a career spanning more than fifty years that a comprehensive discography is almost certainly an impossibility. He made many sessions for Barclay during the time when Quincy Jones was the label's staff arranger and a large number of the recordings were innocent of personnel listings. However I believe all the major dates are included.

I have not attempted to list *all* the labels and serial numbers under which the various tracks have been released – I leave that task to the dedicated discographers.

M.H.

Key to Abbreviations

t	trumpet	cl	clarinet
fh	flugelhorn	bcl	bass clarinet
c	cornet	frh	french horn
tb	trombone	ob	oboe
vtb	valve trombone	tu	tuba
btb	bass trombone	fl	flute

picc	piccolo	b	bass
as	alto saxophone	d	drums
ts	tenor saxophone	perc	percussion
ss	soprano saxophone	cgas	congas
bs	baritone saxophone	arr	arranger
bsax	bass saxophone	cond	conductor
vln	violin	ldr	leader
vb	vibraphone	vcl	vocal
xyl	xylophone		
p	piano	**Record Labels**	
elp	electric piano	Atl	Atlantic
org	organ	BN	Blue Note
acc	accordion	Col	Columbia
g	guitar	OJC	Original Jazz Classics
ban	banjo	Pres	Prestige

1937:

March 9
New York City

EDGAR HAYES AND HIS ORCHESTRA
Bernie Flood, Henry Goodwin, Shelton Hemphill (t); Bob Horton, Clyde Bernhardt, John Haughton (tb); Stanley Palmer, Al Sherrett (as); Crawford Wetherington, Joe Garland (ts); Edgar Hayes (p); Andy Jackson (g); Elmer James (b); Kenny Clarke (d); Orlando Roberson (vcl)
Manhattan Jam
Sylvia (Rejected)
Variety VA 586, Vocalion 3773
Sweet Is The Word For You (vcl)
Just A Quiet Evening (vcl)
Variety 513

May 25
New York City

EDGAR HAYES AND HIS ORCHESTRA
Leonard Davis (t); Joe Britton (tb); Rudy Powell (cl, as) and Roger Boyd (as) replace Hemphill, Houghton, Palmer and Sherrett; Ralph Sawyer (vcl) replaces Roberson
Caravan (2 takes) (New World Records NW 217 only, 1 take)
Edgar Steps Out
Stomping At The Renny
Laughing At Life (vcl Ralph Sawyer & Chorus)
Decca, Brunswick, Swingfan 1003

July 27
New York City

David James (tb) replaces Britton; Kenny Clarke (vb)†
Laughing At Life (vcl Bernie Flood)
High Wide And Handsome (vcl Ruth Ellington)†
Satan Takes A Holiday (Spooky Takes A Holiday)*
Decca, Brunswick, Brunswick 02482*, Swingfan, Coral

September 7
New York City

EDGAR HAYES QUINTET
Rudy Powell (cl); Edgar Hayes (p); Andy Jackson (g); Elmer James (b); Kenny Clarke (d,vb); Bill Darnell (vcl)
Love Me Or Leave Me (vcl)
Blue Skies
So Rare (vcl)

October 11
New York City

Same
Sweetheart
I Know Now (vcl)
When You And I Were Young, Maggie (vcl)
Decca, Brunswick, Swingfan 1003 (both sessions), Coral

Same

EDGAR HAYES AND HIS ORCHESTRA
Bernie Flood, Henry Goodwin, Leonard Davis (t); Robert Horton, Clyde Bernhardt, David James (tb); Roger Boyd (as); Rudy Powell (as,cl); Crawford Wetherington, Joe Garland (ts); Edgar Hayes (p); Andy Jackson (g); Elmer James (b); Kenny Clarke (d); Bill Darnell (vcl)
Queen Isabella
Old King Cole (vcl)
Shindig (vcl)
Let's Love (vcl)
Decca, Brunswick, Swingfan 1003

1938:
January 14,
February 17
New York City

EDGAR HAYES AND HIS ORCHESTRA
Bernie Flood, Henry Goodwin, Leonard Davis (t); Bob Horton, Clyde Bernhardt, David James (tb); Rudy Powell (cl,as); Roger Boyd (as); William Mitchener (ts); Joe Garland (ts,vcl); Edgar Hayes (p,vcl); Eddie Gibbs (g); Frank Darling (b); Kenny Clarke (d,vb); James Clay Anderson, Earlene Howell (vcl)
Meet The Band (vcl EH)
Fugitive From A Harem
Swingin' In The Promised Land
Barbary Coast Blues (vcl EH)
Help Me (Kenny Clarke vb)
Without You (vcl Clyde Bernhardt)
You're My First Thought Every Morning (vcl JCA)
In The Mood
Stardust
Sophisticated Swing
Decca, Brunswick, Swingfan 1003

March 8
Stockholm

KENNY CLARKE KVINTETT
Henry Goodwin (t); Rudy Powell (cl,as); Edgar Hayes (p); Eddie Gibbs (g); Frank Darling (b); Kenny Clarke (d,xyl); James Clay Anderson (vcl)
Once In A While (vcl JCA)

	I Found A New Baby (vcl JCA) **You're A Sweetheart** (vcl JCA) **Sweet Sue** Odeon A-255509, A-255510, D-2952, D-2953, Tax M-8035	
1939: *Arkansas*	SIDNEY BECHET Sidney Bechet (cl); Sonny White (p); Stubby Sebastian (b); Kenny Clarke (d) **Blues**	
Same	Charlie Howard (g) added **Ole Miss** Arkansas Arts Center Jazz Gems 102	
1940: *February 5* *New York City*	SIDNEY BECHET AND HIS NEW ORLEANS FEETWARMERS Sidney Bechet (cl,ss,vcl); Sonny White (p); Charles Howard (g); Ernest Meyers (b,vcl); Kenny Clarke (d) **Indian Summer** (2 takes, second unissued) **Preachin' The Blues** (vcl EM) **One O'Clock Jump** (2 takes, second unissued) Bluebird A XM2-5516 (1 take of each), Stash, HMV, RCA	
Same	SIDNEY BECHET AND HIS RHYTHM **Sidney's Blues** (2 takes) (vcl SB) Bluebird A XM2-5516 (1 take), RCA, HMV	
May 15 *New York City*	MILDRED BAILEY AND HER ORCHESTRA Roy Eldridge (t); Robert Burns, Jimmy Carroll (cl); Irving Horowitz (bcl); Ed Powell (fl); Mitch Miller (ob); Teddy Wilson (p); John Collins (g); Pete Peterson (b); Kenny Clarke (d); Mildred Bailey (vcl); Alec Wilder (arr)	
	How Can I Ever Be Alone	Columbia 35532
	Tennessee Fish Fry	Columbia 35532, Tax M-8020
	Blue (And Broken Hearted)	Columbia 35589
	I'll Pray For You	" "
September 12 *New York City*	BILLIE HOLIDAY AND HER ORCHESTRA Roy Eldridge (t); Georgie Auld, Don Redman (as); Don Byas, Jimmy Hamilton (ts); Teddy Wilson (p); John Collins (g); Al Hall (b); Kenny Clarke (d); Billie Holiday (vcl)	
	I'm All For You (2 takes)	Queen Disc 067
	I Hear Music (2 takes) **It's The Same Old Story** (2 takes) **Practice Makes Perfect** (3 takes) Okeh, CBS, Col.	

1941:

March 11
New York City

SLIM GAILLARD AND HIS FLAT FLOOGIE BOYS
Loumell Morgan (p); Bulee 'Slim' Gaillard (g,vcl); Slam Stewart (b); Kenny Clarke (d)

A Tip On The Numbers	CBS 80049, Okeh 6135, Stash ST 108
Slim Slam Boogie	Okeh 6135, Stash ST 108, Caete 4
Ah Now	Okeh 6295, Stash ST 108
Bassology	" " " "

Col. DO-2639, Tax M-8044

March 21
New York City

BILLIE HOLIDAY WITH EDDIE HEYWOOD AND HIS ORCHESTRA
Shad Collins (t); Leslie Johnakins, Eddie Barefield (as); Lester Young (ts); Eddie Heywood (p); John Collins (g); Ted Sturgis (b); Kenny Clarke (d); Billie Holiday (vcl)

Let's Do It (3 takes, one unissued)	Queen Disc 065
Georgia On My Mind (3 takes, one unissued)	" " "
Romance In The Dark (4 takes, one unissued)	" " "
All Of Me (3 takes, one unissued)	" " "

Col. 2C-34849, MXCO-29940-3, K9-32124, 32060 (Master takes only), Okeh

May 1
New York City

BUDDY JOHNSON
Buddy Johnson (p,ldr); Shad Collins (t); Joe Eldridge, Scoville Brown (as); Kenneth Hollon (ts); Lennie Ware (g); Frank Clarke (b); Kenny Clarke (d); Ella Johnson (vcl)

I'm My Baby's Baby
Now Please Mr Johnson
It's The Gold
Troyon Swing
Southern Exposure
Boogie-Woogie's Mother-In-Law
I'd Be Ever So Grateful
In There

Decca 8546, 8555, 8562, 8573, Swingfan 1021, MCA (F) 510145

May 21
New York City

COUNT BASIE ORCHESTRA
Ed Lewis, Al Killian, Buck Clayton, Harry Edison (t); Dicky Wells, Edward Cuffey, Dan Minor (tb); Earle Warren (as,vcl); Tab Smith (ss,as); Jack Washington (bs); Don Byas, Buddy Tate (ts); Count Basie (p); Freddie Green (g); Walter Page (b); Kenny Clarke (d)

You Betcha My Life (vcl)	Okeh 6221, Queen Disc 015
Down, Down, Down (Take 1)	Epic LN 3169, Queen Disc 33
Down, Down, Down (Take 2)	Queen Disc 015, Okeh 6221

October 6
New York City

ELLA FITZGERALD
Teddy McRae (ts); Tommy Fulford (p); Ulysses Livingston (g); Beverly Peer (b); Kenny Clarke (d); Ella Fitzgerald (vcl)

Jim	Decca 4007, Coral 6.22178
This Love Of Mine	" " " "

Brunswick 03281

Note: The following sessions were recorded at Minton's and Monroe's clubs in New York City during 1941. Exact dates are unknown.

JAM SESSION
Hot Lips Page, Joe Guy (t); Rudy Williams (as); Don Byas, Kermit Scott (ts); 'Tex' (p); Nick Fenton (b); Kenny Clarke (d)

Stompin' At The Savoy	Esoteric 548, Society SOC 996, Swing CLDE 890, Vogue(F) LD-158, Vogue 500114, Everest FS 219, Fresh Sound

CHARLIE CHRISTIAN'S BAND
Joe Guy, Hot Lips Page (t); Kermit Scott, Don Byas (ts); Thelonious Monk (p); Charlie Christian (g); Nick Fenton (b); Kenny Clarke (d)

Up On Teddy's Hill	Esoteric 548, Fresh Sound, Society SOC 996, Swing CLDE 890
Down On Teddy's Hill	(same labels as 'Jam Session' **Stompin' At The Savoy**) plus Xanadu 102

JAM SESSION
Add one or two unknown (t); unknown (ts)

Stompin' At The Savoy	(same labels as 'Jam Session' **Stompin' At The Savoy** above)

CHARLIE CHRISTIAN
Joe Guy (t); Thelonious Monk (p); Charlie Christian (g); Nick Fenton (b); Kenny Clarke (d)
Charlie's Choice (Parts 1, 2, 3)
Stompin' At The Savoy
(Swing To Bop) (Parts 1, 2, 3)
(also Time Life STL-J12)
Guy's Got To Go
Lips Flips
(same labels as 'Jam Session' **Stompin' At The Savoy**)

DON BYAS
Joe Guy (t); Don Byas (ts); Thelonious Monk (p); Unknown (b); Kenny Clarke (d)
I Can't Give You Anything But Love
Indiana
Onyx 208, Musidisc JA 5121

Broadcast

JOE GUY AND HIS ORCHESTRA
Joe Guy (t); Al Sears (ts); Thelonious Monk (p); Nick Fenton (b); Kenny Clarke (d); Viola Jefferson (vcl)
Theme (Epistrophy) (4 takes)
The Sheik Of Araby
Mean To Me
I Got Rhythm
Indiana
I Found A New Baby

Broadcast

Make Groaner (vcl) replaces Jefferson; Guy, Sears out
Theme (Epistrophy) (2 takes)
Sweet Georgia Brown
Everything Happens To Me
Rear Back
Meet Dr Christian
I Understand
Topsy

ROY ELDRIDGE
Roy Eldridge, Joe Guy (t); Unknown (ts); Thelonious Monk (p); Unknown (b); Kenny Clarke (d)
Indiana
Xanadu 123

HOT LIPS PAGE
Hot Lips Page (t); Tiny Grimes (g); Unknown (p,b); Possibly Kenny Clarke (d)
I've Found A New Baby
Add Joe Guy (t); Thelonious Monk (p); Unknown (ts)
Sweet Georgia Brown
Onyx 207 (both sessions)

JAM SESSION
Unknown (t); Don Byas (ts); Charlie Christian (g); Nick Fenton (b); Kenny Clarke (d)
Up On Teddy's Hill
Everest 5233 (plus same labels as 'Jam Session' **Stompin' At The Savoy**)

JAM SESSION
Dizzy Gillespie (t); Don Byas, Unknown (ts); Possibly Kenny Kersey (p); Nick Fenton (b); Kenny Clarke (d)
Stardust (Parts 1, 2)
Kerouac (Parts 1, 2)
Esoteric E55-4, Smithsonian R-004-P2-13455, Everest 5233 (plus same labels as 'Jam Session' **Stompin' At The Savoy**)

JAM SESSION
Joe Guy, Unknown (t); Kermit Scott (ts); Unknown (p); Charlie Christian (g); Nick Fenton (b); Kenny Clarke (d)
Rhythm-a-ning
Xanadu 107 (same labels as 'Jam Session' **Stompin' At The Savoy**)

JAM SESSION
Joe Guy (t,vcl); Thelonious Monk (p); Nick Fenton (b); Kenny Clarke (d)
Rhythm Riff
Nice Work If You Can Get It
Add Al Sears (ts)
Down
I Found A Million Dollar Baby
Xanadu 112 (both sessions)

JAM SESSION
Hot Lips Page (t); Unknown (ts); Thelonious Monk (p); Unknown (b); Kenny Clarke (d)
Baby Lips
Xanadu 123

1946:

April 9
New York City

BILLIE HOLIDAY WITH BILLY KYLE AND HIS TRIO
Billy Kyle (p); Joe Guy (t); Jimmy Shirley (g); Thomas Barney (b); Kenny Clarke (d); Billie Holiday (vcl)

Baby, I Don't Cry Over You	MCA (F) 510086, Decca 23957
I'll Look Around	MCA (F) 510015, ″ ″ Decca 7161, MCA 4009

May 7
New York City

SARAH VAUGHAN WITH ORCHESTRA UNDER THE DIRECTION OF TADD DAMERON
Freddy Webster (t); Hank Ross (bcl); Leroy Harris (as); Leo Parker (bs); 9 strings; Bud Powell (p); Ted Sturgis (b); Kenny Clarke (d); Sarah Vaughan (vcl); Tadd Dameron (arr,cond)
If You Could See Me Now
I Could Make You Love Me
You're Not The Kind
My Kinda Love (2 takes)
Musicraft MVS 504

May 15
New York City

DIZZY GILLESPIE SEXTET
Dizzy Gillespie (t); Sonny Stitt (as); Milt Jackson (vb); Al Haig (p); Ray Brown (b); Kenny Clarke (d); Alice Roberts, Gil Fuller (vcl)

One Bass Hit, Part 1	Musicraft 404
Oop Bop Sh'Bam (vcl)	Musicraft 383, Atlantis ATS 11
A Hand Fulla Gimme (vcl) (vb out)	Musicraft 485, Allegro LP 4032
That's Earl Brother	″ ″

Savoy MG 12020; Prestige P 24030, Delta 11 064

June 10
New York City

DIZZY GILLESPIE AND HIS ORCHESTRA
Dizzy Gillespie, Dave Burns, Raymond Orr, Talib Daawood, John Lynch (t); Alton Moore, Charles Greenlee (tb); Howard Johnson, John Brown (as); Warren Luckey, Ray Abrams (ts); Saul Moore (bs); John Lewis (p); Ray Brown (b); Kenny Clarke (d)

Our Delight	Musicraft 399
Good Dues Blues	

Pres. P-24030, Savoy MG 12020, Atlantis ATS 11

June *New York City* *Spotlite Club*	SARAH VAUGHAN Eddie Davis (ts); Thelonious Monk (p); Ray Brown (b); Kenny Clarke (d) **Don't Blame Me** Hi-Fly (Sw. H-01) (private recording)	
June 18 *New York City* *Broadcast,* *Spotlite Club*	DIZZY GILLESPIE ORCHESTRA Dizzy Gillespie (t,vcl); Dave Burns, Talib Daawood, Kenny Dorham, John Lynch, Elmon Wright (t); Leon Comegys, Charles Greenlee, Alton Moore (tb); Howard Johnson, Sonny Stitt (as); Ray Abrams, Warren Luckey (ts); Leo Parker (bs); Thelonious Monk (p); Milt Jackson (vb); Ray Brown (b); Kenny Clarke (d)	
	Things To Come	Hi-Fly (Sw)H-01
	Things To Come	"
	Second Balcony Jump	"
	Groovin' High	"
	Second Balcony Jump	
	Our Delight	"
	Our Delight	
	One Bass Hit	
	Things To Come	
July 6	Same	
	Unknown Title	"
	One Bass Hit	"
	I Waited For You (theme)	
	Algo Bueno (Woody'n You)	
	Unknown Ballad (incomplete)	
	Day By Day	
	The Man I Love	"
	How High The Moon (incomplete)	
	Unknown Title	
	Things To Come (theme)	
	Shaw 'Nuff (theme, intro)	
	I Waited For You (theme)	
	The Man I Love (incomplete)	
	Oop Bop Sh'Bam	"
	'Round Midnight	"
	Ray's Idea	"
	Cool Breeze	"
	I Waited For You	
	One Bass Hit	
	Note: although some titles appear several times, they are all different versions.	
July 9 *New York*	DIZZY GILLESPIE ORCHESTRA Gordon Thomas (tb); John Lewis (p) replace Greenlee and Monk. James Moody (ts) poss. replaces Abrams. Gill Fuller (arr)	
	One Bass Hit, Part 2	Musicraft 404, Savoy MG 12020, Saga 6920
	Ray's Idea	Musicraft 487, Savoy MG 12020

	Things To Come	Musicraft 447, Savoy MG 12020, Saga 6920
	He Beeped When He Shoulda Bopped	Musicraft 487, Saga 6920
	Prestige P-24030, Allegro LP 3083	
August 23 *New York City*	SONNY STITT QUINTET (THE BEBOP BOYS) Kenny Dorham (t); Sonny Stitt (as); Bud Powell (p); Al Hall (b); Kenny Clarke (d)	
	Serenade To A Square	Savoy MG 9006, MG 12011, WL 50547
	Good Kick	Savoy MG 9006, MG 12011, WL 50547
	Seven Up	Savoy MG 9006, MG 12011, WL 50547
	Blues In Be Bop (Blues À La Bud) (2 takes)	XP 8046, WL 50547
	Diz-iz	XP 8097, MG 9034
	Blues A La Bud (alt. take)	XP 8098, "
	Savoy SJL-2225	

September 5
New York City

KENNY CLARKE AND HIS 52ND STREET BOYS
Fats Navarro, Kenny Dorham (t); Sonny Stitt (as); Ray Abrams (ts); Ed De Verteuil (bs); Bud Powell (p); John Collins (g); Al Hall (b); Kenny Clarke (d); Walter Fuller (arr)
Epistrophy
Oop Bop Sh'Bam
52nd Street Theme
Rue Chaptal (Royal Roost)
(New World 284 also)
Swing 224, 225, 244, RCA LPV-519, Pathé (F)CO-54-16030, Pathé-EMI 251273-2 (CD)

September 6
New York City

FATS NAVARRO AND GIL FULLER'S MODERNISTS (THE BE BOP BOYS)
Fats Navarro, Kenny Dorham (t); Sonny Stitt (as); Morris Lane (ts); Ed De Verteuil (bs); Bud Powell (p); Al Hall (b); Kenny Clarke (d); Gil Fuller (arr)
Webb City (2 parts)
Fat Boy (2 parts)
Boppin' A Riff (2 parts)
Everything's Cool (2 parts)
Jazz Anthology 30-JA-5129, Savoy MG-12011, SJL-2216, Vogue VG 655 650115

Early 1947:
Detroit, Michigan

MILT JACKSON ALL STARS
Milt Jackson (vb); John Lewis (p); Al Jackson (b); Kenny Clarke (d)
Bobbin' With Robin
Autumn Breeze (In A Beautiful Mood)
Sensation 19, Galaxy LP-204

June *New York City*	TADD DAMERON Fats Navarro (t); Ernie Henry (as); Tadd Dameron (p); Curly Russell (b); Kenny Clarke (d); Kay Penton (vcl)	
	A Be-Bop Carol	Musidisc JA 5129, Savoy SJL 2216, Savoy 931
	The Tadd Walk	Musidisc JA 5129, Savoy SJL 2216, Savoy 931
	Gone With The Wind (vcl)	Musidisc JA 5129, Savoy SJL 2216, MG 9023
	That Someone Must Be You	Musidisc JA 5129, Savoy SJL 2216, MG 9024
	A Be-Bop Carol (alt. take)	Musidisc JA 5129, Savoy SJL 2216
July 2 *New York City*	SISTER ROSETTA THARPE WITH THE SAMMY PRICE TRIO Sammy Price (p); George 'Pops' Foster (b); Kenny Clarke (d); Sister Rosetta Tharpe (vcl,g); Marie Knight (vcl)	
	This Train	Decca 48043, DL 8782, Swingtime 104, MCA 1317
	Oh, When I Come To The End End of My Journey	Decca 48043, Swingtime 104, MCA 510148
	Didn't It Rain	Decca 48054, DL 8782 MCA 1317
	Stretch Out Decca 48043, 48043A	Decca 48054, MCA 510148
July 16 *New York City*	COUSIN JOE WITH SAMMY PRICE AND HIS TRIO Sammy Price (p); Danny Barker (g); Pops Foster (b); Kenny Clarke (d); Cousin Joe (vcl)	
	Bad Luck Blues (Oldie Blues)	Decca 48045, MCA 2-4064, Brunswick EP 10630
	Box Car Shorty And Peter Blue Oldie Blues 8008, MCA 1353	Decca 48045
Same	MONETTE MOORE WITH SAMMY PRICE Sammy Price (p); Danny Barker (g); Pops Foster (b); Ali Salaam (Kenny Clarke) (d) **Another Woman's Man** **Please Mr Blues** Decca 48047	
August 22 *New York City*	DIZZY GILLESPIE AND HIS ORCHESTRA Dizzy Gillespie (t,vcl); Dave Burns, Elmon Wright, Matthew McKay, Ray Orr (tp); Ted Kelly, Bill Shepherd (tb); John Brown, Howard Johnson (as); George Nicholas, Joe Gayles (ts); Cecil Payne (bs); John Lewis (p); Al McKibbon (b); Kenny Clarke (d); Kenny Hagood (vcl) **Ow!** **Oop-Pop-A-Da** **Two Bass Hit** **Stay On It** VIC LJM 1009, RCA LPV 519, RCA (F) 731068	

August 27
New York City

KENNY HAGOOD WITH JOHN LEWIS'S ORCHESTRA
Elmon Wright (t); Howard Johnson, Ernie Henry (as); Cecil Payne (bs); John Lewis (p); Nelson Boyd (b); Kenny Clarke (d); Kenny Hagood (vcl)

Goodbye To Love	
Baby I'm Comin' Home	WL 70547
The Way You Look Tonight	"
Foolish Me (unissued)	

Savoy 660, SJL-2225)

December 22
New York City

DIZZY GILLESPIE AND HIS ORCHESTRA
Dizzy Gillespie (t,vcl); Dave Burns, Elmon Wright, Benny Bailey, Lamar Wright Jr. (t); Bill Shepherd, Ted Kelly (tb); Howard Johnson, John Brown (as); Joe Gayles, George Nicholas (ts); Cecil Payne (bs); John Lewis (p); Al McKibbon (b); Kenny Clarke (d); Chano Pozo (conga,vcl); Kenny Hagood (vcl); Tadd Dameron, George Russell, Gil Fuller, Linton Garner (arr)

Algo Bueno (Woody'n You)	VIC 20-3186, LPV 530, HMV 39770
Cool Breeze (vcl DG, KH)	VIC LPV 519
Cubana Be	VIC LJM 1009, LPM 2398
Cubana Bop (vcl CP)	VIC LPV 519

RCA LPV-519, LPV-530, LP-2398, RCA (F) PM-42408

December 29
New York City

SARAH VAUGHAN
Jimmy Jones, (p); John Collins (g); Al McKibbon (b); Kenny Clarke (d); Sarah Vaughan (vcl)

What A Difference A Day Made	LPV 530, VIC 20-3186 RCA RD 7827, Bulldog BDL 1009
Gentleman Friend	Bulldog BDL 1009
Once In A While	
How Am I To Know	

Musicraft 2002, 2006

December 30
New York City

DIZZY GILLESPIE AND HIS ORCHESTRA
Dizzy Gillespie (t,vcl); Dave Burns, Elmon Wright, Benny Bailey, Lamar Wright Jr. (t); Bill Shepherd, Ted Kelly (tb); Howard Johnson, John Brown (as); Joe Gayles, George Nicholas (ts); Cecil Payne (bs); John Lewis (p); Al McKibbon (b); Kenny Clarke (d); Chano Pozo (conga,vcl); Kenny Hagood (vcl); Tadd Dameron, George Russell, Gil Fuller, Linton Garner (arr)

Manteca (vcl CP)	VIC LJM 3046, LJM 1009
Algo Bueno (Woody'n You)	VIC LJM 1009, RCA (F) 75389
Ool Ya Koo (vcl DG, KH)	LPV 530, RCA (F) 741095
Good Bait	VIC LPM 2398
Minor Walk	LPM 2398

1948:
February 28
Paris

DIZZY GILLESPIE BIG BAND
Dizzy Gillespie (t,vcl); Benny Bailey, Dave Burns, Lamar Wright Jr., Elmon Wright (t); Ted Kelly, Bill Shepherd (tb); Howard

Johnson, John Brown (as); Joe Gayles, George Nicholas (ts); Cecil Payne (bs); John Lewis (p); Al McKibbon (b); Kenny Clarke (d); Chano Pozo (conga); Kenny Hagood (vcl)
Oop Pop A Da (vcl DG, KH)
'Round Midnight
Algo Bueno (Woody'n You)
I Can't Get Started
Two Bass Hit
Good Bait
Afro Cubano Suite
Ool Ya Koo (rel DG, KH)
Things To Come
Vogue LD651-30, Pres. 7818

February
Paris

SAMMY PRICE
Sammy Price (p); Georges Hadjo (b); Kenny Clarke (d)

Eiffel Tower	Decca SF 159, Flame 171
Good Paree	Decca SF 160, " "
Low Down Blues	" " " "
Montparnasse	Decca SF 159, " "
Sammy's Boogie	Decca SF 161, " "
Frenchy's Blues	" " " "

Flame 171 = (7", 33 rpm)

March 2
Paris

KENNY CLARKE
Benny Bailey (t); John Brown (as); Cecil Payne (bs); Ralph Schecroun (p); Al McKibbon (b); Kenny Clarke (d)
Confirmation
Jay Mac
Cheryl (À La Colette) (Too Much Horn)
Listen Here (Jumpin' There)
Pres. 7605, Swing 277, 281

March 12
Paris

MICHEL DE VILLERS
Michel De Villers (as); Jean-Claude Fohrenbach (ts); André Persiany (p); Georges Hadjo (b); Kenny Clarke (d)

3ième Etage (unissued)	
Lover Man	Swing 276
The Small Bag	" "
I'm Sorry	Swing 290
Leave Us Leap (unissued)	
The Man I Love (unissued)	

March 17
Paris

THE BE-BOP MINSTRELS
Dick Collins (t); Hubert Fol (as); Dave Kriedt (ts); André Persiany (p); Georges Hadjo (b); Kenny Clarke (d)

Hard To Get (unissued)	
Ralph Goes (unissued)	
I've Got To Be Bop	Swing 278
All The Things You Are	" "

May 4 *Paris*	KENNY CLARKE Dick Collins (t); Hubert Fol (as); Jean-Claude Fohrenbach (ts); Claude Laurence (vln); Jacques Denjean (p); Harry Montaggioni (g); Alf Masselier (b); Kenny Clarke (d)	
	Algerian Cynicism	Swing 284
	Laurenzology	" "
	Doria (cl out) (unissued)	
	I'll Tell You Any (unissued)	
	Tall Boy	Emanon 9600
	Klook Returns (cl out)	Dee Gee 3602
May 5 *Paris*	MICHEL DE VILLERS Claude Dunson (t); Michel De Villers (as); Jean-Claude Fohrenbach (ts); Jacques Denjean (p); Harry Montaggioni (g); Alf Masselier (b); Kenny Clarke (d)	
	Working Eyes (unissued)	
	Stuffy	Swing 282
	Embraceable You (unissued)	
Same	Michel De Villers (as); Jacques Denjean (p); Harry Montaggioni (g); Alf Masselier (b); Kenny Clarke (d)	
	I Surrender Dear	Swing 290
May 14 *Paris*	KENNY CLARKE Howard McGhee (t); Jimmy Heath (as); Hubert Fol (as); Jessie Powell (ts,vcl); John Lewis (p); John Collins (g); Percy Heath (b); Kenny Clarke (d)	
	Maggie's Draw **Out Of Nowhere** **I'm In The Mood For Love** **Sweet And Lovely** Pres. 7605	
August 28 *New York City* *Broadcast,* *Royal Roost*	TADD DAMERON Fats Navarro (t); Allen Eager (ts); Tadd Dameron (p); Curly Russell (b); Kenny Clarke (d); Kenny Hagood (vcl)	
	Good Bait (Parts 1, 2)	Jazzland LP 50, Milestone M 47041
	Anthropology	Jazzland LP 50, Milestone M 47041
	Lady Be Good	Jazzland LP 50, Milestone M 47041
	The Kitchenette Across The Hall	Sneaker TDFN 828, Ozone 5
	The Squirrel	" " " " "
	Pennies From Heaven	" " " " "
	Jumpin' With Symphony Sid (Parts 1, 2)	
August 29 *New York City* *Broadcast,* *Royal Roost*	Same **Our Delight** **The Squirrel** **Dameronia** **The Tadd Walk** Milestone 47041, Sneaker 829, Beppo 505 (both sessions), Ozone 5	

August, September
New York City
Broadcast,
Royal Roost

TADD DAMERON AND HIS ORCHESTRA
Allen Eager, Wardell Gray (ts); Tadd Dameron (p); Curly Russell (b); Kenny Clarke (d)
Now Is The Time
Lady Be Good
Just You, Just Me
Spotlight (E)108

September 4
New York City
Broadcast,
Royal Roost

TADD DAMERON
Fats Navarro (t); Allen Eager (ts); Milt Jackson (vb);* Tadd Dameron (p); Curly Russell (b); Kenny Clarke (d)

Symphonette*	Jazzland JLP 68, Ozone 5
Tadd Walk	Sneaker TDFN 829
The Squirrel	" " "

Milestone 47041, Beppo 505

September 13
New York City

TADD DAMERON
Fats Navarro (t); Allen Eager, Wardell Gray (ts); Tadd Dameron (p); Curly Russell (b); Kenny Clarke (d); Chano Pozo (bongo)*

Jahbero* Take 1	Blue Note 559, BLP 1532, Gazell 2019
Jahbero* Take 2	BLP 1532
Lady Bird Take 1	Blue Note 559, BLP 5004, Gazell 2019, BLP 1532
Lady Bird Take 2	BLP 1532
Symphonette Take 1	" " BN 1564
Symphonette Take 2	" "
I Think I'll Go Away (unissued)	
52nd Street Theme	

Blue Note 84554

October 2
New York City
Broadcast,
Royal Roost

TADD DAMERON
Fats Navarro (t); Rudy Williams (as); Allen Eager (ts); Tadd Dameron (p); Curly Russell (b); Kenny Clarke (d)
Good Bait
The Squirrel
Jumpin' With Symphony Sid (theme)
Beppo 505, Talcrip 10230

Same

ANITA O'DAY
Tadd Dameron (p); Curly Russell (b); Kenny Clarke (d); Anita O'Day (vcl)

What Is This Thing Called Love	Alto 702
How High The Moon (unissued)	

October 9
New York City

Same

September In The Rain	Alto 702
How High The Moon (unissued)	

Talcrip 10230 (both sessions)

Same

TADD DAMERON
Fats Navarro (t); Rudy Williams (as); Allen Eager (ts); Tadd Dameron (p); Curly Russell (b); Kenny Clarke (d)
Dameronia
Tadd Walk Ozone 5
Milestone 47041, Beppo 506, Talcrip 10230, Jazzland JLP 5

October 11
New York City

HOWARD McGHEE
Howard McGhee, Fats Navarro (t); Ernie Henry (as); Milt Jackson (p,vb); Curly Russell (b); Kenny Clarke (d)
The Skunk Take 1
The Skunk Take 2
Boperation (McGhee p,t) BLP 1532
Double Talk, Part I (2 takes)
Double Talk, Part II (2 takes)
BN BST-81531 (Vol. 1), BST-81532 (Vol. 2)
(BLP 1532 – alt. masters of **Double Talk** and **The Skunk**)

October 16
New York City
Broadcast,
Royal Roost

TADD DAMERON
Fats Navarro (t); Rudy Williams (as); Allen Eager (ts); Tadd Dameron (p); Curly Russell (b); Kenny Clarke (d)
Jumpin' With Symphony Sid (theme)
Anthropology (2 parts) Sneaker TDFN 829, Bop 7
Our Delight " " Ozone 5
Tadd Walk " " "
The Squirrel (unissued)
Milestone 47041

October 23
New York City
Broadcast,
Royal Roost

Same
Jumpin' With Symphony Sid (theme)
Our Delight Jazzland JLP 50, Milestone M 47041
The Squirrel Jazzland JLP 50, Milestone M 47041
Good Bait Jazzland JLP 68, Milestone M 47041

Same

Add Kai Winding (tb)
Ep-Pop Jazzland JLP 68, Milestone M 47041

October 25
New York City

EARL COLEMAN WITH THE LINTON GARNER ALL STARS
Allen Eager (ts); Linton Garner (p); Kenny Clarke (d); Earl Coleman (vcl)
You're The One For Me
I Won't Tell A Soul I Love You
Don't Bring Your Troubles To Me
I Hadn't Anyone Till You
I Don't Need You Now
I Give You My Word
Atl. 872 (**Don't Bring** and **I Hadn't Anyone** only; rest unissued)

October 30
New York City
Broadcast,
Royal Roost

TADD DAMERON
Kai Winding (tb); Allen Eager (ts); Tadd Dameron (p); Curly Russell (b); Kenny Clarke (d)
Wahoo (Donby)
The Chase
Lady Be Good
The Squirrel
Jumpin' With Symphony Sid
(theme)
Milestone 47041, Talcrip 10230, Jazzland JLP 68, Ozone 5

November 6
New York City

Same
Anthropology
Tiny's Blues (Gabardine And Serge)
Wahoo
Milestone 47041, Jazzland JLP 68

1948

JAM SESSION
Howard McGhee (t); Jimmy Heath (as); Erroll Garner (p); John Collins (g); Percy Heath (b); Kenny Clarke (d)
I Surrender Dear
Europa Jazz 1020

Same

COLEMAN HAWKINS
Coleman Hawkins (ts); Errol Garner (p); Percy Heath (b); Kenny Clarke (d)
Cocktails For Two
Europa Jazz 1020

1949:
January 18
New York City

TADD DAMERON
Fats Navarro (t); Kai Winding (tb); Sahib Shihab (as); Dexter Gordon (ts); Cecil Payne (bs); Tadd Dameron (p); Curly Russell (b); Kenny Clarke (d); Diego Ibarra (bongo); Vidal Bolado (conga); Rae Pearl (vcl)

Sid's Delight	Affinity AFF 149
Casbah	" " "

Capitol M-11059, Capitol Jazz Classics Vol. 13 052-80852, Cap. 057-60006

January 25
New York City

MILT JACKSON (BLUESOLOGY)
Kenny Dorham (t,p); Julius Watkins (frh); Billy Mitchell (ts); Milt Jackson (vb,p); Kenny Clarke (d)
Conglomeration
Bruz
You Go To My Head
Roll 'em Bags
Faultless
Hey Frenchy
Savoy 12061, SJL-1130, WL 50537

Same	MILT JACKSON QUARTET Milt Jackson (vb); John Lewis (p); Al Jackson (b); Kenny Clarke (d) **Slits** **Baggy Eyes** **In A Beautiful Mood** **Baggy's Blues** Galaxy LP-204, America AM-6072
February 12 *New York City* *Broadcast,* *Royal Roost*	TADD DAMERON Leonard Hawkins (t); Ted Kelly (tb); Sahib Shihab (as); Benjamin Lundy (ts); Cecil Payne (bs); Tadd Dameron (p); Curly Russell (b); Kenny Clarke (d); Carlos Vidal (conga) **Good Bait** } Unissued **Webb's Delight** **Focus** **Wahoo**
February 19 *New York City* *Broadcast,* *Royal Roost*	TADD DAMERON Miles Davis (t); Kai Winding (tb); Sahib Shihab (as); Benjamin Lundy (ts); Cecil Payne (bs); Tadd Dameron (p); John Collins (ban); Curly Russell (b); Kenny Clarke (d); Carlos Vidal (conga) **Focus** **April In Paris** **Good Bait** **Webb's Delight**
February 26 *New York City* *Broadcast,* *Royal Roost*	Same **Miles** **Casbah** Beppo 503, Jazz Live/Cicala 8032 (both sessions) Jungcat R8D 448
March 5 *New York City* *Broadcast,* *Royal Roost*	Same **Good Bait** **The Squirrel**
April 21 *New York City*	TADD DAMERON Miles Davis (t); J.J. Johnson (tb); Sahib Shihab (as); Benjamin Lundy (ts); Cecil Payne (bs); Tadd Dameron (p); John Collins (g); Curly Russell (b); Kenny Clarke (d); Kay Penton (vcl) **John's Delight** Affinity AFF 149 **What's New** " " " **Heaven's Doors Are Wide Open** " " " **Focus** " " " Capitol M-11059, 60015, 052-80852
April 22 *New York City*	MILES DAVIS Miles Davis (t,ldr); J.J. Johnson (tb); Sandy Siegelstein (fh); Bill Barber (tu); Lee Konitz (as); Gerry Mulligan (bs,arr); John Lewis (p,arr); Nelson Boyd (b); Kenny Clarke (d); Gil Evans, John Carisi (arr)

Venus De Milo
Rouge
Boplicity
Israel
Capitol N-16168, T 762, 052-80798, CAPS 1024

May 8
Paris

MILES DAVIS/TADD DAMERON QUINTET
Miles Davis (t); James Moody (ts); Tadd Dameron (p); Barney Spieler (b); Kenny Clarke (d)
Don't Blame Me
Rifftide
The Squirrel (unissued)
Embraceable You
Ornithology
Good Bait
Lady Bird
Perdido (unissued)
All The Things You Are
Crazy Rhythm

May 9, 10 or 11
Paris

Same
Wahoo
Allen's Alley
Embraceable You
Ornithology
All The Things You Are
Col. JC-34804, CBS 82100 (both sessions)

May 14
Paris

Same
Lady Be Good
Don't Blame Me
Allen's Alley
Crazy Rhythm
All The Things You Are
} Unissued

October 20
Paris

SIDNEY BECHET AND HIS ALL-STAR BAND
Bill Coleman (t); Sidney Bechet (ss); Frank 'Big Boy' Goudie (ts); Charlie Lewis (p); Pierre Michelot (b); Kenny Clarke (d)
Orphan Annie's Blues Vogue (F) V5017, LD042
Happy Go Lucky Blues (Black Stick) " " LD044
Klook's Blues (SB, KC only) Vogue (F) V5018
American Rhythm (Klook Klux Klan) " "
Esquire 10.068, 10.085, Dial 301-A, Vogue 501, Vogue VJD 552

Same

Goudie, Coleman out
Out Of Nowhere
Mon Homme
Vogue V5019, VJD 552, Dial 301-A, Esquire 10-077

October 29
Paris

HUBERT FOL
Nat Peck (tb); Hubert Fol (as); Bernard Peiffer (p); Jean Bouchety (b); Kenny Clarke (d)

Love In The Sun	Swing 330
Iambic Pentameter	" 325
Assy Pan Assy	" 330
Robbins Nest	" 325

November 5
Paris

SIDNEY BECHET AND HIS NEW ORLEANS FEETWARMERS
Sidney Bechet (ss); Eddie Bernard (p); Pierre Michelot (b); Kenny Clarke (d)

Wrap Your Troubles In Dreams	Blue Star 152, Esquire 10-189
It Had To Be You	Blue Star 140, Esquire 10-179
Baby Won't You Please Come Home	Blue Star 148, Esquire 10-094
Please Don't Talk About Me When I'm Gone	Blue Star 140, Esquire 10-179
Ooh Boogie	Blue Star 142, Esquire 10-095
After You've Gone	" " " "
I'm Going Way Down Home	Blue Star 148, Esquire 10-094
Margie	Blue Star 152, Esquire 10-089

Atl. LP-118

December 21
Paris

COLEMAN HAWKINS
Nat Peck (tb); Hubert Fol (as); Coleman Hawkins (ts); Jean-Paul Mengeon (p); Pierre Michelot (b); Kenny Clarke (d)

Sih-Sah	Vogue 5025, JL 56, Mode 9863
It's Only A Paper Moon	" 5023, " " " Swingtime ST 1004
Bean's Talking Again	Vogue 5025, JL 56, Mode 9863
Bay-u-bah	" 5024, " " " Swingtime ST 1004
I Surrender Dear (tb,as out)	Vogue 5023, JL 56, Mode 9863
Sophisticated Lady	" 5024, " " "

Vogue LD-005, Pres. 7824

1949
Paris

ANDRE HODEIR AVEC TONY PROTEAU ET SON ORCHESTRE
Personnel incl. Jo Boyer (t); Hubert Rostaing (cl,as); Don Byas (ts); Bernard Peiffer (p); Jean Bouchety (b); Kenny Clarke (d)
Autour D'Un Recif
Swing M33.343

1950:
March 3
Paris

PIERRE MICHELOT
Hubert Fol (as,ts); Raymond Fol (p); Pierre Michelot (b); Kenny Clarke (d)
Out Of Nowhere (unissued)

These Foolish Things	Take 1	Swing 344
" " "	Take 2	(unissued)
" " "	Take 3	(unissued)

April 13 *Paris*	JOHN LEWIS'S MUSIC (ERNIE ROYAL & HIS ALL-STARS) Ernie Royal (t); Ted Kelly (tb); Russell Procope (as); James Moody (ts); Henry Aspar (bs); Raymond Fol (p); Kenny Clarke (d); John Lewis (cond,arr)		
	Pierre (unissued)		
Same	Hubert Fol (bs) replaces Aspar		
	Period Suite (2 parts)	Swing 345	
	Perdido (2 parts)	Swing 361	
May 26 *Paris*	JACK DIEVAL Nat Peck (tb); James Moody (ts); Jack Diéval (p); Emmanuel Soudieux (b); Kenny Clarke (d)		
	Maryvonne		
	Lou-Easy		
	Ouch		
	No		
	Cherokee		
	Swing 354 (**Cherokee** and **Lou-Easy** only; rest unissued)		
June 7 *Paris*	JERRY WIGGINS TRIO Gerald Wiggins (p); Pierre Michelot (b); Kenny Clarke (d)		
	The Wig		
	Orient Express		
	Swing (F)-350		
Same	JERRY WIGGINS Nat Peck (tb); Hubert Fol (as); James Moody (ts); Gerald Wiggins (p); Pierre Michelot (b); Kenny Clarke (d)		
	I'll Get You Yet		
	Be A Good Girl		
	Swing (F) 352, Pathé (F) C054-16029		
June 14 *Paris*	ROY ELDRIDGE Roy Eldridge (t,vcl); Gerald Wiggins (p); Pierre Michelot (b); Kenny Clarke (d)		
	Easter Parade (2 takes)	Vogue 5044	
	Wild Driver (4 takes) (two unissued)	" "	Queen Disc 066
	If I Had You	Vogue 5045	
	Nuts		
	Someone To Watch Over Me (2 takes)	Vogue 5046	
	Goliath Bounce	" "	
	Vogue, Inner City IC-7002		
June 26 *Paris*	ZOOT SIMS Zoot Sims (ts); Gerald Wiggins (p); Pierre Michelot (b); Kenny Clarke (d)		
	Night And Day	Vogue V5048, Prestige PR7817	
	Night And Day (alt. take)	Discovery 148, Prestige 7817	
	Slingin' Hash	Vogue V5048, Discovery 148	
	Slingin' Hash (alt. take)	Prestige 7817	

Tenorly	Vogue V5052, Prestige 7817
I Understand	" " " "
Don't Worry 'Bout Me	Vogue 5054, Prestige 7817
Crystals	" " " "
Zoot And Zoot	Vogue LD 185
The Big Shot	" " "

October 9
Paris

KENNY CLARKE
James Moody (ts); Ralph Schecroun (p); Pierre Michelot (b); Kenny Clarke (d)
Nath (2 takes)
I Can't Get Started
Riffin And Raffin'
St Louis Blues
Embraceable You
In A Rush
Pres. 7605

1951:
April 1
Brussels

JAZZ AT THE BEAUX ARTS
Roy Eldridge, Emile Peiffer (t); Don Byas, James Moody (ts); Roger Asselberghs (bs); Johnny Hot (p); Paul Karthy (g); Paul Dubois (b); Kenny Clarke (d)
Tu Disais Que Tu M'aimais
Move
Laura
Volcano
Robbins' Nest

April 6
Paris

KENNY CLARKE
Dick Collins (t); Jean-Claude Fohrenbach (ts); André Persiany (p); Pierre Michelot (b); Kenny Clarke (d)
I'll Get You Yet
Lady Be Good
All The Things You Are
Klook Returns
Dee Gee 3602 (**Klook Returns** only; rest unissued)

August 8
New York City

CHARLIE PARKER QUINTET
Red Rodney (t); Charlie Parker (as); John Lewis (p); Ray Brown (b); Kenny Clarke (d)

Blues For Alice	Clef EPC 337, Verve VLP 9138, Metro (E) 2356.087, Col (E) SEB 10053, Verve 833268-2
Si Si	Merc/Clef 11103, Clef EPC 336, Verve MGV 8000, Verve VLP 9138, Barclay GM 8516
Swedish Schnapps	Verve MGV 8409 Metro (E) 2356.088, Col (E) 33CX10117

Swedish Schnapps	Merc/Clef 11103, Clef EPC 336, Verve (F) V3HB 8840, Metro (E) 2356.088, Barclay GM 8516
Back Home Blues	Verve (E) VLP 9078, Metro (E) 2356.088, Verve (F) 511023
Back Home Blues	Merc/Clef 11095, Clef EPC 336, Verve MGV 8000, Metro (E) 2356.088
Lover Man	Merc/Clef 11095, Clef EPC 336, Verve MGV 8000, Metro (E) 2356.088, Verve 833268-2

Verve (Japan) UMV-2030, Verve 2-2512, 817447-1
Note: All Charlie Parker Verve recordings are on VERVE 837141-2 (10-CD set)

August 24
New York City

MILT JACKSON QUARTET
Milt Jackson (vb); John Lewis (p); Ray Brown (b); Kenny Clarke (d)
Milt Meets Sid
D And E
Yesterdays
Between The Devil And The Deep Blue Sea
Dee Gee LP-1002, Musicdisc, Savoy SJL-1106, Jazz Anthology JA-5130, Realm RM 119

October 12

SONNY CRISS WITH THE JATP ALL STARS
Sonny Criss (as); Joe Newman (t); Bennie Green (tmb); Eddie 'Lockjaw' Davis (ts); Bobby Tucker (p); Tommy Potter (b); Kenny Clarke (d)
Intermission Riff
How High The Moon
Perdido
Body And Soul
High Jump
Pablo 2310929

1952:
April 1
New York City

ANNIE ROSS
Milt Jackson (vb); Blossom Dearie (p); Percy Heath (b); Kenny Clarke (d); Annie Ross (vcl)
Everytime
The Way You Look Tonight
I'm Beginning To Think You Care For Me
Between The Devil And The Deep Blue Sea
Dee Gee EP.4010, Savoy MG-12060, 12217, Regent MG-6031

April 7
New York City

MILT JACKSON QUINTET
Lou Donaldson (as); Milt Jackson (vb); John Lewis (p); Percy Heath (b); Kenny Clarke (d)
Tahiti
Lillie (2 takes)
Bags' Groove
What's New (2 takes)
Don't Get Around Much Any More (2 takes)
On The Scene
BN 1592, BLP 1509, LA590-H2

April
New York City

MILT JACKSON QUARTET
Milt Jackson (vb); John Lewis (p); Percy Heath (b); Kenny Clark (d)

Softly As In A Morning Sunrise	Hi-Lo 1412
Love Me Pretty Baby	" 1405
Heart And Soul	" "
True Blues	" 1420

Savoy SJL-1106, Musidisc, Jazz Anthology JA-5130

May 9
New York City

MILES DAVIS
Miles Davis (t); J.J. Johnson (tb); Jackie McLean (as); Gil Coggins (p); Oscar Pettiford (b); Kenny Clarke (d)

Dear Old Stockholm	Blue Note BN 1595, BLP 5013, BLP 1501
Chance It (Max Is Making Wax)	BN 1596, BLP 5013, BLP 1501
Donna	Vogue V2222, LDE 028, BN 1595, BLP 5013, BLP 1502
Donna (alt. take)	BN 45-1633, BLP 1501
Woody'n You	BN 1596, BLP 5013, BLP 1502
Woody'n You (alt. take)	BLP 1501
Yesterdays (JJJ, JMcL out)	BN 1597, BLP 5013, BLP 1501
How Deep Is The Ocean (JJJ, JMcL out)	BN 1597, BLP 5013, BLP 1501

June
New York City

JAZZ INC.
Miles Davis (t); J.J. Johnson (tb); Zoot Sims (ts); Milt Jackson (vb,p); Percy Heath (b); Kenny Clarke (d)
Unknown titles

November 1
New York City

CHARLIE PARKER WITH THE MILT JACKSON QUARTET
Charlie Parker (as); Milt Jackson (vb); John Lewis (p); Percy Heath (b); Kenny Clarke (d)

How High The Moon	Jap. Odeon EDR 9015C, Atlantis ATS 12

Embraceable You
52nd Street Theme (theme)
Klacto (E) MG-101, Transark 1001

December 22 *New York City*	MODERN JAZZ QUARTET Milt Jackson (vb); John Lewis (p); Percy Heath (b); Kenny Clarke (d)	
	All The Things You Are	Prestige 7421, 7749
	La Ronde	" 7425, "
	Vendome	" " "
	Rose Of The Rio Grande	" 7421, "
	Pres. 7059, 24005, Original Jazz Classics 125	

1953:

January 20 *New York City* *Birdland*	STAN GETZ QUARTET Stan Getz (ts); Duke Jordan (p); Bill Crow (b); Kenny Clarke (d)	
	Yesterdays	
	Strike Up The Band	
	Queen Disc 013	
February 19 *New York City*	MILES DAVIS ALL STARS PLAY AL COHN Miles Davis (t); Sonny Truitt (tb); Al Cohn, Zoot Sims (ts); John Lewis (p); Leonard Gaskin (b); Kenny Clarke (d)	
	Floppy	Prestige LP7168
	Same (Truitt out)	
	Tasty Pudding	" "
	Willie The Wailer	" "
	For Adults Only	" "
	Pres. LP-154, P-24054, 7025, OJC 053	
April 29 *New York City*	MAT MATHEWS Mat Mathews (acc); Herbie Mann (fl,ts); Benny Weeks (g); Percy Heath (b); Kenny Clarke (d)	
	Owl Eyes	
	Study In Purple	
	There's A Small Hotel (fl,ts out)	
	Laura (fl,ts,g out)	
	Brunswick BL 54013	
May 9 *New York City*	CHARLIE PARKER QUARTET Charlie Parker (as); John Lewis (p); Curly Russell (b); Kenny Clarke (d)	
	Cool Blues	Okiedoke (no number)
	Star Eyes	
	Moose The Mooche	" "
	Theme (Lullaby Of Birdland)	" "
Same	Add Candido (conga)	
	Broadway	" "
	Theme (Lullaby Of Birdland)	
	Klacto (E) MG-100, Col. JC-34831 (all six titles), Jap. Odeon EDR 9015C	
June 22 *New York City*	J.J. JOHNSON SEXTET Clifford Brown (t); J.J. Johnson (tb); Jimmy Heath (ts,bs); John Lewis (p); Percy Heath (b); Kenny Clarke (d)	

Capri	Blue Note 1621, BLP 5028, BLP 1505
Capri (alt. take)	BLP 1506
Turnpike	Blue Note 1621, BLP 5028 BLP 1505
Turnpike (alt. take)	BLP 1506
Lover Man	BLP 5028, BLP 1505
Get Happy	BLP 5028, BLP 1505
Get Happy (alt. take)	BN-LA267-G, BST 84428
Sketch One	BLP 5028, BLP 1505
It Could Happen To You (CB, JH out)	BLP 5028, BLP 1505

June 25
New York City

MODERN JAZZ QUARTET
Milt Jackson (vb); John Lewis (p); Percy Heath (b); Kenny Clarke (d)
The Queen's Fancy
Delaunay's Dilemma
Autumn In New York
But Not For Me
Pres. LP-7057, 24005, 7425, 7749, OJC 057

June
New York City

KAI WINDING AND HIS BIRDLANDERS
Howard McGhee (t); Kai Winding (tb); Eddie Shu (ts); John Lewis (p); Percy Heath (b); Kenny Clarke (d)
Perdido
That's A Plenty
Get Happy
Hot And Cool Blues
MGM E-231

July 6
New York City

MAT MATHEWS
Mat Mathews (acc); Herbie Mann (fl,ts); Benny Weeks (g); Percy Heath (b); Kenny Clarke (d)
Maya
The Nearness Of You
Bags' Groove
Brunswick BL 54013

September 9
New York City

MAT MATHEWS
Mat Mathews (acc); Herbie Mann (fl); Benny Weeks (g); Percy Heath (b); Kenny Clarke (d)
I Can't Believe That You're In Love With Me
Brunswick BL 58057

September 19
New York City

KING PLEASURE
John Lewis (p); Percy Heath (b); Kenny Clarke (d); King Pleasure (vcl); Dave Lambert Singers (vcl trio)
Sometimes I'm Happy
This Is Always
Pres. PR-24097, 7586, 860, 7128, 0JC 217

September 22
Boston

CHARLIE PARKER (AT STORYVILLE)
Charlie Parker (as); Herb Pomeroy (t); Sir Charles Thompson (p); Jimmy Woode (b); Kenny Clarke (d)
Now's The Time
Don't Blame Me
Dancing On The Ceiling
Cool Blues
Groovin' High
Blue Note BT 85108

October 7
Hackensack, N.J.

SONNY ROLLINS WITH THE MODERN JAZZ QUARTET
Sonny Rollins (ts); Milt Jackson (vb); John Lewis (p); Percy Heath (b); Kenny Clarke (d)
In A Sentimental Mood
The Stopper
Almost Like Being In Love
No Moe
Pres. PR-24096, 874, 7029, OJC 011

October 10
New York City

JAZZ STUDIO ONE
Joe Newman (t); Bennie Green (tb); Frank Foster, Paul Quinichette (ts); Hank Jones (p); Johnny Smith (g); Eddie Jones (b); Kenny Clarke (d)
Tenderly
Let's Split
Decca DL-8058

October 21
New York City

CAL TJADER QUARTET
Cal Tjader (vb); Hank Jones (p); Al McKibbon (b); Kenny Clarke (d)
Minority
I Want To Be Happy
Love Me Or Leave Me
Tangerine
Savoy MG-12054, MG 9036

October 27
New York City

CHARLES MINGUS OCTET
Ernie Royal (t); Willie Dennis (tb); Eddie Caine (as,fl); Teo Macero (ts); Danny Bank (bs); John Lewis (p); Jackson Wiley (cello); Charles Mingus (b); Kenny Clarke (d); Janet Thurlow (vcl); Spaulding Givens (arr)
Eclipse (vcl) (New World 216 only)
Debut DEB 198
Blue Tide
Pink Topsy
Miss Bliss
Debut EP-450 OJC 115

October 31
New York City
Broadcasts,
Birdland

MODERN JAZZ QUARTET
Milt Jackson (vb); John Lewis (p); Percy Heath (b); Kenny Clarke (d)
Vendome
Lily

	The Queen's Fancy **Bags' Groove** **All The Things You Are** **La Ronde** Session SR-110
December 15 *New York City*	KENNY DORHAM Kenny Dorham (t); Jimmy Heath (as,ts); Walter Bishop Jr. (p); Percy Heath (b); Kenny Clarke (d) **An Oscar For Oscar** **Be My Love** (2 takes) **Darn That Dream** (2 takes) **I Love You** (2 takes) **Ruby My Dear** (2 takes) **Osmosis** Debut DLP-9, OJC 113, Jap. Vij.5006 M
December 24 *New York City*	KING PLEASURE John Lewis (p); Percy Heath (b); Kenny Clarke (d); King Pleasure (vcl) **Parker's Mood** **What Can I Say After I Say I'm Sorry** Pres. 7586, PR-24077, 880, 240, 7119, OJC 217
1953 *New York City*	HAL MITCHELL Hal Mitchell (t); Allen Harris (org); George Duvivier (b); Kenny Clarke (d) **Confidentially** **Mitch's Blues** Debut 104
1954: *January 20* *New York City*	ART FARMER'S NEW JAZZ STARS Art Farmer (t); Sonny Rollins (ts); Horace Silver (p); Percy Heath (b); Kenny Clarke (d) **Soft Shoe** **Confab In Tempo** **I'll Take Romance** **Wisteria** Pres. P-24032, LP 177
April 3 *New York City*	MILES DAVIS QUINTET Miles Davis (t); Dave Shildkraut (as); Horace Silver (p); Percy Heath (b); Kenny Clarke (d)

Solar	Prestige LP 185, 7076, 7457, 24077
You Don't Know What Love Is	Prestige LP 185, 7076, 7352
Love Me Or Leave Me	" " "
I'll Remember April	" " 7054, OJC-093

April 29
New York City

MILES DAVIS ALL-STAR SEXTET
Miles Davis (t); J.J. Johnson (tb); Lucky Thompson (ts); Horace Silver (p); Percy Heath (b); Kenny Clarke (d)

Blue 'n' Boogie	Prestige EP 1358, LP 182, 7076, 24077
Walkin'	45-157, EP 1357, LP 182, 7076, 24077

Note: All titles from 7076 on OJC 213

April 30
New York City

URSO-BROOKMEYER QUINTET
Bob Brookmeyer (vtb); Phil Urso (ts); Horace Silver (p); Percy Heath (b); Kenny Clarke (d)
Chiketa
Ozzie's Ode
Stop Watch
Wizzard's Gizzard
Savoy 2236, MG-12056

May 5
New York City

FRANK FOSTER QUINTET
Benny Powell (tb); Frank Foster (ts); Gildo Mahones (p); Percy Heath (b); Kenny Clarke (d)
Little Red
How I Spent The Night
Blues For Benny
Out Of Nowhere
Gracias
The Heat's On
BN BLP-5043

May 12
New York City

GEORGE WALLINGTON AND HIS BAND
Dave Burns (t); Jimmy Cleveland (tb); Frank Foster (ts); Danny Bank (bs); George Wallington (p); Oscar Pettiford (b); Kenny Clarke (d)
Summertime (5 takes)
Festival (4 takes)
Christina (3 takes)
Frankie And Johnny (2 takes)
Baby Grand (4 takes)
Bumpkins (7 takes)
BN BNP-5045, B-6503, BN (Japan) 71003, K28P 9276

May 19
New York City

ART FARMER QUINTET
Art Farmer (t); Gigi Gryce (as); Horace Silver (p); Percy Heath (b); Kenny Clarke (d)

A Night At Tony's	(Pres. P-24032 also)
Blue Concept	(" " ")
Deltitnu	
Stupendous-Lee	

Pres. LP-7085, OJC 072

June 2
New York City

CATS VERSUS CHICKS
Cats: Clark Terry (t); Urbie Green (tb); Lucky Thompson (ts); Horace Silver (p); Tal Farlow (g); Percy Heath (b); Kenny Clarke (d)

Chicks: Norma Carson (t); Corky Hale (harp); Terry Pollard (vb); Mary Osborne (g); Bonnie Wetzel (b); Elaine Leighton (d)
The Man I Love
Mamblues
Cat Meets Chick
Anything You Can Do
MGM E-3614, E225

June 16
New York City

MILT JACKSON QUINTET
Henry Boozier (t); Milt Jackson (vb); Horace Silver (p); Percy Heath (b); Kenny Clarke (d)
Opus De Funk
I've Lost Your Love
Buhaina
Soma
Pres. P-7059, P-24048, OJC 125

June 29
New Jersey

MILES DAVIS QUINTET
Miles Davis (t); Sonny Rollins (ts); Horace Silver (p); Percy Heath (b); Kenny Clarke (d)

Airegin	Prestige LP 187, LP 7109, OJC 245
Oleo	
But Not For Me	915, Met MEP 385
But Not For Me	LP 7109, P 24077
Doxy	LP 187, LP 7109

Pres. 24012, PR 7847, LP 16-3

August 11
New York City

THAD JONES QUINTET
Thad Jones (t); Frank Wess (fl,ts); Hank Jones (p); Charles Mingus (b); Kenny Clarke (d)
Ellusive
Sombre Intrusion
Bitty Ditty
I'll Remember April
(Chazzanova) (Wess out)
You Don't Know What Love Is
(Wess out)
Debut DLP-12, American AM-6054, Pres. MPP-2506

August 24
New York City

JAY AND KAI
J.J. Johnson, Kai Winding (tb); Billy Bauer (g); Charles Mingus (b); Kenny Clarke (d)
Blues For Trombone
What Is This Thing Called Love
Lament
The Major

August 26

Wally Cirillo (p) replaces Bauer
Bernie's Tune
Reflections
Co-op

Blues In Twos
Savoy SJL-2232, Realm RM 167, Savoy MG 12010

August
New York City
JULIUS WATKINS
Julius Watkins (frh); Frank Foster (ts); George Butcher (p); Perry Lopez (g); Oscar Pettiford (b); Kenny Clarke (d)
I Have Known
Linda Dalia
Perpetuation
Leete
BN BLP-5053

September 24
New York City
J.J. JOHNSON
J.J. Johnson (tb); Wynton Kelly (p); Charles Mingus (b); Kenny Clarke (d); Sabu Martinez (conga)
Jay
Old Devil Moon
Too Marvellous For Words
Coffee Pot
It's You Or No-one
Time After Time
BN BLP-5057, BLP-1505 (Vol. 1), BLP-1506 (Vol. 2)

October 6
New York City
CARMEN McRAE
Mat Mathews (acc); Herbie Mann (fl,ts); Mundell Lowe (g); Wendell Marshall (b); Kenny Clarke (d); Carmen McRae (vcl)
Easy To Love
If I'm Lucky
Old Devil Moon
Tip Toe Gently
Bethlehem BCP-6004, BCP 1023, Affinity AFF 97

November 1
Los Angeles
KENNY CLARKE ALL STARS
Frank Morgan (as); Walter Benton (ts); Milt Jackson (vb,vcl); Gerald Wiggins (p); Percy Heath (b); Kenny Clarke (d)
Sonor
Strollin'
Blues Mood
I've Lost Your Love MG 12061
Skoot (vcl MJ)
Savoy MG-12006, SJL 2242

December 23
New York City
MODERN JAZZ QUARTET (DJANGO)
Milt Jackson (vb); John Lewis (p); Percy Heath (b); Kenny Clarke (d)
I'll Remember April
Django LP 7057, ST 7425, 7749
One Bass Hit " " "
Milano " " "
Pres. LP-7057, PR-24005, OJC 057

December 24
New Jersey
MILES DAVIS ALL STARS
Miles Davis (t); Milt Jackson (vb); Thelonious Monk (p); Percy Heath (b); Kenny Clarke (d)

	Bags' Groove	Prestige LP 196, LP 7109, LP 7457
	Bags' Groove	P 24077
	Bemsha Swing	Prestige LP 200, LP 7150
	Swing Spring	Prestige LP 196, LP 7150
	The Man I Love	Prestige LP 200
	The Man I Love	P 24077
	Prestige LP 16-3, PR 7650	
1954 *New York City*	JOHN MEHEGAN TRIO John Mehegan (p); Charles Mingus (b); Kenny Clarke (d) **Blues Too Much** **Thou Swell** **The Boy Next Door** **Cherokee** Savoy XP-8130, MG-15054	
1955:		
January 9 *New York City*	MODERN JAZZ QUARTET Milt Jackson (vb); John Lewis (p); Percy Heath (b); Kenny Clarke (d) **La Ronde Suite** (pts. 1–4) Pres. LP-5057, Pres. 24005, ST 7425, 7749, OJC 057	
January 20 *Birdland,* *New York City*	MODERN JAZZ QUARTET Milt Jackson (vb); John Lewis (p); Percy Heath (b); Kenny Clarke (d) **What's New** **I'll Remember April** **Django**	
January 23 *Birdland,* *New York City*	Same **Concorde** **Yesterdays** **One Bass Hit** Alto AL-716 (both sessions)	
January 30 *New York City*	Same **Bags' Groove** **What's New** **One Bass Hit** **Django** **Concorde** **Milt Meets Sid** Session SR-111 (**Bags' Groove** on Alto)	
Same	CHARLES MINGUS/WALLY CIRILLO QUARTET Teo Macero (ts); Wally Cirillo (p); Charles Mingus (b); Kenny Clarke (d) **Transeason (Transocean)** **Rose Geranium** **Level Seven** **Smog L.A.** Savoy MG-15055, SJL-1113	

February 6
New York City

MODERN JAZZ QUARTET
Milt Jackson (vb); John Lewis (p); Percy Heath (b); Kenny Clarke (d)

D & E	Session SR 111
Yesterdays	" "
Bluesology	" "
Autumn In New York	" SR 112
Autumn Nocturne	" "
Milt Meets Sid	" "
Summertime	" "

February 7
New York City

KENNY CLARKE ALL STARS
Henry Coker (tb); Frank Wess (fl,ts); Charlie Fowlkes (bs); Milt Jackson (vb,p); Eddie Jones (b); Kenny Clarke (d); Ernie Wilkins (arr)

Klook's Nook	Savoy MG 12006
Inhibitions	" " "
Baggin' The Blues	" " "
Telefunken Blues	" " "
Telefunken Blues (alt. take)	" MG 12061

February 26
New York City

JOHNNY COSTA
Johnny Costa (p); Gene Ramey (b); Kenny Clarke (d)
Tea For Two
Begin The Beguine
Caravan
Flamingo
Savoy MG-12052, MG-15056

March 7
New York City

DUKE JORDAN TRIO
Duke Jordan (p); Oscar Pettiford (b); Kenny Clarke (d)
Sometimes I'm Happy
Embraceable You
Jor-du
Oh Yeah
Savoy MG-12145

Same

GIGI GRYCE QUARTET
Gigi Gryce (as) overdubbed on above session
Sometimes I'm Happy
Embraceable You
Jor-du
Oh Yeah
Savoy MG-12146, SJL-2231

March 30
New York City

KENNY CLARKE/ERNIE WILKINS SEPTET
Eddie Bert (tb); Ernie Wilkins (as,ts,arr); George Barrow (ts,bs); Cecil Payne (bs); Hank Jones (p); Wendell Marshall (b); Kenny Clarke (d)
Summer Evening
Oz The Wizzard
I Dig You The Most
Pru's Blooze

Same

KENNY CLARKE
Same
Plenty For Kenny
Cute Tomato
Now's The Time (d solo) BYG 529606
Savoy MG-12007 (both sessions) London C15008

May 27
New York City

RALPH SHARON SEXTET
J.R. Monterose (ts); Teddy Charles (vb); Ralph Sharon (p); Joe Puma (g); Charles Mingus (b); Kenny Clarke (d)
Manhattan
Two Sleepy People
Have You Met Miss Jones
Man On The Couch
Just Because We're Kids
Darn That Dream
Mood For Mitch
There's A Small Hotel
Love Walked In
Can't Get Out Of This Mood
Plutocrat At The Automat
Slightly Oliver
London LL-1488

May 31
New York City

EDDIE BERT QUARTET
Eddie Bert (tb); Hank Jones (p); Wendell Marshall (b); Kenny Clarke (d)
Fragile
Stompin' At The Savoy
I Should'A Said
See You Later
Three Bass Hit
What'd Ya Say
Billie's Bounce
Savoy MG-12015, WL 70539

June 6
New York City

J.J. JOHNSON QUINTET
J.J. Johnson (tb); Hank Mobley (ts); Horace Silver (p); Paul Chambers (b); Kenny Clarke (d)
Daylie Double
You're Mine You
Pennies From Heaven
Groovin'
Viscosity
A Portrait of Jenny
BN BLP-1506, BLP-5070

June 14
New York City

CARMEN McRAE
Dick Katz (p); Mundell Lowe (g); Wendell Marshall (b); Kenny Clarke (d); Carmen McRae (vcl)
Just One Of Those Things
Sometimes I'm Happy
Love Is Here To Stay

I Can't Get Started
This Will Make You Laugh
Decca DL-8173

Same

LEE KONITZ WITH WARNE MARSH
Lee Konitz (as); Warne Marsh (ts); Sal Mosca (p); Billy Bauer (g); Oscar Pettiford (b); Kenny Clarke (d)
Two Not One
There Will Never Be Another You
Donna Lee
Don't Squawk
Topsy
I Can't Get Started
Background Music (All Of Me)

June 15
New York City

Ronnie Ball (p) replaces Mosca
All The Things You Are
I Saw You Last Night
Ronnie's Line
Atl. LP-1217 (both sessions), 50298, 90050-1

June 15
New York City

GENE AMMONS ALL STARS
Art Farmer (t); Lou Donaldson (as); Gene Ammons (ts); Freddie Redd (p); Addison Farmer (b); Kenny Clarke (d)
Juggernaut
Woofin' And Tweetin'
Pres. LP-7050, OJC 014

June 16
New York City

CARMEN McRAE
Mat Mathews (acc); Herbie Mann (fl); Dick Katz (p); Mundell Low (g); Wendell Marshall (b); Kenny Clarke (d); Carmen McRae (vcl)

My One And Only Love	Decca DL 8173
Yardbird Suite	" " "
Give Me The Simple Life	" " "
I'll Remember April	" " "
You Took Advantage Of Me	" ED 2281

June 22
New York City

EDDIE BERT QUARTET
Eddie Bert (tb); Joe Puma (g); Clyde Lombardi (b); Kenny Clarke (d)
It's Only Sunshine
Bert Tram
One For Tubby
Opicana
Savoy MG-12019

June 28
New York City

KENNY CLARKE (BOHEMIA AFTER DARK)
Nat Adderley (c); Donald Byrd (t); Julian 'Cannonball' Adderley (as); Jerome Richardson (fl,ts); Horace Silver (p); Paul Chambers (b); Kenny Clarke (d)
With Apologies To Oscar

Hear Me Talkin' To Ya (JR out)
Willow Weep For Me (NA, DB out)
Bohemia After Dark
Chasm
Late Entry (DB out)
Savoy SJL-2206, MG 12017, WL 70531, ZD 70816 (CD only)

July 14
New York City

JULIAN 'CANNONBALL' ADDERLEY
Nat Adderley (c); Julian 'Cannonball' Adderley (as); Hank Jones (p); Paul Chambers (b); Kenny Clarke (d)
Spontaneous Combustion
Still Talkin' To Ya
A Little Taste
Caribbean Cutie
Flamingo (NA out)
Savoy SJL-2206, MG-12018, SJC-401, WL 70531, ZD 70816 (CD only)

Same

Cannonball Adderley out
We'll Be Together Again
Savoy MG-12017, SJL-2206

July 21
New York City

JULIAN 'CANNONBALL' ADDERLEY
Nat Adderley (c); Jimmy Cleveland (tb); Julian 'Cannonball' Adderley (as); Jerome Richardson (ts,fl); Cecil Payne (bs); John Williams (p); Paul Chambers (b); Kenny Clarke (d)
Hurricane Connie
Cynthia's In Love
The Song Is You
Purple Shades
EmArcy MGS-6043, (E) EJL-102

July 21 & 27
New York City

MONK PLAYS DUKE ELLINGTON
Thelonious Monk (p); Oscar Pettiford (b); Kenny Clarke (d)
Mood Indigo
It Don't Mean A Thing
Sohisticated Lady
I Got It Bad And That Ain't Good
Black And Tan Fantasy
I Let A Song Go Out Of My Heart
Solitude
Caravan
Riverside RLP-12-201, Milestone M-47052, OJC 024

July 26
New York City

NAT ADDERLEY QUINTET
Nat Adderley (c); Jerome Richardson (fl,ts); Hank Jones (p); Wendell Marshall (b); Kenny Clarke (d)
Porky Pork
Kussin's Buzzin'
Big E
Ann Springs

I Married An Angel
You Better Go Now
Savoy MG-12021, SJL-1128

Same

KENNY CLARKE
Nat Adderley (c); Hank Jones (p); Paul Chambers (b); Kenny Clarke (d)
We'll Be Together Again
Savoy SJL-2206, MG-12017

July 29
New York City

JULIAN 'CANNONBALL' ADDERLEY
Nat Adderley (c); J.J. Johnson (tb); Julian 'Cannonball' Adderley (as); Jerome Richardson (fl,ts,bs); Cecil Payne (bs); John Williams (p); Paul Chambers (b); Kenny Clarke (d)
Cannonball
Nat's Everglade
You'd Be So Nice To Come Home To
EmArcy MG-36043, Mercury EMS-2-404

August 2
New York City

ERNIE WILKINS: FLUTES & REEDS
Ernie Wilkins (as,arr); Jerome Richardson, Frank Wess (fl,ts); Hank Jones (p); Eddie Jones (b); Kenny Clarke (d)
Stereophonic
Doing The Thing
Shorty George
Bouncing With Boots
That's A Woman
Blues In Coldwater Flat
Savoy MG-12022

August 4
New York City

THE TRIO
Hank Jones (p); Wendell Marshall (b); Kenny Clarke (d)
We're All Together
Odd Number
When Hearts Are Young
There's A Small Hotel
Cyrano
Now's The Time
My Funny Valentine
We Could Make Such Beautiful Music
Savoy MG-12023

September 1
New York City

EDDIE BERT
Eddie Bert (tb); J.R. Monterose (ts); Hank Jones (p); Clyde Lombardi (b); Kenny Clarke (d)

Crosstown	Savoy MG 12019
Slow Crosstown	" " 12029
Steady Eddie	" " "
Bronx Line	" " "
Wishbone	" " "
Manhattan Suite	" " 12019
Conversation	" " "

September 6
New York City

JOHNNY MEHEGAN
Johnny Mehegan (p); Kenny Clarke (d)

Lullaby Of Birdland	Savoy	MG	12028
Everytime We Say Goodbye	"	"	"
Blue Skies	"	"	"
Little White Lies	"	"	"
My Heart Stood Still	"	"	"
Nice Work If You Can Get It	"	"	"
At Long Last Love	"	"	"
The Song Is You	"	"	"
Round About Midnight	"	"	"
Night And Day	"	"	"
Crazy Rhythm	"	"	12029
I'll Take Romance	"	"	"

September 27
New York City

CHUZ ALFRED QUINTET
Ola Hanson (tb); Chuz Alfred (ts); Chuck Lee (p); Vinnie Burke (b); Kenny Clarke (d)
A Message From Home
Manta Wray
I Can't Get Started
Harlequin
Love Comes To Mehitabel Brown
Chuz Duz
Savoy MG-12030

September 29
New York City

DONALD BYRD
Donald Byrd (t); Frank Foster (ts); Hank Jones (p); Paul Chambers (b); Kenny Clarke (d)

If I Love Again	Savoy	MG	12029,	SJC	1101
Gotcha Goin' n' Comin'	"	"	12032,	"	"
Winterset	"	"	"	"	"
Long Green	"	"	"	"	"
Star Eyes	"	"	"	"	"
Someone To Watch Over Me	"	"	"	"	"

October 6
New York City

AL CAIOLA
Bernie Privin (t); Hank Jones (p); Al Caiola (g); Clyde Lombardi (b); Kenny Clarke (d)
Love Letters
There Will Never Be Another You
Deep In A Dream
You Are Too Beautiful

October 11
New York City

Same
Thunderbird
Everything Happens To Me
I've Got A Crush On You
I've Got It Bad
Savoy MG-12033 (both sessions)

October 12
New York City

URBIE GREEN QUINTET
Urbie Green (tb,vb); Dave McKenna (p); Jimmy Raney (g); Percy Heath (b); Kenny Clarke (d)
Paradise
You Are Too Beautiful
Am I Blue
It's Too Late Now
Dirty Dan
Reminiscent Blues
Thou Swell
One For Dee
Warm Valley (p solo)
Frankie And Johnny
(tb & p only)
Limehouse Blues (p solo)
ABC-Paramount ABC-101, Fresh Sound

October 22
New York City

GIGI GRYCE'S ORCHESTRA
Art Farmer (t); Jimmy Cleveland (tb); Gunther Schuller (frh); Bill Barber (tu); Gigi Gryce (as); Danny Bank (bs); Horace Silver (p); Oscar Pettiford (b); Kenny Clarke (d); Ernestine Anderson (vcl)
Speculation
In A Meditating Mood
Social Call (vcl)
Kerry Dance
Savoy SJL-2231, Signal S1201, BYG (F) S 29153

October 28
New York City

MILT JACKSON
Frank Wess (fl,ts); Milt Jackson (vb); Hank Jones (p); Eddie Jones (b); Kenny Clarke (d)
Opus De Funk
Opus Pocus
You Leave Me Breathless
Opus And Interlude
Savoy MG-12036, SJL-1116, WL 70501

November 3
New Jersey

HANK JONES
Donald Byrd, Matty Dice (t)*; Hank Jones (p); Eddie Jones (b); Kenny Clarke (d)

Summer's Gone	Realm R27152,	Eros ERC 50067
Don't Blame Me	"	"
An Evening At Papa Joe's*	"	"
Almost Like Being In Love	"	"
And Then Some*	"	"
Hank's Pranks	"	"

Savoy MG-12037, MG 12053

November 3
New York City

HANK JONES
Jerome Richardson (fl,ts); Hank Jones (p); Wendell Marshall (b); Kenny Clarke (d)
Wine And Brandy
Little Girl Blue (JR out)

Alpha (JR out)
Crystal (unissued)
Savoy MG-12053

November 8
New York City

ERNIE WILKINS' TOP BRASS
Donald Byrd, Ray Copeland, Ernie Royal, Idrees Sulieman, Joe Wilder (t); Hank Jones (p); Wendell Marshall (b); Kenny Clarke (d); Ernie Wilkins (arr)
Top Brass Medley: Willow Weep For Me; Imagination; It Might As Well Be Spring; The Nearness of You; Taking A Chance On Love
Trick Or Treat
58 Market Street
Speedway
Dot's What
Savoy MG-12044, 2237

November 17
New York City

JOHNNY COATES
Johnny Coates (p); Wendell Marshall (b); Kenny Clarke (d)
Between The Devil And The Deep Blue Sea
Skylark
Stompin' At The Savoy
Coates Oats
Savoy MG-12082

November 22
New York City

MIKE CUOZZO
Mike Cuozzo (ts); Eddie Costa (vb); Ronnie Ball (b); Vinnie Burke (b); Kenny Clarke (d)
There Will Never Be Another You
What Is This Thing Called Love
Nancy
An Evening At Papa Joe's
Undecided (or Under-sided)
Walk Up
Savoy MG-12051

November 29
New York City

MARLENE PAUL
Joe Wilder (t); Herbie Mann (fl); Hank Jones (p); Eddie Jones (b); Kenny Clarke (d); Marlene Paul (vcl)
Snuggled On Your Shoulder
We Could Make Such Beautiful Music Together
With Every Breath I Take
Deep In A Dream
You Leave Me Breathless
Savoy MG-12058

Same
New York City

KENNY CLARKE
Joe Wilder (t); Hank Jones (p); Wendell Marshall (b); Kenny Clarke (d)
How High The Moon
(Wilder's Moon)
I Think Of You With Every
Breath I Take
Savoy MG-12053, MG-12073

December 14
New York City

AL CAIOLA
Romeo Penque (fl,bcl,English horn); Hank Jones (p); Al Caiola (g); Clyde Lombardi (b); Kenny Clarke (d)
Don't Worry 'bout Me
Indian Summer
Moments Like This
Drambuie
Savoy MG-12057

December 20
New York City

MARLENE PAUL
Joe Wilder (t); Herbie Mann (fl); Hank Jones (p); Eddie Jones (b); Kenny Clarke (d); Marlene Paul (vcl)
Accent On Youth
Some Other Time
If I Love Again
Two Cigarettes In The Dark
Without A Word Of Warning
Savoy MG-12058

Same

HANK JONES
Paul out
Bluebird
Savoy 4511, MG-12053, MG-12125

December 27
New York City

AL CAIOLA
Bernie Privin (t); Ronnie Ball (p); Al Caiola (g); Clyde Lombardi (b); Kenny Clarke (d)
Serenade In Blue
Black And Blue
Blue The Night
Early Autumn
Savoy 12057

Late 1955
New York City

ETHEL ENNIS
Hank Jones (p); Eddie Biggs (g); Abie Baker (b); Kenny Clarke (d); Ethel Ennis (vcl)
You Better Go Now
I've Got You Under My Skin
Love For Sale
Dreamer Dreamer
Blue Prelude
Casually
Hey Jacques
Lullaby For Losers

Say It Ain't So, Joe
Blue Willow
Bon Voyage
Jubilee JLP-1021

1955
New York City

MUSIC MINUS ONE
Don Abney (p); Jimmy Raney (g); Oscar Pettiford (b); Kenny Clarke (d)
Poor Butterfly
I May Be Wrong
Fine And Dandy
Embraceable You
Lady Be Good
Three Little Words
I Cover The Waterfront
Too Marvellous For Words
Music Minus One 2

Same

MODERN JAZZ QUARTET
Milt Jackson (vb); John Lewis (p); Percy Heath (b); Kenny Clarke (d)
Two Degrees East, Three Degrees West
Between The Devil And The Deep Blue Sea
Angel Eyes
Bluesology
God Bless You Merry Gentlemen
Delaunay's Dilemma
Bess
Bags' Groove
Ozone LP-16/1005

Same

SPOTLIGHT ON PERCUSSION
Narrated by Al 'Jazzbo' Collins; Kenny Clarke (d solo)
Jazz
Vox DL-180

1956:
January 5
New York City

MILT JACKSON
Lucky Thompson (ts); Milt Jackson (vb); Wade Legge (p); Wendell Marshall (b); Kenny Clarke (d)

Come Rain Or Come Shine	Savoy	MG	12042
They Can't Take That Away From Me	″	″	12061
Wild Man	″	″	12042
Soulful	″	″	12061
Fred's Mood	″	″	12042
Flamingo	″	″	12061

Savoy SJL-2204

January 17
New York City

MILT JACKSON SEXTET
Lucky Thompson (ts); Milt Jackson (vb); John Lewis (p); Skeeter Best (g); Oscar Pettiford (b); Kenny Clarke (d)
Hello
Bright Blues
How High The Moon (Atl. SD2-319 also)
Atl. LP-1242

January 19
New York City

JOE WILDER
Joe Wilder (t); Hank Jones (p); Wendell Marshall (b); Kenny Clarke (d)
Cherokee
My Heart Stood Still
Prelude To A Kiss
Six Bit Blues
Mad About The Boy
Darn That Dream
Savoy MG-12063

January 21
New York City

MILT JACKSON
Milt Jackson (vb); John Lewis (p); Barry Galbraith (g); Oscar Pettiford (b); Kenny Clarke (d); 5 woodwinds
So In Love (Atl. SD2-319 also)
Midnight Sun (unissued)
They Didn't Believe Me
Solitude
Atl. LP-1242

January 23
New York City

MILT JACKSON
Lucky Thompson (ts); Milt Jackson (vb); Hank Jones (p); Wendell Marshall (b); Kenny Clarke (d)

Lover	Savoy MG 12070
Can't Help Lovin' That Man	" " "
The Lady Is A Tramp	" " "
Angel Face	" " "
Sometimes I'm Happy	" " "
What's New	" " "
Now's The Time	" " 12080
In A Sentimental Mood	" " "
Mood Indigo	" " "
Azure	" " "
Minor Conception	" " "
Soul In 3/4	" " "

Savoy SJL-2204, WL 70821

January 30
New York City

THE JAZZ MESSAGE
Donald Byrd (t); John LaPorta (as); Horace Silver (p); Wendell Marshall (b); Kenny Clarke (d)
Budo
I Married An Angel
The Jazz Message (Freedom For All)
Savoy 2247

February 3
New York City

MAT MATHEWS
Julius Watkins (fh); Mat Mathews (acc); Joe Puma (g); Oscar Pettiford (b); Kenny Clarke (d)
As Time Goes By
I Only Have Eyes For You
Later On
Dawn DLP-1104, Fresh Sound FSR 563

February 6
New York City

KENNY CLARKE (KLOOK'S CLIQUE)
Donald Byrd (t); John LaPorta (as); Ronnie Ball (p); Wendell Marshall (b); Kenny Clarke (d)
Will Wail
Volcano
La Porta-thority
I Hear A Rhapsody
Yesterdays
Play Fiddle Play
Savoy MG 12065

February 8
New York City

KENNY CLARKE/HANK MOBLEY
Donald Byrd (t); Hank Mobley (ts); Ronnie Ball (p); Doug Watkins (b); Kenny Clarke (d)

There Will Never Be Another You	Savoy MG 12064
Cattin'	" " "
Madeline (t out)	" " "
When I Fall In Love	" " "

Savoy SJL-1125

February 27
New York City

THE BIRDLAND STARS
Conte Candoli, Kenny Dorham (t); Phil Woods (as); Al Cohn (ts); Hank Jones (b); Kenny Clarke (d)
Two Pairs Of Aces
Roulette
A Bit Of Blues
Ah Funky New Baby
Last Lap
Phil 'er Up
Conte's Condolences
For Kicks Only
Hip Boots
Minorin' The Blues
Birdland Fantasy
Playboy
RCA Victor LPM-1327, LPM-1328

March 5
New York City

FRANK FOSTER
Benny Powell, Henry Coker (tb); Frank Wess (fl,ts); Frank Foster (ts); Kenny Burrell (g); Eddie Jones (b); Kenny Clarke (d)

Serenata	Savoy MG 12078
Dill Pickles	" " "
Hard Sock Dance	" " "
Dancing On The Ceiling	" " "

	Alternative	" " "
	Stop Gap	" " "
	Savoy 2249	
March 7	FRANK WESS	
New York City	Same	
	What'd Ya Say	Savoy MG 12072
	Salvation	" " 12078
	Apron Strings	" " "
	Casa De Marcel	" " "
	Lazy Sal	" " 12072
	Unknown (unissued)	
	Excursion	" " 12078
	Savoy 2249	

March 12
New York City

MORT HERBERT SEXTET
Don Stratton (t); Mike Cuozzo (ts); Sahib Shihab (fl,bs); Ronnie Ball (p); Mort Herbert (b); Kenny Clarke (d)
Swiss Movement
Night People
I've Got You Under My Skin
Son Of The Preacher
Savoy MG-12073

March 21
New York City

RONNIE BALL
Willie Dennis (tb); Ted Brown (ts); Ronnie Ball (p); Wendell Marshall (b); Kenny Clarke (d)
Pennie Packer
Feathered Bed
Little Quail
Sweet And Lovely
Prez Sez
Ghost Of A Chance
Citrus Season
Savoy MG-12075

March
New York City

VARIOUS ARTISTS/KNOW YOUR JAZZ
DONALD BYRD QUINTET
Donald Byrd (t); Joe Roland (vb); Billy Taylor (p); Oscar Pettiford (b); Kenny Clarke (d)
Stella By Starlight
ABC Paramount ABC 115

Same

JIMMY CLEVELAND QUARTET
Jimmy Cleveland (tb); Billy Taylor (p); Oscar Pettiford (b); Kenny Clarke (d)
Embraceable You
ABC Paramount ABC 115

Same

GIGI GRYCE QUARTET/SEXTET
Gigi Gryce (as); Tony Scott (cl)*; Mundell Lowe (g)*; Billy Taylor (p); Oscar Pettiford (b); Kenny Clarke (d)
Come Rain Or Come Shine

In A Mellotone*
ABC Paramount ABC 115

Same

MUNDELL LOWE QUARTET/QUINTET
Mundell Lowe (g); Tony Scott (cl); Billy Taylor (p)*; Oscar Pettiford (b); Kenny Clarke (d)
If I Love Again
How About You*
ABC Paramount ABC 115

Same

JOE ROLAND QUARTET
Joe Roland (vb); Billy Taylor (p); Oscar Pettiford (b); Kenny Clarke (d)
Laura
ABC Paramount ABC 115

Same

CHARLIE ROUSE QUARTET
Charlie Rouse (ts); Billy Taylor (p); George Duvivier (b); Kenny Clarke (d)
But Not For Me
ABC Paramount ABC 115

Same

TONY SCOTT QUINTET
Tony Scott (cl); Mundell Lowe (g); Billy Taylor (p); Oscar Pettiford (b); Kenny Clarke (d)
The Nearness Of You
ABC Paramount ABC 115

April 3
New York City

RAY BRYANT
Ray Bryant (p); Wyatt Reuther (b); Kenny Clarke (d)
You're My Thrill
Off Shore
Pawn Ticket
Cry Me A River
Philadelphia Bound
Goodbye
Epic LN-3279

April 23
New York City

JOHNNY COATES
Johnny Coates (p); Wendell Marshall (b); Kenny Clarke (d)
Let's Get Lost
Love Is The Sweetest Thing
Little Girl Blue
Ding Dong The Witch Is Dead
If I Love Again
Savoy MG-12082

April 30
Hackensack,
New Jersey

KENNY CLARKE (KENNY CLARKE MEETS THE DETROIT JAZZMEN)
Pepper Adams (bs); Tommy Flanagan (p); Kenny Burrell (g); Paul Chambers (b); Kenny Clarke (d)
Cottontail
But Not For Me (KB, KC only)
(unissued)

Your Host
Tricrotism
Tom's Thumb
Savoy SJL-1111

May 3
New York City

BERNIE PRIVIN (BROTHERS AND OTHER MOTHERS VOL. 2)
Bernie Privin (t); Toots Mondello, Romeo Penque (as); Al Cohn, Jerry Sanfino (ts); Wolf Payne (bs); Bernie Leighton (p); Clyde Lombardi (b); Kenny Clarke or Osie Johnson (d)*
But Not For Me
I'm Gonna Sit Right Down
And Write Myself A Letter
The Sheik Of Araby
More Than You Know
Soon
Do You Ever Think Of Me?
Sugar
Savoy SJL-2236, Regent MG 6027
(* It is not known which drummer plays on which titles)

Same

PHINEAS NEWBORN
Phineas Newborn (p); Calvin Newborn (g); Oscar Pettiford (b); Kenny Clarke (d)
Daahoud
All The Things You Are
Love And Live (unissued)
Barbados
Afternoon In Paris

May 4

Calvin Newborn out
Celia
Embraceable You (unissued)
Land's End (unissued)
I'm Beginning To See The Light
They Can't Take That Away From Me (unissued)
Atl. LP-1235 (both sessions) Atl. (Japan) P7562A

May 9
Hackensack,
New Jersey

KENNY CLARKE (KENNY CLARKE MEETS THE DETROIT JAZZMEN)
Pepper Adams (bs); Tommy Flanagan (p); Kenny Burrell (g); Paul Chambers (b); Kenny Clarke (d)
You Turned The Tables On Me
Afternoon In Paris
Apophthegm
Savoy SJL-1111, MG 12083, WL 70515

May 21
New York City

JOHNNY COATES
Johnny Coates (p); Wendell Marshall (b); Kenny Clarke (d)
Sha-da-ga-da
Lucky Day
If There Is Someone Lovelier
Than You

	Unknown	
	Savoy MG-12082	
May 29	MORT HERBERT SEXTET	
New York City	Joe Wilder (t); Bobby Jaspar (ts); Sahib Shihab (fl,bs); Dick Katz (p); Mort Herbert (b); Kenny Clarke (d)	
	Blues For Fred and Fay	
	Mitch's Carol	
	That's All (unissued)	
	Savoy MG-12073	
May 29	INTRODUCING KENNY BURRELL	
New York City	Tommy Flanagan (p); Kenny Burrell (g); Paul Chambers (b); Kenny Clarke (d); Candido Camero (conga)	
	Weaver Of Dreams	Blue Note BLP 1523
	This Time The Dream's On Me	" " " "
	Takeela	" " " "
	Fugue 'n Blues	" " " "
	Delilah	" " " "
	Rhythmorama (Burrell, Clarke, Camero only)	" " " "
	Blues For Skeeter	" " " "
	But Not For Me (g solo)	Blue Note BLP 1543
	Get Happy	" " " "
June 14	BERNIE PRIVIN AND HIS ORCHESTRA	
New York City	Bernie Privin (t); Toots Mondello, Romeo Penque (as); Al Cohn, Jerry Sanfino (ts); Wolf Payne (bs); Bernie Leighton (p); Clyde Lombardi (b); Kenny Clarke or Osie Johnson (d)*	
	My Heart Stood Still	
	How Long Has This Been Going On?	
	I Can't Believe That You're In Love With Me (unissued)	
	Please Don't Talk About Me When I'm Gone (unissued)	
	(* It is not known which drummer plays on which titles)	
	Regent MG 6027	
June 20	FRANK WESS/KENNY BURRELL	
New York City	Frank Wess (fl); Kenny Burrell, Freddie Green (g); Eddie Jones (b); Kenny Clarke (d)	
	Wess Side	Savoy MG 12085, SJL 1120
	Kansas City Side	" " " " "
	East Wind	" " " " "
	Over The Rainbow	" " " " "
	Southern Exposure	" " " " "
July 2	THE HORACE SILVER QUINTET	
New York City	Joe Gordon (t); Hank Mobley (ts); Horace Silver (p); Doug Watkins (b); Kenny Clarke (d)	
	To Beat Or Not To Beat	
	Shoutin' Out	

How Long Has This Been Going On
Epic LA-16006, LN-3326

July 11
New York City

DICK HYMAN/LEONARD FEATHER AND THEIR ORCHESTRA (HIFI SUITE: FROM PICCOLO TO TUBA IN RHYTHM)
Thad Jones (t); Benny Powell (tb); Jerome Richardson (as,picc); Frank Wess (ts,fl); Phil Bodner (bs,oboe); Dick Hyman (p); Oscar Pettiford (b); Kenny Clarke (d)
Bass Reflex

Same

Add Bill Barber (tu)
Reverberations
Tweeter
Woofer
MGM E-3494 (both sessions)

July 13
New York City

JAY AND KAI
J.J. Johnson, Kai Winding (tb); Dick Katz (p); Bill Brown (b); Kenny Clarke (d)
To Close For Comfort
'S Wonderful
Tromboniums In Motion
How High The Moon
Violets For Your Furs
Col. CL-973

July 18
New Jersey

FRANK WESS
Jimmy Cleveland, Henry Cooper, Benny Powell, Bill Hughes (tb); Frank Wess (fl); Ronnell Bright (p); Freddie Green (g); Eddie Jones (b); Kenny Clarke (d); Frank Foster (arr)

You'll Do	Savoy MG 12086, WL 70523
Wanting You	" " " " "
Lo Fi	" " " " "
Unknown (unissued)	
Unknown (unissued)	
Don't Blame Me	" " "
Crackerjack	" " "

July 23
New York City

HANK MOBLEY
Donald Byrd (t); Hank Mobley (ts); Barry Harris (p); Doug Watkins (b); Kenny Clarke (d)
B For BB
Space Flight
Blues Number Two
Savoy SJL-1125

August 14, 16, 23
New York City

MARY ANN McCALL WITH THE ERNIE WILKINS ORCHESTRA
Joe Wilder (t); George Barrow, Seldon Powell, Zoot Sims (ts); Sol Moore (bs); Nat Pierce (p); Wendell Marshall (b); Kenny Clarke (d); Mary Ann McCall (vcl); Ernie Wilkins (arr,cond)

	Shake Down The Stars	Regent MG 6040
	You Can Depend On Me	" " "
	Easy Living	" " "
	Mean To Me	" " "
	In My Solitude	" " "
	I Thought About You	" " "
	Deep Purple	" " "
	'Deed I Do	" " "
	It's You Or No One	" " "
	It's Been So Long	" " "
	Something I Dreamed Last Night	" " "
	It Must Be True	Regent MG 6046

August 21
New York City

HANK JONES QUARTET
Babby Jaspar (fl,ts); Hank Jones (p); Paul Chambers (b); Kenny Clarke (d)
Sunday At Savannah
Moonlight Becomes You
Relaxin' At Camarillo
Minor Contention
Spontaneous Combustion
Savoy MG-12087, WL 70504

1956
New York City

MAT MATHEWS
Herbie Mann (fl,ts); Mat Mathews (acc); Joe Puma (g); Oscar Pettiford (b); Kenny Clarke (d)
The Puritan
What A Difference A Day Made
How Deep Is The Ocean
Dawn 1104, Fresh Sound FSR 563

Same

MAT MATHEWS
Art Farmer (t); Gigi Gryce (as); Mat Mathews (acc); Dick Katz (p); Oscar Pettiford (b); Kenny Clarke (d)
Not So Sleepy
Knights At The Castle
Now See How You Are (MM, OP only)
Summertime (MM, OP only)
Dawn 1104, Fresh Sound FSR 563

September 24
Paris

JAZZ INTERNATIONAL
Jimmy Deuchar (t); Billy Byers (tb); Allen Eager (ts); Martial Solal (p); Benoît Quersin (b); Kenny Clarke (d)
Cinerama
Trianon
Kenny Special
Illusion
Vogue
Love Me Or Leave Me
Byers' Blues
Vogue LAE-12029, Swing LDM-30048

October 26
Paris

JAZZ INTERNATIONAL
Roger Guérin (t); Nat Peck, Billy Byers (tb); René Urtreger (p); Pierre Michelot (b); Kenny Clarke (d)
'Round Midnight
When Lights Are Low

Same

Martial Solal (p) replaces Urtreger
On A Riff
Philips 77312, Epic LN-3376 (both sessions)

November 21
Paris

JAZZ INTERNATIONAL (KENNY CLARKE PLAYS ANDRE HODEIR)
Billy Byers (tb); Hubert Rostaing (as); Armand Migiani (bs); Martial Solal (p); Jean Warland (b); Kenny Clarke (d); André Hodeir (arr)
Oblique
Jeru
Eronel
Tahiti

November 30
Paris

Roger Guérin (t) replaces Rostaing
Bemsha Swing
Blue Serge
Swing Spring
The Squirrel
Cadenze
Philips 77312, Epic LN-3376 (both sessions)

December 4
Paris

JOHN LEWIS & SACHA DISTEL (AFTERNOON IN PARIS)
Barney Wilen (ts); John Lewis (p); Sacha Distel (g); Percy Heath (b); Kenny Clarke (d)
Bags' Groove
All The Things You Are
Willow Weep For Me
Versailles 12005, Atl. LP-1267, Oriole (E) MG-20036

1956
Paris

ZOOT SIMS QUARTET
Zoot Sims (ts); Martial Solal (p); Pierre Michelot (b); Kenny Clarke (d)
It Had To Be You
Europa Jazz 1007

1956–1958
Paris

JACQUES HELIAN ET SON ORCHESTRE
Ernie Royal, Jean Baissart, Edmond Harnie, Janot Morales, Pierre Thibaut, Albert Vanneque (t); Bill Tamper, Raymond Fonseque, Luis Fuentes (tb); Michel Cassez, Bob Garcia, Georges Blanc, Jean-Louis Chautemps (saxes); Sadi (vb,bongo); Paul Piguilem (g); Jean Warland (b); Kenny Clarke (d); Humberto Canto (perc); Jacques Hélian (cond); Ernie Royal (t solo –1)

When Your Lover Has Gone (1)	CPT 8626-21,	Pathé (F)	PG 601
Est-ce Un Péché (It's No Sin) (1)	CPT 8627-21,	"	"
A La Kenton	CPT 8851-21,	"	PG 625

Embrasse-Moi Vite (I Wanna Love You)	CPT 9193-21,	"	PG 655
Bing Bang Blues (The Blacksmith Blues)	CPT 9210-21,	"	PG 664
Lullaby Of Birdland	Pathé (F) G1138		
Train Boogie	" "		
Sixteen Tons	" G1201		
Lola, Lola	" "		
Learning The Blues	" EG 188		
Slue Foot	" "		
Rock Around The Clock	" AT 1074		
Stranger In Paradise	" "		

Note: Several other titles were recorded by the orchestra in this period with short solo passages by Ernie Royal and drum backing by Kenny Clarke

1957:

January 2
Paris

HENRI RENAUD TRIO
Henri Renaud (p); Jean Warland (b); Kenny Clarke (d)
You Are Too Beautiful
Beautiful Love
Klook's Clock
Wallington's Special
What Is There To Say
Duc-Thomson (F)450V052

January 8
Paris

HENRI RENAUD ORCHESTRA
Fernand Verstraete (t); Charles Verstraete, Billy Byers (tb); Allen Eager (ts); Jean-Louis Chautemps (ts,bs); Henri Renaud (p); Jean Warland (b); Kenny Clarke (d)
Meet Quincy Jones
The Greatest Lie
Mac Zooto
The Tabou Trot
Dillon
Duc-Thomson (F)300V027

March 10
Paris

Same
Jack Of Diamonds
I Love You Baby
Sally Go Round The Sunshine
Every Day I Have The Blues
Nobody Knows The Trouble I've Seen
I've Been Lonesome, I've Been Worried
Let Us Run
Lonesome Road
Great Day
When I've Been Drinking
Vanguard VRS-7022

May 13
Paris

BROTHER JOHN SELLERS
Guy Lafitte (ts); Georges Arvanitas (p); Pierre Michelot (b); Kenny Clarke (d); Brother John Sellers (b)
Lucy Mae Blues
Love Is A Story
Railroad Man
He Came All The Way Down
Col. (F)ESDF-1157

May 23
Paris

EDDIE BARCLAY & HIS ORCHESTRA
Roger Guérin, Fred Gérard, Maurice Thomas, Henri Vanecke (t); Charles Huss, Andre Paquinet, Benny Vasseur (tb); Gabriel Vilain (btb); Raymond Guiot (fl); Mickey Nicolas, Jo Hrasko (as); Marcel Hrasko, Lucky Thompson (ts); William Boucaya (bs); Stéphane Grappelli (vln); Michel Hauser (vb); Art Simmons (p); Pierre Cavalli (g); Jean Bouchety (b); Kenny Clarke (d); 16 strings; choir of 8; Quincy Jones (arr,cond)
Quand Je Monte Chez Toi Barclay (F)72249, 82138
United Artists UAL 3023, UAS 6023, Fresh Sound FSR 514

June 17
Paris

SIDNEY BECHET/MARTIAL SOLAL QUARTET
Sidney Bechet (ss); Martial Solal (p); Pierre Michelot (b); Kenny Clarke (d)
All The Things You Are
Embraceable You
Wrap Your Troubles in Dreams
All Of Me
Rose Room
It Don't Mean A Thing
Vogue (F) LDM-30065, Inner City IC-7008

June 24
Paris

EDDIE BARCLAY & HIS ORCHESTRA
Roger Guérin, Fred Gérard, Maurice Thomas, Henri Vanecke (t); Charles Huss, André Paquinet, Benny Vasseur (tb); Gabriel Vilain (btb); Mickey Nicolas, Jo Hrasko (as); Marcel Hrasko, Lucky Thompson, William Boucaya (bs); Raymond Guiot (fl); Michel Hausser (vb); Art Simmons (p); Pierre Cavalli (g); Jean Bouchety (b); Kenny Clarke (d); Stéphane Grappelli (vln); 16 strings; choir of 8 vocalists; Quincy Jones (arr,dir)
Tu Joues Avec Le Feu Barclay (F) 82138
Un P'tit Bout de Femme (Manhattan) Barclay (F) 72133, 82138
Tout Doucement (unissued)

c. July
Paris

Ne M'Laissez Pas Comme Ca Barclay (F) 72133, 82138
Place Blanche " " " "
All titles on Barclay 82138 also on United Artists UAL 2023, UAS 6023, Fresh Sound FSR 514

July 13
Paris

MARTIAL SOLAL AND SON ORCHESTRE
Roger Guérin, Christian Bellest, Fred Gérard, Thomas Garric (t); Billy Byers, Nat Peck, Charles Verstraete, Guy Destrangues (tb);

Hubert Rostaing, Jean Aldegon (as); Lucky Thompson, Jacques Ferrier (ts); Michael Cassiz (bs); Pierre Gossez (bsax); Martial Solal (p); Pierre Michelot (b); Kenny Clarke (d)
Blouse Bleue
Fantasque
Alhambra
Swing (F) LDM-30099

July 18
Paris

STEPHANE GRAPPELLI
Stéphane Grappelli (vln); Raymond Fol (p,harpsichord); Guy Pedersen (b); Kenny Clarke (d)
Coquette
Willow Weep For Me
This Can't Be Love
My Funny Valentine
Blue Room

July 22

Pierre Michelot (b) replaces Pedersen
Thou Swell
By All Means
Shine
I've Found A New Baby
Barclay (F)-84066

September 16
Paris

JUNE RICHMOND WITH QUINCY JONES ORCHESTRA
Roger Guérin (t); Billy Byers (tb); Jo Hrasko (cl,as); Lucky Thompson, Marcel Hrasko (ts); Henri Renaud (p); Guy Pedersen (b); Kenny Clarke (d); 13 strings; Quincy Jones (arr,cond)
I've Got A Right To Sing The Blues
Sleep
Everybody's Doin' It Now
Between The Devil And The Deep Blue Sea
Barclay (F) EP70105

September 23
Paris

KENNY CLARKE
Bernard Hulin, Ack van Rooyen (t); Billy Byers, Nat Peck (tb); Hubert Fol (as); Lucky Thompson, Pierre Gossez (ts); Armand Migiani (bs); Maurice Vander (p); Pierre Michelot (b,arr); Kenny Clarke (d)
Love Me Or Leave Me
Fun For Four
Fantasy For Bass
Jackie My Little Cat
Col. (F) ESDF-1176, Swingtime SW 8411

September 26
Paris

KENNY CLARKE
Lucky Thompson (ts); Martial Solal (p); Pierre Michelot (b); Kenny Clarke (d)
Now's The Time
The Squirrel
Stompin' At The Savoy

Four
Col. (F) ESDF-1176, Swingtime SW 8411

October 8 *Paris*	EDDIE BARCLAY Roger Guérin, Fred Gérard, Maurice Thomas, Fernand Verstraete (t); André Paquinet, Charles Huss, Benny Vasseur (tb); Gabriel Vilain (btb); Mickey Nicolas, Jo Hrasko (as); Don Byas, Pierre Gossez or Georges Grenu (ts); William Boucaya (bs); Michel Hausser (vb); Art Simmons (p); Pierre Cavalli (g); Jean Bouchety (b); Kenny Clarke (d); Stéphane Grappelli (vln); unknown strings; Quincy Jones (arr,cond)	
	Et Voilà	Barclay (F) 72249, 82138
	Avec Ces Yeux-Là	Barclay (F) 82138
October 17 *Paris*	**Nuages** (unissued) **Aime-Moi** **Quand J'y Pense**	
October 18 *Paris*	**Numero 13** (rejected)	
	Quincy Boogie	Barclay (F) 72180
	Tout Doucement	Barclay (F) 72133, 72180
	Quelque Chose En Toi (vln out)	Barclay (F) 82138
	All titles on Barclay 82138 also on United Artists UAL 3023, UAS 6023 and Fresh Sound FSR 514	
November 12 *Paris*	KENNY CLARKE (KENNY CLARKE PLAYS CHRISTIAN CHEVALIER) Roger Guérin (t); Benny Vasseur (tb); Pierre Gossez, Mickey Nicolas (as); George Grenu (ts); Armand Migiani (bs); Maurice Vander (p); Pierre Michelot (b); Kenny Clarke (d) **Dream Time** **Gold Fish** Col. (F) ESDF-1222, Swingtime SW 8411	
Same	KENNY CLARKE Ack van Rooyen (t); Nat Peck (tb); Hubert Fol, Jean Aldegon (as); Georges Grenu (ts); Armand Migiani (bs); Maurice Vander (p); Pierre Michelot (b); Kenny Clarke (d) **Black Knight** Col. (F) ESDF-1222, Swingtime SW 1141	
Same	KENNY CLARKE Jean Liesse (tp); Nat Peck (tb); Hubert Fol, Jean Aldegon (as); Tony Scott (cl,ts); Armand Migiani (bs); Raymond Fol (p); Pierre Michelot (b); Kenny Clarke (d) **Jean-Paul** Col. (F) ESDF-1222, Swingtime SW 1141	
November 30 *Paris*	MILES DAVIS/BARNEY WILEN QUARTET (LIVE AT THE OLYMPIA THEATRE) Miles Davis (t); Barney Wilen (ts); René Urtreger (p); Pierre Michelot (b); Kenny Clarke (d) **Bags' Groove**	

Tune Up (unissued)
Four
Rollins' Tune (unissued)
Walkin' (unissued)
'Round About Midnight (unissued)
Valsajane
Live Television Broadcast; Carlyne Music CAR-006

December 4/5
Paris
MILES DAVIS (ASCENSEUR POUR L'ECHAFAUD)
Same
Nuit Sur Les Champs-Elysées (4 takes)
Assassinat (3 takes)
Motel
Final (3 takes)
Ascenseur
Le Petit Bal (2 takes)
Sequence Voiture (2 takes)
Générique Polydor 816411-1
L'Assassinat De Carala
Sur L'Autoroute
Julien Dans L'Ascenseur
Florence Sur Les Champs-Elysées
Diner Au Motel
Evasion De Julien
Visite Du Vigile
Au Bar Du Petit Bac
Chez Le Photographe Du Motel
Blue 'n' Boogie
Fontana 836305-2 (CD only)
(Last eleven titles on Col. CL-1268, Mercury 6444701, 812107-1, and Fontana 660213)

December 8
Amsterdam
Radio broadcast
MILES DAVIS/BARNEY WILEN QUINTET
Same
OMS 7003

December
Paris
TV broadcast
MILES DAVIS/BARNEY WILEN QUINTET
Same
Lady Bird (unissued)

Paris
BUD POWELL QUINTET
Clark Terry (t); Barney Wilen (ts); Bud Powell (p); Eric Peter (b); Kenny Clarke (d)
No Problem
Miguel's Party
Europa Jazz 1007, Denon (CD) DC 8519

Same
STUFF SMITH QUINTET
Stéphane Grappelli, Stuff Smith (vln); Raymond Fol (p); Pierre

Michelot (b); Kenny Clarke (d)
How High The Moon
Europa Jazz 1014

1958:
January 11
Paris

EDDIE BARCLAY & HIS ORCHESTRA
Roger Guérin, Fred Gérard, Maurice Thomas, Fernand Verstraete (t); André Paquinet, Charles Huss, Benny Vasseur (tb); Gabriel Vilain (btb); Mickey Nicolas, Jo Hrasko (as); Don Byas, Pierre Gossez or George Grenu (ts); William Boucaya (bs); Michel Hausser (vb); Art Simmons (p); Pierre Cavalli (g); Jean Bouchety (b); Kenny Clarke (d); Stéphane Grappelli (vln); unknown strings; Quincy Jones (arr,cond)

Sermonette	Barclay (F)	72249, 82138
Craven	"	82138
Numéro 13	"	72249, 82138
Pas Moi	"	82138

All titles on Barclay (F) 82138 also on United Artists UAL 3023, UAS 6023 and Fresh Sound FSR 514

February 13, 14
Paris

MILT JACKSON (PARIS SESSION – JAZZ SUR SEINE)
Barney Wilen (ts); Milt Jackson (p); Percy Heath (b); Kenny Clarke (d); Gana M'Bow (conga)
Swing 39
Vamp
Menilmontant
John's Groove
BBB (Bags' Barney Blues)
Swingin' Paris Rhythm (Jazz Sur Seine)
J'ai Ta Main
Nuages
La Route Enchantée
Que Reste-t-il De Nos Amours
Minor Swing
Epistrophy
Philips 77127, (E) BBL-7459

June 23

JAZZ LEGACY, BADEN BADEN, THE CONCERT, 23.6.1958
HANS KOLLER QUARTET
Hans Koller (ts); Roland Kovac (p); Peter Trunk (b); Kenny Clarke (d)
Fallin' In Love

Same

ZOOT SIMS QUARTET
Zoot Sims (ts); Roland Kovac (p); Peter Trunk (b); Kenny Clarke (d)
Allen's Alley
Tangerine

Same

ZOOT SIMS/HANS KOLLER QUINTET
Zoot Sims, Hans Koller (ts); Roland Kovac (p); Peter Trunk (b); Kenny Clarke (d)
All The Things You Are

Same

ZOOT SIMS/HANS KOLLER QUARTET
Zoot Sims, Hans Koller (cl); Peter Trunk (b); Kenny Clarke (d)
Minor Meeting For Two Clarinets

Same

WILLIE DENNIS/ZOOT SIMS SEXTET
Willie Dennis (tb); Zoot Sims, Hans Koller (ts); Roland Kovac (p); Peter Trunk (b); Kenny Clarke (d)
Blue Night
I'll Remember April

Same

ZOOT SIMS SEPTET
Zoot Sims, Adi Feuerstein, Gerd Husemann, Hans Koller (as); Roland Kovac (p); Peter Trunk (b); Kenny Clarke (d)
Open Door

Same

HELMUT BRANDT QUARTET
Helmut Brandt (bs); Roland Kovac (p); Peter Trunk (b); Kenny Clarke (d)
I Surrender Dear

Same

WILLIE DENNIS/ZOOT SIMS SEPTET
Willie Dennis (tb); Zoot Sims, Hans Koller (ts); Helmut Brandt (bs); Roland Kovac (p); Peter Trunk (b); Kenny Clarke (d)
Trottin'

Same

WILLIE DENNIS QUARTET
Willie Dennis (tb); Roland Kovac (p); Peter Trunk (b); Kenny Clarke (d)
These Foolish Things

Same

JAM SESSION
Stu Hamer (t); Willie Dennis (tb); Adi Feuerstein, Gerd Husemann, Zoot Sims (ts); Hans Koller (as); Helmut Brandt (bs); Roland Kovac, Lasse Werner (p); Peter Trunk (b); Kenny Clarke (d)
Walkin'
Jazzline JL 20829, Delta 11098

July 7
Paris

SARAH VAUGHAN
Zoot Sims, Jo Hrasko, William Boucaya, Marcel Hrasko (saxes); Michel Hausser (vb); Ronnell Bright (p); Pierre Cullaz (g); Richard Davis (b); Kenny Clarke (d); unknown strings; Quincy Jones (arr,cond)
Please Be Kind
The Midnight Sun Will Never Set
Day By Day
Misty Mercury 830669-2
I'll Close My Eyes

Same

Pierre Michelot (b) replaces Davis
I'm Lost
Love Me

	That's All Mercury MG-20370 (both sessions)
December 2 *Baden Baden*	JAZZ LEGACY BADEN BADEN (Unreleased radio tapes) OSCAR PETTIFORD SEPTET Oscar Pettiford (b,cello); Hans Koller, Helmut Brandt, Rudi Flieri, Johnny Feigli (bs); Hans Hammerschmid (p); Kenny Clarke (d) **Low Idea**
Same	OSCAR PETTIFORD QUARTET Oscar Pettiford (b); Hans Koller (ts); Attila Zoller (g); Kenny Clarke (d) **Blues In The Closet** Jazzline 20827
December 19 *Paris*	BOBBY JASPAR Bobby Jaspar (fl); Michel Hausser (vb,xyl); Paul Rovère (b); Kenny Clarke (d); Humberto Canto (bongo)* **Cliff Cliff*** **Waiting For Irene** **Chasin' The Bird*** **Phenyl-Ysopropil-Amine** **Mysterioso** **Jeu De Cartes** **Lullaby Of The Leaves** **Speak Low** Barclay (F) 84063, Fresh Sound
December 21 *Paris*	ART BLAKEY Lee Morgan (t); Benny Golson (ts); Bobby Timmons (p); Jymie Merritt (b); Art Blakey (d); Kenny Clarke (d); Gana M'Bow (conga) **A Night In Tunisia** **Ending With The Theme** RCA (F) 430045, FXL3, 7052
1958:	
	STAN GETZ QUARTET Stan Getz (ts); Martial Solal (p); Pierre Michelot (b); Kenny Clarke (d) **Ghost Of A Chance** **They All Fall In Love** — Denon CD 33C38 7679 **All God's Children Got Rhythm** — " " " " **Broadway** — " " " " **East Of The Sun And West Of The Moon** — " " " " Europa Jazz 1008, I Giganti del Jazz No. 20. (All except **They All Fall In Love** on Bandstand BDLP 1503)
Same	STAN GETZ QUINTET Stan Getz (ts); Martial Solal (p); Jimmy Gourley (g); Pierre Michelot (b); Kenny Clarke (d) **Topsy**

'Round About Midnight
Europa Jazz 1008, I Giganti del Jazz No. 20, Bandstand BDLP 1503

Same

JOE TURNER
Benny Waters (ts); Joe Turner (p); Jimmy Woode (b); Kenny Clarke (d); Big Joe Turner (vcl)
Flip, Flop And Fly Denon CD DC 8530
Cherry Red
Europa Jazz 1026

Same

JOE TURNER
Buck Clayton (t); Vic Dickenson (tb); Alix Combelle, Benny Waters (ts); Joe Turner (p); Jimmy Woode (b); Kenny Clarke (d); Stuff Smith (vln); Big Joe Turner (vcl)
Shake Rattle & Roll
Europa Jazz 1014

Same

CHET BAKER QUARTET
Chet Baker (t); Georges Arvanitas (p); Guy Pedersen (b); Kenny Clarke (d)
Milestones
Europa Jazz 1007, Denon CD DC 8516

Same

JAMES MOODY QUARTET
James Moody (ts); Henri Renaud (p); Pierre Michelot (b); Kenny Clarke (d)
You Go To My Head
Don't Blame Me
Europa Jazz 1050

1959:
March 4
Paris

LESTER YOUNG
Lester Young (ts); René Urtreger (p); Jimmy Gourley (g); George Joyner (Jamil Nasser) (b); Kenny Clarke (d)
I Didn't Know What Time It Was
Oh Lady Be Good
Almost Like Being In Love
Three Little Words
I Cover The Waterfront
I Can't Get Started
Indiana
Pennies From Heaven
New D.B. Blues
Lullaby Of Birdland
There'll Never Be Another You
Tea For Two
Verve MGV-8378, 2304-489

March 11
Paris

LESTER YOUNG
Idrees Sulieman (t); Lester Young (ts); René Urtreger (p); Jimmy Gourley (g); Pierre Michelot (b); Kenny Clarke (d)

D.B. Blues (unissued)
– private recording
There Will Never Be Another You (unissued broadcast)

March

LESTER YOUNG
Lester Young (ts); Jimmy Gourley (g); Harold Kaufmann (p); Jean-Marie Ingrand (b); Kenny Clarke (d)
I Cover The Waterfront
Kenny Clarke on Prez
There'll Never Be Another You
Philology 214W6

April 15

ANDY AND THE BEY SISTERS
Kenny Dorham (t); Barney Wilen (ts); Andy Bey (p,vcl,arr); Paul Rovère (b); Kenny Clarke (d); Geraldine Bey, Salome Bey (vcl)
Bye Bye Blackbird
Fascinating Rhythm
Scoubidou
Smooth Sailin'
Fontana 464451

April
Paris

BARNEY WILEN QUINTET (UN TEMOIN DANS LA VILLE)
Kenny Dorham (t); Barney Wilen (ts,ss); Duke Jordan (p); Gilbert Rovère (b); Kenny Clarke (d)
Un Témoin Dans La Ville
Le Pendaison
Mélodie Pour Les Radio-Taxis
Poursuite En Métro
Ambiance Pourpre
Préméditation Dans L'Appartement
La Vie N'Est Qu'Une Lutte
Complainte Du Chauffeur
Sur L'Antenne
Blues De L'Attente
SOS Radio-Taxis
Final Au Jardin D'Acclimatation
Fontana (F) 660226-HR

August
Paris

CHET BAKER QUARTET
Chet Baker (t); Georges Arvanitas (p); Guy Pedersen (b); Kenny Clarke (d)
Milestones — I Giganti del Jazz 8; Europa Jazz EJ1007, Denon DC 8516

December 12
Paris

BUD POWELL (BUD IN PARIS)
Barney Wilen (ts); Bud Powell (p); Pierre Michelot (b); Kenny Clarke (d)
Shaw 'Nuff
Oleo

	Autumn In New York **John's Abbey** Xanadu 102	
1959	STAN GETZ QUINTET Stan Getz (ts); René Urtreger (p); Jimmy Gourley (g); Jean-Marie Ingrand (b); Kenny Clarke (d)	
	Dear Old Stockholm	Denon CD 8520, Denon CD 33C38 7679
	Lady Bird	Denon CD 33C38 7679
	Cherokee	(Europa Jazz 1050 only)
	Europa Jazz EJ-1008, Bandstand BDLP 1503 (except Cherokee)	
1959–1960 *Paris*	ANDRE HODEIR (JAZZ ET JAZZ) Nat Peck (tb); Raymond Guiot (fl); Georges Grenu (ts); Jean-Pierre Drouet (vb,bongo); Pierre Michelot (b); Kenny Clarke (d); André Hodeir (arr,cond) **Trope A Saint-Trop** **Flautando** **Osymetrios 2** Fontana 680-208, Philips PHM-200-073, PHS-60, 0-073	
Early 1960: *Paris*	LES DOUBLE-SIX (RECONTRENT QUINCY JONES) Art Simmons (p); Pierre Michelot (b); Kenny Clarke (d); Monique Guérin (Aldebert), Louis Aldebert, Ward Swingle, Jean-Louis Conrozier, Roger Guérin (vcl); Mimi Perrin (vcl,ldr) **For Lena And Lennie (En Flanant Dans Paris)** **Rat Race (La Course Au Rat)** **Meet Benny Bailey (Au Bout Du Fil)** Open Records OP-18	
January *Paris*	ART SIMMONS Clark Terry (t); Eric Dixon (fl,ts); Art Simmons (p); Elek Bacsik (g); Michel Gaudry (b); Kenny Clarke (d); Billie Poole (vcl) **No Problem** **Don't Ever Leave Me** **Et Tu Me Regardes** Duc-Thomson 450-V-254, DRG Swing SW 8406	
February *Paris*	CLARK TERRY Clark Terry (t); Quentin Jackson (tb,vcl); Elek Bacsik (g); Art Simmons (p); Michel Gaudry (b); Kenny Clarke (d) **In A Mellow Tone** **Don't Worry 'Bout Me** **Ol' Zulu** **Travelling All Alone** Duc-Thomson (F) 450-V-255, DRG Swing 8406	
February 25 *Cologne*	DON BYAS (DON WAILS WITH KENNY) Don Byas (ts); Eddie Busnello (as); Chris Kellens (tb); Fats Sadi (vb); Francy Boland (p); Jean Warland (b); Kenny Clarke (d)	

Tampico
Bell Hop
More Than You Know
Col. (Ger.) C-41-368 (45 rpm EP), Swingtime SW 8411

March 12
Paris

BUD POWELL
Bud Powell (p); Pierre Michelot (b); Kenny Clarke (d)
Confirmation
Xanadu 102

March 20
Baden Baden

JAZZ LEGACY BADEN BADEN
OSCAR PETTIFORD TRIO
Oscar Pettiford, (b,cello); Don Byas (ts); Kenny Clarke (d)
Blues It
Indiana
Cello For Cello Twins
Jazzline 20827

Same

DON BYAS QUARTET (HELLO BADEN BADEN)
Don Byas, Hans Koller (ts); Oscar Pettiford (b); Kenny Clarke (d)
Blues In The Closet
Jazzline 20828

April 2
Essen, Germany

BUD POWELL
Bud Powell (p); Oscar Pettiford (b); Kenny Clarke (d)
Shaw 'Nuff
Blues In The Closet
Willow Weep For Me
John's Abbey
Salt Peanuts
(see next session for label details)

Same

COLEMAN HAWKINS WITH THE OSCAR PETTIFORD TRIO
Coleman Hawkins (ts); Bud Powell (p); Oscar Pettiford (b); Kenny Clarke (d)
All The Things You Are
Yesterdays
Stuffy
Just You, Just Me
Fantasy 6015, Black Lion (G) BL-278084, BL-159, Fontana 688600 ZL/ZY, Storyville SLP 4112, Black Lion BLP 60105 (CD 760105)

April 20
Paris

GAIL MITCHELL
Sahib Shihab (fl,as); Bart Taylor (p); Pierre Michelot (b); Kenny Clarke (d)
Frankie And Johnny
Bill Bailey, Won't You Please Come Home
Some Of These Days
Gone With The Wind
Ducretet-Thomson (F) 460-V-500

June 15 *Paris*	BUD POWELL Bud Powell (p); Pierre Michelot (b); Kenny Clarke (d) **Get Happy** **John's Abbey** Xanadu 102
July *Paris*	LOU BENNETT (AMEN) Lou Bennett (org); Jimmy Gourley (g); Jean-Marie Ingrand (b); Kenny Clarke (d) **Sister Sadie** **So What** **Jubilation** (J-MI out) **Brother Daniel** **On Green Dolphin Street** **Amen** RCA (F)-430050, 900 078, Viking VIK-3037
October 7 *Cologne*	Jimmy Gourley (g) out **Satin Doll** **What A Difference A Day Made** Col. (G) C-41334
October 14 *Paris* *Theatre des Champs-Elysées*	BUD POWELL TRIO (MEMORIAL OSCAR PETTIFORD) Bud Powell (p); Pierre Michelot (b); Kenny Clarke (d) **Buttercup** **John's Abbey** **Sweet And Lovely** **Crossin' The Channel** Vogue (F) EPL-7942, Xanadu 102, Vogue VJD 546
1960	STEPHANE GRAPPELLI Stéphane Grappelli (vln); René Urtreger (p); Jean-Marie Ingrand (b); Kenny Clarke (d) **Parisian Thoroughfare** **Nuages** Europa Jazz EJ-1047
1961:	
February 14 *Cologne*	DUSKO GOJKOVIC/KENNY CLARKE OCTET Dusko Gojkovic (t,fh); Derek Humble (as); Carl Drevo (ts); Heinz Kretschmer (bcl); Bubi Aderhold (bs); Francy Boland (p,arr); Jean Warland (b); Kenny Clarke (d) **La Campimania** **You're Too Beautiful** **Lullaby Of The Leaves** **Doo-doosh** **Mr X** **That's All** Radio-Tele Beograd LPV-4201
April 14 *Paris*	BUD POWELL TRIO Bud Powell (p); Pierre Michelot (b); Kenny Clarke (d)

There Will Never Be Another You
Thelonious
'Round Midnight
Night In Tunisia
Ah! Moore (Monk's Mood)
Dance Of The Infidels (Shaw 'Nuff) Duke (I) D-1012
Lover Man
52nd Street Theme
ESP-Disk 1066

May 18, 19
Cologne

KENNY CLARKE/FRANCY BOLAND (THE GOLDEN EIGHT)
Dusko Gojkovic (t); Raymond Droz (alto horn); Christian Kellens (baritone horn); Derek Humble (as); Carl Drevo (ts); Francy Boland (p,arr); Jimmy Woode (b); Kenny Clarke (d)
La Campimania
Gloria
High Notes
Softly As In A Morning Sunrise
The Golden Eight
Strange Meeting
You'd Be So Nice To Come Home To
Dorian 0437
Poor Butterfly
Basse Cuite
A Ball For Othello Col. CS-9114, CBS 52736
Blue Note BLP-4092, BST-84092 (Jap.), 71035

Spring 1961
Paris

LUCKY THOMPSON QUARTET
Lucky Thompson (ts); Martial Solal (p); Peter Trunk (b); Kenny Clarke (d)
Lord, Lord, Am I Ever Gonna Know
Candid CM-8019, Barnaby/Candid Jazz BR-5021

October 12
Laren, Holland

JAZZ PICTURES AT AN EXHIBITION
Pim Jacobs (p); Wim Overgaauw (g); Ruud Jacobs (b); Kenny Clarke (d); Rita Reys (vcl)
I'm Gonna Sit Right Down And Write Myself A Letter
Autumn Leaves
Poor Butterfly
Can't We Be Friends
I Get A Kick Out Of You
I Remember Clifford
Cherokee
Tangerine
What's New
Speak Low
Philips P-08062-L

December 13
Cologne

KENNY CLARKE/FRANCY BOLAND (JAZZ IS UNIVERSAL)
Benny Bailey, Roger Guérin, Jimmy Deuchar, Ahmed Muvaffak Falay (t); Nat Peck, Ake Persson (tb); Derek Humble (as); Zoot Sims, Carl Drevo (ts); Sahib Shihab (bs); Francy Boland (p,arr); Jimmy Woode (b); Kenny Clarke (d)
Box 703, Washington D.C.
The Styx
Gloria
Los Bravos
Charon's Ferry
Volutes
Last Train From Overbrook
Atl. LP-1401

December 15
Paris

DON BYAS/BUD POWELL (A TRIBUTE TO CANNONBALL)
Idrees Sulieman (t); Don Byas (ts); Bud Powell (p); Pierre Michelot (b); Kenny Clarke (d)
Just One Of Those Things
Jackie My Little Cat
Cherokee
I Remember Clifford
Good Bait
Jeannine
All The Things You Are
Jackie
Myth
Col. JC-35755

December 17
Paris

BUD POWELL TRIO (PORTRAIT OF THELONIOUS)
Bud Powell (p); Pierre Michelot (b); Kenny Clarke (d)
Thelonious
Ruby My Dear
There Will Never Be Another You
Off Minor
I Ain't No Foolin'
No Name Blues
Squatty
Monk's Mood
Cherokee (unissued)
Col. CL-2292

December 21
Cologne

GEORGE GRUNTZ (JAZZ SOUND TRACK FOR THE FILM 'MENTAL CRUELTY')
Raymond Court (t); Marcel Peeters (fl,as); Barney Wilen (ts,ss); George Gruntz (p); Karl Theodor Geier (b); Kenny Clarke (d)
Main Theme
Blues And Theme
Students' Hang-out
Morning After The Wedding Night
Music For Night Children
Jazz Appreciation

Jazz Appreciation II
Good-Time Joe
Swiss Tease
Romance
Spanish Castles
Nick And Marlene
Proposal
Final Theme
Decca (G)-LF 1612

1961
Paris
MAURICE VANDER
Maurice Vander (p); Pierre Michelot (b); Kenny Clarke (d)
Take The 'A' Train
Willow Weep For Me
Walkin'
Autumn Leaves
I'll Remember April
The Nearness Of You
Django
Blue Lester
Philips (F) 680212

1961
KENNY CLARKE/FRANCY BOLAND QUINTET
Sahib Shihab (fl,bs,vcl); Fats Sadi (vb,vcl); Francy Boland (p); Kenny Clarke (d); Joe Harris (perc,vcl)
The Top
Tin Tin Deo
Night Lady
Ya Ya Blues
Jay Jay
Europa Jazz EJ-1030

1962:
February
Paris
ELEK BACSIK
Elek Bacsik (g); Pierre Michelot (b); Kenny Clarke (d)
Take Five
Blue Rondo A La Turk
Willow Weep For Me
My Old Flame
On Green Dolphin Street
Milestones
Fontana (F) 680221, Philips PHS 600079, Philips PHM 200-079

May 10
London
RAY PREMRU GROUP
Eddie Blair (t); Ray Premru (btb); Bob Efford (bcl,oboe,ts); Kenny Napper (b); Kenny Clarke (d)
Conversations: 1 Small Talk
2 Slow Talk
3 Folk Talk
Col. (E) 33-SX-1452

1962
Paris
BUD POWELL 62
Bud Powell (p); Pierre Michelot (b); Kenny Clarke (d)

Shaw 'Nuff
Loverman
There Will Never Be Another You
Monk's Mood
Night In Tunisia
'Round Midnight
Thelonious
52nd Street Theme
CY Records CYL 6462

1962
Paris

BEN WEBSTER QUINTET (Rare Live Performance)
Ben Webster (ts); John Lewis (p); Milt Jackson (vb); Unknown (b); Kenny Clarke (d)
Confirmation
Lady Be Good
The Nearness Of You
Poutin'
Danny Boy
Billie's Bounce
Cottontail
Jazz Anthology JA 5159

1963:

January 3
Koblenz, Germany

LOU BENNETT
Lou Bennett (org); Jimmy Gourley (g); Kenny Clarke (d)
No Smokin'
Low Life
Impulse A (S)-36

January 25
Cologne, Germany

KENNY CLARKE/FRANCY BOLAND BIG BAND
Benny Bailey, Idrees Sulieman, Jimmy Deuchar, Ahmed Muvaffak Falay, Roger Guérin, Edmund Arnie (tp); Ake Persson Nat Peck, Erich Kleinschuster, Raymond Katarzynski, Frederic 'Keg' Johnson (tb); Derek Humble (as); Carl Drevo, Ronnie Scott, Billy Mitchell (ts); Sahib Shihab (fl,bs); Francy Boland (p,arr); Jimmy Woode (b); Kenny Clarke (d); Joe Harris (tympani); Fats Sadi (bongos)
Long Note Blues
Get Out Of Town
Sonor
Speedy Reeds
Old Stuff
Om Mani Padme Hum
Atl. LP-1404

January 26
Cologne, Germany

Night Lady
I'm So Scared Of Girls When They're Good Looking
A Ball For Othello
Sabbath Message
Now Hear My Meanin'
Johnny One Note
Col. CS 9114

March 1
Paris

ALICE BABS AND DUKE ELLINGTON
Duke Ellington (p); Gilbert Rovère (b); Kenny Clarke (d); Alice Babs (vcl)
La De Doody Do
I Didn't Know About You
Take Love Easy
I'm Beginning To See The Light — Reprise 454

Same

Add Unknown (cl); Unknown (as; Gerard Badini (ts)
The C Jam Blues
Reprise R-5024, Telestar 11100 (both sessions)

May 23
Paris

DEXTER GORDON (OUR MAN IN PARIS)
Dexter Gordon (ts); Bud Powell (p); Pierre Michelot (b); Kenny Clarke (d)
Scrapple From The Apple
Willow Weep For Me
Broadway
Stairway To The Stars
A Night In Tunisia
BN BLP-4146, BST-84146

Same

Our Love Is Here To Stay

Same

Gordon out
Like Someone In Love
BN BST 84430

July 8
Paris

DIZZY GILLESPIE ET LES DOUBLE SIX
Dizzy Gillespie (t); Bud Powell (p); Pierre Michelot (b); Kenny Clarke (d); Les Double Six: Mimi Perrin, Claudine Barge, Christiane Legrand, Ward Swingle, Robert Smart, Jean-Claude Briodin, Eddy Louiss (vcl)
One Bass Hit
Two Bass Hit
Emanon
Blue 'n' Boogie
The Champ
Tin Tin Deo
Groovin' High
Ow!
Hot House
Anthropology
Philips PHM 200-106, PHS-600-106

1963
Paris

LOU BENNETT
Lou Bennett (org); Memphis Slim (p,vcl); René Thomas (g); Unknown (b); Kenny Clarke (d); Charles 'Big' Jones, Vin Morris, Swingle Singers (vcl); Choir with unknown piano
That Preaching Man
Glory Glory Hallelujah
Jericho

Echoes
Elijah
Sauveur, Ayez Pitié De Nous
Nobody Knows The Trouble I've Seen
This Train
Que Feras-Tu?
Bel Air (F) 411052

1964:
London

THE BEBOP LEGENDS
J.J. Johnson (tb); Sonny Stitt (as); Howard McGhee (t); Walter Bishop Jr. (p); Tommy Potter (b); Kenny Clarke (d)
Introduction
Buzzy
Lover Man
Now's The Time
Jazz Up JU-302

February 13
Cologne

JOHNNY GRIFFIN
Johnny Griffin (ts); Francy Boland (p); Jimmy Woode (b); Kenny Clarke (d)
Scrabble
Summertime
Old Stuff
Night Lady
Little Man, You've Had A Busy Day
All The Things You Are
Philips (G) P-48071-L, Emarcy SRE 66001, MGE 26001

March 21
Cologne

FATS SADI (HIS VIBES AND FRIENDS)
Fats Sadi (vb); Francy Boland (p); Jimmy Woode (b); Kenny Clarke (d)
The Same
Ensadinado
Goodbye
Night Lady
All Of You
Blue Sunrise
Gamal Sady 'n' Em
Ridin' High
Saba SB-15111-ST

May 8, 9
Cologne

SAHIB SHIHAB
Ake Persson (tb); Sahib Shihab (fl,as,bs); Francy Boland (p); Jimmy Woode (b); Kenny Clarke (d); Joe Harris (bongo)

Lillemor	Argo LP(S) 742
Please Don't Leave Me	" " "
Waltz For Seth	" " "
Campi's Idea	" " "
Herr Fixit	" " "

Chess CH-9182

October 10
Milan, Italy

ROLAND KIRK
Roland Kirk (ts,stritch,manzello,siren); Tete Montoliu (p); Tommy Potter (b); Kenny Clarke (d)
All By Myself
I Remember Clifford
Private Recordings

1964–1965
Cologne

SAHIB SHIHAB (COMPANIONSHIP)
Sahib Shihab (fl,bs); Fats Sadi (vb); Francy Boland (p); Jimmy Woode (b,vcl); Kenny Clarke (d); Joe Harris (perc)
Om Mani Padme Hum
Bohemia After Dark
Jay-Jay
Calypso Blues
Balafon
Insensatez
Invitation
Con Alma
Yah-Yah Blues
Serenata
Just Give Me Time
Born To Be Blue
Sconsolato
Vogue LDVS-17243

1965:
January 31
Villingen, Germany

NATHAN DAVIS QUINTET (HAPPY GIRL)
Nathan Davis (ts,ss,fl); Woody Shaw (t); Larry Young (p); Jimmy Woode (b); Kenny Clarke (d)
Happy Girl
The Flute In The Blues
Spring Can Really Hang You Up The Most
Theme From Zoltan
Exolution
Along Came Byrd
Mister E
Saba SB 15025

May 7
Paris

NATHAN DAVIS (PEACE TREATY)
Woody Shaw (t); Nathan Davis (as,ts); Jean-Louis Chautemps (bs); René Urtreger (p); Jimmy Woode (b); Kenny Clarke (d)
Klook's Theme
Peace Treaty
Now Let M'Tell Ya
Sconsolato
Ruby My Dear
Kansas City Special
SFP (F) 10003

May 13
Paris

STUFF SMITH LIVE IN PARIS 1965
Stuff Smith (vln); Joe Turner (p); Jimmy Woode (b); Kenny Clarke (d)

How High The Moon
Bugle Call Blues
Fresh Sound FC 120

September 1
Villingen, Germany

NATHAN DAVIS (THE HIP WALK)
Carmell Jones (t); Nathan Davis (fl,ts,ss); Francy Boland (p); Jimmy Woode (b); Kenny Clarke (d)
The Hip Walk
While Children Sleep
Train Of Thought
Yesterdays
That Kay Cee Thing
Carmell's Black Forest Waltz
B's Blues
Saba (G) SB-15063

September 25
Alten Bahnhof
von Rolandseck

CLARKE–BOLAND SEXTETT (MARCEL MARCEAU) SWING IM BAHNHOF
Sahib Shihab (fl); Fats Sadi (vb,marimba,bongo); Francy Boland (p); Jimmy Woode (b,vcl); Kenny Clarke (d); Joe Harris (perc)
Invitation
Just Give Me Time
Con Alma
Serenata
Sconsolato
Yah Yah Blues
Born To Be Blue
Insensatez
Calypso Blues
Balafon For Marcel Marceau
CBS BPG-S 62681

November
Paris

EARL HINES ORCHESTRA
Earl Hines (p); Roy Eldridge (t); Don Byas, Ben Webster (ts); Stuff Smith (vln); Jimmy Woode (b); Kenny Clarke (d)
Boogie Woogie On The St Louis Blues
France's Concert FC 101

Same

EARL HINES/KENNY CLARKE DUO
Earl Hines (p); Kenny Clarke (d)
You're The Cream In My Coffee
France's Concert FC 101

1966:
January
Paris

LOU BENNETT
Lou Bennett (org); René Thomas (g); Kenny Clarke (d)
Pieter's Waltz
Repetition
Meeting

Same

Add Donald Byrd (t); (PARIS JAZZ ALL STARS)
Pentacostal Feeling
Echoes
That Preachin' Man
Easy Living
Philips (F) 70325

February 28
Cologne

CARL DREVO & THE CLARKE–BOLAND BIG BAND (SWING, WALTZ, SWING!)
Benny Bailey, Jimmy Deuchar, Dusko Gojkovic, Shake Keane (t); Ake Persson, Nat Peck (tb); Derek Humble (as); Carl Drevo, Sal Nistico (ts); Sahib Shihab (bs,fl); Francy Boland (p); Jimmy Woode (b); Kenny Clarke (d); Fats Sadi (perc)
Frühlingsstimmen op.410
My Favourite Things
Schön Ist Die Welt
Wives And Lovers
Rosenkavalier op.59
Claudia
By Strauss
Kaiserwalzer
Just Give Me Time
Keep On Keeping On
Philips 840 246 PY

October
Cologne,
Villingen

JONNY TEUPEN (PLAY HARP)
Sahib Shihab (fl); Jonny Teupen (harp); Francis Coppietors (cembalo); Jimmy Woode, John Fischer (b); Kenny Clarke, Stuff Combe (d); Blanche Birdsong (vcl); Barock String Quartet
Bourree
Menuett
Fugato
Konzert Für Harfe und Orchester, 3.Satz
Prelude
Minuetto Per Un Arpa
Gavotte
Barock On Harp
Barockin' The Blues
Konzert Für Harfe Und Orchester 1 Und 2 Satz
Menuett No. 2
Etude In C
Pavane
Intrada
Andante
Saba (G) SB-15117-ST

1967:
February 18
Cologne

FRANCY BOLAND TRIO (OUT OF THE BACKGROUND)
Francy Boland (p,arr); Jimmy Woode (b); Kenny Clarke (d); Fats Sadi (bongo)
Dark Eyes

Dia-bleu
Gloria
You Just Hit The One You Say You Love
Wolf-gang
Father Klook
Rosa De Luxe
You Don't Know What Love Is
Espresso Loco
Saba SB-15137, MPS 15070-ST

May 28
Brussels, Belgium

FRANCY BOLAND (FLIRT AND DREAM)
Ake Persson, Nat Peck (tb); Francy Boland (p,arr); Jimmy Woode (b); Kenny Clarke (d); Fats Sadi, Jean Warland (perc); 21 strings under the direction of Fernand Terby, René Costy and Roger Speguel
Double Play Gal
Clown Princess
A Blue Girl In A Red Sunrise
Claudia
Turkish Girl
Pretty And Childlike
In The Darkness
But Supposin'
A Girl Mad As Birds
Lillemor
The Shape Seemed Familiar
Saba SB-15136-ST

June 16
Cologne

FRANCY BOLAND (MUSIC FOR THE SMALL HOURS)
Sahib Shihab (fl,vcl); Francy Boland (p,arr); Fats Sadi (vb, bongo); Jimmy Woode (b,vcl); Kenny Clarke (d); Joe Harris (perc)
Ebony Samba
Lush Life
Tin Tin Deo
Please Don't Leave
The Man From Potter's Crossing
Wives And Lovers
Ensadino
Lorraine
Day By Day
Love Hungry
Col. (G) SMC-74324

June 18
Cologne

KENNY CLARKE/FRANCY BOLAND (SAX NO END)
Benny Bailey, Idrees Sulieman, Jimmy Deuchar (t); Shake Keane (t,fh); Ake Persson, Nat Peck, Eric van Lier (tb); Derek Humble (as); Carl Drevo, Johnny Griffin, Ronnie Scott, Eddie 'Lockjaw' Davis (ts); Sahib Shihab (bs); Francy Boland (p); Jimmy Woode (b); Kenny Clarke (d); Fats Sadi (perc)
New Box MPS BAB 9003

Sax No End MPS BAB 9003
Griff's Groove
Lockjaw Blues
The Turk
Milkshake MPS BAB 9003
Pieter's Waltz
Griff 'n' Jaws
Pres. 7634, MPS 15138, MC 25102 (Vol. 2)

July 31
Cologne

KENNY CLARKE/FRANCY BOLAND (OUT OF THE FOLK BAG)
Torolf Molgaard (tb) replaces Persson; Davis (ts) out
Nice Bunch
Greensleeves
Funiculi, Funicula
Nights In Warsaw
I Don't Want Nothin'
The Turk
Here The Good Wind Comes
Return
Dear Old Stockholm
Col. SMC-74323

September 9
Cologne

FRANCY BOLAND
Idrees Sulieman (t); Ake Persson (tb); Sahib Shihab (bs); Francy Boland (p); Jimmy Woode (b); Kenny Clarke (d)
The Turk's Bolero
Vogue LDVS-17243

Same

KENNY CLARKE/FRANCY BOLAND (GOING CLASSIC)
Francy Boland (p); Jimmy Woode (b); Kenny Clarke (d)
Nights In Warsaw
I'm All Smiles
Myriam Doll
Lonely Girl
Dierdre's Blues
Night Lady
Gamal Sady 'n' Em
The Girl And The Turk
Like Someone In Love
Deutsche Vogue LDVS 17242

October 18
Zurich

SONNY STITT AND THE GIANTS
Howard McGhee (t); Sonny Stitt (as); Walter Davis Jr. (p); Tommy Potter (b); Kenny Clarke (d)
Night Work
Matter Horns
Lover Man
Satin Doll
Don't Blame Me
Hello
Black Lion ITC28.484-4U, BLP-30154

December 18 *Cologne*	MARK MURPHY Jimmy Deuchar (t); Ake Persson (tb); Derek Humble (as); Ronnie Scott (ts); Sahib Shihab (bs); Francy Boland (p); Jimmy Woode (b); Kenny Clarke (d); Mark Murphy (vcl) **Jump For Joy** **I Don't Want Nothin'** **Why And How** **Alone Together** **You Fascinate Me So** **Hopeless** **Sconsolato** **My Ship** **Just Give Me Time** **I Get Along Without You Very Well** Saba MPS/ST-15151, Pausa PR-7023
December 19 or 20 *Cologne*	FRANCY BOLAND Sahib Shihab (fl); Francy Boland (p); Jimmy Woode (b); Kenny Clarke (d); Milt Jackson (vcl) **I'm A Fool To Want You** Vogue LDVS-17243
1967 *Prague*	KENNY CLARKE/FRANCY BOLAND (OPEN DOOR) Benny Bailey (t,fh); Idrees Sulieman, Jimmy Deuchar, Dusko Gojkovic (t); Ake Persson, Nat Peck, Eric Van Lier (tb); Derek Humble (as); Johnny Griffin, Ronnie Scott, Tony Coe (ts); Sahib Shihab (fl,bs); Francy Boland (p,arr); Jimmy Woode (b); Kenny Clarke, Kenny Clare (d) **New Box** **A Rosa Negra** **Duas Rosas** **Milkshake** **All Blues Suite** **Open Door** **Dia Blues** **Total Blues** Muse 5056
1967 *London*	LEE KONITZ Lee Konitz (as) dubbed onto 1959 recording of: Don Abney (p); Oscar Pettiford (b); Kenny Clarke (d) **Three Little Words** Music Minus One 4017
1967 *London*	GEORGE CHISHOLM Stan Roderick (t); George Chisholm (tb); Roy Willox (as); Al Newman (fl,ts); prob. Max Harris (p); Frank Clarke (b); Kenny Clarke (d) **Ghost Of A Chance** **You Turned The Tables On Me** Col. (E) SX-6195

1967 *Paris*	NORMANDO MARQUEZ Normando Marquez (g,vcl); Stéphane Grappelli (vln); Jean-Pierre Mengeon (celeste); Pierre Michelot (b); Kenny Clarke (d) **On A Fait L'Amour** **Balancon Con Bossa** Decca 79431 (45 rpm)
1968: *Paris*	HAMPTON HAWES (PIANO IMPROVISATION) Hampton Hawes (p); Jimmy Woode (b); Kenny Clarke (d) **Fly Me To The Moon** (2 takes) **Autumn Leaves** (2 takes) Moon MLP 005-1
May 13, 14 *Cologne*	KENNY CLARKE/FRANCY BOLAND (ALL SMILES) Benny Bailey (t,fh); Idrees Sulieman, Jimmy Deuchar, Sonny Grey (t); Ake Persson, Nat Peck, Eric Van Lier (tb); Derek Humble (as); Johnny Griffin, Ronnie Scott, Tony Coe (ts); Sahib Shihab (fl,bs); Dave Pike (vb); Francy Boland (p,arr); Jimmy Woode (b); Kenny Clarke, Kenny Clare (d) **Let's Face The Music And Dance** **I'm All Smiles** **You Stepped Out Of A Dream** **I'm Glad There Is You** **Get Out Of Town** — MPS BAB 9003 **By Strauss** **When Your Lover Has Gone** **Gloria** — MPS BAB 9003 **Sweet And Lovely** — " " " **High School Cadets** MPS LP-15214-ST, 88018-2, 2222726-3, Pres. 7699, MPS 29686
June 9 *Cologne*	KENNY CLARKE/FRANCY BOLAND Sahib Shihab (fl,bs); Fats Sadi (vb,marimba,bongo); Francy Boland (p); Jimmy Woode (b); Kenny Clarke (d) **Seeds** **Pieter's Waltz** **Set Up** **Who'll Buy My Dream** **Jay Jay** **Another Samba** **My Kinda World** **Uma Fita De Tres Cores**
Same	Jean Warland (b) replaces Jimmy Woode **Mauve** **The Wild Man** Vogue (G) LDVS-17165 (both sessions)
June 28, 29 *Cologne*	KENNY CLARKE/FRANCY BOLAND (FACES) Benny Bailey (t,fh); Idrees Sulieman, Jimmy Deuchar, Dusko Gojkovic (t); Ake Persson, Nat Peck, Eric Van Lier (tb); Derek

Humble (as); Johnny Griffin, Ronnie Scott, Tony Coe (ts); Sahib Shihab (fl,bs); Fats Sadi (vb,bongo); Francy Boland (p,arr); Jimmy Woode (b); Kenny Clarke, Kenny Clare (d)
Vortographs
Solarisation
Panchromatic
Macrographic
Poly. 583739, MPS 15218 ST

July 17
Rome

CLARKE/BOLAND BIG BAND (MORE)
Unlisted personnel; probably same as June 28, 29
Seven Golden Men
Je M'En Fous
Your Smile
Questi Vent Anni Miei
Passerella Di 8 1/2
Roma Nun Fa La Stupida Stasera
More
Canto D'Amore
Voglio Bene Al Mondo
La Hora De La Verdad
Saxology
Campi SJG-12006

August 27
Cologne

JOHNNY GRIFFIN BAND
Benny Bailey (t,fh); Ake Persson (tb); Johnny Griffin (ts); Sahib Shihab (bs); Francy Boland (p); Jimmy Woode (b); Kenny Clarke, Kenny Clare (d)
Foot Patting
Please Send Me Someone To Love
The Turk's Bolero
Deep Eight
A Handful Of Soul
The Jamfs Are Coming
Out Of Breath (Lady Heavybottom's Waltz)
Young Blood (E) SSYB-11, Vogue LD-16164

August 28,29
Cologne

KENNY CLARKE/FRANCY BOLAND (LATIN KALEIDOSCOPE)
Benny Bailey, Idrees Sulieman, Dusko Gojkovic, Milo Pavlovic (t); Ake Persson, Nat Peck, Eric Van Lier (tb); Derek Humble, Phil Woods (as); Johnny Griffin, Tony Coe, Ronnie Scott (ts); Sahib Shihab (bs,as); Francy Boland (p); Jimmy Woode, Jean Warland (b); Kenny Clarke, Kenny Clare (d); Shake Keane, Albert Heath, Tony Inzalaco, Sabu Martinez (perc)
Un Graso De Areia
Duas Rosas
A Rosa Negra
Uma Fita De Tres Cores
Olhos Negros
Ramo De Flores

Fiebre Cuban
Mambo De Las Brujas
Strano Sueno
Cara Bruja
Crepusculo Y Aurora
Pres. 7760, MPS 152 13, BASF BMP 29685-7, Polydor (G) 583726

September 4, 5
Cologne

GITTE HAENNING WITH THE KENNY CLARKE–FRANCY BOLAND BIG BAND (OUT OF THIS WORLD)
Idrees Sulieman, Derek Watkins (t); Dusko Gojkovic, Benny Bailey (t,flh); Ake Persson, Nat Peck (tb); Eric Van Lier (btb); Derek Humble (as); John Surman (ss,bs); Tony Coe (ts,cl); Johnny Griffin, Ronnie Scott (ts); Francy Boland (p); Jimmy Woode (b); Kenny Clarke, Kenny Clare (d); Gitte Haenning (vcl)
My Kinda World
A Sack Full Of Dreams
A World Without Love
Go To Hell
Imagination
Please Send Me Someone To Love
Out Of This World
Marriage Is For Old Folks
I Love The Life I Live
November Girl
(Hr ZU)SHZE-280 veraBra 20

December 2, 3
Cologne

KENNY CLARKE/FRANCY BOLAND (FELLINI 712)
Benny Bailey, Dusko Gojkovic (t,fh); Idrees Sulieman, Jimmy Deuchar (t); Ake Persson, Nat Peck (tb); Eric van Lier (btb); Derek Humble (as); Sahib Shihab (fl,as,ss); Johnny Griffin, Ronnie Scott (ts); Tony Coe (ts,cl); Francy Boland (p); Jean Warland (b); Kenny Clarke, Kenny Clare (d)
Villa Radieuse
'Tween Dusk And Dawn In Via Urbana
Rosata At Popolo Square
Po-583727, MPS 15073-ST

1968
Germany

CLARKE/BOLAND BIG BAND (17 MEN & THEIR MUSIC)
Shake Keane (t) replaces Gojkovic; Don Menza (ts) replaces Coe; Jimmy Woode (b) replaces Warland; add Fats Sadi (perc)
Resurrection
Woody Nightshade
New Eye
Mauve
The 18th Man
Klook's Report
Hopeless
Shihab, Humble & Co.
You Dig It
The Griffin
Kenny & Kenny
Campi SJG-12004

1969:

January *Paris*	HAMPTON HAWES/MARTIAL SOLAL (KEY FOR TWO) Hampton Hawes, Martial Solal (p); Pierre Michelot (b); Kenny Clarke (d) **Key For Two** **Stella By Starlight** **Spring Can Really Hang You Up The Most** **Bags' Groove** (MS out) **Lover Come Back To Me** **Fly Me To The Moon** **The Theme** **Godchild** **Three For Two** (HH out) Byg (F) 529125
February 11 *London* *Live at Ronnie Scott's Club*	KENNY CLARKE/FRANCY BOLAND (LIVE AT RONNIE SCOTT'S) Benny Bailey, Dusko Gojkovic (t,fh); Idrees Sulieman, Tony Fisher (t); Ake Persson, Nat Peck (tb); Eric van Lier (btb); Derek Humble (as); Sahib Shihab (fl,as,ss); Johnny Griffin, Ronnie Scott (ts); Tony Coe (ts,cl); Francy Boland (p); Ron Mathewson (b); Kenny Clarke, Kenny Clare (d) **Box 703** **Griff's Groove** **Volcano** **Love Which To No Loved One Permits Excuse For Loving** **Now Hear My Meanin'** **And Thence We Issued Out Again To See The Stars** Polydor 24-4501
February 28 *London*	Same **You Stepped Out Of A Dream** **Fellini 712** **The Girl And The Turk** **Kenny And Kenny** **Rue Chaptal** **I Don't Want Nothin'** **Sax No End** Po 583055, MPS 88019-2, BASF 2229728-4 (both sessions), BASF 12007 ST
May 27 *Cologne*	KENNY CLARKE/FRANCY BOLAND (ALL BLUES) Benny Bailey, Idrees Sulieman, Tony Fisher (t); Dusko Gojkovic (t,fh); Ake Persson, Nat Peck (tb); Eric van Lier (btb); Derek Humble (as); Sahib Shihab (as,ss,fl); Tony Coe (ts,cl); Johnny Griffin, Ronnie Scott (ts); Francy Boland (p); Jean Warland (1), Jimmy Woode (2) (b); Kenny Clarke, Kenny Clare (d) **The Wild Man** (2) **The Jamfs Are Coming** (2) **At Ronnie's** (1) **All Blues (1)**

Open Door (1)
Dia-bleu (2)
Total Blues (2)
MPS 15288

May 28
Cologne

KENNY CLARKE/FRANCY BOLAND (MORE SMILES)
Jean Warland (b) out
Johnny One Note
Lullaby Of The Leaves
Bei Dir War Es Immer So Schön
My Favourite Things MPS BAB 9003
Just In Time " " "
All Through The Night
November Girl MPS BAB 9003
My Heart Belongs To Daddy
Love For Sale
MPS CRM-746, 15053-ST, MPS 2222726-3, BASF 25102

September 5
Cologne

KENNY CLARKE/FRANCY BOLAND (AT HER MAJESTY'S PLEASURE: THE SECOND GREATEST JAZZ BIG BAND IN THE WORLD)
Derek Watkins, Kenny Wheeler (t) replace Tony Fisher; Dusko Gojkovic out
Pentonville
Wormwood Scrubs
Doing Time
Broadmoor
Holloway
Reprieve
Going Straight
Black Lion 28416, BL-131, Polydor Select 2460131

1969
Warsaw, Poland

KENNY CLARKE/FRANCY BOLAND (FAMOUS ORCHESTRA)
Benny Bailey, Idrees Sulieman, Tony Fisher (t); Dusko Gojkovic (t,fh); Ake Persson, Nat Peck (tb); Eric van Lier (btb); Derek Humble (as); Sahib Shihab (ss,bs); Tony Coe (ts,cl); Johnny Griffin, Ronnie Scott (ts); Francy Boland (p); Jimmy Woode (b); Kenny Clarke, Kenny Clare (d)
Tarantas Drive
Old Stuff
Sunday At Ten
Sabbath Message
Funiculi-Funicula
Greensleeves
I Don't Want Nothin'
The Good Wind Is Here
The Turk
Nights In Warsaw
Supraphon 15988, 55988 (stereo)

1969
Paris

LOU BENNETT (ECHOES AND RHYTHMS OF MY CHURCH)
Lou Bennett (org); Art Simmons (p); René Thomas (g); Gilbert Rovère (b); Kenny Clarke (d); the Dean Sisters, Charles 'Big' Jones, Vin Morris (vcl); Dean Cooper (arr,dir)

	That Preachin' Man **Jericho** **Elijah**
Same	Simmons out **Sauveur, Ayez Pitié De Nous** **Nobody Knows The Trouble I've Seen** **Que Feras-tu?**
Same	Dean Sisters out **Glory, Glory Hallelujah** **Echoes** **This Train** (vcl Memphis Slim) Bel Air (F) 30-PA-7024 (all sessions) Note: This is a modified version of the 1963 recording on Bel Air (F) 411052
1970: *April 24* *Cologne*	EDDIE DAVIS (TOUGH TENORS AGAIN 'N' AGAIN) Eddie 'Lockjaw' Davis, Johnny Griffin (ts); Francy Boland (p); Jimmy Woode (b); Kenny Clarke (d) **Again 'n' Again** **Tin Tin Deo** **If I Had You** **Jim Dawg** **When We Were One** **Gigi** Saba 2120742, MPS 15283, Pausa PR-7063, CRM 742
July 7 *Cologne*	KENNY CLARKE Ake Persson (tb); Sahib Shihab (fl,bs); Jimmy Woode (b,vcl); Kenny Clarke (d) **Dijdar** **Talk Some Yak-ee-dak**
July	Benny Bailey (t,fh) replaces Persson **Companionship** **Stoned Ghosts** **CT + CB** Vogue LDVS-17243 (both sessions)
September 30 *Cologne*	CLARKE/BOLAND BIG BAND (OFF LIMITS) Benny Bailey, Rick Kiefer, Art Farmer, Dusko Gojkovic (t,fh); Ake Persson, Nat Peck, Eric van Lier (tb); Derek Humble (as); Billy Mitchell, Ronnie Scott (ts); Tony Coe (cl,ts); Sahib Shihab (fl,bs); Francy Boland (p); Jimmy Woode (b); Kenny Clarke, Kenny Clare (d) **Wintersong** **Astrorama** **Osaka Calling** **Our Kind Of Sabi** **Sahara**

Exorcisme
Endosmose
Polydor 2310147

November 3
London

CARMEN McRAE AND THE KENNY CLARKE/FRANCY BOLAND BIG BAND (NOVEMBER GIRL)
Benny Bailey, Idrees Sulieman, Art Farmer, Dusko Gojkovic (t,fh); Ake Persson, Nat Peck, Eric van Lier (tb); Derek Humble (as); Billy Mitchell, Ronnie Scott (ts); Tony Coe (cl,ts); Sahib Shihab (fl,bs); Francy Boland (p); Jimmy Woode (b); Kenny Clarke, Kenny Clare (d); Dizzy Gillespie (snare d)
November Girl
Just Give Me Time
'Tis Autumn
A Handful Of Soul
Dear Death
I Don't Want Nothin'
You're Getting To Be A Habit With Me
My Kinda World
Black Lion 28498-4U, Jazz Man JAZ-5004

December 13
Paris

STEPHANE GRAPPELLI (IN PARIS)
Stéphane Grappelli (vln); Marc Hemmeler (p,org)*; Jack Sewing (b); Kenny Clarke (d)
Tea For Two
Danny Boy
Let's Do It
Coltrane
I Hear Music
Dany
Smoke Gets In Your Eyes
Gary
A Flower For Kenny*
Satin Doll
Let's Fall In Love (2 takes) (unissued)

Same

Hemmeler out (Grappelli on p)
Dear Ben

Same

Sewing out (Clarke on p)
Body And Soul
RCA (F) 730107, CL-37197 (all sessions)

1970
Prob. Italy
Radio or TV broadcast

JOHNNY GRIFFIN MEETS DEXTER GORDON (Jazz Undulation)
Johnny Griffin, Dexter Gordon (ts); Hampton Hawes (p); Jimmy Woode (b); Kenny Clarke (d)

Body And Soul	Lotus (It) ORL 8247
All The Things You Are	" " " "
Blues Up And Down	" " " "

1971:

June 14
Cologne

STAN GETZ/FRANCY BOLAND – THE CLARKE–BOLAND BIG BAND (CHANGE OF SCENES)
Benny Bailey, Rick Kiefer, Art Farmer, Ack van Rooyen, Manfred Schoof (t,fh); Ake Persson, Albert Mangelsdorff, Eric Van Lier (tb); Herb Geller (as,oboe,Eng.horn,fl); Stan Getz, Ronnie Scott (ts); Tony Coe (cl,ts); Stan Sulzmann (ts,ss,fl); Sahib Shihab (ss,bs,fl); Francy Boland (p); Jean Warland (b); Kenny Clarke, Kenny Clare (d); Tony Inzalaco (perc)
Extravagances
Symptones
Quiproquos
Escarmouches
Touchstone
Provocations
Verve 2304034

1971?
Paris

EDDY LOUISS
Eddy Louiss (org); René Thomas (g); Kenny Clarke (d)
No Smoking
You've Changed
I Don't Want Nothing
Nardis
Blue Tempo
Groovin' High
RCA, Cy Records CY-3004

1972:

September 6
Paris

JIMMY GOURLEY & THE PARIS HEAVYWEIGHTS
Jimmy Gourley (g); René Urtreger (p); Luigi Trussardi (b); Kenny Clarke (d); Humberto Canto (perc)
Tafira Alta
Repetition
Pannonica
Sean's Dream
52e Rue Est RECD 002

November 12, 13
Paris

STEPHANE GRAPPELLI (SATIN DOLL)
Stéphane Grappelli (vln); Eddy Louiss (org); Marc Hemmeler (p); Jimmy Gourley (g); Guy Pedersen (b); Kenny Clarke (d)
Satin Doll (JG out)
On The Sunny Side Of The Street (JG, MH out)
Body And Soul (Take 1 – EL out)
Ain't Misbehavin' (EL out)
Mack The Knife
Body And Soul (Take 2 – MH, JG out)
Pennies From Heaven (JG out)
The Girl From Ipanema
My Funny Valentine (SG & EL only)
Blue Moon (EL out)

The Lady Is A Tramp (JG out)
Exactly Like You (JG, EL out)
Ebb Tide (MH, JG out)
You Took Advantage Of Me (EL out)
Lover Man (EL out)
I Didn't Know What Time It Was (EL, MH out)
In A Mellow Tone (SG, EL, KC only)
Halleluia (MH out)
Festival (F) FLD596 (except **Halleluia** on FLD 629), Vanguard VSD-81/82 (except **Halleluia**)

1973:
February 22, 23
Paris

OSCAR PETERSON/STEPHANE GRAPPELLI
Stéphane Grappelli (vln); Oscar Peterson (p); Niels-Henning Orsted-Pedersen (b); Kenny Clarke (d)

Them There Eyes	America (F) AM 6129
Flamingo	" " " "
Makin' Whoopee	" " " "
Looking At You	" " " "
Walking My Baby Back Home	" " " "
My One And Only Love	" " " "
Thou Swell	" " " "
I Won't Dance	America (F) AM 6131
The Folks Who Live On The Hill	" " " "
Autumn Leaves	" " " "
My Heart Stood Still	" " " "
Blues For Musidisc	" " " "
If I Had You	" " " "

Pres. PR-24041

April 13
Paris

DIZZY GILLESPIE (THE GIANT)
Dizzy Gillespie (t); Johnny Griffin (ts); Kenny Drew (p); Niels-Henning Orsted-Pedersen (b); Kenny Clarke (d); Humberto Canto (conga,tumbas)
Stella By Starlight
I Waited For You
Girl Of My Dreams
Fiesta Mo-jo
Serenity
The Source
Manteca
Alone Together
Brother 'K'
Wheatleigh Hall
America (F) 30 AM-6133, (F) 30 AM-6135, Pres. PR-24047, Jazz Man JAZ-5017

July 7
Montreux,
Switzerland

HAMPTON HAWES (PLAYIN' IN THE YARD)
Hampton Hawes (p,elp); Bob Cranshaw (b); Kenny Clarke (d)

Playin' In The Yard
Double Trouble
Pink Peaches
De De
Stella By Starlight
Pres. P-10077

Same

DEXTER GORDON (BLUES A LA SUISSE)
Dexter Gordon (ts); Hampton Hawes (p,elp); Bob Cranshaw (b,elb); Kenny Clarke (d)
Gingerbread Boy
Blues A La Suisse
Some Other Spring
Secret Love
Pres. P-10079

Same

GENE AMMONS AND FRIENDS AT MONTREUX
Gene Ammons (ts); Hampton Hawes (elp); Bob Cranshaw (b); Kenny Clarke (d); Kenneth Nash (cgas)
Yardbird Suite
Since I Fell For You
New Sonny's Blues
Sophisticated Lady

Same

Add Nat Adderley (c); Julian 'Cannonball' Adderley (as); Dexter Gordon (ts)
Treux Bleu
Pres. P-10078 (both sessions)

1974:
January 7
London

AL HAIG (INVITATION)
Al Haig (p); Gilbert 'Bibi' Rovère (b); Kenny Clarke (d)
Enigma
Sambalhasa
Linear Motion
Invitation
If You Could See Me Now
Day Dream
Holy Land
Sawbo City Blues
Spotlite (E) AH-4

1975:
October 3
Rome

KENNY CLARKE: JAZZ A CONFRONTO
Cicci Santucci (t); Enzo Scoppa (ts); Enrico Pieranunzi (p); Roberto Della Grotta (b); Kenny Clarke (d)
Close The Door
I Am Louis Armstrong
Big Bang
Jay Jay
Waiting
New April
Nudibranco

Via Sistina
Horo HLL101-20

November 3
Paris

SONNY GREY (SKIPPIN')
Sonny Grey (t); Alain Hatot (ts); Mal Waldron (p); Gus Nemeth (b); Kenny Clarke (d)
Skippin'
Journey Without End
The Fire Now
Anthony
Numera Mai 9/8

1976:
November
Paris

AMERICAN ELECTIONS 1976
Ambrose Jackson (t); Steve Lacy (ss); Bobby Few (p); Saheb Sarbib (b); Kenny Clarke (d)
Rue Chaptal (Tenor Madness)
Summertime
Radio Broadcast: O.R.T.F.-Eurovision; unissued

December 9
Copenhagen

HOWARD McGHEE QUINTET (JUST BE THERE)
Howard McGhee (t); Per Goldschmidt (bs); Horace Parlan (p); Mads Vinding (b); Kenny Clarke (d)

Jazz Exchange (Take 1)	SteepleChase SCS 1204
You're Something Else (Take 2)	" " " "
Wee Dot	" " " "
You're Something Else (Take 1)	
Jazz Exchange (Take 2)	
Into It	SteepleChase SCS 1204
Just Be There	" " " "

SteepleChase SCCD-31204

December 10
Copenhagen

IDREES SULIEMAN QUINTET (BIRD'S GRASS)
Idrees Sulieman (t,flh); Per Goldschmidt (ts); Horace Parlan (p); Niels-Henning Orsted-Pedersen (b); Kenny Clarke (d)
Wee
The Summer Knows
Billie's Bounce
All Your Words
Loneliness Is A Mutual Feeling
SteepleChase SCS 1202

December
Ludwigsburg, Germany

BENNY BAILEY (SERENADE TO A PLANET)
Benny Bailey (t,flh); Ferdinand Povel (ts); Joe Haider (p); Isla Eckinger (b); Kenny Clarke (d)
Aquarian Moods
The Kicker
You Tell Me
Little B
Serenade To A Planet
Neptunis
Ego 4004

1977:	
May 16	NOAH HOWARD FEATURING KENNY CLARKE (RED STAR) Richard Williams (t); Noah Howard (as); Bobby Few (p); Guy Pedersen (b); Kenny Clarke (d) **Creole Girl** **Lovers** **Red Star** Merc 9101903
October 22 *Pittsburgh, Penn.*	PITTSBURGH JAZZ SEMINAR Abraham Laboriel (b); Kenny Clarke (d) **Demonstration** (drum solo) **Demonstration** (bass and drums)
Same	CARNEGIE MUSIC HALL Woody Shaw (t); Dexter Gordon (ts); Nathan Davis (reeds); Terry Pollard (vb); Mike Longo (p); Abraham Laboriel (b); Kenny Clarke (d) **It's You Or No One** **Unknown** National Public Radio Broadcast: Jazz Alive
1980:	
June 10, 11 *Paris*	KENNY CLARKE LIVE IN PARIS Roger Guérin (t,fh); Bob Garcia (ts); Maurice Vander (p); Marc Fosset (g); Patrice Caratini (b); Kenny Clarke (d) **Jay Jay** **Bluette Pour Petulia** **Satin Doll** **Night In Tunisia** **That's All** **Now's The Time** (unissued) **Afternoon In Paris** (unissued) **3 à 5** (unissued) MP-211, NAD 1000
1981:	
March 27, 28 *Paris*	KENNY CLARKE LIVE IN PARIS Walter Davis Jr. (p); Pierre Michelot (b); Kenny Clarke (d) **'Round About Midnight** **Monk's Mood** MP-211
1981 *Paris*	JEUX DE MAINS Henry Byrs (p); Roland Lobligeois (b); Kenny Clarke (d) **Jeux De Mains** **Mission Impossible** **Laura** **Bleusette** **Carioca** **Five Guys** **Blouse De Dentiste**

The Good Life
Jeux De Mains (reprise)
Frogsy Music FM 18360

1983:

September 16, 17 *New York*	PIECES OF TIME Kenny Clarke, Andrew Cyrille, Milford Graves, Famoudou Don Moye (d, perc) **Laurent** **Nibaldi Isle** **No 11** **Energy Cycles** **Drum Song For Leadbelly** **Pieces Of Time (Personal Statements)** Soul Note SN-1078

1984:

June 29 *New York City*	THE PERCUSSION TRIO WITH KENNY CLARKE (A NIGHT OF PERCUSSION) Same Private recording of live concert from Irving Plaza, NYC
Autumn 1984 *Paris*	PATRICE GALAS TRIO Patrice Galas (org); Michel Valera (g); Kenny Clarke (d) **Pepette** **Some Day My Prince Will Come** **Ma Muse S'Amuse** **It's You Or No One** **Septembre** **We Fix** MCM 3001

Sources

Bielefelder Jazz Katalog: Manfred Scheffner (ed) (Vereinigte Motor-Verlage, Stuttgart, various editions)

Bruyninckx, Walter: *Modern Jazz, Be-Bop/Hard Bop, West Coast* (Vols 1 to 4) (Mechelen, Belgium)

Bruyninckx, Walter: *Progressive Jazz, Free-Third Stream, Fusion* (Vol. 1, A–D) (Mechelen, Belgium)

Bruyninckx, Walter: *60 Years of Recorded Jazz, 1917–1977* (Mechelen, Belgium, 1978)

Callis, John: *Charlie Christian 1939–1941: A Discography* (London: A Tony Middleton Publication, 1978)

Carr, Ian: *Miles Davis: A Biography* (London: Quartet, 1982; New York: Quill, 1984)

Chilton, John: *Bill Coleman on Record* (London: Steve Lane, 1966)

Cooper, Harry: *A Discography of Charlie Parker* (Cambridge, Ma: WHRB, 1980)

Delaunay, Charles : *New Hot Discography*, Walter E. Schaap and George Avakian (eds) (New York: Criterion, 1948)

Evensmo, Jan: *The Guitars of Charlie Christian, Robert Norman, Oscar Aleman*, Jazz Solography Series vol. 4 (Hosle, Norway: 1976)

Evensmo, Jan: *The Tenor Saxophone and Clarinet of Lester Young 1936–1942*, Jazz Solography Series vol. 5 (Hosle, Norway: nd)

Harrison, Max; Alun Morgan; Ronald Atkins; Michael James; Jack Cooke: *Modern Jazz: The Essential Records, A Critical Selection* (London: Aquarius Books, 1975)

Jepsen, Jorgen Grunnet: *Discography of Count Basie* (New York: Debut Records, 1959)

Jepsen, Jorgen Grunnet: *Jazz Records 1942–1968: A Discography* (11 vols) (Copenhagen, Denmark: Knudsen, 1963–70)
Mauerer, Hans J.: *A Discography of Sidney Bechet* (Copenhagen, Denmark: Knudsen, 1969)
Priestley, Brian, 'Miles Davis Discography', in Carr, Ian: *Miles Davis: A Biography*, op. cit.
Priestley, Brian: *Mingus: A Critical Biography* (includes discography) (London: Quartet Books, 1982)
Millar, Jack: *Born to Sing: A Discography of Billie Holiday* (Copenhagen, Denmark: Jazzmedia Aps, *c.* 1979)
Raben, Erik: *Jazz Records 1942–80* (Vol. 1 A–Ba) (Copenhagen: Stainless/Wintermoon, 1989)
Ruppli, Michel: *Atlantic Records: A Discography* (4 vols) (Westport, Connecticut: Greenwood Press, 1979)
Ruppli, Michel: *Prestige Jazz Records 1949–1969: A Discography* (Copenhagen: Knudsen, 1972)
Ruppli, Michel: *The Savoy Label: A Discography* (Westport, Connecticut: Greenwood Press, 1980)
Rust, Brian: *Jazz Records 1897–1942* (2 vols) (New Rochelle, New York: Arlington House, 1978)
Scherman, Bo; Carl A. Hallstrom: *A Discography of Count Basie* (Copenhagen, Denmark: Knudsen, nd)
Van Eyle, Wim; Henk Zwartenkot; Gerard Bielderman; Jan Mulder; Rien Wisse; Herman Openeer: *The Dutch Jazz and Blues Discography 1916–1980* (Holland: Spectrum, 1981)

Index